T0366472

APPIAN

II

LCL 3

APPIAN

ROMAN HISTORY

VOLUME II

EDITED AND TRANSLATED BY

BRIAN McGING

HARVARD UNIVERSITY PRESS

CAMBRIDGE, MASSACHUSETTS

LONDON, ENGLAND

2019

Library of Congress Control Number 2019940172
CIP data available from the Library of Congress

ISBN 978-0-674-99648-9

Composed in ZephGreek and ZephText by
Technologies 'N Typography, Merrimac, Massachusetts.
Printed on acid-free paper and bound by
Maple Press, York, Pennsylvania

CONTENTS

ROMAN HISTORY

ΑΠΠΙΑΝΟΥ ΡΩΜΑΪΚΗ ΙΣΤΟΡΙΑ

APPIAN'S ROMAN HISTORY

VIII

ΛΙΒΥΚΗ[1]

1. Καρχηδόνα τὴν ἐν Λιβύῃ Φοίνικες ᾤκισαν ἔτεσι πεντήκοντα πρὸ ἁλώσεως Ἰλίου, οἰκισταὶ δ' αὐτῆς ἐγένοντο Ζῶρός τε καὶ Καρχηδών, ὡς δὲ Ῥωμαῖοι καὶ αὐτοὶ Καρχηδόνιοι νομίζουσιν, Διδώ, γυνὴ Τυρία, ἧς τὸν ἄνδρα κατακαίνει Πυγμαλίων, Τύρου τυραννεύων,

2 καὶ τὸ ἔργον ἐπέκρυπτεν. ἡ δὲ ἐξ ἐνυπνίου τὸν φόνον ἐπέγνω καὶ μετὰ χρημάτων πολλῶν καὶ ἀνδρῶν, ὅσοι Πυγμαλίωνος τυραννίδα ἔφευγον, ἀφικνεῖται πλέουσα

3 Λιβύης ἔνθα νῦν ἐστιν Καρχηδών. ἐξωθούμενοι δ' ὑπὸ τῶν Λιβύων ἐδέοντο χωρίον ἐς συνοικισμὸν λαβεῖν, ὅσον ἂν βύρσα ταύρου περιλάβοι. τοῖς δὲ ἐνέπιπτε μέν τι καὶ γέλωτος ἐπὶ τῇ τῶν Φοινίκων μικρολογίᾳ καὶ ᾐδοῦντο ἀντειπεῖν περὶ οὕτως βραχυτάτου· μάλιστα δ' ἠπόρουν, ὅπως ἂν πόλις ἐν τηλικούτῳ διαστήματι γένοιτο, καὶ ποθοῦντες ἰδεῖν, ὅ τι ἐστὶν

---

[1] Ἀππιανοῦ Λιβυκὴ ἤτοι τὰ Καρχηδονιακά V Ἀππιανοῦ Ῥωμαϊκῶν Λιβυκή BJ

2

BOOK VIII
PART 1

THE AFRICAN BOOK[1]

1. The Phoenicians founded Carthage, in Africa, fifty years before the fall of Troy. Its founders were Zorus and Carchedon, or, as the Romans and Carthaginians themselves believe, Dido, a Tyrian woman, whose husband was murdered by Pygmalion, tyrant of Tyre. Although he tried to cover up the deed, she saw the murder in a dream, and, taking plenty of money, and men who were trying to escape the tyranny of Pygmalion, came by ship to Africa, landing where Carthage now stands. They were driven off by the Africans, but, for the purposes of founding a settlement, asked to be given as much land as an ox hide would enclose. The Africans laughed at the modest proposal of the Phoenicians, but were ashamed to refuse such a trifling request. They were particularly intrigued to know how a town could be built within such a small radius, and so desiring to see the nature of their ingenuity, they agreed

2

3

---

[1] The title is reported in V as "Appian's African Book, or, Carthaginian History." Other manuscripts have "Appian's African Book of Roman History." Photius (*Bibl.* 57) calls it the "African, Carthaginian, and Numidian Book."

αὐτοῖς τοῦτο τὸ σοφόν, συνέθεντο δώσειν καὶ ἐπώμο-
4 σαν. οἳ δὲ τὸ δέρμα περιτέμνοντες ἐς ἱμάντα ἕνα
στενότατον περιέθηκαν, ἔνθα νῦν ἐστιν ἡ Καρχηδονίων ἀκρόπολις· καὶ ἀπὸ τοῦδε Βύρσα ὀνομάζεται.
5   2. Χρόνῳ δ', ἐντεῦθεν ὁρμώμενοι καὶ τῶν περιοίκων
ἀμείνους ὄντες ἐς χεῖρας ἐλθεῖν ναυσί τε χρώμενοι
καὶ τὴν θάλασσαν οἷα Φοίνικες ἐργαζόμενοι, τὴν πό-
6 λιν τὴν ἔξω τῇ Βύρσῃ περιέθηκαν. καὶ δυναστεύοντες
ἤδη Λιβύης ἐκράτουν καὶ πολλῆς θαλάσσης ἐκδή-
μους τε πολέμους ἐστράτευον ἐς Σικελίαν καὶ Σαρδὼ
καὶ νήσους ἄλλας, ὅσαι τῆσδε τῆς θαλάσσης εἰσί,
καὶ ἐς Ἰβηρίαν· πολλαχῇ δὲ καὶ ἀποικίας ἐξέπεμπον·
ἥ τε ἀρχὴ αὐτοῖς ἐγένετο δυνάμει μὲν ἀξιόμαχος τῇ
7 Ἑλληνικῇ, περιουσίᾳ δὲ μετὰ τὴν Περσικήν. ἑπτακοσίοις δ' αὐτοὺς ἔτεσιν ἀπὸ τοῦ συνοικισμοῦ Ῥωμαῖοι
Σικελίαν ἀφείλοντο καὶ Σαρδὼ μετὰ Σικελίαν, δευ-
8 τέρῳ δὲ πολέμῳ καὶ Ἰβηρίαν. ἔς τε τὴν ἀλλήλων ἐμβαλόντες μεγάλοις στρατοῖς, οἳ μέν, Ἀννίβου σφῶν
ἡγουμένου, τὴν Ἰταλίαν ἐπόρθουν ἑκκαίδεκα ἔτεσιν
ἑξῆς, οἳ δὲ Λιβύην, Κορνηλίου Σκιπίωνος τοῦ πρε-
σβυτέρου σφῶν στρατηγοῦντος, μέχρι τὴν ἡγεμονίαν
Καρχηδονίους ἀφείλοντο καὶ ναῦς καὶ ἐλέφαντας καὶ
9 χρήματα σφίσιν ἐπέταξαν ἐσενεγκεῖν ἐν χρόνῳ. δεύ-
τεραί τε σπονδαὶ Ῥωμαίοις καὶ Καρχηδονίοις αἵδε
διέμειναν ἐς ἔτη πεντήκοντα, μέχρι λύσαντες αὐτὰς
τρίτον πόλεμον καὶ τελευταῖον ἀλλήλους ἐπολέμη-
σαν, ἐν ᾧ Καρχηδόνα Ῥωμαῖοι κατέσκαψαν, Σκιπίωνος τοῦ νεωτέρου σφῶν στρατηγοῦντος, καὶ ἐπάρατον

to give the land, and swore an oath on it. The Phoenicians 4
cut the hide into one very thin strip and laid it around what
is now the acropolis of Carthage. It is from this that it gets
its name, "The Hide."

2. Using this as their base they proved better than their 5
neighbors at fighting, and, being Phoenicians, plied the
sea with their ships; and over the course of time they extended the city outside The Hide. While making them- 6
selves masters of Africa, they came to dominate much of
the sea as well, and fought overseas campaigns in Sicily,
Sardinia, and other Mediterranean islands, as well as Iberia. They sent out colonies to many places. Their empire
matched the Greeks in power and was second in wealth
after Persia. Seven hundred years after the founding of the 7
city, the Romans took Sicily from them, then Sardinia, and
in a second war, Iberia too. Then they set about invading 8
each other's territory with great armies: the Carthaginians
under the command of Hannibal ravaged Italy for sixteen
consecutive years, and the Romans, with the elder Cornelius Scipio as their general, attacked Africa until they deprived Carthage of its dominance, ships, and elephants,
and imposed an indemnity on them to be paid within a
fixed time. This was the second treaty between Rome and 9
Carthage, and it lasted fifty years, until they broke its
terms and fought a third and final war against each other.
In this war, under the command of the younger Scipio,
Rome razed Carthage to the ground and declared it

ἔγνωσαν. αὖθις δ᾽ ᾤκισαν ἰδίοις ἀνδράσιν, ἀγχοτάτω
μάλιστα τῆς προτέρας, ὡς εὔκαιρον ἐπὶ Λιβύῃ χω-

10 ρίον. τούτων τὰ μὲν ἀμφὶ Σικελίαν ἡ Σικελικὴ γραφὴ
δηλοῖ, τὰ δ᾽ ἐν Ἰβηρίᾳ γενόμενα ἡ Ἰβηρική, καὶ ὅσα
Ἀννίβας ἐς Ἰταλίαν ἐσβαλὼν ἔπραξεν, ἡ Ἀννιβαϊκή·
τὰ δ᾽ ἐν Λιβύῃ γενόμενα ἀπ᾽ ἀρχῆς ἥδε συνάγει.

11 3. Ἤρξαντο δ᾽ αὐτῶν ἀμφὶ τὸν Σικελικὸν πόλεμον
οἱ Ῥωμαῖοι, ναυσὶ πεντήκοντα καὶ τριακοσίαις ἐπιπλεύσαντες ἐς Λιβύην καὶ πόλεις τινὰς ἑλόντες καὶ
στρατηγὸν ἐπὶ τῇ δυνάμει καταλιπόντες Ἀτίλιον
Ῥῆγλον, ὃς ἄλλας τε πόλεις διακοσίας προσέλαβεν,
αἳ Καρχηδονίων ἔχθει πρὸς αὐτὸν μετετίθεντο, καὶ

12 τὴν χώραν ἐπιὼν ἐπόρθει. Καρχηδόνιοι δὲ Λακεδαιμο-
νίους στρατηγὸν ᾔτουν, οἰόμενοι δι᾽ ἀναρχίαν κακο-
πραγεῖν. οἱ μὲν δὴ Ξάνθιππον αὐτοῖς ἔπεμπον, ὁ δὲ
Ἀτίλιος, ἀμφὶ λίμνῃ στρατοπεδεύων, ὥρᾳ καύματος
περιώδευε τὴν λίμνην ἐπὶ τοὺς πολεμίους, ὅπλων τε
βάρει καὶ πνίγει καὶ δίψῃ καὶ ὁδοιπορίᾳ κακοπαθῶν

13 καὶ βαλλόμενος ἀπὸ κρημνῶν ἄνωθεν. ὡς δ᾽ ἐπλησία-
σεν περὶ ἑσπέραν καὶ ποταμὸς αὐτοὺς διεῖργεν, ὁ μὲν
εὐθὺς ἐπέρα τὸν ποταμόν, ὡς καὶ τῷδε τὸν Ξάνθιππον
ἐκπλήξων, ὁ δὲ συντεταγμένην τὴν στρατιὰν ἐπαφ-
ίησι διὰ τῶν πυλῶν, ἐλπίσας κεκμηκότος καὶ κακοπα-
θοῦντος περιέσεσθαι καὶ τὴν νύκτα πρὸς τῶν νικών-

---

[2] M. Atilius Regulus had been consul in 267 and was made
suffect consul in 256, to replace Q. Caedicius, who had died in
office.

cursed. They regarded the site, however, as strategically important with regard to Africa, and recolonized it with their own people, very close to the site of the earlier settlement. Of these events, the Sicilian Book explains the Sicilian part, the Iberian Book what happened in Iberia, and the Hannibalic Book sets out Hannibal's actions when he invaded Italy. The present book narrates developments in Africa right from the beginning. 10

3. The Romans initiated events in the course of the Sicilian war, when they sent an expedition of three hundred and fifty ships against Africa, captured some towns, and left Atilius Regulus in command of their forces.[2] He took possession of an additional two hundred towns—they went over to his side out of hatred for the Carthaginians—and plundered the land as he advanced. Thinking that their misfortune was due to a lack of leadership, they asked the Spartans for a general, and were sent Xanthippus. Atilius was encamped near a lake and in the heat of the day marched round the lake against the enemy. The men were suffering badly, what with the weight of their weapons, the stifling heat, the lack of water, the tiring march, and the missiles that were being fired at them from the crags above. When he got close to the Carthaginians, toward evening, Atilius immediately crossed the river that separated the two armies, intending that precisely this maneuver would shock Xanthippus. But the latter marshaled his forces and sent them out through the gates expecting to overcome a tired and distressed enemy, and that darkness would be to the advantage of the victor. 11

12

13

APPIAN

14 των ἔσεσθαι. τῇσδε μὲν οὖν τῆς ἐλπίδος ὁ Ξάνθιππος
    οὐκ ἀπέτυχεν· ἀπὸ γὰρ τρισμυρίων ἀνδρῶν, οὓς ὁ
    Ἀτίλιος ἦγεν, ὀλίγοι μόλις αὐτῶν ἐς Ἀσπίδα πόλιν
    διέδρασαν, οἱ δὲ λοιποὶ πάντες, οἳ μὲν ἀπώλοντο, οἱ
    δ' ἐζωγρήθησαν.

15 4. Καὶ μετ' αὐτῶν ὁ στρατηγὸς Ἀτίλιος, ὕπατος
    γεγονώς, αἰχμάλωτος ἦν. τόνδε μὲν δὴ μετ' οὐ πολὺ
    κάμνοντες οἱ Καρχηδόνιοι σὺν οἰκείοις πρέσβεσιν
    ἔπεμψαν ἐς Ῥώμην, ἐργασόμενον σφίσι διαλλαγὰς ἢ
    ἐπανήξοντα· καὶ ὁ Ἀτίλιος Ῥῆγλος, ἐν ἀπορρήτῳ τοῖς
    τέλεσι Ῥωμαίων ἐπισκήψας ἐγκρατῶς ἔχεσθαι τοῦ
    πολέμου, ἐπανῆλθεν ἐς λύμην ἕτοιμον, καὶ αὐτὸν οἱ
    Καρχηδόνιοι καθείρξαντες ἐν γαλεάγρᾳ κέντρα πάν-
16 τοθεν ἐχούσῃ διέφθειραν. Ξανθίππῳ δὲ τὸ εὐτύχημα
    ξυμφορῶν ἦρξε· Καρχηδόνιοι γὰρ αὐτόν, ἵνα μὴ δο-
    κοίη Λακεδαιμονίων ἔργον εἶναι τοσοῦτον, ὑποκρινά-
    μενοι τιμᾶν δωρεαῖς πολλαῖς καὶ προπέμπειν ἐπὶ τρι-
    ήρων ἐς Λακεδαίμονα τοῖς τριηράρχοις ἐνετείλαντο
17 μετὰ τῶν συμπλεόντων Λακώνων καταποντίσαι. ὁ μὲν
    δὴ δίκην ἔδωκε τήνδε εὐπραξίας, καὶ τάδε ἦν τοῦ
    πρώτου πολέμου Ῥωμαίοις περὶ Λιβύην εὐπραγήματά
    τε καὶ ἀτυχήματα, μέχρι Καρχηδόνιοι Σικελίας Ῥω-
    μαίοις ἀπέστησαν. ὅπως δὲ ἀπέστησαν, ἐν τῇ Σικε-
    λικῇ γραφῇ δεδήλωται.

18 5. Μετὰ δὲ τοῦτο Ῥωμαίοις μὲν καὶ Καρχηδονίοις
    εἰρηναῖα ἦν ἐς ἀλλήλους, Λίβυες δ', ὅσοι Καρχη-
    δονίων ὄντες ὑπήκοοι συμμεμαχήκεσαν αὐτοῖς ἐπὶ
    Σικελίαν, καὶ Κελτῶν, ὅσοι μεμισθοφορήκεσαν, ἐγ-

8

And Xanthippus was not disappointed in his expectation.   14
For only a small number of the thirty thousand troops led
by Atilius escaped, with difficulty, to the town of Aspis; all
the rest were either killed or captured.

4. Among the latter was Atilius, their commanding of-   15
ficer, a former consul, now a prisoner of war. When the
Carthaginians got tired of the war, they sent him to Rome
along with their own envoys: he was to broker a peace or
return to Carthage. In private conversation Atilius Regulus pressed Rome's top officials to continue fighting vigorously, and then returned, prepared to undergo torture.
The Carthaginians executed him by shutting him up in a
cage fitted throughout with spikes. As for Xanthippus, his   16
success was the beginning of his downfall. For the Carthaginians did not want Sparta to get the credit for such an
achievement. They pretended to honor Xanthippus with
many gifts and to send him back to Sparta on warships, but
in fact they ordered the ships' captains to throw him and
his fellow Spartans overboard. This was the penalty he   17
paid for his success, and these were the triumphs and
failures of Rome's first war in Africa. Eventually the Carthaginians abandoned Sicily to the Romans. I have explained in my Sicilian history how this happened.

5. After this, there was peace between Carthage and   18
Rome, but those of Carthage's African subjects who had
served on her side in Sicily, along with some Celtic mercenaries, now fought a particularly ferocious war against

APPIAN

κλήματά τινα μισθῶν καὶ ὑποσχέσεων ἐς τοὺς Καρχηδονίους ἔχοντες, ἐπολέμουν αὐτοὺς μάλα καρτερῶς.

19 οἳ δὲ Ῥωμαίους ἐς συμμαχίαν ὡς φίλους ἐκάλουν, καὶ
αὐτοὺς οἱ Ῥωμαῖοι ξενολογεῖν ἐς μόνον τόνδε τὸν
πόλεμον ἀπὸ τῆς Ἰταλίας ἐφῆκαν· ἀπείρητο γὰρ ἐν

20 ταῖς σπονδαῖς καὶ τόδε. ἔπεμψαν δὲ καὶ διαλλα-
κτῆρας, οἷς οἱ Λίβυες οὐχ ὑπήκουον, ἀλλὰ τὰς πόλεις
ἐδήλωσαν ὑπηκόους εἶναι Ῥωμαίων, εἰ θέλοιεν· οἳ δ'

21 οὐκ ἐδέξαντο. Καρχηδόνιοι δὲ ναυτικῷ πολλῷ ταῖς
πόλεσιν ἐφεδρεύοντες τὴν ἀγορὰν αὐτῶν ἀφηροῦντο
τὴν ἐκ τῆς θαλάσσης. ἀσπόρου δὲ καὶ τῆς γῆς ὡς ἐν
πολέμῳ γενομένης Λιβύων μὲν διὰ τὸν λιμὸν ἐκράτουν, ἐμπόρους δ', ὅσοι παρέπλεον, ἐλῄστευον ἐξ
ἀπορίας· τοὺς δὲ Ῥωμαίων καὶ κτείνοντες ἔβαλλον ἐς

22 τὸ πέλαγος, ἵνα λανθάνοιεν. καὶ διέλαθον ἐπὶ πολύ.
γνωσθέντος δὲ τοῦ γιγνομένου ποινὴν αἰτούμενοι δι-
ωθοῦντο, μέχρι Ῥωμαίων ἐπιστρατεύειν αὐτοῖς ψηφι-
σαμένων Σαρδὼ ποινὴν ἔδωκαν. καὶ τόδε ταῖς προ-
τέραις συνθήκαις ἐνεγράφη.

23   6. Οὐ πολὺ δὲ ὕστερον οἱ Καρχηδόνιοι στρατεύου-
σιν ἐς Ἰβηρίαν καὶ αὐτὴν κατὰ μέρος ὑπήγοντο, μέχρι Ζακανθαίων ἐπὶ Ῥωμαίους καταφυγόντων Καρχηδονίοις ὅρος ἐν Ἰβηρίᾳ γίνεται, μὴ διαβαίνειν τὸν
Ἴβηρα ποταμόν. καὶ τάσδε αὖ τὰς σπονδὰς ἔλυσαν
Καρχηδόνιοι, περάσαντες Ἀννίβου σφῶν ἡγουμένου.

24 διαβάντες δέ, ὁ μὲν Ἀννίβας, διαστρατηγεῖν ἑτέροις
τὰ ἐν Ἰβηρίᾳ καταλιπών, ἐς τὴν Ἰταλίαν ἐσέβαλεν·

10

the Carthaginians. The source of their grievance against
Carthage was pay and promises. The Carthaginians called   19
on Rome, in the name of friendship, for military assistance, and the Romans allowed them, for this war only, to
recruit mercenaries from Italy, as this too had been pro-
hibited in the treaty. They also sent mediators, whom the   20
Africans refused to recognize; instead, they undertook to
make their towns subject to Rome, if the Romans would
accept them. The Romans declined. By blockading the   21
towns with a large fleet, the Carthaginians cut off the rebels' seaward food supply, and with the land unsown because of the war, they starved the Africans into submission. But the Carthaginians carried out raids on passing
merchants, as they too were short of supplies. They even
killed Roman merchants and threw their bodies into the
sea to avoid detection, and they succeeded in this for a
long time. But when the facts emerged, and Rome de-   22
manded compensation, they refused to pay, until the Romans voted to declare war against them, and they handed
over Sardinia as compensation. This clause was added to
the previous treaty.

6. A short time later, the Carthaginians campaigned in   23
Iberia, and began to subdue it little by little, until the
people of Saguntum sought the protection of Rome. A
boundary is fixed for the Carthaginians in Iberia, by which
they were not to cross the river Ebro. But this treaty too
the Carthaginians broke when they crossed the Ebro under the command of Hannibal.[3] After making the crossing,   24
he left others in command in Iberia, while he himself in-

---

[3] See *Hann.* 3.10–12; *Ib.* 7.25.

APPIAN

στρατηγοὶ δὲ Ῥωμαίων ἐν Ἰβηρίᾳ, Πούπλιός τε Κορνήλιος Σκιπίων καὶ Γναῖος Κορνήλιος Σκιπίων, ἀλ-
λήλοιν ἀδελφώ, λαμπρὰ ἔργα ἀποδεικνυμένω θνήσκε-
25 τον ἄμφω πρὸς τῶν πολεμίων. καὶ οἱ μετ᾽ αὐτοὺς
στρατηγοὶ κακῶς ἔπρασσον, μέχρι Σκιπίων, ὁ Που-
πλίου Σκιπίωνος τοῦδε τοῦ περὶ Ἰβηρίαν ἀναιρεθέντος υἱός, ἐπιπλεύσας καὶ δόξαν ἅπασιν ἐμβαλών, ὡς
ἥκοι κατὰ θεὸν καὶ δαιμονίῳ χρῷτο συμβούλῳ περὶ
ἁπάντων, ἐκράτει τε λαμπρῶς καὶ ἐπὶ δόξης ἐκ τοῦδε
πολλῆς γενόμενος τὴν μὲν στρατηγίαν τοῖς ἐς διαδο-
χὴν ἐπιπεμφθεῖσι παρέδωκεν, ἐς δὲ Ῥώμην ἐπανελθὼν ἠξίου πεμφθῆναι στρατηγὸς ἐς Λιβύην, ὡς ἀναστήσων Ἀννίβαν ἐξ Ἰταλίας καὶ Καρχηδονίοις δίκην
ἐπιθήσων ἐν τῇ πατρίδι.

26   7. Τῶν δὲ πολιτευομένων οἱ μὲν ἀντέλεγον οὐ χρῆ-
ναι, κεκενωμένης ἄρτι τῆς Ἰταλίας τοσοῖσδε πολέμοις
καὶ πορθουμένης ἔτι πρὸς Ἀννίβου καὶ Μάγωνος ἐν
πλευραῖς ἐπ᾽ αὐτὴν Λίγυάς τε καὶ Κελτοὺς ξενολο-
γοῦντος, ἐς Λιβύην στρατεύειν οὐδὲ τὴν ἀλλοτρίαν
χειροῦσθαι, πρὶν τὴν οἰκείαν ἀπαλλάξαι τῶν παρόν-
27 των· οἱ δὲ ᾤοντο Καρχηδονίους νῦν μὲν ἀδεεῖς ὄντας
ἐφεδρεύειν τῇ Ἰταλίᾳ, οὐδὲν ἐνοχλουμένους οἴκοι, πολέμου δὲ οἰκείου σφίσι γενομένου καὶ Ἀννίβαν μετα-

---

4 The campaigns in Iberia of P. Cornelius Scipio (consul 218)
and his brother, Cn. Cornelius Scipio Calvus (consul 222), are
recounted by Appian at *Ib.* 14.54–17.64. They were killed in 211.

12

vaded Italy. The Roman generals in Iberia, Publius Cornelius Scipio and Gnaeus Cornelius Scipio, two brothers,
performed brilliant deeds before both died at the hands
of the enemy.[4] Their successors in the command did not   25
do well, until Scipio, the son of this Publius Scipio who
was killed in Iberia, sailed there and instilled in everyone
the belief that he was coming with divine approval and had
access to heaven-sent advice in all matters.[5] He achieved
a brilliant dominance, and as a result won great glory.
Handing over the command to those sent to succeed him,
he returned to Rome, where he asked to be given a command and sent to Africa, in order to force Hannibal to
leave Italy and punish the Carthaginians in their own
country.

7. Some of Rome's leading politicians, however, spoke   26
against Scipio, arguing that, when Italy had recently been
depleted by such extensive wars and was still being devas-
tated by Hannibal, and while Mago was recruiting Ligurian and Celtic mercenaries for an attack on its flank,[6] they
should not be sending an expedition against Africa or trying to conquer foreign territory before freeing their own
from its present dangers. Others thought that the Cartha-   27
ginians felt secure in occupying Italy at the present time
precisely because they faced no threat at home, and would
recall Hannibal if they had to fight a war in their own land.

[5] P. Cornelius Scipio Africanus, who brought the war against
Hannibal to an end with his victory at the battle of Zama in 202,
was elected consul in 205 and given the province of Sicily, and
then Africa too.

[6] Liguria in northwest Italy is seen by Appian as lying on Italy's western flank.

APPIAN

28 πέμψεσθαι. οὕτω μὲν ἐκράτησε πέμπειν ἐς Λιβύην
Σκιπίωνα, οὐ μὴν συνεχώρησαν αὐτῷ καταλέγειν
στρατὸν ἐξ Ἰταλίας πονουμένης ἔτι πρὸς Ἀννίβου·
ἐθελοντὰς δέ, εἴ τινες εἶεν, ἐπέτρεψαν ἐπάγεσθαι καὶ
τοῖς ἀμφὶ τὴν Σικελίαν ἔτι οὖσι χρῆσθαι· τριήρεις τε
ἔδοσαν αὐτῷ κατασκευάσασθαι δέκα καὶ πληρώματα
29 αὐταῖς λαβεῖν, ἐπισκευάσαι δὲ καὶ τὰς ἐν Σικελίᾳ. καὶ
χρήματα οὐκ ἔδωκαν, πλὴν εἴ τις ἐθέλοι τῷ Σκιπίωνι
κατὰ φιλίαν συμφέρειν. οὕτως ἀμελῶς ἥπτοντο τοῦδε
τοῦ πολέμου τὰ πρῶτα, μεγίστου σφίσι καὶ ἀξιοτιμο-
τάτου μετ' ὀλίγον γενομένου.

30 8. Ὁ δὲ Σκιπίων, ἔνθους ὢν ἐπὶ Καρχηδόνι ἐκ πολλοῦ καί τινας ἱππέας τε καὶ πεζούς, ἐς ἑπτακισχιλίους
μάλιστα, ἀθροίσας, διέπλευσεν ἐς Σικελίαν, ἔχων
ἀμφ' αὑτὸν ἀρτιγενείους ἐπιλέκτους τριακοσίους, οἷς
31 εἴρητο χωρὶς ὅπλων ἕπεσθαι. Σικελῶν δὲ αὖ τριακοσίους καταγράψας εὐδαίμονας ἐκέλευσεν ἥκειν ἐς
ἡμέραν ῥητήν, ἐσκευασμένους ὅπλοις τε καὶ ἵπποις,
ὅτι δύναιντο, καλλίστοις. ὡς δὲ ἀφίκοντο, προύθηκεν,
εἴ τις ἑαυτοῦ θέλοι[2] τὸν στρατευσόμενον ἀντιδοῦναι.
32 δεξαμένων δὲ πάντων ἤγαγεν ἐς μέσον τοὺς τριακοσίους τοὺς ὅπλων ἐρήμους καὶ ἐς τούσδε ἐκείνοις
προσέταξε μετασκευάσασθαι. οἱ δ' ἑκόντες παρεδίδο-
33 σαν ὅπλα καὶ ἵππους. καὶ περιῆν τῷ Σκιπίωνι τριακοσίους νέους Ἰταλιώτας ἔχειν ἀντὶ Σικελιωτῶν, κάλ-

[2] εἴ τις ‹τὰ › ἑαυτοῦ ‹θέσθαι› θέλοι aut lac. ante ἑαυτοῦ
Goukowsky

The latter view prevailed, that is, to send Scipio to Africa, 28
but they would not allow him to conscript an army from
Italy, as it was still suffering at the hands of Hannibal:
instead they gave him permission to recruit volunteers, if
there were any, and to use the troops still in Sicily. They
also gave him authority to build ten triremes, collect crews
for them and refit the triremes in Sicily. But they granted 29
no funding for this, apart from any voluntary contributions
made to Scipio as a result of personal friendship. Such was
the indifference with which Rome undertook this war in
the beginning, although it soon became huge in scale and
brought them the greatest glory.

8. Scipio had long enjoyed divine inspiration in the war 30
against Carthage, and after collecting a force of about
seven thousand infantry and cavalry, he sailed for Sicily.
He brought in his company three hundred specially chosen young men, whom he ordered to escort him without
arms. He then conscripted another three hundred wealthy 31
Sicilians, and ordered them to come on a particular day,
fitted out with their finest possible arms and horses. When
they arrived, he offered them the choice of substituting
someone to serve in their place.[7] As they all accepted the 32
offer, he introduced the three hundred young men who
did not have weapons, and ordered the Sicilians to exchange their gear with them. They willingly handed over
their arms and horses. In this way Scipio succeeded in 33
getting three hundred Italian youths instead of Sicilians,

[7] The Greek must mean something like this, but it is elliptical
enough to think that there might be a lacuna in the text.

λιστα ἵπποις καὶ ὅπλοις ἀλλοτρίοις ἐσκευασμένους
καὶ χάριν εὐθὺς ἐπὶ τῷδε εἰδότας· οἷς δὴ καὶ προθυ-
μοτάτοις ἐς πάντα χρώμενος διετέλει.

34   9. Καρχηδόνιοι δὲ ταῦτα πυνθανόμενοι Ἀσρούβαν
μὲν τὸν Γέσκωνος ἐπὶ θήραν ἐλεφάντων ἐξέπεμπον,
Μάγωνι δ᾽ ἀμφὶ τὴν Λιγυστίνην ξεναγοῦντι πεζοὺς
ἀπέστελλον ἐς ἑξακισχιλίους καὶ ἱππέας ὀκτακοσίους
καὶ ἐλέφαντας ἑπτὰ καὶ προσέτασσον αὐτῷ μεθ᾽
ὅσων δύναιτο ἄλλων ἐσβαλεῖν ἐς Τυρρηνίαν, ἵνα τὸν
35   Σκιπίωνα περισπάσειεν ἐκ Λιβύης. Μάγων μὲν δὴ
καὶ τότε ἐβράδυνεν, Ἀννίβᾳ τε συνελθεῖν οὐ δυνάμενος πολὺ διεστῶτι καὶ τὸ μέλλον αἰεὶ προορώμενος·
Ἀσρούβας δ᾽ ἀπὸ τῆς θήρας ἐπανελθὼν κατέλεγεν
Καρχηδονίων τε καὶ Λιβύων ἐς ἑξακισχιλίους πεζοὺς
ἑκατέρων καὶ ἱππέας ἑξακοσίους δούλους τε ἠγόραζε
πεντακισχιλίους, ⟨ὅσους⟩[3] τὸ ναυτικὸν ἐρέσσειν, καὶ
παρὰ τῶν Νομάδων ἔλαβε δισχιλίους ἱππέας καὶ ξέ-
νους ἐμισθοῦτο καὶ πάντας ἐγύμναζεν, διακοσίους
σταδίους ἀποσχὼν ἀπὸ Καρχηδόνος.

36   10. Νομάδων δὲ τῶν ἐν Λιβύῃ δυνάσται μὲν ἦσαν
κατὰ μέρη πολλοί, Σύφαξ δ᾽ ὑπὲρ ἅπαντας, καὶ τιμὴν
37   εἶχε πρὸς τῶν ἄλλων ἐπιφανῆ. Μασσυλίων δ᾽ αὖ, γέ-
νους ἀλκίμου, παῖς ἦν τοῦ βασιλέως Μασσανάσσης,
ὃς ἐτέθραπτο μὲν ἐν Καρχηδόνι καὶ ἐπεπαίδευτο, ὄντι
δ᾽ αὐτῷ καὶ τὸ σῶμα καλῷ καὶ τὸν τρόπον ἀρίστῳ,
Ἀσρούβας ὁ Γέσκωνος, οὐδενὸς Καρχηδονίων δεύτερος, ἐνεγγύησε τὴν θυγατέρα, καίπερ ὄντι Νομάδι,
Καρχηδόνιος ὤν. ὡς δ᾽ ἐνεγγύησεν, ἐπήγετο ἐς Ἰβη-

equipped magnificently with horses and weapons belonging to others, and immediately grateful to him thereafter. And to be sure, he continued to enjoy their warmest support in all matters.

9. When news of these events got to Carthage, they 34 dispatched Hasdrubal, son of Gisco, to hunt for elephants, and sent about six thousand infantry, eight hundred cavalry, and seven elephants to Mago, who was recruiting mercenaries in Liguria. They ordered him to invade Etruria with these and whatever other forces he could muster, with the purpose of getting Scipio to leave Africa. But 35 even then Mago delayed, as he was too far away from Hannibal to be able to join forces with him, and was always one to prevaricate. When Hasdrubal returned from his hunting expedition, he enlisted about six thousand infantry from both Carthaginians and Africans, purchased five thousand slaves as rowers for the fleet, got two thousand cavalry from Numidia, and hired some mercenaries. He put the whole force into training two hundred stades away from Carthage.

10. There were many local Numidian princes in Africa, 36 of whom the most senior was Syphax. He was held in particularly high esteem by the others. Then there was 37 Massinissa, son of the king of the Massylians, a brave people. He had been brought up and educated in Carthage, and because he was handsome and of noble character, Hasdrubal the son of Gisco, first among Carthaginians, betrothed his daughter to him, although Massinissa was a Numidian and Hasdrubal a Carthaginian. After the betrothal, Hasdrubal brought the young man with him while

---

3 ὅσους add. Goukowsky

38 ρίαν στρατηγῶν τὸ μειράκιον. Σύφαξ δὲ κνιζόμενος
ὑπ᾽ ἔρωτος ἐπὶ τῇ παιδὶ τὰ Καρχηδονίων ἐλεηλάτει
καὶ Σκιπίωνι διαπλεύσαντι πρὸς αὐτὸν ἐξ Ἰβηρίας

39 συνέθετο συμμαχήσειν ἐπὶ Καρχηδονίους ἰόντι. αἰ-
σθόμενοι δ᾽ οἱ Καρχηδόνιοι καὶ μέγα ποιούμενοι ἐς
τὸν πρὸς Ῥωμαίους πόλεμον Σύφακα προσλαβεῖν ἐξ-
έδοσαν αὐτῷ τὴν παρθένον ἀγνοούντων καὶ ὄντων ἐν

40 Ἰβηρίᾳ Ἀσρούβου τε καὶ Μασσανάσσου. ἐφ᾽ οἷς ὁ
Μασσανάσσης ὑπεραλγῶν συνετίθετο καὶ ὅδε ἐν
Ἰβηρίᾳ τῷ Σκιπίωνι, λανθάνων, ὡς ᾤετο, Ἀσρούβαν.

41 ὁ δ᾽ αἰσθόμενος βαρέως μὲν ἔφερεν ὑπὲρ τοῦ μειρα-
κίου καὶ τῆς θυγατρός, ὑβρισμένοιν ἀμφοῖν, ἡγεῖτο
δ᾽ ὅμως τῇ πατρίδι συμφέρειν ἐκποδὼν Μασσανάσσην ποιήσασθαι καὶ ἐπανιόντι ἐς Λιβύην ἐξ Ἰβηρίας
ἐπὶ θανάτῳ τοῦ πατρὸς συνέπεμπε προπομποὺς ἱππέας, οἷς εἴρητο ἀφανῶς ἐπιβουλεύειν αὐτῷ καὶ κτείνειν, ὅπῃ δύναιντο, Μασσανάσσην.

42   11. Ὁ δὲ αἰσθόμενος ἐξέφυγέν τε καὶ τὴν πατρῴαν
ἀρχὴν ἐκρατύνετο, ἱππέας ἀθροίζων, οἷς ἡμέρας τε
καὶ νυκτὸς ἦν ἔργον ἀκοντίοις πολλοῖς χρωμένους
ἐπελαύνειν αἰεὶ καὶ ἀναχωρεῖν καὶ αὖθις ἐπελαύνειν,

43 καὶ ὅλως ἐστὶν αὐτοῖς ἡ μάχη φυγὴ καὶ δίωξις. ἴσα-
σιν δὲ καὶ λιμὸν φέρειν οἱ Νομάδες οἵδε καὶ πόᾳ χρῆσθαι πολλάκις ἀντὶ σίτου· καὶ τὸ πάμπαν ὑδροποτοῦ-
σιν. ὅ τε ἵππος αὐτοῖς κριθῆς μὲν οὐδ᾽ ὅλως γεύεται,

44 ποηφαγῶν αἰεί, πίνει δὲ διὰ πολλοῦ. τοιούτους ὁ
Μασσανάσσης ἐς δισμυρίους συναγαγὼν ἐξῆγεν ἐπὶ
θήρας ἢ λεηλασίας ἑτέρων ἐθνῶν· ἅπερ ᾤετο καὶ ἔργα

he was in command in Iberia. Now, Syphax, who felt love's   38
sting for the girl, began to raid Carthaginian territory and
came to an agreement with Scipio, who had sailed from
Iberia to meet him, that he would give him military assistance when he attacked Carthage. When the Carthagin-   39
ians learned of this, they thought it was very important to
get Syphax on their side in the war against Rome, and so
handed over the young woman to him, without telling
Hasdrubal or Massinissa, who were in Iberia. Massinissa   40
was extremely annoyed at this, and so he too made an
agreement with Scipio in Iberia. He thought he had kept   41
it secret from Hasdrubal, but in fact Hasdrubal found out,
and although he was offended on behalf of the young man,
and of his own daughter—they had both been insulted—
he nevertheless thought it would be for the good of his
country to do away with Massinissa. So when the latter
returned from Iberia to Africa on the death of his father,
Hasdrubal sent a squadron of cavalry to escort him, with
orders to devise and execute a plot to kill him in secret,
however they could manage it.

11. But Massinissa found out and escaped. He then   42
took possession of his father's kingdom, and gathered a
force of cavalry, training them day and night to fire volleys
of javelins, repeatedly advancing, retiring and advancing
again. Battle for them is all about flight and pursuit. These   43
Numidians know how to put up with hunger, often eating
grass instead of bread, and drinking only water. Their
horses do not even know what oats taste like, but eat grass
the whole time, and drink rarely. Massinissa collected   44
about twenty thousand of such men, and would lead them
out on hunting expeditions or raiding parties on other
peoples, activities he regarded as both proper work and

45 καὶ γυμνάσια εἶναι. Καρχηδόνιοι δὲ καὶ Σύφαξ, νομίζοντες ἐπὶ σφᾶς εἶναι τὴν παρασκευὴν τοῦ μειρα-
κίου (οὐ γὰρ ἠγνόουν, ἃ ἐλελυπήκεσαν αὐτόν), ἔκριναν προτέρῳ τῷδε πολεμεῖν, ἔστε καθέλωσιν, καὶ τότε
Ῥωμαίοις ἀπαντᾶν.

46   12. Σύφαξ μὲν οὖν καὶ Καρχηδόνιοι πλείους ἦσαν
παρὰ πολύ, μετὰ δὲ ἁμαξῶν καὶ παρασκευῆς βαρείας
καὶ τρυφῆς ἐστρατεύοντο· Μασσανάσσης δὲ πόνων
τε πᾶσιν ἐξῆρχε καὶ ἱππικὸν μόνον εἶχε καὶ ὑποζύ-
47 γιον οὐδὲ οὐδὲ ἀγοράν. ὅθεν ῥᾳδίως ὑπέφευγέ τε καὶ
ἐπεχείρει καὶ ἐς τὰ ὀχυρὰ ἀνεπήδα· πολλάκις τε καὶ
καταλαμβανόμενος διεσκίδνη τὸ στράτευμα, ὅπῃ δυνηθεῖεν ἀποφεύγειν κατὰ μέρη, καὶ σὺν ὀλίγοις αὐτὸς
ὑπεκρύπτετό ποι, μέχρι συνέλθοιεν αὐτῷ νυκτὸς ἢ
μεθ᾽ ἡμέραν ἐς τὸ συγκείμενον. τρίτος δέ ποτε ἐν
σπηλαίῳ κρυπτόμενος ἔλαθε, τῶν πολεμίων περὶ τὸ
48 σπήλαιον στρατοπεδευόντων. οὐδὲ ἔστιν, ὅτε ἐστάθμευεν ἐν στρατοπέδῳ, ἀλλὰ καὶ μάλιστ᾽ ἐστρατήγει
λανθάνειν, ὅποι ποτὲ εἴη· ὅθεν οὐκ εἶχον αὐτῷ συνεχῶς προεπιχειρεῖν οἱ πολέμιοι, ἀλλ᾽ ἠμύνοντο ἐπι-
49 όντα. ἀγορὰ δ᾽ ἦν αὐτῷ καθ᾽ ἑκάστην ἡμέραν, ὅ τι
περὶ ἑσπέραν καταλάβοι χωρίον ἢ κώμην ἢ πόλιν,
ληζομένῳ τε πάντα καὶ διαρπάζοντι καὶ μεριζομένῳ
τοῖς συνοῦσιν· ὅθεν αὐτῷ πολλοὶ τῶν Νομάδων ἐπε-
φοίτων, μισθοὺς μὲν οὐ διδόντι τεταγμένους, τὰς δ᾽
ὠφελείας πολὺ πλείονας ἔχοντες.

50   13. Καὶ Μασσανάσσης μὲν Καρχηδονίοις οὕτως
ἐπολέμει, ὁ δὲ Σκιπίων, ἐπεί οἱ πάντα εὐτρεπῆ γε-

training. Syphax and the Carthaginians, believing that the   45
young man was making preparations against them—for
they were well aware how much they had annoyed him—
decided to fight and destroy him first, and then face the
Romans.

12. Syphax and the Carthaginians had many more men,   46
but their army moved with wagons and heavy baggage and
luxury goods. Massinissa on the other hand set an example
in all forms of hard work, and only had cavalry, no transport animals or supplies to carry. This made it easy for him   47
to withdraw or attack or quickly occupy strong positions.
Often, even when surprised, he would split his force to let
them escape in groups, however they could manage. He
himself would hide somewhere with a few men, until the
others would join him at night or during the day at an
agreed location. On one occasion, he and two others hid
in a cave and escaped detection, even though the enemy
were encamped outside the cave. He never took up quar-   48
ters in a camp, but his special skill as a general was always
to keep his position secret. As a result, his enemy could
never launch a sustained attack against him, but had to
defend themselves against his attacks. He gathered sup-   49
plies each day, at whatever place he happened to reach
toward evening, either village or town, by seizing everything as plunder and dividing it among his men. As a result, many Numidians made their way to join to him, in
spite of the fact that he paid no set wages: instead, they
had the booty, which was worth much more.

13. While Massinissa was making war on the Cartha-   50
ginians in this way, Scipio, when he had everything ready

APPIAN

γένητο ἐν Σικελίᾳ, ἔθυε Διὶ καὶ Ποσειδῶνι καὶ ἐς Λιβύην ἀνήγετο ἐπὶ νεῶν μακρῶν μὲν δύο καὶ πεντήκοντα, φορτίδων δὲ τετρακοσίων· κέλητές τε καὶ
51 λέμβοι πολλοὶ συνείποντο αὐτῷ. καὶ στρατιὰν ἦγε
πεζοὺς μὲν ἑξακισχιλίους ἐπὶ μυρίοις, ἱππέας δὲ χιλίους καὶ ἑξακοσίους. ἐπήγετο δὲ καὶ βέλη καὶ ὅπλα
52 καὶ μηχανήματα ποικίλα καὶ ἀγορὰν πολλήν. καὶ
Σκιπίων μὲν ὧδε διέπλει, Καρχηδόνιοι δὲ καὶ Σύφαξ
πυνθανόμενοι ἔγνωσαν ἐν τῷ παρόντι ὑποκρίνασθαί
τε ⟨πρὸς⟩[4] Μασσανάσσην καὶ ἐς φιλίαν ὑπαγαγέ-
53 σθαι, μέχρι ὅτου Σκιπίωνος ἐπικρατήσαιεν. ὁ δ' οὐκ
ἠγνόει μὲν ἐξαπατώμενος, ἀντενεδρεύων δὲ καὶ μη-
νύων πάντα τῷ Σκιπίωνι ἧκε πρὸς τὸν Ἀσρούβαν ὡς
συνηλλαγμένος μετὰ τῶν ἰδίων ἱππέων. καὶ ἐστρατοπέδευον οὐ μακρὰν ἀπ' ἀλλήλων Ἀσρούβας τε καὶ
Σύφαξ καὶ Μασσανάσσης περὶ Ἰτύκην πόλιν, ἐς ἣν
ὁ Σκιπίων καταχθεὶς ὑπ' ἀνέμων καὶ αὐτὸς ἐστρατο-
54 πέδευσε περὶ αὐτήν. οὐ πολὺ δ' ἀπεῖχεν ὁ Ἀσρούβας
αὐτοῦ, στρατιὰν ἔχων ἐς δισμυρίους πεζοὺς καὶ ἱππέας ἑπτακισχιλίους καὶ ἐλέφαντας ἑκατὸν ἐπὶ τεσσαράκοντα.

55   14. Σύφαξ μὲν οὖν, εἴτε δείσας, εἴτε ἄπιστος ἐς
ἑκατέρους γιγνόμενος παρὰ μέρος, ἐσκήψατό τι λυ-
πεῖν τὴν ἀρχὴν αὐτοῦ τοὺς ὁμόρους βαρβάρους καὶ
ἀνεζεύγνυεν ἐς τὰ οἰκεῖα· Σκιπίων δὲ κατ' ὀλίγους
ἔπεμπεν ἐπιχειρεῖν τῷ Ἀσρούβᾳ, καί τινες αὐτῷ καὶ
56 τῶν πόλεων προσεχώρουν. νυκτὸς δὲ λαθὼν ὁ Μασσανάσσης ἧκεν ἐπὶ τὸ στρατόπεδον τοῦ Σκιπίωνος

in Sicily, sacrificed to Zeus and Poseidon, and set sail for Africa with a fleet of fifty-two warships and four hundred transports, followed by a multitude of skiffs and galleys. He was leading an army of sixteen thousand infantry and 51 one thousand six hundred cavalry, and also carrying missiles, weapons, various kinds of siege engines, and plentiful supplies. When the Carthaginians and Syphax learned 52 that Scipio was sailing across to Africa, they decided to pretend for the moment to take Massinissa as a friend, until they had defeated Scipio. He was aware of the deception, 53 however, and laid a countertrap, which he explained fully to Scipio, by going to Hasdrubal with his own cavalry as if they had an alliance. Hasdrubal, Syphax, and Massinissa made camp not far from each other near the town of Utica, where Scipio had been driven by winds and where he too had camped nearby. Not far away from him 54 was Hasdrubal with an army of about twenty thousand infantry, seven thousand cavalry and one hundred and forty elephants.

14. Either out of fear or because he was being faithless 55 to each of his adversaries in turn, Syphax now made an excuse that his barbarian neighbors were despoiling his principality, and he broke camp to return home. Scipio sent his men in small detachments to attack Hasdrubal, and some of the towns joined him. During the night Massinissa came to Scipio's camp in secret, and after greeting 56

---

[4] πρὸς add. Reiske

καὶ δεξιωσάμενος αὐτὸν ἐδίδασκε τῆς ἐπιούσης ἔς τι
χωρίον ἀπὸ τριάκοντα σταδίων Ἰτύκης, ἔνθα πύργος
ἔστιν Ἀγαθοκλέους, ἔργον τοῦ Συρακοσίων τυράννου,
57 μὴ πλείους πεντακισχιλίων ἐνεδρεῦσαι. ἅμα δ' ἡμέρᾳ
τὸν Ἀσρούβαν ἔπειθε τὸν ἵππαρχον Ἄννωνα πέμψαι
τό τε πλῆθος τῶν ἐχθρῶν ἐπισκεψόμενον καὶ ἐς Ἰτύκην ἐσδραμούμενον, μή τι πλησιαζόντων πολεμίων
νεωτερίσειαν· καὶ αὐτὸς ὑπισχνεῖτο, εἰ κελεύοιτο, ἔψε-
58 σθαι. Ἄννων μὲν δὴ χιλίους ἦγεν ἐπιλέκτους ἱππέας
Καρχηδονίους καὶ Λιβύων τι πλῆθος, Μασσανάσσης
δὲ Νομάδας τοὺς ἑαυτοῦ· ὡς δ' ἐπὶ τὸν πύργον ἀφίκοντο καὶ ὁ Ἄννων ἐξίππευσεν ἐς τὴν Ἰτύκην σὺν
ὀλίγοις, μέρος τι τῆς ἐνέδρας ἐξεφαίνετο, καὶ ὁ Μασσανάσσης ἐκέλευσε τὸν τεταγμένον ἐπὶ τοῖς ἱππεῦσι
τῶν Καρχηδονίων ἐπιδραμεῖν αὐτοῖς, ὡς οὖσιν ὀλίγοις, καὶ αὐτὸς ἐκ βραχέος εἵπετο ὡς ἐπιβοηθήσων.
59 ἐν μέσῳ δὲ τῶν Λιβύων γενομένων ἥ τε πλείων ἐνέδρα κατεφαίνετο, καὶ συνηκόντισαν αὐτοὺς ἑκατέρωθεν οἵ τε Ῥωμαῖοι καὶ ὁ Μασσανάσσης πλὴν τετρα-
60 κοσίων, οἳ ἐλήφθησαν αἰχμάλωτοι. Μασσανάσσης
δ', ἐπεὶ τοῦτο ἐξετετέλεστο, ἀπήντα τῷ Ἄννωνι κατὰ
σπουδὴν ὡς φίλος ἐπανιὼν καὶ συλλαβὼν αὐτὸν ἀπῆγεν ἐς τὸ τοῦ Σκιπίωνος στρατόπεδον καὶ ἀντέδωκεν
Ἀσρούβᾳ τῆς μητρὸς τῆς ἑαυτοῦ.
61   15. Σκιπίων δὲ καὶ Μασσανάσσης τὴν χώραν ἐπόρθουν καὶ Ῥωμαίων ἐξέλυον, ὅσοι δεθέντες ἔσκαπτον
ἐν τοῖς ἀγροῖς, ἐξ Ἰβηρίας ἢ Σικελίας ἢ ἀπ' αὐτῆς
62 τῆς Ἰταλίας πεμφθέντες ὑπὸ Ἀννίβου. πολιορκοῦσι δ'

him, advised him to set an ambush next day of not more than five hundred troops at a spot about thirty stades from Utica, where there is a tower built by the Syracusan tyrant, Agathocles.[8] At dawn he persuaded Hasdrubal to send 57 Hanno, his commander of cavalry, to assess the size of the enemy army and make a rapid entry into Utica, to prevent the citizens, encouraged by the presence of the enemy, from trying to bring down the government. He promised he would follow himself, if ordered. So Hanno took one 58 thousand select Carthaginian cavalry and a detachment of Africans, while Massinissa led out his own Numidians. When they arrived at Agathocles' tower and Hanno rode off to Utica with a few men, a section of the ambush party suddenly revealed themselves. Massinissa ordered the officer in charge of the Carthaginian cavalry to attack them, since there were only a few of them, while he himself 59 followed closely, as if ready to assist. When the Africans were out in the open, the main body of the ambush appeared, and both the Romans and Massinissa shot down and killed all the Africans, except four hundred who were taken prisoner. With this accomplished, Massinissa hurried to meet Hanno, returning like a friend, but he arrested him and led him off to Scipio's camp, where he gave him to Hasdrubal in exchange for his own mother.

15. Scipio and Massinissa then ravaged the land, and 61 freed the Roman chain gangs digging in the fields, who had been sent there by Hannibal from Iberia, Sicily and

[8] Agathocles was born in 361/0, and by 316 he had established himself as tyrant of Syracuse. He declared himself king in 305. Most of his career was spent in fighting Carthage and trying to bring the Greeks of Sicily and southern Italy under his rule. He was assassinated in 289/8.

αὐτοῖς πόλιν μεγάλην, ᾗ ὄνομα ἦν Λόχα, καὶ πολλὰ
δεινὰ πάσχουσιν οἱ μὲν Λοχαῖοι προστιθεμένων τῶν
κλιμάκων ἐπεκηρυκεύοντο ἐκλείψειν τὴν πόλιν ὑπό-
σπονδοι, καὶ ὁ Σκιπίων ἀνεκάλει τῇ σάλπιγγι τὴν
63 στρατιάν· ἡ δ᾽ οὐχ ὑπήκουεν ὑπὸ ὀργῆς ὧν ἐπεπόνθε-
σαν, ἀλλ᾽ ἐπιβάντες τοῖς τείχεσι καὶ γύναια καὶ παιδία κατέσφαττον· ὁ δὲ τοὺς μὲν ἔτι ὄντας Λο χαίων
ἀφῆκεν ἀπαθεῖς, τὴν δὲ στρατιὰν τὴν λείαν ἀφείλετο
καὶ τοὺς λοχαγούς, ὅσοι συνεξήμαρτον, ἐκλήρωσεν
ἐν τῷ μέσῳ καὶ τρεῖς τοὺς λαχόντας ἐκόλασε θανάτῳ.
64 καὶ τάδε πράξας αὖθις ἐληλάτει. Ἀσρούβας δ᾽ αὐτοὺς
ἐνήδρευε, Μάγωνα μὲν τὸν ἵππαρχον ἐπιπέμψας ἐκ
65 μετώπου, αὐτὸς δὲ ὄπισθεν ἐπιών· οἱ δ᾽ ἐν μέσῳ γενόμενοι τὸ ἔργον ἐμερίσαντο καὶ ἐς ἑκατέρους αὐτῶν
ἑκάτερος ἐπιστραφεὶς πεντακισχιλίους τῶν Λιβύων
ἀπέκτειναν καὶ χιλίους καὶ ὀκτακοσίους ἔλαβον αἰχμαλώτους, τοὺς δὲ λοιποὺς ἐς τὰς πέτρας κατήραξαν.
66   16. Καὶ ὁ Σκιπίων εὐθὺς ἐπὶ τοῖσδε προσέβαλλεν
Ἰτύκῃ κατὰ γῆν καὶ κατὰ θάλασσαν, δύο μὲν πεντήρεσιν ἐζευγμέναις πύργον ἐπιθείς, ὅθεν τριπήχη
βέλη καὶ λίθους μεγάλους ἐς τοὺς πολεμίους ἠφίει,
καὶ πολλὰ μὲν ἔλυπει, πολλὰ δ᾽ ἀντέπασχε θραυο-
μένων τῶν νεῶν, χώματα δ᾽ ἐπαίρων μέγιστα καὶ κριοῖς τὸ τεῖχος, ὅτε προσπελάσειε, τύπτων δρεπάνοις τε
περισπῶν, ὅσαι βύρσαι περὶ αὐτὸ καὶ ἄλλα σκεπα-
67 στήρια ἦν. οἱ δὲ τὰ μὲν χώματα ὑπετάφρευον καὶ τὰ
δρέπανα βρόχοις παρῆγον καὶ τοὺς κριοὺς τῆς ὁρμῆς
ἐξέλυον, ἐπιβάλλοντες ἐπικαρσίας δοκούς· ἐς δὲ τὰς

Italy itself. Scipio's men suffered badly while besieging a 62
large town called Locha, but when they brought the scal-
ing ladders up against the walls, the inhabitants of the
town sent a message saying that they were willing to leave
under a truce. Although Scipio ordered the trumpets to
sound a withdrawal of the army, the soldiers were angry 63
at what they had suffered and, refusing to obey the order,
climbed the walls and slaughtered the women and children. The surviving Lochaeans were released unharmed
by Scipio, but he confiscated the army's booty, made all
the centurions who had joined in committing the offense
draw lots in public and punished with death the three on
whom the lot fell. This done, he returned to plundering. 64
Hasdrubal set a trap for the Romans, ordering Mago, his
commander of cavalry, to launch a frontal attack, while he
himself came up from the rear. The Romans were caught 65
in the middle, but they divided the task among themselves, each group turning to face either Hasdrubal or
Mago, and killed five thousand Africans, took one thousand eight hundred prisoners and drove the rest onto the
rocks.

16. As for Scipio, immediately after this, he attacked 66
Utica by land and sea. From a tower placed on two quinqueremes tied together he fired three-cubit long missiles
and huge stones at the enemy, inflicting but also suffering
much damage, with the ships taking a battering. He also
constructed huge siege mounds and, when he could get
near enough, pounded the wall with rams and used hooks
to pull off the leather awnings and other protective cover-
ings on it. The defenders dug mines under the mounds, 67
deflected the hooks with nooses and lessened the impact
of the rams by dropping beams across them. They would

27

μηχανὰς ἐξεπήδων μετὰ πυρός, ὅτε πνεῦμα φυλά-
ξειαν ἐς αὐτὰς ἐπίφορον· ὅθεν ὁ Σκιπίων ἀπογνοὺς
οὕτως αἱρήσειν τὴν πόλιν ἐς πολιορκίαν αὐτῆς καθ-
ίστατο.

68   17. Σύφαξ δέ, τῶν γιγνομένων πυνθανόμενος, ἧκε
μετὰ τοῦ στρατοῦ καὶ οὐ μακρὰν ἐστάθμευεν ἀπὸ
69 Ἀσρούβου. ἔτι δ' ὑποκρινόμενος εἶναι φίλος ἑκατέροις
καὶ τρίβειν τὸν πόλεμον ἐγνωκώς, μέχρι νῆές τε ἕτε-
ραι ναυπηγούμεναι πρὸς τῶν Καρχηδονίων ἐπιγένοι-
ντο καὶ μισθοφόροι τινὲς Κελτῶν καὶ Λιγύων ἐπέλ-
70 θοιεν, ἐπεχείρει διαιτᾶν διαλύσεις· καὶ ἐδικαίου μήτε
Ῥωμαίους Λιβύης μήτε Καρχηδονίους Ἰταλίας ἐπιβαίνειν ἐπὶ πολέμῳ, ἔχειν δὲ Ῥωμαίους Σικελίαν καὶ
Σαρδὼ καὶ εἴ τινας ἄλλας νήσους ἔχουσι, καὶ Ἰβη-
ρίαν· ἢν δέ τις ἀπειθῇ, τοῖς πειθομένοις ἔφη συμ-
71 μαχήσειν. ἅμα δὲ ταῦτ' ἔπρασσε καὶ Μασσανάσσην
ἐπείρα μεταθέσθαι πρὸς αὐτόν, τήν τε Μασσυλίων
ἀρχὴν αὐτῷ βεβαιώσειν ὑπισχνούμενος καὶ τῶν θυ-
γατέρων τριῶν οὐσῶν δώσειν ἐς γάμον, ἢν ἂν ἐθέλῃ.
72 ἔφερε δ' ὁ ταῦτα λέγων χρυσίον, ἵνα, εἰ μὴ πείσειε,
δῴη τῶν θεραπευτήρων αὐτοῦ τῷ κτείνειν Μασσανάσσην ὑπισχνουμένῳ. ὁ μὲν δὴ μὴ πείθων ἔδωκέ τινι τὸ
χρυσίον ἐπὶ τῷ φόνῳ· ὁ δὲ λαβὼν ἔδειξε τῷ Μασσανάσσῃ καὶ τὸν δόντα ἤλεγξε.

73   18. Σύφαξ δ', οὐ προσδοκῶν ἔτι λήσειν, φανερῶς
τοῖς Καρχηδονίοις συνεμάχει πόλιν τε ἐν μεσογείῳ
Θολοῦντα, Ῥωμαίων παρασκευὴν καὶ σῖτον πολὺν
ἔχουσαν, ἐκ προδοσίας εἷλε καὶ τοὺς φρουροῦντας

also make sorties against the siege engines with fire, whenever they observed the wind blowing in the right direction against them. The situation caused Scipio to despair of capturing the city in this way, and he settled down to besiege it.

17. When Syphax heard of what was happening, he 68 came with his army and established his quarters near Hasdrubal. Still pretending to be friends with both Romans 69 and Carthaginians, and intending to drag out the war until the new ships being built by the Carthaginians were finished and certain Celtic and Ligurian mercenaries had arrived, he set about trying to negotiate a settlement. His 70 proposal was that the Romans should not invade Africa, and the Carthaginians should not invade Italy, but that the Romans should keep Sicily, Sardinia and whatever islands they presently had, and Iberia. If one side rejected these terms, and the other complied, he said he would make an alliance with the compliant party. At the same time 71 as he was doing this, he was also trying to change Massinissa's allegiance over to himself. He promised he would strengthen Massylian power, and give him whichever of his three daughters he would like to marry. In case he 72 could not persuade Massinissa, the messenger was also bringing gold to pay a servant of his to kill him. In fact, he did not persuade him, and so he gave the money to someone to carry out the murder. But the man who accepted the money showed it to Massinissa and exposed the donor.

18. Realizing that he could no longer keep his position 73 secret, Syphax now openly joined the Carthaginian side. He arranged the betrayal and capture of the inland town of Tholous, where the Romans kept a large supply of

αὐτὴν ἔκτεινεν, οὐκ ἐθελήσαντας ἀπελθεῖν ὑποσπόν-
δους, συμμαχίαν τε ἄλλην πολλὴν Νομάδων μετεπέμ-
74 πετο. καὶ οἱ μισθοφόροι παρῆσαν αὐτοῖς ἤδη, καὶ
αἱ νῆες εὐτρεπῶς εἶχον, ὥστε ἔγνωστο πολεμεῖν Σύφακα μὲν ὁρμώμενον ἐπὶ τοὺς πολιορκοῦντας Ἰτύκην,
Ἀσρούβαν δ' ἐπὶ τὸ Σκιπίωνος στρατόπεδον· τὰς δὲ
ναῦς ἔδει ταῖς ναυσὶν ἐπιπλεῖν καὶ γίγνεσθαι ταῦτα
τῆς ἐπιούσης ἡμέρας ἅπαντα ὁμοῦ, ἵνα μὴ διαρκέ-
σειαν αὐτοῖς οἱ Ῥωμαῖοι διὰ τὴν ὀλιγότητα.

75   19. Ὧν ἤδη νυκτὸς οὔσης ὁ Μασσανάσσης παρά
τινων Νομάδων πυθόμενος μετέδωκε τῷ Σκιπίωνι. ὁ
76 δὲ ἔδεισε καὶ ἠπόρει, μὴ ἐς πολλὰ αὐτῷ διαιρούμενος
ὁ στρατὸς ἀσθενέστερος ἐς πάντα γίγνηται. τοὺς οὖν
ἡγεμόνας αὐτίκα νυκτὸς ἐπὶ τὴν σκέψιν ἐκάλει καὶ
ἀπορούντων ἀπάντων ἐπὶ πολὺ σύννους γενόμενος εἶ-
πεν· "Τόλμης καὶ ταχυτῆτος ἡμῖν, ὦ φίλοι, δεῖ καὶ
μάχης ἐξ ἀπογνώσεως. φθάσωμεν ἐπελθόντες τοῖς
πολεμίοις. ὅσα δ' ἐν τῷδε πλεονεκτήσομεν, μάθετε
77 ἤδη. ἐκείνους μὲν ἐκπλήξει τὸ ἀδόκητον τῆς ἐφόδου
καὶ τὸ παράδοξον τοῦ ἔργου, τῶν ὀλιγωτέρων προεπι-
χειρούντων· ἡμεῖς δ' οὐκ ἐς πολλὰ διῃρημένῃ τῇ
στρατιᾷ χρησόμεθα, ἀλλὰ ἀθρόᾳ, οὐδ' ἐπάξομεν αὐτὴν ἅπασι τοῖς ἐχθροῖς, ἀλλ' οἷς ἂν ἐπιλεξώμεθα
78 πρώτοις. σταθμεύουσι δ' ἐφ' ἑαυτῶν ἕκαστοι, καὶ
ἐσμεν αὐτοῖς κατὰ μέρος ἰσόμαχοι, τόλμῃ δὲ καὶ
εὐτυχίᾳ προύχομεν. καὶ ἢν ὁ θεὸς δῷ τῶν πρώτων
ἐπικρατῆσαι, τῶν ἄλλων καταφρονήσομεν. οἷς δ' ἐπι-
χειρητέον ἐστὶ πρώτοις καὶ τίς ὁ καιρὸς ἢ τρόπος

equipment and food, and killed the garrison troops when they refused to leave under truce. He also sent for another large force of Numidian allies. Now that the mercenaries had arrived and the ships were ready, the decision was made to join battle: Syphax was to attack the Romans besieging Utica, Hasdrubal the camp of Scipio, the ships were to engage the Roman fleet, and all parts of the operation were to take place simultaneously next day, so that the Romans would not be able to deal with them, given their lack of manpower. 74

19. It was already night when Massinissa learned of these plans from certain Numidians, and informed Scipio. Scipio did not know what to do, and was afraid that, as he had divided up his army into many sections, it would be too weak overall. So he immediately summoned his officers to a meeting in the night to consider the situation, but they too were all at a loss. After reflecting for a long time, he spoke: "My friends, what we need is daring and speed, and we must fight in desperation. I propose that we attack first, rather than the enemy. Just consider what advantages we will gain by doing this. The unexpectedness of the attack, and the extraordinary nature of the situation in which the smaller force is the first to attack, will shock them. For our part, we will not divide up our army into separate sections, but will keep it together, and we will not lead it out against the combined forces of our enemy, but only against those we select to attack first. They are all quartered in separate camps, and we can match each of them individually, as we are superior to them in daring and good fortune. And if the god grants us victory against the first we take on, we will be able to disdain the others. I will, if you are agreeable, give you my opinion on which ones we should 75 76 77 78

APPIAN

ἔσται τῆς ἐπιχειρήσεως, ἢν ἀρέσκῃ, τὰ τῆς γνώμης
ἐρῶ."

79   20. Συνθεμένων δὲ πάντων, "Ὁ μὲν καιρός," εἶπεν,
"Εὐθὺς ἐπιχειρεῖν ἀπὸ τοῦδε τοῦ συλλόγου, νυκτὸς
ἔτι οὔσης, ὅτε καὶ τὸ ἔργον ἐστὶ φοβερώτερον καὶ
ἀνέτοιμα τὰ ἐκείνων καὶ οὐδεὶς τῶν συμμάχων αὐτοῖς
δύναται βοηθεῖν ἐν σκότῳ, φθάσομέν τε οὕτως αὐτῶν
τὰ βουλεύματα μόνως, ἐγνωκότων ἡμῖν τῆς ἐπιούσης
80 ἡμέρας ἐπιθέσθαι. τριῶν δ᾽ αὐτοῖς ὄντων στρατοπέδων, αἱ μὲν νῆές εἰσι πόρρω, καὶ οὐκ ἔστιν ναυσὶ
νυκτὸς ἐπιχειρεῖν, Ἀσρούβας δὲ καὶ Σύφαξ οὐ μα-
81 κρὰν ἀπ᾽ ἀλλήλων. καὶ τούτοιν Ἀσρούβας μέν ἐστι
τὸ τοῦ πολέμου κεφάλαιον, Σύφαξ δὲ οὐκ ἂν νυκτὸς
ἐπιτολμήσειε τῷ πόνῳ, βάρβαρος ἀνὴρ καὶ τρυφῆς
82 γέμων καὶ δέους. φέρε οὖν, ἡμεῖς μὲν ἐπὶ Ἀσρούβαν
μετὰ παντὸς ἴωμεν τοῦ στρατοῦ, Μασσανάσσην δὲ
τόνδε ἐπιτάξωμεν ἐφεδρεύειν τῷ Σύφακι, ἢν ἄρα καὶ
83 παρὰ δόξαν ἐξίῃ τοῦ στρατοπέδου. πεζοὶ δὲ χωρῶμεν
ἐπὶ τὸν χάρακα τοῦ Ἀσρούβου καὶ περιστάντες ἐπι-
χειρῶμεν ἐκ παντὸς μέρους σὺν ἐλπίδι τε χρηστῇ
καὶ τόλμῃ θρασυτάτῃ τούτων γὰρ τὰ παρόντα δεῖται
84 μάλιστα. τοὺς δ᾽ ἱππέας (οὐ γὰρ ἔστιν αὐτοῖς χρῆσθαι νυκτὸς ἔτι οὔσης) προπέμψω πορρωτέρω κυ-
κλοῦσθαι τὸ στρατόπεδον τῶν πολεμίων, ἵνα, εἰ μὲν
βιασθείημεν, ὑποδέχοιντο ἡμᾶς καὶ ἐς φιλίους κατα-
φεύγοιμεν, εἰ δ᾽ ἐπικρατοίημεν, ἐκφεύγοντας ἐκείνους
διώκοιεν καὶ διαχρῷντο."

85   21. Ταῦτ᾽ εἰπὼν καὶ τοὺς ἡγεμόνας ἐκπέμψας ὁπλί-

target first, and what the timing and means of our attack will be."

20. They all agreed, and he continued: "The right time 79 to attack is immediately after this meeting, while it is still night. That is when the battle will be more frightening and the enemy not ready for it, and none of their allies will be able to offer assistance in the darkness. This is the only way to act first ahead of their plans to attack us tomorrow. They have three separate camps. The ships are some dis- 80 tance away and it is not possible to launch a naval attack at night. Hasdrubal and Syphax are not far from each other, and of these two, Hasdrubal is the spearhead of 81 their war effort, while Syphax will not risk trouble at night, since he is a barbarian, a man burdened with luxury and fear. Come on, then, let us attack Hasdrubal with our 82 entire force, and give Massinissa here the job of keeping watch on Syphax, just in case he leaves his camp unexpectedly. I suggest we use our infantry to attack Hasdrubal's 83 palisade, and by surrounding it come at them from all quarters. Above all, the situation needs our best hopes and most audacious courage. As you cannot use cavalry at 84 night, I will send them to circle the enemy camp further out, so that if we are forced back, they can take us into their lines and we have a refuge among friends; and if we win, they can pursue the enemy and destroy them in flight."

21. With these words, he sent the officers off to arm the 85

APPIAN

σαι τὸν στρατὸν αὐτὸς ἐθύετο Τόλμῃ καὶ Φόβῳ, μηδὲν ὡς ἐν νυκτὶ πανικὸν οἱ γενέσθαι, ἀλλὰ τὸν στρατὸν αὐτῷ θρασύτατόν τε <. . .>[5] μάλιστα ὀφθῆναι.
86 τρίτης δὲ ἤδη φυλακῆς ἠρέμα τῇ σάλπιγγι ὑπεσή-
μαινε, καὶ μετὰ σιγῆς βαθυτάτης στρατὸς τοσοῦτος
ἐβάδιζεν, ἕως οἱ μὲν ἱππεῖς περιέστησαν ἐν κύκλῳ
τοὺς πολεμίους, οἱ πεζοὶ δ' ἐπὶ τὴν τάφρον αὐτῶν
87 ἀφίκοντο. βοῇ δὲ τότε παμμιγεῖ καὶ σάλπιγξιν ἀθρό-
αις καὶ βυκανήμασιν ἐς κατάπληξιν χρώμενοι τοὺς
μὲν φύλακας ἐξέωσαν ἐκ τῶν φυλακτηρίων, τὴν δὲ
τάφρον ἔχουν καὶ τὰ σταυρώματα διέσπων· οἱ δ' εὐ-
τολμότατοι προδραμόντες ἐνέπρησάν τινας σκηνάς.
88 καὶ οἱ Λίβυες μετ' ἐκπλήξεως ἀνεπήδων τε ἐξ ὕπνου
καὶ τὰ ὅπλα μετελάμβανον καὶ ἐς τὰς τάξεις ἀτάκτως
ἐφέροντο καὶ τῶν παραγγελλομένων διὰ τὸν θόρυβον
οὐ κατήκουον, οὐδ' αὐτοῦ τοῦ στρατηγοῦ τὸ ἀκριβὲς
89 τῶν γιγνομένων εἰδότος. ἀναπηδῶντας οὖν αὐτοὺς οἱ
Ῥωμαῖοι καὶ ὁπλιζομένους ἔτι καὶ ταρασσομένους
κατελάμβανον καὶ σκηνὰς πλέονας ἐνεπίμπρασαν
90 καὶ τοὺς ἐν ποσὶν ἀνήρουν. τοῖς δ' ἦν ἥ τε βοὴ τῶν
ἐχθρῶν καὶ ἡ ὄψις καὶ τὰ ἔργα φοβερώτατα ὡς ἐν
νυκτὶ καὶ ἀγνωσίᾳ τοῦ γινομένου κακοῦ· ἡγούμενοί τε
εἰλῆφθαι τὸ στρατόπεδον καὶ τὸ πῦρ τῶν ἐμπεπρη-
σμένων σκηνῶν δεδιότες ἐξέπιπτον ἑκόντες ἐξ αὐτῶν
καὶ ἐς τὸ πεδίον ὡς ἀσφαλέστερον ἐωθοῦντο· ὅθεν
κατὰ μέρος, ὅπῃ τύχοιεν, ἀκόσμως διεδίδρασκον καὶ
ἐς τοὺς Ῥωμαίων ἱππέας, οἳ κύκλῳ περιεστήκεσαν,
ἐμπίπτοντες ἀπέθνησκον.

troops, while he himself sacrificed to Courage and Fear, praying that there would be no panic in the night, but that his soldiers would be seen at their very bravest and ⟨. . .⟩[9] It was now the third watch, when he gave the signal with 86 muted trumpet, and the army, large as it was, advanced in the deepest silence, until the cavalry had encircled the enemy and the infantry had arrived at the trench of the enemy camp. Then with a mixture of shouting and trum- 87 pets and horns all sounding together to create confusion, they drove the guards from the pickets, leveled the trench and tore down the stockade. The most daring ran ahead and set fire to some tents. The Africans were in a state of 88 chaos, leaping up out of bed and arming themselves, try- ing to get into rank amid the confusion, and unable to hear their orders because of the noise; their general did not even know exactly what was happening. So, the Romans 89 caught them getting up, still arming themselves, and in disarray; and they burned more of the tents and killed all they met. The night, and ignorance of the disaster as it was 90 unfolding, made the noise of the enemy, their appearance, and actions even more frightening for the Africans. They believed their camp had been captured and, in fear of the burning tents, were glad to escape from them and press forward to the apparently greater safety of the plain. But here, with scattered groups running around in confusion and in all directions, they fell into the path of the Roman cavalry surrounding them, and died.

[9] There seems to be a short lacuna in the text at this point.

---

[5] Lac. ind. Mend.

91   22. Σύφαξ δέ, νυκτὸς μὲν ἔτι τῆς βοῆς αἰσθόμενος
καὶ τὸ πῦρ ὁρῶν, οὐκ ἐπεξῆλθεν, ἀλλὰ τῶν ἱππέων
τινὰς ἐπικουρεῖν ἔπεμψεν Ἀσρούβᾳ, οἷς ὁ Μασσανάσ-
92 σης ἐπιπεσὼν ἄφνω πολὺν ἐργάζεται φόνον. ἅμα δ᾽
ἡμέρᾳ μαθὼν ὁ Σύφαξ Ἀσρούβαν μὲν ἤδη φυγόντα,
τῆς δὲ στρατιᾶς αὐτοῦ τοὺς μὲν ἀπολωλότας, τοὺς δ᾽
εἰλημμένους ὑπὸ τῶν πολεμίων, τοὺς δὲ διερριμμέ-
νους καὶ τὸ στρατόπεδον αὐτῇ παρασκευῇ Ῥωμαίους
ἔχοντας ἀνεζεύγνυε φεύγων ἐς τὰ μεσόγεια μετὰ θορύβου, πάντα καταλιπών, οἰόμενος εὐθὺς ἀπὸ τῆς
Καρχηδονίων διώξεως αὐτῷ τὸν Σκιπίωνα ἐπανιόντα
ἐπιστήσεσθαι· ὅθεν καὶ τοῦδε τὸν χάρακα καὶ τὴν ἐν
αὐτῷ παρασκευὴν εἷλε Μασσανάσσης.

93   23. Καὶ Ῥωμαῖοι διὰ τόλμης μιᾶς, ἐν ὀλίγῳ μέρει
νυκτός, δύο στρατοπέδων καὶ δύο στρατῶν πολὺ μει-
94 ζόνων ἐκράτησαν ὁμοῦ. ἀπέθανον δὲ Ῥωμαίων μὲν
ἀμφὶ τοὺς ἑκατὸν ἄνδρας, τῶν δ᾽ ἐχθρῶν ὀλίγῳ δέον-
τες τρισμύριοι· καὶ αἰχμάλωτοι ἐγένοντο δισχίλιοι
καὶ τετρακόσιοι. τῶν δὲ ἱππέων ἑξακόσιοι ἐπανιόντι
τῷ Σκιπίωνι ἑαυτοὺς παρέδοσαν. καὶ τῶν ἐλεφάντων
95 οἳ μὲν ἀνῄρηντο, οἳ δὲ ἐτέτρωντο. Σκιπίων δέ, ὅπλων
τε καὶ χρυσοῦ καὶ ἀργύρου καὶ ἐλέφαντος πολλοῦ καὶ
ἵππων ἄλλων τε καὶ Νομαδικῶν κεκρατηκὼς καὶ διὰ
μιᾶς τῆσδε νίκης, λαμπροτάτης δὴ γενομένης, ἐς
γόνυ τὰ Καρχηδονίων καταβαλὼν ἅπαντα, ἀριστεῖα
τῷ στρατῷ διεδίδου καὶ τῶν λαφύρων τὰ ἀξιολο-
96 γώτατα ἐς Ῥώμην ἔπεμπε. καὶ τὸν στρατὸν ἐγύμναζε

22. As for Syphax, while it was still night, although he heard the shouting and saw the fire, he did not venture out, but sent a force of cavalry to help Hasdrubal. These were caught in a surprise attack by Massinissa who inflicts heavy losses on them. At dawn, when Syphax learned that Hasdrubal had already fled, and that the enemy had either killed, captured, or dispersed his army, and that the Romans were now in possession of his camp, equipment and all, he withdrew and fled inland in disorder, leaving everything behind, as he thought that Scipio would return immediately after he had finished pursuing the Carthaginians and attack him. As a result, Massinissa captured his palisade and the equipment in it.

23. So it was that the Romans in one bold stroke, and in a short period of the night, simultaneously became master of two camps and defeated two armies much bigger than theirs. The Romans lost about one hundred men killed, the enemy just short of thirty thousand killed and two thousand four hundred captured. Six hundred cavalry surrendered to Scipio when he got back, and some elephants were killed, some wounded. Scipio became master of a large supply of weapons, gold, silver, ivory, and horses (both Numidian and other), and having brought Carthage to its knees through this one brilliant victory, he distributed prizes for valor to the army, but sent the most spectacular of the spoils to Rome. He then put the army

φιλοπόνως, προσδοκῶν Ἀννίβαν τε αὐτίκα ἀπὸ τῆς
Ἰταλίας καὶ Μάγωνα⁶ ἀπὸ Λιγυστίνων ἐπελεύσεσθαι.

97   24. Καὶ Σκιπίων μὲν περὶ ταῦτα ἦν, Ἀσρούβας δέ,
ὁ στρατηγὸς ὁ Καρχηδονίων, ἐν μὲν τῇ νυκτομαχίᾳ
μεθ᾽ ἱππέων πεντακοσίων τετρωμένος εἰς Ἀνδὰν κατέφυγεν, ἔνθα μισθοφόρους τέ τινας ἐκ τῆς μάχης
ἐκπεσόντας καὶ Νομάδας συνέλεγε καὶ δούλους εἰς

98   ἐλευθερίαν συνεκάλει· πυθόμενος δ᾽, ὅτι Καρχηδόνιοι
θάνατον αὐτοῦ κατέγνωσαν ὡς κακῶς ἐστρατηγη-
κότος καὶ Ἄννωνα τὸν Βουμίλχαρος εἵλοντο στρατηγεῖν, ἴδιον αὐτοῦ τὸν στρατὸν ἐποίει καὶ κακούργους
προσελάμβανε καὶ ἐλῄζετο ἐς τὰς τροφὰς καὶ ἐγύμναζεν, οὓς εἶχεν, ἀμφὶ τρισχιλίους ἱππέας, πεζοὺς δὲ
ὀκτακισχιλίους, ὡς ἐν μόνῳ τῷ μάχεσθαι τὰς ἐλπίδας

99   ἔχων. ὁ μὲν δὴ ταῦτα ποιῶν Ῥωμαίους ὁμοῦ καὶ Καρχηδονίους ἐπὶ πολὺ ἐλάνθανε, Σκιπίων δ᾽ ἐπῆγεν αὐτῇ
Καρχηδόνι τὸν στρατὸν ὡπλισμένον καὶ σοβαρῶς ἐς

100   μάχην προυκαλεῖτο, οὐδενὸς ἐξιόντος. Ἀμίλχαρ δὲ ὁ
ναύαρχος ναυσὶν ἑκατὸν ἐσπευσμένως εἰς τὸν ναύ-
σταθμον ἀνήγετο τοῦ Σκιπίωνος, ἐλπίσας αὐτόν τε
φθάσειν ἐπανιόντα καὶ τὰς οὔσας ἐκεῖ Ῥωμαίων
εἴκοσι τριήρεις ῥᾳδίως ταῖς ἑκατὸν αἱρήσειν.

101   25. Καὶ ὁ Σκιπίων ἰδὼν αὐτοῦ τὸν ἀπόπλουν πρού-
πεμπέ τινα τὸν ἔσπλουν τοῦ λιμένος ἐμφράξαι στραγ-
γύλοις πλοίοις ἐπ᾽ ἀγκυρῶν ἐκ διαστήματος, ἵνα ὡς
διὰ πυλῶν αἱ τριήρεις ἐκθέοιεν, ὅτε καιρὸς εἴη, καὶ τὰ
πλοῖα τοῖς κέρασι συνδῆσαί τε καὶ ἁρμόσαι πρὸς

102   ἄλληλα, ἵνα ἀντὶ τείχους ᾖ. καταλαβὼν δὲ τὸ ἔργον

into rigorous training, expecting the immediate arrival of
Hannibal from Italy and of Mago from Liguria.

24. So much for Scipio's actions. Meanwhile, the Car- 97
thaginian general, Hasdrubal, who had been wounded in
the night battle, fled to Anda with five hundred cavalry.
Here, he enrolled some mercenaries and Numidians who
had escaped from the battle, and invited slaves to join him
with the promise of freedom. When he found out that the 98
Carthaginians had sentenced him to death for his incom-
petent performance as general, and had appointed Hanno
son of Bomilcar to the command, he formed his own private army, even taking on criminals, and resorting to raiding for supplies. As he believed his only hope lay in fighting, he set about training the men he had, about three
thousand cavalry and eight thousand infantry. For a long 99
time, neither Rome nor Carthage noticed what he was
doing. Scipio led his men in arms against Carthage itself,
and although he imperiously challenged the enemy to
battle, nobody emerged from the town. Hamilcar, the ad- 100
miral, set sail for Scipio's anchorage in a hurry with one
hundred ships, expecting to get there before Scipio returned, and to capture easily the twenty Roman warships
there with his own one hundred.

25. When Scipio saw him sail off, he sent somebody 101
ahead to block the entrance of the harbor with merchantmen anchored at intervals, so that, when the opportunity
arose, the triremes could dash out as if making sorties
through gates. He was also to have them roped together
at the bow and attached to each other so as to function like
a wall. On his arrival, finding the work ⟨. . .⟩ he went into 102

---

6 Μάγωνα edd: Ἄννωνα codd.

⟨. . .⟩ ἥπτετο τοῦ πόνου. καὶ βαλλομένων τῶν Καρχηδονίων ἀπό τε τῶν πλοίων καὶ ἀπὸ τῆς γῆς καὶ ἀπὸ
τοῦ τείχους αἱ νῆες ἐθραύοντο καὶ καμοῦσαι περὶ
103   ἑσπέραν ἀπέπλεον. ἀπιούσαις δ᾽ αὐταῖς αἱ Ῥωμαίων
ἐπέκειντο, ἐκθέουσαί τε διὰ τῶν διαστημάτων καί,
ὅτε βιάζοιντο, ὑποχωροῦσαι· μίαν δὲ καὶ ἀνεδήσαντο
104   κενὴν ἀνδρῶν καὶ πρὸς τὸν Σκιπίωνα ἀνήγαγον. μετὰ
δὲ τοῦτο ἐχείμαζον ἄμφω. καὶ Ῥωμαίοις μὲν ἦν ἐκ
θαλάσσης ἀγορὰ δαψιλής, Ἰτυκαῖοι δὲ καὶ Καρχηδόνιοι λιμώττοντες ἐλήστευον τοὺς ἐμπόρους, μέχρι
Ῥωμαίων νῆες ἄλλαι, πεμφθεῖσαι τῷ Σκιπίωνι, ἐφώρ-
μουν τοῖς πολεμίοις καὶ τὰς λῃστρικὰς ἐκώλυον. οἱ δ᾽
ἔκαμνον ἤδη σφόδρα τῷ λιμῷ.

105   26. Τοῦ δ᾽ αὐτοῦ χειμῶνος, ἐγγὺς ὄντος Σύφακος,
Μασσανάσσης ᾔτησεν ἐπὶ τῇ ἰδίᾳ στρατιᾷ τὸ τρίτον
τῆς Ῥωμαϊκῆς παρὰ Σκιπίωνος καὶ λαβών, ἡγουμέ-
106   νου τῶν Ῥωμαίων Λαιλίου, τὸν Σύφακα ἐδίωκεν. ὁ δὲ
ὑπέφευγεν, μέχρι καθορώμενος περί τινι ποταμῷ συν-
ετάσσετο ἐς μάχην. οἱ μὲν οὖν Νομάδες ἑκατέρωθεν,
ὥσπερ ἔθος αὐτοῖς, πολλὰ καὶ ἀθρόα ἠφίεσαν ἐπ᾽
ἀλλήλοις, οἱ δὲ Ῥωμαῖοι προβαλλόμενοι τὰς ἀσπίδας
107   ἐπῄεσαν. Σύφαξ δὲ Μασσανάσσην ἰδὼν ἵετο ἐπ᾽
αὐτὸν ὑπὸ ὀργῆς· ὁ δ᾽ ἀντεπήλασεν γεγηθώς, καὶ
ἀγῶνος πολλοῦ περὶ ἄμφω γενομένου τραπέντες οἱ
τοῦ Σύφακος ἐς φυγὴν τὸν ποταμὸν ἐπέρων, ἔνθα τις
αὐτοῦ τὸν Σύφακος ἵππον ἔβαλεν· ὁ δ᾽ ἀπεσείσατο

battle.[10] The Carthaginians were hit by missiles fired from the ships, from the land and from the walls, and toward evening their ships sailed off, battered and exhausted. As they withdrew, the Romans fell on them, rushing out through the gaps between the merchant vessels, and then when forced back, retreating by the same route. They even managed to get a line on one crewless ship, and bring it back to Scipio. After this, both sides went into winter quarters. The Romans were well supplied by sea, but the inhabitants of Utica and Carthage were starving and turned to raiding merchant ships, until new ships sent to Scipio from Rome blockaded the enemy and stopped the piracy. The Carthaginians now began to suffer terribly from hunger.

26. During the same winter, since Syphax was in the vicinity, Massinissa asked Scipio for a third of the Roman army to add to his own. Scipio agreed, and with Laelius in command of the Roman troops, Massinissa set off in pursuit of Syphax.[11] Syphax withdrew until he was sighted near a river and formed up for battle. The Numidians on both sides followed their usual practice of firing many concentrated volleys at each other, while the Romans advanced with their shields to the front. Catching sight of Massinissa, Syphax rushed at him in anger, but Massinissa was pleased to meet his attack. There was a fierce fight around them, and then Syphax's men turned in flight and began to cross the river. Here, when somebody shot Syph-

103

104

105

106

107

[10] There is a lacuna in the text here, but there may not be much missing.

[11] Syphax was captured in 203. C. Laelius became consul in 190. He had been serving with Scipio since 206.

τὸν δεσπότην, καὶ ὁ Μασσανάσσης ἐπιδραμὼν εἷλεν
108 αὐτόν τε Σύφακα καὶ τὸν ἕτερον αὐτοῦ τῶν υἱῶν. καὶ
τούσδε μὲν εὐθὺς ἔπεμπε Σκιπίωνι, ἀπέθανον δ' ἐν τῇ
μάχῃ Σύφακος μὲν ἐς μυρίους ἄνδρας, Ῥωμαίων δὲ
πέντε καὶ ἑβδομήκοντα, Μασσανάσσου δὲ τριακόσιοι. καὶ αἰχμάλωτοι Σύφακος ἐγένοντο τετρακισχί-
109 λιοι. τούτων ἦσαν Μασσύλιοι δισχίλιοι καὶ πεντακόσιοι, τῶν εἰς Σύφακα ἀπὸ Μασσανάσσου μεταστάντων·
καὶ αὐτοὺς ὁ Μασσανάσσης ἐπὶ τῷδε ᾔτησεν παρὰ
Λαιλίου καὶ λαβὼν κατέσφαξεν.

110   27. Μετὰ δὲ τοῦτο Μασσυλίους καὶ τὴν χώραν τὴν
Σύφακος ἐπῄεσαν, τοὺς μὲν αὖθις εἰς τὴν ἀρχὴν τὴν
Μασσανάσσου καθιστάμενοι, τοὺς δὲ προσποιούμε-
νοί τε καὶ τοὺς ἀπειθοῦντας αὐτῶν καταστρεφόμενοι.
111 ἀφίκοντο δ' αὐτοῖς καὶ ἐκ Κίρτης πρέσβεις, τὰ
βασίλεια τοῦ Σύφακος παραδιδόντες, ἰδίᾳ δὲ πρὸς
Μασσανάσσην ἕτεροι παρὰ Σοφωνίβας, τῆς Σύφακος γυναικός, τὴν ἀνάγκην τοῦ γάμου διηγούμενοι.
112 Σοφωνίβαν μὲν οὖν ἄσμενος εἶχε λαβὼν ὁ Μασ-
σανάσσης· καὶ αὐτήν, ἐπανιὼν πρὸς Σκιπίωνα αὐτός,
113 ἐν Κίρτῃ κατέλιπε, προορώμενος ἄρα τὸ μέλλον. Σκιπίων δ' ἤρετο Σύφακα· "Τίς σε δαίμων ἔβλαψε, φίλον
ὄντα μοι καὶ αὐτὸν ἐπὶ Λιβύην ἐλθεῖν προτρέψαντα,
ψεύσασθαι μὲν θεούς, οὓς ὤμοσας, ψεύσασθαι δὲ
μετὰ τῶν θεῶν Ῥωμαίους καὶ μετὰ Καρχηδονίων ἀντὶ
Ῥωμαίων ἑλέσθαι πολεμεῖν, τῶν ἐπὶ Καρχηδονίους
114 οὐ πρὸ πολλοῦ σοι βεβοηθηκότων;" ὁ δ' εἶπεν· "Σο-
φωνίβα, Ἀσρούβα θυγάτηρ, ἧς ἐγὼ ἤρων ἐπ' ἐμῷ

ax's horse, it threw its rider and Massinissa galloped up to capture Syphax himself and one of his sons. He immedi- 108 ately sent them off to Scipio. Syphax lost about ten thousand men killed in the battle, the Romans seventy-five, Massinissa three hundred. Four thousand of Syphax's men were captured, of whom two thousand five hundred were 109 Massylians, who had changed sides from Massinissa to Syphax. For this reason, when Massinissa asked Laelius for them, and his request was accepted, he executed them.

27. After this, they invaded the territory of the Massyl- 110 ians and of Syphax. The former they placed back under the rule of Massinissa, the latter they won over by persuasion or reduced by force those who refused to comply. Ambassadors also came to them from the town of Cirta, to 111 hand over the palace of Syphax.[12] Others came personally to Massinissa from Sophoniba, the wife of Syphax, to explain how the marriage was forced on her. Massinissa re- 112 ceived her graciously and married her, but when he himself returned to Scipio, he left her in Cirta, predicting, no doubt, what would happen. "What divinity so befuddled 113 you, you who are my friend," Scipio asked Syphax, "that when you personally asked me to come to Africa, you chose to fight alongside the Carthaginians rather than the Romans, who only shortly before had helped you against the Carthaginians, in the process perjuring yourself before the gods by whom you swore an oath, and not just the gods, but perjuring yourself before the Romans as well?" He 114 replied: "It was Sophoniba, Hasdrubal's daughter, with

[12] Cirta is the modern town of Constantine in Algeria, renamed and rebuilt by the emperor Constantine in AD 313.

κακῷ. φιλόπατρις δ᾽ ἐστὶν ἰσχυρῶς καὶ ἱκανὴ ἅπαντά
τινα πεῖσαι, πρὸς ἃ βούλεται. αὕτη με καὶ ἐκ τῆς
ὑμετέρας φιλίας ἐς τὴν τῆς ἑαυτῆς μετέθηκε πατρίδος
καὶ ἐς τόδε συμφορᾶς ἐκ τοσῆσδε εὐδαιμονίας κατέ-
115 βαλεν. σοὶ δὲ παραινῶ (χρὴ γάρ, ὑμέτερον γενόμενον
καὶ Σοφωνίβας ἀπηλλαγμένον, νῦν γε ὑμῖν εἶναι βέβαιον)· φύλασσε Σοφωνίβαν, μὴ Μασσανάσσην ἐς
ἃ βούλεται, μεταγάγῃ. οὐ γὰρ δή, μὴ τὸ γύναιόν
ποτε ἕληται τὰ Ῥωμαίων, ἐλπίζειν ἄξιον· οὕτως ἐστὶν
ἰσχυρῶς φιλόπολις."

116   28. Ταῦθ᾽ ὁ μὲν ἔλεγεν, εἴτ᾽ ἀληθεύων, εἴτε ζηλοτυ-
πούμενος καὶ Μασσανάσσην ἐς τὰ μέγιστα βλά-
πτων· ὁ δὲ Σκιπίων Σύφακα μέν, συνετόν τε φαινόμε-
νον καὶ τῆς χώρας ἔμπειρον, ἐπὶ τὰ κοινὰ ἐπήγετο καὶ
γνώμης καὶ συμβουλῆς μετεδίδου, οἷόν τι καὶ Κροίσῳ
τῷ Λυδῷ Κῦρος ἐχρῆτο· Λαιλίου δ᾽ ἀφικομένου καὶ
ταὐτὰ περὶ τῆς Σοφωνίβας πυθέσθαι παρὰ πολλῶν
λέγοντος ἐκέλευσε τὸν Μασσανάσσην τὴν Σύφακος
117 γυναῖκα παραδοῦναι. παραιτουμένου δὲ ἐκείνου καὶ τὰ
περὶ αὐτῆς ἄνωθεν, ὡς ἐγένετο, διηγουμένου τραχύ-
τερον ὁ Σκιπίων ἐκέλευεν αὐτὸν μηδὲν ἀφαιρεῖσθαι
βίᾳ τῶν Ῥωμαϊκῶν λαφύρων, ἀλλ᾽ εἰς τὸ μέσον κατα-
118 θέντα αἰτεῖν καὶ πείθειν, εἰ δύναιτο. ᾤχετο οὖν ὁ
Μασσανάσσης μετά τινων Ῥωμαίων παραδώσων αὐτοῖς τὴν Σοφωνίβαν. κρύφα δὲ αὐτῇ φέρων φάρμακον
πρῶτος ἐνέτυχεν καὶ τὰ παρόντα προύθηκεν, ἢ πιεῖν
ἢ Ῥωμαίοις δουλεύειν ἑκοῦσαν, οὐδέν τε εἰπὼν ἔτι
119 ἐξήλασεν τὸν ἵππον. ἡ δέ, τῇ τροφῷ δείξασα τὴν

whom I had the misfortune to fall in love. She is a woman
fiercely patriotic and capable of persuading anyone to do
what she wants. It was she who turned me away from your
friendship to that of her own country, and cast me down
from a state of such prosperity to my present misfortune.
I have advice for you—and now that my allegiance is yours   115
and I am free of Sophoniba, I must be steadfast on your
behalf: make sure that Sophoniba does not seduce Massinissa into adopting her plans. For she is so fiercely loyal
to her own city that there is no point expecting her ever to
choose Rome's side."

28. This was what he said, either because he was telling   116
the truth or because he was jealous of Massinissa and was
trying to hurt him as much as possible. As Syphax had
shown himself to be intelligent and well informed about
the country, Scipio brought him in for consultations, and
shared his opinions and advice, in the same way as Cyrus
had consulted Croesus the Lydian. When Laelius arrived
and said that he had heard the same things about Sophoniba from many people, Scipio ordered Massinissa to
hand over Syphax's wife. But Massinissa raised objections,   117
and although he explained how things had happened in
relation to her from the beginning, Scipio ordered him
more severely not to try to appropriate any of the Roman
spoils, but once they had been deposited publicly as a
prize, to make his request and establish his case, if he
could. So Massinissa went off with a company of Romans   118
to hand over Sophoniba to them. But secretly he brought
her poison and, meeting her before the others, explained
the situation: she must either drink the poison, or willingly
serve the Romans as a slave. He said nothing more and   119

APPIAN

κύλικα καὶ δεηθεῖσα μηδὲν ὀδύρασθαι καλῶς ἀπο-
120 θανοῦσαν, ἔπιεν τοῦ φαρμάκου. καὶ αὐτὴν ὁ Μασσανάσσης τοῖς ἥκουσι Ῥωμαίων ἐπιδείξας καὶ θάψας
βασιλικῶς ὑπέστρεφεν πρὸς Σκιπίωνα. ὁ δὲ αὐτὸν
ἐπαινέσας τε καὶ παρηγορήσας, ὅτι πονηρᾶς γυναικὸς ἀπηλλάγη, ἐστεφάνωσε τῆς ἐφόδου τῆς ἐπὶ Σύ-
121 φακα καὶ ἐδωρήσατο πολλοῖς. ἀχθέντος δ᾽ ἐς Ῥώμην
τοῦ Σύφακος, οἱ μὲν ἠξίουν περισώζειν ἄνδρα ἐν
Ἰβηρίᾳ φίλον καὶ σύμμαχον αὐτοῖς γενόμενον, οἱ δὲ
κολάζειν, ὅτι τοῖς φίλοις ἐπολέμησεν. ὁ δὲ ὑπὸ λύπης
νοσῶν ἀπέθανεν.

122   29. Ἀσρούβας δὲ ἐπειδὴ καλῶς τοὺς συνόντας ἐγύ-
μνασεν, ἔπεμπέ τινα πρὸς Ἄννωνα, τὸν στρατηγὸν
τῶν Καρχηδονίων, ἀξιῶν αὐτῷ τὸν Ἄννωνα κοινωνῆ-
σαι τὴν στρατηγίαν καὶ ὑποδεικνύς, ὅτι πολλοὶ Σκιπίωνι σύνεισιν Ἴβηρες ἄκοντες, οὓς ἐάν τις χρυσίῳ
καὶ ὑποσχέσεσι διαφθείρῃ, τὸ στρατόπεδον ἐμπρή-
σουσι τὸ Σκιπίωνος. ἔφη δὲ καὶ αὐτός, εἰ προμάθοι
123 τὸν καιρόν, ἥξειν ἐπὶ τὸ ἔργον. ταῦτα μὲν Ἀσρούβας·
ὁ δὲ Ἄννων ἐς μὲν τὸν Ἀσρούβαν ἐπανούργει, τοῦ
δ᾽ ἐγχειρήματος οὐκ ἀπήλπισεν, ἀλλ᾽ ἄνδρα πιστὸν
μετὰ χρυσίου καθάπερ αὐτόμολον εἰς τὸ Σκιπίωνος
στρατόπεδον κατέπεμψεν, ὃς πιθανὸς ὢν ἐντυχεῖν
ἑκάστῳ διέφθειρε πολλοὺς ἡμέραν τε συνθέμενος
αὐτοῖς ἐπανῆλθεν. καὶ τὴν ἡμέραν ὁ Ἄννων τῷ Ἀσ-
124 ρούβᾳ μετέφερεν. Σκιπίωνι δὲ θυομένῳ κίνδυνον τὰ
ἱερὰ ἐδήλου ἐμπρησμοῦ· καὶ περιπέμψας εἰς ἅπαν τὸ

rode off. She showed the cup to her nurse, told her not to grieve for her as she was dying a noble death, and drank the poison. The Romans had now arrived and Massinissa displayed her dead body to them, gave her a royal burial and returned to Scipio. Scipio praised him and, comforting him with the thought that he was rid of a wicked woman, he awarded him a crown for his attack on Syphax and showered him with gifts. When Syphax was brought to Rome, some thought that they should spare him for being their friend and ally in Iberia, others argued for punishing him on the grounds that he had gone to war against their friends. But Syphax himself fell ill and died of grief.[13]

29. When Hasdrubal had his men in a high state of training, he sent a messenger to Hanno, the Carthaginian commander, proposing that Hanno share the command with him, and pointing out that there were many Iberians serving with Scipio against their will, who could be bribed with money and promises to set fire to Scipio's camp. He said that he himself would assist in the operation, if he was told the time beforehand. Such was Hasdrubal's proposal. Hanno intended to double-cross Hasdrubal, but he did not dismiss the plan of action. He sent someone he trusted to Scipio's camp with money, as if he was a deserter. This man was convincing when talking with anyone and he corrupted many of them; after fixing a day with them, he returned to Hanno, who communicated the date to Hasdrubal. But when Scipio was offering sacrifice, the victims revealed a danger of fire, and so he sent instructions

[13] The story of the beautiful Sophoniba is recounted most famously, and in more romantic detail, by Livy (30.12–15).

στρατόπεδον, εἴ πού τι λάβρον εὕρισκε πῦρ, κατ-
έπαυεν. καὶ αὖθις ἐπὶ πολλὰς ἡμέρας ἐθύετο.

125   30. Ὡς δ᾽ οὐκ ἀνίει τὰ ἱερὰ τὸν ἐμπρησμὸν ὑποδει-
κνύοντα, ὃ μὲν ἐβαρυθύμει καὶ μεταστρατοπεδεῦσαι
διεγνώκει, ἱππέως δὲ Ῥωμαίου θεράπων Ἴβηρ, ὑπο-
νοήσας τι περὶ τῶν συνθεμένων, ὑπεκρίνατο συνειδέ-
ναι, ἕως τὸ πᾶν ἔμαθεν καὶ ἐμήνυσε τῷ δεσπότῃ· ὃ δὲ
αὐτὸν ἐς τὸν Σκιπίωνα ἤγαγεν, καὶ τὸ πλῆθος ἠλέγ-
χετο· καὶ πάντας ὁ Σκιπίων ἔκτεινεν καὶ ἐξέρριψε πρὸ
126   τοῦ στρατοπέδου. αἴσθησις δ᾽ ἦν Ἄννωνι μὲν ὀξεῖα
πλησίον ὄντι, καὶ οὐκ ἦλθεν ἐπὶ τὸ συγκείμενον, Ἀσρούβας δ᾽ ἀγνοῶν ἀφίκετο. ὡς δὲ τὸ πλῆθος εἶδε τῶν
νεκρῶν, εἴκασε τὸ συμβὰν καὶ ἀνεχώρει. καὶ αὐτὸν ὁ
Ἄννων ἐς τὸ πλῆθος διέβαλεν, ὡς ἀφίκοιτο Σκιπίωνι
127   διδοὺς ἑαυτόν, ὃ δὲ οὐ λάβοι. Ἀσρούβας μὲν δὴ καὶ
ἐκ τοῦδε τοῖς Καρχηδονίοις ἦν μᾶλλον διὰ μίσους·
ὑπὸ δὲ τὸν αὐτὸν καιρὸν Ἀμίλχαρ μὲν ἄφνω ταῖς Ῥωμαίων ναυσὶν ἐπιπλεύσας μίαν ἔλαβεν τριήρη καὶ
φορτίδας ἕξ, Ἄννων δ᾽ ἐπιθέμενος τοῖς πολιορκοῦσιν
128   Ἰτύκην ἀπεκρούσθη. Σκιπίων δέ, χρονίου τῆς πολιορκίας οὔσης, ταύτην μὲν διέλυσεν οὐδὲν ἀνύων, τὰς δὲ
μηχανὰς ἐς Ἱππῶνα πόλιν μετετίθει· καὶ οὐδενὸς οὐδ᾽
ἐνταῦθα προκόπτοντος αὐτῷ, κατακαύσας ὡς ἄχρηστα τὰ μηχανήματα τὴν χώραν ἐπέτρεχεν, τοὺς μὲν
εἰς φιλίαν ἐπαγόμενος, τοὺς δὲ ληζόμενος.

129   31. Καρχηδόνιοι δ᾽ ἐπὶ ταῖς κακοπραγίαις δυσφο-
ροῦντες αἱροῦνται στρατηγὸν αὐτοκράτορα Ἀννίβαν,
τὸν δὲ ναύαρχον ἔπεμπον ἐπὶ νεῶν, ἐπισπέρχειν αὐτὸν

around to the whole camp that everyone was to put out any fire they found ablaze.

30. He sacrificed again for many days, but the victims continued to indicate fire, at which he became disheartened and decided to move camp. But the Iberian servant of a Roman cavalryman got some inkling of the plot, and pretended to be part of it until he found out the whole plan. He informed his master who brought him to Scipio, and provided evidence against the whole group. Scipio executed them all and threw their bodies out in front of the camp. Hanno, who was nearby, quickly learned of this and did not come to the rendezvous—unlike Hasdrubal, who turned up in ignorance, although when he saw the pile of corpses, he guessed what had happened and withdrew. Hanno now abused him in public, accusing him of coming in order to surrender to Scipio, but Scipio would not accept him. As a result, Hasdrubal was even more hated at Carthage. About the same time, Hamilcar made a sudden descent on the Roman fleet, and captured one trireme and six merchantmen, while Hanno attacked those besieging Utica, but was beaten off. Scipio, however, raised the siege, as it had lasted so long and achieved nothing, and moved his siege engines against the town of Hippo. Here too he made no progress, and burning the engines as useless, he overran the country, winning some people as friends, and plundering the land of others.

31. The Carthaginians, disheartened by their failures, now choose Hannibal as supreme commander, and sent their admiral with a flotilla to press him to take passage

130 ἐπὶ τὴν διάβασιν. ἅμα δὲ ταῦτ’ ἔπρασσον καὶ ἐς τὸν
Σκιπίωνα περὶ εἰρήνης ἐπρεσβεύοντο, ἡγούμενοι τούτοιν πάντως ἂν ἑνὸς τυχεῖν, ἢ τὴν εἰρήνην ἕξειν, ἢ
131 χρόνον διατρίψειν, ἕως ἀφίκοιτο ὁ Ἀννίβας. Σκιπίων
μὲν οὖν αὐτοῖς ἀνοχάς τε ἔδωκεν, καὶ τὴν δαπάνην
τοῦ στρατοῦ λαβὼν πρεσβεύειν ἐφῆκεν ἐς Ῥώμην· οἱ
δὲ ἐπρέσβευον καὶ τειχῶν ἐκτὸς ἐστάθμευον, ὡς ἔτι
πολέμιοι, ἀχθέντες τε ἐπὶ τὴν βουλὴν ἐδέοντο συγ-
132 γνώμης τυχεῖν. τῶν δὲ βουλευτῶν οἱ μὲν τῆς Καρχηδονίων ἀπιστίας ὑπεμίμνησκον, ὁσάκις συνθοῖντο καὶ
παραβαῖεν ὅσα τε Ἀννίβας δράσειε δεινὰ Ῥωμαίους
καὶ τοὺς Ῥωμαίων συμμάχους ἔν τε Ἰβηρίᾳ καὶ Ἰτα-
133 λίᾳ· οἱ δὲ τὸ τῆς εἰρήνης χρήσιμον οὐ Καρχηδονίοις
μᾶλλον ἢ σφίσιν ὑπεδείκνυον ἔσεσθαι, τῆς Ἰταλίας
τοσοῖσδε πολέμοις ἐκτετρυμένης, τό τε τοῦ μέλλοντος
περιδεὲς ἐπεξῄεσαν, ἐπιπλευσομένων ἐπὶ τὸν Σκιπίωνα αὐτίκα σὺν μεγάλοις στρατοῖς Ἀννίβου τε ἐξ
Ἰταλίας καὶ Μάγωνος ἐκ Λιγύων καὶ Ἄννωνος ἀπὸ
Καρχηδόνος.

134   32. Ἐφ’ οἷς ἀποροῦσα ἡ βουλὴ συμβούλους ἔπεμψε
τῷ Σκιπίωνι, μεθ’ ὧν ἔμελλε κρινεῖν τε καὶ πράξειν, ὅ
135 τι δοκιμάσειεν συνοίσειν. ὁ δὲ ἐς τὴν εἰρήνην τοῖς
Καρχηδονίοις ἐπὶ τοῖσδε συνέβη· Μάγωνα μὲν ἀποπλεῖν ἐκ Λιγύων αὐτίκα καὶ τοῦ λοιποῦ Καρχηδονίους
μὴ ξενολογεῖν μηδὲ ναῦς ἔχειν μακρὰς πλείους τριάκοντα μηδὲ πολυπραγμονεῖν τι πέραν ὧν ἔχουσιν
ἐντὸς τῶν λεγομένων Φοινικίδων τάφρων, ἀποδοῦναι
δὲ Ῥωμαίοις, ὅσους αἰχμαλώτους αὐτῶν ἔχουσι καὶ

home. At the same time, they also sent an embassy to   130
Scipio to discuss peace, thinking to achieve at least one of
two things: either to have peace, or to win time until the
arrival of Hannibal. Scipio granted them a ceasefire, and   131
making them pay the expenses of his army, he allowed
them to send an embassy to Rome. Their ambassadors,
however, were treated as if they were still hostile, and
quartered outside the city walls, but when introduced to
the senate, they begged for forgiveness. Some of the sen-   132
ators kept reminding them of the Carthaginians' duplicity,
how often they had made treaties and broken them, and
of the terrible damage inflicted by Hannibal on Rome and
her allies in Iberia and Italy. Others pointed out that they   133
themselves needed the benefits of peace just as much as
the Carthaginians, Italy having been exhausted by so many
wars; and they explained in detail their fears for the future,
with Scipio facing immediate attack from the large armies
about to arrive with Hannibal from Italy, Mago from Liguria, and Hanno from Carthage.

32. The senate were at a loss about what to do in the   134
situation, and sent advisers for Scipio with whom he was
to consult and decide what he regarded as the best course
of action to take. Scipio made peace with the Carthagin-   135
ians on the following terms: Mago should leave Liguria
immediately and the Carthaginians should not recruit
mercenaries in future; the Carthaginians should have no
more than thirty warships; they should not interfere at all
outside the territory they held within the so-called Phoenician Trenches; they should return all Roman prisoners

αὐτομόλους, ἀργυρίου τε αὐτοῖς τάλαντα χίλια καὶ
ἑξακόσια ἐσενεγκεῖν ἐν χρόνῳ, ἔχειν δὲ Μασσανάσσην Μασσυλίους τε καὶ τῆς Σύφακος ἀρχῆς, ὅσα
136 δύναιτο. τάδε μὲν συνέθεντο ἀλλήλοις, καὶ πρέσβεις
διέπλεον, οἱ μὲν ἐς Ῥώμην, τοὺς ὑπάτους ὁρκιοῦντες,
οἱ δ᾿ ἀπὸ Ῥώμης ἐς Καρχηδόνα, καὶ τὰ τέλη τῶν
137 Καρχηδονίων αὐτοῖς ὤμνυεν. Μασσανάσσῃ δὲ Ῥωμαῖοι χαριστήρια τῆς συμμαχίας στέφανόν τε ἀπὸ
χρυσοῦ καὶ σφραγῖδα χρυσῆν ἔπεμπον καὶ ἐλεφάντι-
νον δίφρον καὶ πορφύραν καὶ στολὴν Ῥωμαϊκὴν καὶ
ἵππον χρυσοφάλαρον καὶ πανοπλίαν.
138   33. Γιγνομένων δ᾿ ἔτι τούτων ὁ Ἀννίβας ἄκων ἐς
Καρχηδόνα ἔπλει, τὴν ἐς τοὺς ἄρχοντας ἀπιστίαν τοῦ
139 δήμου καὶ ταχυεργίαν ὑφορώμενος. ἀπιστῶν δ᾿ ἔτι
τὰς σπονδὰς ἔσεσθαι καί, εἰ γένοιτο, εὖ εἰδὼς οὐκ ἐς
πολὺ βεβαίους ἐσομένας ἐς Ἀδρυμητὸν Λιβύης κατήγετο πόλιν καὶ σῖτον συνέλεγεν ἐπί τε ὠνὴν ἵππων
περιέπεμπεν, καὶ τὸν δυνάστην τῶν Νομάδων τῶν
140 καλουμένων Ἀρεακιδῶν ἐς φιλίαν ὑπήγετο. καὶ τετρακισχιλίους ἱππέας αὐτομόλους αὐτῷ προσφυγόντας,
οἳ Σύφακος ὄντες τότε ἐγίγνοντο Μασσανάσσου, κατ-
ηκόντισεν ὑποπτεύσας· τοὺς δ᾿ ἵππους διέδωκε τῷ
141 στρατῷ. ἦλθε δὲ καὶ Μεσότυλος αὐτῷ δυνάστης ἕτερος μετὰ χιλίων ἱππέων καὶ Οὐερμίνας, Σύφακος υἱὸς
ἕτερος, ἔτι τῶν πλεόνων τῆς πατρῴας ἀρχῆς ἐπικρα-
τῶν. πόλεις τε Μασσανάσσου τὰς μὲν ὑπήγετο, τὰς
142 δ᾿ ἐβιάζετο. Νάρκην δ᾿ ἐνήδρευσεν ὧδε. ἀγορᾷ χρώ-

and deserters; they should pay Rome one thousand six hundred talents of gold within a specified time; Massinissa should rule the Massylians and have as much of Syphax's kingdom as he could manage. These were the terms of 136 their agreement. Carthaginian ambassadors then sailed to Rome to administer the oath to the consuls, and Roman ambassadors sailed to Carthage, to receive the oath of the Carthaginian magistrates. As a mark of their gratitude 137 for his military assistance, the Romans sent Massinissa a golden crown and a golden signet ring and an ivory chair and a purple robe and a Roman toga and a horse with gold harness and a suit of armor.

33. While this was happening, Hannibal set sail for 138 Carthage against his will, suspicious of the people's distrust of their leaders and of their impetuous nature. Fur- 139 thermore, he did not believe there would be a treaty, or if there was one, he was certain it would not last long. He landed at the town of Hadrumetum in Africa, where he collected grain and sent out for the purchase of horses;[14] and he won the friendship of the prince of the Areacidae, a Numidian people. When four hundred cavalrymen fled 140 to him as deserters—they had served Syphax but were now with Massinissa—he shot them down, as he did not trust them. He distributed their horses among his own soldiers. Another prince, called Mesotylus, came to him 141 with one thousand cavalry, and also Verminas, another son of Syphax, who was still master of most of his father's kingdom. Some of Massinissa's towns Hannibal won over peacefully, others by using violence. For the town of 142

[14] Hadrumetum, modern Sousse in Tunisia, was renamed Susa in the eighth century AD under Arab control.

μενος ἐσέπεμπεν ὡς ἐς φίλους. ὅτε δ' ἔδοξεν ἐπιθέσθαι, πλείους ἔπεμπε ξιφίδια ἐπικρύπτοντας, οἷς εἴρητο τὰ δίκαια ποιεῖν ἐς τοὺς πιπράσκοντας, μέχρι σαλπίγγων ἀκούσειαν, τότε δ' ἐπιχειρεῖν τοῖς ἐντυχοῦσι καὶ τὰς πύλας οἱ φυλάσσειν.

143   34. Οὕτω μὲν ἑάλω Νάρκη, Καρχηδονίων δὲ ὁ δῆμος, ἄρτι τὰς συνθήκας πεποιημένοι καὶ Σκιπίωνος αὐτοῖς ἔτι παρόντος, οὔπω τῶν ἰδίων πρέσβεων ἀπὸ Ῥώμης ἀνεστροφότων, ἀγορὰν Σκιπίωνος ὑπ' ἀνέμων κατενεχθεῖσαν ἐς Καρχηδόνα διήρπασαν καὶ τοὺς παραπέμποντας αὐτὴν ἔδησαν, πολλὰ τῆς βουλῆς ἀπειλούσης καὶ παραινούσης μὴ λύειν συνθήκας ἄρτι γεγενημένας. οἱ δὲ καὶ ταῖς συνθήκαις ἐπεμέμφοντο ὡς ἀδίκως γενομέναις καὶ τὸν λιμὸν ἔφασαν ἐνοχλεῖν

144   ὑπὲρ τὰς παραβάσεις. Σκιπίων μὲν οὖν οὐκ ἠξίου πολέμου κατάρχειν μετὰ σπονδάς, ἀλλ' ᾔτει δίκας ὡς φίλους ἁμαρτόντας· οἱ δὲ καὶ τοὺς πρέσβεις αὐτοῦ κρατεῖν ἐπενόουν, ἕως ἀφίκοιντο αὐτοῖς οἱ ἀπὸ Ῥώμης.

145   ἀλλὰ τούσδε μὲν Ἄννων τε ὁ Μέγας καὶ Ἀσρούβας ὁ Ἔριφος ἐξείλοντο τοῦ πλήθους καὶ προύπεμπον δύο τριήρεσιν· ἕτεροι δὲ Ἀσρούβαν τὸν ναύαρχον ἔπεισαν, ὁρμοῦντα περὶ τὴν Ἀπόλλωνος ἄκραν, ὅταν ἀποστῶσιν αἱ προπομποὶ τριήρεις, ἐπιθέσθαι τοῖς τοῦ

146   Σκιπίωνος. καὶ ὃ μὲν ἐπέθετο, καὶ τῶν πρέσβεών τινες ἐκ τοξευμάτων ἀπέθανον· οἱ δὲ λοιποὶ τιτρωσκόμενοί τε καὶ ἐρέσσοντες ἔφθασαν ἐς τὸν λιμένα τοῦ σφε-

Narce, he set an ambush in the following manner. Availing of their market, he traded with them as with friends. When he decided to attack, he sent a larger number of people with hidden daggers, ordering them to behave properly toward the merchants until they heard the trumpets, when they should attack everyone they encountered and guard the gates for him.

34. That was how Narce was captured. Although they had only just made the agreement, and Scipio was still present, and their own ambassadors had not yet returned from Rome, the ordinary people of Carthage seized some of Scipio's supplies that had been driven by the wind into the city, and arrested the escort detail. The Carthaginian council issued repeated threats against them and warned them not to break a treaty recently agreed, but the people criticized the treaty as illegally concluded, and said that hunger was more troubling than treaty infringements. Scipio did not think it right to begin a war when they were under treaty, but he demanded satisfaction as if from friends who had made a mistake. The Carthaginian people, however, even intended to seize and hold Scipio's representatives until their own ambassadors returned from Rome. But Hanno the Great and Hasdrubal the Kid took them away from the crowd and escorted them off on two triremes. Another party, however, persuaded Hasdrubal the admiral, who was anchored off the promontory of Apollo, to attack Scipio's representatives when the escorting triremes stood off. He carried out the attack, and some of the Roman representatives were shot and killed. The others, although wounded, took to their oars and got to the harbor of their own camp just before Hasdrubal,

143

144

145

146

τέρου στρατοπέδου καὶ ἐξήλαντο τῆς νεὼς ἤδη λαμβανομένης. παρὰ τοσοῦτον ἦλθον αἰχμάλωτοι γενέσθαι.

147   35. Ὧν οἱ ἐν ἄστει Ῥωμαῖοι πυθόμενοι τοὺς πρέσβεις τοὺς Καρχηδονίων, οἳ περὶ τῆς εἰρήνης ἔτι παρῆσαν, ἐκέλευον ἀποπλεῖν αὐτίκα ὡς πολεμίους. καὶ οἳ μὲν ἐξέπλεον καὶ ὑπὸ τοῦ χειμῶνος ἐς τὸ τοῦ
148 Σκιπίωνος στρατόπεδον κατήγοντο· Σκιπίων δὲ τῷ ναυάρχῳ, πυθομένῳ περὶ αὐτῶν, ὅ τι δέοι ποιεῖν, "Οὐδὲν ὅμοιον," ἔφη, "Ταῖς Καρχηδονίων ἀπιστίαις, ἀλλ'
149 ἀπόπεμπε ἀπαθεῖς." μαθοῦσα δὲ ἡ γερουσία τὸν δῆμον ὠνείδιζε τῇ συγκρίσει καὶ συνεβούλευε καὶ νῦν δεηθῆναι Σκιπίωνος τὰ μὲν συγκείμενα φυλάσσειν, δίκας δὲ τῶν ἡμαρτημένων παρὰ Καρχηδονίων λα-
150 βεῖν. οἳ δὲ καὶ αὐτῇ τῇ γερουσίᾳ δυσχεραίνοντες ἐκ πολλοῦ διὰ τὴν κακοπραγίαν, ὡς οὐκ εὖ τὰ συμφέροντα προορωμένῃ, καὶ ὑπὸ ἀνδρῶν δημοκόπων ἐρεθιζόμενοί τε καὶ ἐς ἀλόγους ἐλπίδας ἐπαιρόμενοι τὸν Ἀννίβαν ἐκάλουν μεθ' ἧς ἔχει στρατιᾶς.

151   36. Ὁ δέ, ὁρῶν τὸ μέγεθος τοῦ πολέμου, Ἀσρούβαν αὐτοὺς ἐκέλευε σὺν τῇ παρούσῃ δυνάμει καλεῖν. Ἀσρούβας μὲν δὴ τῆς καταδίκης αὐτῷ λυθείσης παρεδίδου τὸν στρατὸν Ἀννίβᾳ καὶ οὐδ' ὡς ἐπιφαίνεσθαι τοῖς Καρχηδονίοις ἐθάρρει, ἀλλ' ἐκρύπτετο ἐν τῇ πό-
152 λει· Σκιπίων δὲ ναῦς τῇ Καρχηδόνι ἐπιστήσας εἶργεν αὐτοὺς ἀγορᾶς ἀπὸ θαλάσσης, οὐκ εὐποροῦντας οὐδ' ἀπὸ τῆς γῆς, ἀσπόρου διὰ τὸν πόλεμον γενομένης.
153 τῶν δ' αὐτῶν ἡμερῶν Ἀννίβου καὶ Σκιπίωνος ἱππομα-

and jumped out of the ship just as it was being captured. That was how close they came to being made prisoners.

35. When they got to hear of these events at Rome, 147 they ordered the Carthaginian ambassadors, who were still there in connection with the peace negotiations, to leave immediately as enemies. And so they sailed off, but they were driven by the stormy weather into the camp of Scipio. When his admiral asked him what he should do 148 with them, Scipio replied, "Nothing like the treacherous Carthaginians. Send them off unharmed." On hearing 149 this, the Carthaginian council rebuked the people for the contrast between their behavior and Scipio's, and advised them even now to beg Scipio to abide by the terms of the agreement, and accept reparation from the Carthaginians for their misconduct. But they had been complaining 150 about the council itself for some time, because Carthage was doing so badly and the council was no good at providing for their best interests. Excited now by rabble-rousers and stimulated into unrealistic hopes, they summoned Hannibal and his army.

36. Hannibal could see the scale of the war, and or- 151 dered the Carthaginians to call for Hasdrubal and the force he had at his disposal. Once Hasdrubal's conviction had been quashed, he handed over his army to Hannibal, but did not dare even then to appear in public in Carthage, and remained in hiding in the city. Scipio now blockaded 152 Carthage with his ships and prevented them from being supplied by sea; nor did they have plentiful supplies from the land, which had remained unsown because of the war. In the same period, Scipio got the better of it in a sea 153

APPIAN

χία γίνεται περὶ Ζάμαν, ἐν ᾗ Σκιπίων ἐπλεονέκτει· καὶ
ταῖς ἐπιούσαις ἀκροβολίσματα ἦν ἐς ἀλλήλους, ἕως
αἰσθόμενος ὁ Σκιπίων Ἀννίβαν ἰσχυρῶς τε ἀπορού-
μενον καὶ περιμένοντα ἀγορὰν φερομένην νυκτὸς
ἔπεμψε Θέρμον χιλίαρχον ἐπὶ τοὺς ἄγοντας αὐτήν.
154 καὶ λόφον ὁ Θέρμος ἐν στενῇ διόδῳ καταλαβὼν
ἔκτεινε τῶν Λιβύων ἐς τετρακισχιλίους καὶ ἐζώγρη-
σεν ἑτέρους τοσούσδε καὶ τὴν ἀγορὰν ἧκε φέρων τῷ
Σκιπίωνι.

155   37. Ὁ δ' Ἀννίβας, εἰς ἔσχατον ἀφιγμένος ἀπορίας
καὶ τὸ παρὸν ἐπινοῶν, ὅπως δύναιτο διαθέσθαι, πρέσβεις ἐς Μασσανάσσην ἔπεμπεν, ὑπομιμνήσκων τε
τῆς ἐν Καρχηδόνι διατριβῆς καὶ παιδεύσεως καὶ
παρακαλῶν ἔτι ⟨νῦν⟩[7] οἱ συναγαγεῖν ἐς συνθήκας
Σκιπίωνα· τὰ γὰρ πρότερα τοῦ δήμου καὶ τῶν ἀνοη-
156 τοτέρων τοῦ δήμου ἁμαρτήματα γενέσθαι. ὃ δὲ τῷ
ὄντι τεθραμμένος τε καὶ πεπαιδευμένος ἐν Καρχηδόνι
καὶ τὸ ἀξίωμα τῆς πόλεως αἰδούμενός τε καὶ φίλος
ὢν ἔτι πολλοῖς ἐκεῖθεν ἐδεήθη τοῦ Σκιπίωνος καὶ
συνήγαγεν αὐτοὺς αὖθις ἐς τοιάσδε συνθήκας, ὥστε
Καρχηδονίους τάς τε ναῦς καὶ τοὺς ἄνδρας, οὓς ἔλαβον Ῥωμαίοις ἀγορὰν φέροντας, ἀποδοῦναι καὶ τὰ
ἡρπασμένα ἅπαντα ἢ τῶν ἀπολωλότων τιμήν, ἣν ἂν
ὁρίσῃ Σκιπίων, ποινήν τε τοῦ ἀδικήματος χίλια τάλαντα εἰσενεγκεῖν.

157   38. Τάδε μὲν ἦν τὰ συγκείμενα· καὶ γενομένων
ἀνοχῶν, μέχρις αὐτὰ μάθωσι Καρχηδόνιοι, ὁ μὲν Ἀν-

battle that he and Hannibal fought near Zama. In the following days, they continued to skirmish with each other, until Scipio received word that Hannibal was seriously short of supplies and waiting to be resupplied during the night. So Scipio sent a military tribune called Thermus to attack the supply train.[15] Thermus occupied a hill in a narrow defile, where he killed about four thousand Africans, captured the same number, and returned to Scipio with the supplies.

    37. Hannibal was now facing desperate shortages, and after considering how he might deal with the situation facing him, he sent envoys to Massinissa, reminding him of the time he spent in Carthage and his education there, and in addition asking him even now to get Scipio to agree to terms. For, so he argued, what happened previously was the fault of the common people, and indeed of the more stupid element among them. Massinissa, who had in fact been brought up and educated at Carthage, and respected the reputation of the city, and still had many friends there, begged Scipio for this favor, and succeeded in getting them to agree a new treaty on the following terms: the Carthaginians were to return the ships and men they had captured bringing supplies to the Romans; they were to return or pay for the loss of everything seized, at a price to be determined by Scipio; and they were to pay a one thousand talent indemnity as a penalty for their offense.

    38. These were the terms of the treaty, and a cease-fire came into operation to give the Carthaginians time to hear

154

155

156

157

---

[15] Q. Minucius Thermus became consul in 193.

---

7 νῦν add. Goukowsky

νίβας ἐξ ἀέλπτου περιεσώζετο, Καρχηδονίων δ᾽ ἡ μὲν
βουλὴ τὰ συμβάντα ὑπερησπάζετο καὶ παρεκάλει
τὸν δῆμον ἐμμεῖναι τοῖς ἐγνωσμένοις, τήν τε κακοπραγίαν σφῶν τὴν ἐς ἅπαντα διηγουμένη καὶ τὴν
παροῦσαν ἀπορίαν στρατοῦ τε καὶ χρημάτων καὶ
158 ἀγορᾶς· οἱ δέ, οἷον ὄχλος, ἀφρόνως ἡγοῦντο τοὺς
στρατηγοὺς σφῶν δι᾽ ἑαυτοὺς ταῦτα Ῥωμαίοις συν-
τίθεσθαι, ἵνα δι᾽ ἐκείνων δυναστεύσωσι τῆς πατρίδος·
ὃ καὶ Ἀννίβαν νῦν καὶ Ἀσρούβαν οὐ πρὸ πολλοῦ
ποιῆσαί τε καὶ τὸ στρατόπεδον νυκτὸς ἐγχειρίσαντα
τοῖς πολεμίοις μετ᾽ ὀλίγον καὶ ἑαυτὸν ἐθελῆσαι τῷ
Σκιπίωνι ἐνδοῦναι, ἐπὶ τῷδε προσπελάσαντα, κρύπτε-
159 σθαί τε νῦν ἐν τῇ πόλει. βοῆς δ᾽ ἐπὶ τούτῳ καὶ θορύβου γενομένου τὴν ἐκκλησίαν τινὲς καταλιπόντες
ἐζήτουν Ἀσρούβαν περιιόντες. ὃ δ᾽ ἔφθασε μὲν ἐς τὸν
τοῦ πατρὸς τάφον καταφυγὼν καὶ φαρμάκῳ διαχρη-
σάμενος αὐτόν· οἱ δὲ κἀκεῖθεν αὐτοῦ τὸν νέκυν ἐξελόν-
τες καὶ τὴν κεφαλὴν αὐτοῦ ἀποτεμόντες περιέφερον
ἐπὶ δόρατος ἀνὰ τὴν πόλιν.

160 39. Ἀσρούβας μὲν δὴ καὶ τὸ πρῶτον ἀδίκως ἐξ-
επεπτώκει καὶ τὸ δεύτερον ψευδῶς διεβέβλητο ὑπὸ
Ἄννωνος καὶ τότε πρὸς Καρχηδονίων οὕτως ἀνῄρητο
161 καὶ οὕτως ἀποθανὼν ὑβρίζετο· Καρχηδόνιοι δὲ ἐπέστελλον Ἀννίβᾳ λῦσαι τὰς ἀνοχὰς καὶ πολεμεῖν
Σκιπίωνι, κρῖναι δ᾽ ὅτι τάχιστα τὸν πόλεμον μάχῃ
διὰ τὴν ἀπορίαν. ὃ μὲν δὴ πέμψας ἔλυσε τὰς ἀνοχάς,
καὶ Σκιπίων Πάρθον τε, μεγάλην πόλιν, αὐτίκα προσ-
πεσὼν εἷλε καὶ πλησίον Ἀννίβου μετεστρατοπέδευεν.

what had been agreed. This was an unexpected source of deliverance for Hannibal, and the Carthaginian council was delighted at the agreement, and urged the people to stand by the decisions made, explaining both their wretched situation overall and their current shortage of men, money, and supplies. But, like the rabble they were, they stupidly believed that their generals had made this treaty for their own benefit, so that they could secure control of the country through the Romans. They said that Hannibal was now doing what Hasdrubal had done not long before, when he handed his camp to the enemy at night, and shortly after approached Scipio in person in an attempt to surrender; and he was now hiding in Carthage. Shouting and confusion followed, and some left the assembly to go and look for Hasdrubal. But he escaped ahead of them to the tomb of his father, where he killed himself by taking poison. The mob dragged his body away even from there, cut off his head and carried it round the city on a spear.

39. So it was that Hasdrubal in the first place was exiled unjustly; second, was slandered by the lies of Hanno, and on the present occasion was brought to his death in this way by the Carthaginians, and treated with ignominy in this way on his death. The Carthaginians then ordered Hannibal to break the ceasefire and wage war on Scipio; and because they were so short of supplies, they told him to end the war decisively in battle. So he sent word that he was breaking the truce. Scipio immediately attacked and captured the large town of Parthus, and moved camp

APPIAN

162 ὁ δὲ ἀνεζεύγνυεν, τρεῖς τοῖς Ῥωμαίοις κατασκόπους
ἐπιπέμψας, οὓς ὁ Σκιπίων ἔλαβέν τε καὶ οὐκ ἔκτεινεν,
ὥσπερ ἔθος τοὺς κατασκόπους κτείνειν, ἀλλ' ἐς τὸ
στρατόπεδον καὶ τὰς ὁπλοθήκας καὶ τὰ μηχανήματα
περιαχθῆναι κελεύσας καὶ τὴν στρατιὰν γυμναζο-
163 μένην ἰδεῖν ἀπέλυσε φράζειν Ἀννίβᾳ περὶ ἑκάστων. ὁ
δὲ ἠξίωσεν ἔτι συνελθεῖν ἐς λόγους Σκιπίωνι καὶ συν-
ελθὼν ἔλεγε Καρχηδονίους ἀγανακτῆσαι τῇ πρότερον
εἰρήνῃ διὰ τὰ χρήματα καί, εἰ τοῦτο ἐκλυθείη, Σικελίας δὲ μόνον ἀξιοῖεν οἱ Ῥωμαῖοι καὶ Ἰβηρίας καὶ
νήσων, ὅσων ἄρχουσι, κρατεῖν, ἔσεσθαι τὰς συν-
164 θήκας βεβαίους. ὁ δέ, "Πολύ," ἔφη, "Κέρδος Ἀννίβᾳ
τῆς φυγῆς ἔσται τῆς ἐξ Ἰταλίας, εἰ ταῦτα προσλάβοι
παρὰ Σκιπίωνος." καὶ ἀπηγόρευε πέμπειν ἔτι πρὸς
αὐτόν. διαπειλησάμενοί τε ἀλλήλοις ἀνεζεύγνυον ἑκάτερος ἐς τὸ αὑτοῦ στρατόπεδον.

165   40. Πόλις δ' ἐγγὺς ἦν Κίλλα καὶ παρ' αὐτὴν λόφος
εὐφυὴς ἐς στρατοπεδείαν, ὃν ἐπινοῶν ὁ Ἀννίβας προ-
λαβεῖν ἔπεμπέ τινας διαγράφειν τὸ στρατόπεδον, καὶ
166 εὐθὺς ἀναστήσας ἐβάδιζεν ὡς ἔχων τὸν λόφον. Σκιπίωνος δ' αὐτὸν φθάσαντός τε καὶ προλαβόντος, ἀπο-
ληφθεὶς ἐν πεδίῳ μέσῳ καὶ ἀνύδρῳ διετέλει τὴν νύκτα
πᾶσαν ὀρύσσων φρέατα, καὶ ὁ στρατὸς αὐτῷ διαμώ-
μενος τὴν ψάμμον ὀλίγον καὶ θολερὸν ἔπινον ἐπιμόχθως ἀθεράπευτοί τε καὶ ἄσιτοι, καὶ ἐν τοῖς ὅπλοις

---

16 Cornelius Nepos (*Hann.* 6) is responsible for naming the

near Hannibal. Hannibal withdrew, but sent three spies 162
against the Romans, whom Scipio captured, but, although
it is customary to execute spies, he did not kill them, and
instead ordered that they be brought around the camp, the
armory and the siege engines, and watch the army training. He then released them to tell Hannibal all the details.
Hannibal asked for a further meeting, and when they 163
met he said it was the money that had annoyed the Carthaginians about the previous treaty, and if this clause
could be taken out, and Rome be satisfied with controlling
Sicily, Iberia, and whatever islands were presently under
their rule, the treaty would hold securely. Scipio replied, 164
"Hannibal would benefit greatly by his escape from Italy
if he could win these additional concessions from Scipio";
and he told him to send no more messages. After some
mutual recriminations, they both returned to their own
camp.

40. There was a town called Cilla nearby, and near 165
it was a ridge naturally suited for locating a camp.[16] Hannibal devised a plan to occupy the ridge, and sending
some men to map out the camp, immediately upped and
marched off as if he was already in possession of the ridge.
But because Scipio had anticipated him and already oc- 166
cupied it, Hannibal was cut off in the middle of a waterless
plain and spent the whole night digging wells. By clearing
away the sand, his army succeeded with great difficulty in
getting a little muddy water to drink, but throughout the
night they went without food, and with no care for their

battle that follows the battle of Zama, but it seems to have taken
place near the town of Sicca (mod. Le Kef), fifty miles away from
Zama.

63

167 ἔνιοι, διενυκτέρευσαν. ὧν ὁ Σκιπίων αἰσθανόμενος
προσέβαλεν ἅμα ἕῳ κεκμηκόσιν ἐξ ὁδοῦ καὶ ἀγρυπνίας καὶ ἀνυδρίας. Ἀννίβας δ᾽ ἤχθετο μέν, οὐχ, ὅτε
βούλοιτο, συνιὼν ἐς μάχην, ἑώρα δέ, εἴτε μένοι κατὰ
χώραν, κακοπαθήσων ὑπὸ τῆς ἀνυδρίας, εἴτε φεύγοι,
τὰ φρονήματα τῶν ἐχθρῶν ἀναστήσων καὶ πολλὰ
πεισόμενος ὑπ᾽ αὐτῶν ἐπικειμένων. ὅθεν ἀναγκαῖον ἦν
168 αὐτῷ μάχεσθαι. καὶ παρέτασσεν αὐτίκα ἄνδρας μὲν
ἐς πεντακισμυρίους, ἐλέφαντας δὲ ὀγδοήκοντα. ἵστη
δὲ πρώτους μὲν τοὺς ἐλέφαντας, ἐκ διαστημάτων, ἐφ᾽
169 ὅλου τοῦ μετώπου, φοβερώτατα σκευάσας. καὶ ὑπ᾽
αὐτοῖς ἦν τὸ τρίτον τῆς στρατιᾶς, Κελτοὶ καὶ Λίγυες·
τοξόται τε αὐτοῖς ἀναμεμίχατο πάντῃ καὶ σφενδο-
170 νῆται Μαυρούσιοί τε καὶ Γυμνήσιοι. τούτων δ᾽ ὄπισθεν ἡ δευτέρα τάξις ἦν, Καρχηδόνιοί τε καὶ Λίβυες.
τρίτοι δ᾽, ὅσοι ἐξ Ἰταλίας εἵποντο αὐτῷ· οἷς δὴ καὶ
μάλιστα ὡς πλέον δεδιόσιν ἐθάρρει. ἡ δ᾽ ἵππος περὶ
τὰ κέρατα ἦν.

171 41. Οὕτω μὲν Ἀννίβας ἐξέτασσε, Σκιπίωνι δ᾽ ἦσαν
‹πεζοὶ μὲν›[8] ἀμφὶ τοὺς δισμυρίους καὶ τρισχιλίους,
ἱππεῖς δ᾽ Ἰταλῶν καὶ Ῥωμαίων χίλιοι καὶ πεντακόσιοι. συνεμάχει δὲ Μασσανάσσης ἱππεῦσι Νομάσι
πολλοῖς καὶ Δακάμας ἕτερος δυνάστης ἱππεῦσιν ἑξα-
172 κοσίοις. τὸ μὲν οὖν πεζὸν ἐς τρεῖς καὶ ὅδε τάξεις
ἐπέταττεν ὁμοίως Ἀννίβᾳ, λόχους δ᾽ ὀρθίους ἐποιεῖτο
πάντας, ἵνα δι᾽ αὐτῶν οἱ ἱππεῖς εὐχερῶς διαθέοιεν.
173 ἐφίστη δ᾽ ἑκάστῳ λόχῳ προμάχους κατὰ μέτωπον, οἳ
ξύλα παχέα διπήχεα μάλιστα, πυκνὰ καὶ τὰ πολλὰ

physical condition, some of them even in arms. When 167
Scipio realized this, he launched an attack at dawn when
the enemy were exhausted from their march, and from
lack of sleep and water. Although Hannibal was annoyed
at the prospect of joining battle when he did not want to,
he also saw that if he stayed where he was, his men would
suffer badly from dehydration, and if he fled, he would lift
the spirits of his enemy and take heavy casualties as they
pressed home their attack. For these reasons, he had no
choice but to fight. So he immediately drew up his army 168
in battle order, fifty thousand men and eighty elephants.
He stationed the elephants in front at intervals along the
whole line, decked out to create maximum fear. Behind 169
them were Celts and Ligurians, a third of his army, and
mixed in with them at all points were archers and Moorish
and Balearic slingers. Behind them was the second rank, 170
made up of Carthaginians and Africans. Those who had
followed Hannibal from Italy formed the third rank: he
had particular confidence in these, as they had most to
fear. The cavalry were stationed on the wings.

41. This was Hannibal's battle order. Scipio had about 171
twenty-three thousand infantry, and one thousand five
hundred Italian and Roman cavalry. Fighting alongside
him were Massinissa with a large force of Numidian cavalry, and another prince, called Dacamas, with six hundred cavalry. Scipio too, like Hannibal, divided his infan- 172
try into three ranks, but he arranged them all in columns,
so that the cavalry could easily gallop between them. At 173
the front of each column he posted sappers with thick
beams about two cubits long, heavy and most of them

---

[8] πεζοὶ μὲν add. Viereck-Roos

αὐτῶν σεσιδηρωμένα, ἔμελλον ὡς καταπέλτας ἐκ χει-
174 ρὸς ἐς τοὺς ἐλέφαντας ἐπιόντας ἀφήσειν. παρήγγελτο
δ' αὐτοῖς τε καὶ τοῖς ἄλλοις πεζοῖς ἐκκλίνειν τὴν ὁρμὴν τῶν θηρίων καὶ περιθέοντας ἀκοντίζειν ἐς αὐτὰ
συνεχῶς καὶ προσπελάζοντας, ὅτε δύναιντο, ὑποτέ-
175 μνειν τὰ νεῦρα. οὕτω μὲν οἱ πεζοὶ διετετάχατο τῷ
Σκιπίωνι· τοὺς δ' ἱππέας τοὺς μὲν Νομαδικοὺς ἐπέ-
στησε τοῖς κέρασιν, εἰθισμένους τὴν τῶν ἐλεφάντων
ὄψιν καὶ ὀδμὴν φέρειν, τοὺς δὲ Ἰταλικοὺς διὰ τὸ ἄη-
θες ὀπίσω πάντων, ἑτοίμους ἐπελθεῖν διὰ τῶν διαστημάτων, ὅτε τὴν πρώτην τῶν ἐλεφάντων ὁρμὴν ὑπομεί-
176 νειαν οἱ πεζοί. παρ' ἕκαστον δὲ τῶν ἱππέων τῶνδε
ὑπηρέτης ἦν πολλὰ ἀκόντια φέρων, οἷς ἐπενόει τὰ
θηρία ἀμύνεσθαι. οὕτω μὲν αὐτῷ καὶ ἡ ἵππος εἶχεν,
παρεδίδους δὲ τὸ μὲν δεξιὸν Λαιλίῳ, τὸ δὲ λαιὸν
177 Ὀκταουίῳ. ἐν δὲ τοῖς μέσοις ἤστην αὐτός τε καὶ Ἀννίβας, κατὰ δόξαν ἀλλήλων, ἔχοντες ἀμφ' αὑτοὺς
ἱππέας ἐπικουρεῖν, ὅπῃ τι πονούμενον ἴδοιεν, ὁ μὲν
Ἀννίβας τετρακισχιλίους, ὁ δὲ Σκιπίων δισχιλίους·
καὶ τοὺς τριακοσίους Ἰταλούς, οὓς αὐτὸς ὥπλισεν ἐν
Σικελίᾳ.
178   42. Ἐπεὶ δὲ ἕτοιμα ἦν αὐτοῖς, ἐπέτρεχε τοὺς ἰδίους
ἐπισπέρχων ἑκάτερος, ὁ μὲν Σκιπίων τοὺς θεοὺς
κατακαλῶν ἐν ὄψει τῶν στρατευομένων, ἐς οὓς οἱ
Καρχηδόνιοι παρεσπονδήκεσαν, ὁσάκις ἔλυον τὰ

---

17 Laelius was a quaestor in 202. Appian (or his source) seems
to be wrong in placing Cn. Octavius at the battle of Zama. Octa-

cased in iron: their job was to throw them at the oncoming elephants like catapult bolts. He ordered them and the 174 other foot soldiers to avoid the impact of the animals by running round and continually throwing javelins at them, or getting close, when they could, and cutting their hamstrings. Such was the disposition of Scipio's infantry. With 175 regard to his cavalry, he stationed the Numidians on the wings, as they were well used to tolerating the sight and smell of elephants, but the Italians, who were not, he kept right at the rear, ready to attack through the gaps between the columns, when the infantry had withstood the first charge of the elephants. Each of these cavalrymen had an 176 attendant with a good supply of missiles for the purpose of fighting off the animals. This was how Scipio organized his cavalry; and he put Laelius in command of the right wing, Octavius of the left.[17] Scipio himself and Hannibal 177 both took up position in the center, out of mutual respect, both with a division of cavalry in attendance, to send as reinforcements wherever they saw their line under pressure: Hannibal had four thousand, Scipio two thousand, and the three hundred Italians he had equipped himself in Sicily.

42. When they had everything ready, each commander 178 rode along their lines encouraging the men. In the sight of his troops, Scipio called on the gods, with whom the Carthaginians had broken faith every time they violated

vius had been in command of a fleet since his praetorship in 205, and Livy (30.36.3–6) indicates that Scipio employed him after the battle, but not during it, when Laelius commanded the left wing and Massinissa the right (Livy 30.33.2).

συγκείμενα, καὶ τὴν στρατιὰν ἀξιῶν μὴ ἐς τὸ πλῆθος
τῶν πολεμίων ἀφορᾶν, ἀλλ' ἐς τὴν ἀρετὴν τὴν αὐτῶν,
ᾗ καὶ πρότερον τῶνδε τῶν ἐχθρῶν πλειόνων ὄντων
ἐπεκράτησαν ἐν τῇδε τῇ γῇ· εἰ δ' ἔστι καὶ τοῖς νικη-
σασιν ἐπὶ τῷ μέλλοντι φόβος ἢ δέος ἢ ἀμφιβολία,
πόσῳ ταῦτα τοῖς νενικημένοις πλεονάζειν ἀνάγκη.
179 οὕτω μὲν ὁ Σκιπίων ἠρέθιζέ τε καὶ παρηγόρει τῆς
ὀλιγότητος· ὁ δ' Ἀννίβας τῶν τε ἐν Ἰταλίᾳ γεγονότων
ἔργων ὑπεμίμνησκεν αὐτούς, ὡς λαμπρὰ καὶ μεγάλα
πράξειαν, οὐκ ἐπὶ Νομάσιν, ἀλλ' ἐπὶ πᾶσιν Ἰταλοῖς
κατὰ τὴν Ἰταλίαν, καὶ τὴν ὀλιγότητα τῶν ἐχθρῶν
αὐτόθεν ἑστὼς ἐπεδείκνυεν καὶ παρεκάλει μὴ χείρους
180 ὀλιγωτέρων ἐν οἰκείᾳ γῇ πλέονας ὄντας ὀφθῆναι. τὸν
δὲ κίνδυνον τοῦ παρόντος ἀγῶνος καὶ τὸ μέγεθος
ἑκάτερος τοῖς ἰδίοις ὑπερεπῆρεν, Ἀννίβας μέν, ὅτι
Καρχηδόνα καὶ Λιβύην ἅπασαν ὁ ἀγὼν ὅδε κρινεῖ, ἢ
δούλην εὐθὺς ἡσσωμένων εἶναι ἢ εἰς τὸ ἔπειτα ἄρχειν
ἁπάντων, ὧν ἐπεκράτουν, Σκιπίων δ', ὅτι νικωμένοις
μὲν οὐδ' ἀναχώρησίς ἐστιν ἀσφαλής, ἐπικρατοῦσι δὲ
ἀρχὴ μεγάλη προσγίγνεται καὶ ἀνάπαυλα πόνων τῶν
παρόντων καὶ ἐς τὰ οἰκεῖα ἀπόπλους καὶ ἐς τὸ μέλλον
εὔκλεια.
181   43. Οὕτω παροξύνας τοὺς ἰδίους ἑκάτερος ἐς τὸν
ἀγῶνα συνῄεσαν, Ἀννίβας μὲν σαλπίγγων κατάρξας,
182 Σκιπίων δ' ἀντηχεῖν κελεύσας. συνιόντων δ' αὐτῶν οἱ
μὲν ἐλέφαντες κατῆρχον τῆς μάχης, ἐς τὸ φοβερώτατον ἐσκευασμένοι καὶ τοῖς κέντροις ἐξοτρυνόμενοι
πρὸς τῶν ἐπικαθημένων· περιθέοντες δ' αὐτοὺς οἱ Νο-

the treaties. He asked them to concentrate not on the size of the enemy army, but on their own courage, which had led them to victory before, even though outnumbered, over this very enemy, in this very land. If fear, anxiety, and doubt about the future, he said, affect even those who have been victorious, how much more must they weigh on those who have been defeated. These were the words 179 Scipio used to encourage his men and play down the importance of their small numbers. Hannibal, on the other hand, reminded his troops of their achievements in Italy, of their great and brilliant exploits, not against Numidians, but against all Italians throughout Italy. From where he was actually standing he pointed to the small number of the enemy, and urged his men not to be seen worsted, when they were in the majority, by a smaller army in their own land. Both Scipio and Hannibal exaggerated to their 180 own side the significance and danger of the coming battle. Hannibal claimed that this battle would be decisive for Carthage and the whole of Africa: either immediate slavery if defeated, or permanent mastery over all they controlled. Scipio said there was nowhere safe to withdraw if they were defeated, but that if they won, there would be a great increase in their empire, a rest from their present labors, and they could sail off home to immortal fame.

43. Each commander fired up their own troops in this 181 way and then joined battle. Hannibal began with a trumpet blast, Scipio ordering a counterblast, and then they 182 came together, the elephants the first into action, decked out to create maximum fear and urged on by the goads of their mahouts. The Numidian cavalry kept circling around

μάδες ἱππεῖς ἐσηκόντιζον ἀθρόως, μέχρι τρωθέντας
τε καὶ φεύγοντας καὶ δυσπειθῶς ἔτι ἔχοντας ἀπήγα-
183 γον ἐκ τῆς μάχης οἱ ἐπιβάται. καὶ τάδε μὲν ἦν περὶ
τοὺς ἀμφὶ τὰ κέρατα ἐλέφαντας· οἱ δ' ἐν μέσῃ τῇ
φάλαγγι τοὺς Ῥωμαίων πεζοὺς κατεπάτουν, ἀπείρους
τε μάχης τοιᾶσδε ὄντας καὶ βαρεῖς ὑπὸ τῆς ὁπλίσεως
καὶ παρ' αὐτὸ φεύγειν εὐκόλως ἢ διώκειν οὐ δυναμένους, ἕως ὁ Σκιπίων τοὺς ἱππέας τοὺς Ἰταλικούς,
ὀπίσω τεταγμένους καὶ κουφότερον ἐσκευασμένους,
ἐπαγαγὼν ἀποβῆναι τῶν ἵππων ταρασσομένων ἐκέλευσεν καὶ τοὺς ἐλέφαντας περιθέοντας ἐσακοντίζειν.
184 πρῶτός τε αὐτὸς ἀποβὰς ἔτρωσε τὸν προπηδῶντα τῶν
ἐλεφάντων. θαρρησάντων δὲ τῶν ἄλλων καὶ τιτρω-
σκόντων ἤδη πανταχόθεν αὐτούς, καὶ οἵδε ὑπεχώρουν
καί, γενομένης τῆς μάχης καθαρᾶς θηρίων, ὁ ἀγὼν
ἐγίγνετο μόνων ἀνδρῶν τε καὶ ἵππων.
185   44. Τὸ μὲν οὖν δεξιὸν τὸ Ῥωμαίων, οὗ Λαίλιος
ἐπεστάτει, τρέπεται τοὺς ἐναντίους Νομάδας, Μασσανάσσου βαλόντος αὐτῶν τὸν δυνάστην Μασσάθην·
ὀξέως δ' αὐτοὺς ὁ Ἀννίβας ἐπιδραμὼν συνέτασσε τὴν
186 μάχην. τὸ δὲ λαιόν, ἔνθα Ῥωμαίων μὲν Ὀκτάουιος
ἐπεστάτει, τῶν δὲ πολεμίων Κελτοὶ καὶ Λίγυες ἦσαν,
ἐπόνει μάλα καρτερῶς ἑκατέροις. καὶ Σκιπίων μὲν
ἔπεμπε Θέρμον τὸν χιλίαρχον ἐπικουρεῖν μετ' ἐπι-
λέκτων· Ἀννίβας δ', ἐπεὶ τὸ λαιὸν συνέστησεν, ἐς
τοὺς Λίγυας καὶ Κελτοὺς μεθίππευεν, ἐπάγων ἅμα
τὴν δευτέραν τάξιν Καρχηδονίων τε καὶ Λιβύων.
187 κατιδὼν δ' αὐτὸν ὁ Σκιπίων ἀντιπαρῆγε μεθ' ἑτέρου

70

them firing volleys of missiles, until the mahouts led them off the battlefield, wounded, routed, and already turning disobedient. This is what happened to the elephants stationed on the wings. The ones in the center of the phalanx trampled the Roman infantry who had no experience of this type of fighting, and were prevented by the weight of their armor from easily falling back or pursuing the enemy. Eventually, Scipio brought up the Italian cavalry, who were stationed at the rear and more lightly armed, and ordered them to dismount from their agitated horses, and circle round the elephants on foot and shoot them. He himself was the first to dismount and wound the elephant at the head of the charge. This encouraged the others, who now began to inflict damage on the elephants from all sides, until these ones also withdrew. With the battle now clear of elephants, it became solely a contest of men and horses.

44. The Roman right wing, commanded by Laelius, rout the Numidians facing them, Massinissa killing their prince, Massathes, with a missile; but Hannibal came up quickly and restored order to their battle line. On the left, where Octavius commanded the Romans, and on the enemy side the Celts and Ligurians were stationed, both armies were struggling resolutely. Scipio sent the military tribune, Thermus, to offer assistance with an elite company. When Hannibal had steadied his left wing, he rode off to the Celts and Ligurians, taking with him his second rank, made up of Carthaginians and Africans. Scipio observed him and matched his move with another cohort.

στίφους. δύο δὲ στρατηγῶν ἀρίστων ἐς ἀγῶνα συνιόντων ἔρις ἦν τῶν ὑφ' ἑκατέρῳ λαμπρὰ καὶ δέος, καὶ
προθυμίας οὐδετέροις τι ἐνέλιπεν, σφοδροῦ καὶ ὀξέος
ὄντος πόνου τε καὶ παρακελεύσεως.

188   45. Μακρᾶς δὲ καὶ ἀκρίτου τῆς μάχης οὔσης οἱ
στρατηγοί, τοὺς κάμνοντας ἐλεοῦντες, ὥρμων ἐπ' ἀλλήλους ὡς ἐν σφίσι τῆς κρίσεως ταχυτέρας ἐσομένης.
189 καὶ ἠκόντισαν ὁμοῦ, Σκιπίων μὲν Ἀννίβου τὴν
ἀσπίδα, ὁ δ' Ἀννίβας ἔτυχε τοῦ ἵππου. καὶ ὁ ἵππος
ὑπὸ τῆς πληγῆς ἐξέφερεν ὀπίσω τὸν Σκιπίωνα, μέχρι
περιβὰς ἕτερον ἵππον αὖθις ἐς τὸν Ἀννίβαν ἠκόντι-
σεν. ἀλλ' ἀπέτυχεν αὐτοῦ καὶ τότε, τὸν δὲ ἱππέα τὸν
190 ἐγγὺς ἔβαλεν. ἧκε δ' ἐν τούτῳ καὶ Μασσανάσσης
πυθόμενος. καὶ οἱ Ῥωμαῖοι τὸν στρατηγὸν ὁρῶντες
στρατιωτικῶς σφῶν ὑπερμαχόμενον, καρτερώτερον
ἔτι τοῖς πολεμίοις ἐνέπεσον καὶ ἐτρέψαντο καὶ φεύγοντας ἐδίωκον· οὐδὲ προσιππεύοντος αὐτοῖς τοῦ Ἀννίβου καὶ δεομένου στῆναι καὶ τῆς μάχης αὖθις ἐς
191 πεῖραν ἐλθεῖν ἔτι ἐπείθοντο. ἀπογνοὺς οὖν αὐτῶν ὁ
Ἀννίβας τοὺς ἐξ Ἰταλίας οἱ συνελθόντας, ἐφεδρεύον-
τας ἔτι καὶ ἀτρεμοῦντας, ἦγεν ἐπὶ τὴν μάχην, ἐλπίσας Ῥωμαίοις ἅτε διώκουσιν ἀσυντακτοτέροις ἐπιπε-
192 σεῖσθαι. οἳ δὲ τὸ ἐνθύμημα αὐτοῦ θεασάμενοι μετὰ
σπουδῆς ἀλλήλους ἐκ τῆς διώξεως ἀνεκάλουν καὶ
συνετάσσοντο αὖθις ἐς μάχην. οὔτε δὲ ἵππων σφίσι
παρόντων οὔτε ἀκοντίων ἔτι ὄντων ξίφεσιν ἐς ἀλ-
193 λήλους ἐχρῶντο καὶ συνεπλέκοντο. φόνος τε ἦν πολὺς
ἐνθάδε μάλιστα καὶ τραύματα μέγιστα καὶ πιπτόντων

With two of the best generals thus meeting in battle, the men under their command both competed with, and had awed respect for them, neither side lacking eagerness, but fighting ferociously and encouraging each other loudly.

45. With the battle long and undecided, the generals took pity on their weary troops and kept rushing at each other, as if they would decide the issue more quickly by their personal intervention. They hurled javelins at the same time, Scipio hitting Hannibal's shield, Hannibal hitting Scipio's horse, which, in spite of taking such a blow, managed to carry him away to the rear. Here Scipio changed horses and returned to fire another javelin at Hannibal, but missed for a second time and hit the rider beside Hannibal. In the meantime, Massinissa arrived on the scene, having heard what was going on. When the Romans saw their general fighting like a common soldier on their behalf, they fell on the enemy with even greater ferocity and putting them to flight, set off in pursuit. Even though Hannibal rode along side them and begged them to stand and return to the fight, they still disobeyed. He gave up on them, but then set about leading the Italians who had accompanied him from Italy into battle; they were still holding their position in reserve, and Hannibal was hoping to fall on the Romans in the middle of their disorderly pursuit. But the Romans saw what he was planning, urgently called each other back from the pursuit, and reformed into battle order. As they no longer had their horses and had run out of missiles, they used their swords to engage with the enemy. Here was a place of particularly heavy slaughter and the worst wounds, of dying men

188

189

190

191

192

193

στόνος καὶ ἀναιρούντων μεγαλαυχία, μέχρι ποτὲ καὶ
τούσδε ἐτρέψαντο οἱ Ἰταλοὶ καὶ φεύγουσιν εἵποντο,
κρίσις τε ἦν λαμπρὰ τοῦ πολέμου.

194   46. Καὶ ὁ Ἀννίβας, ἐν τῇ φυγῇ θεασάμενος ἱππέων
Νομάδων πλῆθος συναλέν,[9] προσδραμὼν ἠξίου μὴ
προλιπεῖν αὐτὸν καὶ πείσας ἐπῆγε τοῖς διώκουσιν,
195 ἐλπίσας ἐργάσεσθαί τινα παλινδίωξιν. πρώτοις δὲ
Μασσυλίοις ἐντυχὼν ἐμάχετο, καὶ μόνος ἦν ἔτι οὗτος
ὁ ἀγὼν Μασσανάσσου καὶ Ἀννίβου συνεστώτων. φερομένων δὲ καὶ τῶνδε ἐπ᾽ ἀλλήλους ὑπὸ προθυμίας ἐς
μὲν τὴν ἀσπίδα ὁ Μασσανάσσης ἠκόντισε βαλών, ὁ
196 δὲ Ἀννίβας καὶ τότε ἔτυχε τοῦ ἵππου. καὶ ὁ Μασσανάσσης ἐκπεσὼν πεζὸς ἐπὶ τὸν Ἀννίβαν ὥρμα τόν
τε ἐπελαύνοντά οἱ πρὸ τῶν ἄλλων ἱππέα βαλὼν ἀπέ-
197 κτεινεν. καὶ τῶν λοιπῶν τὰ ἀκόντια ἐς τὸν ἐλεφαντι-
στὴν ἐκδεχόμενος ἓν τῶν ἐμπεπηγότων ἐξεῖλκε καὶ
ἀκοντίσας ἐς τὸν Ἀννίβαν αὖθις οὐδ᾽ ὡς ἐπετύγχανεν,
ἀλλὰ τὸν ἐγγὺς ἱππέα καὶ ὧδε ἀπέκτεινεν. ἕτερον δ᾽
ἐξέλκων ἐς τὸν βραχίονα ἐτρώθη καὶ ὑπεχώρησεν ἐκ
198 τῆς μάχης ἐπ᾽ ὀλίγον. Σκιπίων δὲ πυθόμενος ἔδεισε
περὶ τῷ Μασσανάσσῃ καὶ ἐς τὸ ἔργον ἠπείγετο· καὶ
εὗρε τὸν Μασσανάσσην ἐς τὴν μάχην αὖθις ἐπὶ ἵπ-
199 που φερόμενον ἑτέρου, τὸ τραῦμα ἐπιδήσαντα. ὅ τε
ἀγὼν ἦν ἴσος αὖθις αὐτοῖς καὶ πάνυ καρτερός, αἰ-
δουμένων τοὺς στρατηγοὺς ἑκατέρων, ἕως ὁ Ἀννίβας
ἐπί τινος λόφου θεασάμενος Ἴβηρας καὶ Κελτοὺς
200 συνεστῶτας ἐξίππευσεν ὡς κἀκείνους ἐπάξων. τότε
γὰρ οἱ μαχόμενοι, τῆς μὲν αἰτίας οὐ συνιέντες, τὴν δ᾽

groaning and their killers boasting. Eventually, the Italians put these to flight too and chased them as they fled, thus brilliantly bringing about the decisive moment of the war.

46. While in flight, Hannibal noticed a force of Numidian cavalry huddled together, and hurrying over, begged them not to desert him. He won them over, and led them against the pursuing Romans, hoping to turn the tide of battle. The Massylians were the first he met and fought, and another single combat took place between the contestants, this time between Massinissa and Hannibal. They too engaged eagerly with each other, Massinissa hitting Hannibal's shield with his spear, Hannibal on this occasion also hitting Massinissa's horse. As Massinissa had been thrown from his horse, he rushed against Hannibal on foot, and hit and killed a horseman who was driving down on him ahead of the others. Taking the missiles of the rest on his elephant-hide shield, he pulled out one of those embedded in it and threw it back at Hannibal, but, like Scipio, missed him and killed the cavalryman next to him. As he was pulling out another missile, he was wounded in the arm, and withdrew from the battle for a short time. When Scipio heard this he was worried about Massinissa and hurried to the scene of the action, but found him riding back into battle on another horse having bandaged up his wound. With both sides greatly admiring the two commanders, once again the battle was evenly balanced and very fierce, until Hannibal spotted a group of Iberians and Celts who had gathered on a hill, and rode off to collect them too. Those who were still fighting did not understand

194

195

196

197

198

199

200

---

9 συναλέν Goukowsky: συνελάς V: συνεστὼς rell.

ἀποχώρησιν αὐτοῦ φυγὴν ὑπολαβόντες εἶναι, τὸν
ἀγῶνα μεθῆκαν ἑκόντες καὶ ἔφυγον ἀκόσμως, οὐχ
201 ᾗπερ ἑώρων Ἀννίβαν, ἀλλ' ὅπῃ τύχοιεν ἕκαστοι. καὶ
οἱ μὲν οὕτω διελύθησαν, Ῥωμαῖοι δ' αὐτούς, ὡς τετελεσμένης τῆς μάχης, ἐδίωκον ἀτάκτως, οὐδ' αὐτοὶ τῆς
Ἀννίβου προαιρέσεως συνιέντες.

202   47. Ὁ δ' ἐπανῄει πεφραγμένος Ἴβηρσι καὶ Κελτοῖς ἀπὸ τοῦ λόφου. καὶ ὁ Σκιπίων αὖθις ἐκ τῆς
διώξεως τοὺς Ῥωμαίους ἀνεκάλει μετὰ σπουδῆς, καὶ
παρέτασσε πολὺ πλείονας τῶν ἀπὸ τοῦ λόφου κατα-
βεβηκότων· ὅθεν αὐτῶν οὐ δυσχερῶς περιεγίνετο.
203 Ἀννίβας δέ, καὶ τῆσδε τῆς πείρας τελευταίας γενομένης ἀποτυχών, ἔφευγεν ἤδη σαφῶς ἀπογνοὺς
ἅπαντα. καὶ αὐτὸν ἐδίωκον ἱππεῖς ἄλλοι τε πολλοὶ καὶ
Μασσανάσσης, περιώδυνος ὢν ἐκ τοῦ τραύματος αἰεί
τε πλησιάζων καὶ μέγα ποιούμενος αἰχμάλωτον Ἀν-
204 νίβαν ἀγαγεῖν Σκιπίωνι. τὸν δὲ νὺξ ἐρύσατο, καὶ σκο-
ταῖος μετ' εἴκοσιν ἱππέων, τῶν δυνηθέντων σὺν αὐτῷ
συνανύσαι τὸν δρόμον, ἐς πόλιν κατέφυγεν, ᾗ ὄνομα
Θῶν, ἔνθα Βρεττίων ἔγνω καὶ Ἰβήρων ἱππέας πολ-
205 λοὺς ἀπὸ τῆς ἥττης συμπεφευγότας. δείσας οὖν περὶ
μὲν τῶν Ἰβήρων ὡς βαρβάρων ταχυέργων, περὶ δὲ
Βρεττίων ὡς Ἰταλῶν ὁμοεθνῶν Σκιπίωνι, μὴ ἐς συγγνώμην ὧν ἐξήμαρτον ἐς τὴν Ἰταλίαν, προσαγάγω-
σιν αὐτὸν τῷ Σκιπίωνι, λαθὼν ἐξέφυγε μεθ' ἑνὸς ἱπ-
206 πέως, ᾧ μάλιστ' ἐπίστευε. σταδίους δ' ἀνύσας ἐς
τρισχιλίους δύο νυξί τε καὶ ἡμέραις, ἧκεν ἐς πόλιν
ἐπὶ θαλάσσης Ἀδρυμητόν, ἔνθα τι μέρος ἦν αὐτῷ

the reason for Hannibal's temporary withdrawal, and assumed that he had in fact fled. So they decided to abandon the fight and made their escape in disorder, not retreating to where they saw Hannibal, but each in whatever direction they could manage. The scattering of these men led the Romans to think that the battle was over, and they went after them in disorderly pursuit, they too failing to understand Hannibal's plan.

47. Reinforced by the Iberians and Celts, Hannibal returned to the fray from the hill. Scipio again hurriedly recalled the Romans from their pursuit and formed them into battle order. He had many more men than those who had come down from the hill, and so he was able to overcome them without difficulty. This was Hannibal's final effort, and when it failed, he turned to flight, now clearly in complete despair. Among the many cavalrymen chasing him was Massinissa, who, in spite of the pain from his wound, kept close to him, making a big effort to capture him and take him to Scipio. But Hannibal was saved by the arrival of night, and, under cover of darkness, found refuge in the town of Thon, along with the twenty horsemen who had been able to match his pace. Here he became aware of a large number of Bruttian and Iberian cavalrymen who had also escaped from the defeat. Fearing the Iberians as impetuous barbarians, and the Brutii as fellow countrymen of Scipio, who might deliver him to Scipio to win pardon for their crimes against Italy, he secretly slipped away with one particularly trusted horseman. After traveling nearly three thousand stades in two days and two nights, he came to the town of Hadrumetum on the coast, where part of his army was guarding sup-

201

202

203

204

205

206

στρατιᾶς σιτοφυλακοῦν. περιπέμπων δ᾽ ἐς τὰ πλησίον καὶ τοὺς ἐκ τῆς μάχης διαφυγόντας ἀναλαμ-
βάνων ὅπλα καὶ μηχανήματα εἰργάζετο.

207   48. Σκιπίων δὲ νίκην ἀρίστην νενικηκὼς τὰ μὲν
ἄχρηστα τῆς λείας ἐνεπίμπρη διαζωσάμενος αὐτός,
ὥσπερ εἰώθασι Ῥωμαίων οἱ στρατηγοί, χρυσίου δ᾽
ἐς Ῥώμην τάλαντα δέκα καὶ ἀργυρίου δισχίλια καὶ
πεντακόσια καὶ ἐλέφαντα εἰργασμένον καὶ τοὺς ἐπιφανεῖς τῶν αἰχμαλώτων ἔπεμπε καὶ Λαίλιον ἐξαγγε-
208   λοῦντα περὶ τῆς νίκης, ἐπὶ νεῶν <. . .> τὰ δὲ λοιπὰ
ἀποδόμενος τὴν τιμὴν ἐπιδιεῖλε τῷ στρατῷ καὶ δῶρα
τοῖς ἀριστεύσασιν ἐδίδου καὶ Μασσανάσσην ἐστε-
209   φάνου καὶ τότε. καὶ τὰς πόλεις ἐπιὼν ἐχειροῦτο. τὸ
μὲν δὴ τέλος τῆς Ἀννίβου τε καὶ Σκιπίωνος ἐν Λιβύῃ
μάχης, τότε πρῶτον ἀλλήλοις ἐς χεῖρας ἐλθόντων,
τοῦτ᾽ ἦν, ἀπέθανον δὲ Ῥωμαίων μὲν δισχίλιοι καὶ
πεντακόσιοι, Μασσανάσσου δ᾽ ἔτι πλείονες καὶ τῶν
210   πολεμίων δισμύριοι καὶ πεντακισχίλιοι. αἰχμάλωτοι
δ᾽ ἐλήφθησαν ὀκτακισχίλιοι καὶ πεντακόσιοι. καὶ
Ἴβηρες ηὐτομόλησαν πρὸς Σκιπίωνα τριακόσιοι καὶ
Νομάδες πρὸς Μασσανάσσην ὀκτακόσιοι.

211   49. Οὔπω δὲ οὔτε Καρχηδόνιοι τῶνδε οὔτε Ῥωμαῖοι
πυθόμενοι, οἱ μὲν ἐπέστελλον Μάγωνι, ξενολογοῦντι
ἔτι Κελτούς, ἐσβαλεῖν εἰς τὴν Ἰταλίαν, εἰ δύναιτο, ἢ
ἐς Λιβύην μετὰ τῶν μισθοφόρων καταπλεῦσαι, οἱ δέ,

18 Allowing nine stades to the mile (see note to *Ib.* 1.4), Appian thinks that Hannibal traveled some 330 miles, but Hadru-

plies.[18] Sending around to the neighboring country, and collecting those who had escaped from the battle, he began to manufacture weapons and siege engines.

48. After this unique victory, Scipio girded himself for sacrifice, as is the custom for Roman generals, and personally made a burnt offering of the unusable plunder. On ⟨. . .⟩ ships he transported to Rome ten talents of gold, two thousand five hundred of silver, some carved ivory, and the most distinguished prisoners, and sent Laelius to announce the victory. The rest he put up for sale and divided the proceeds up among his army. He awarded prizes for outstanding courage and, on this occasion too, crowned Massinissa. He also went round subduing the towns. Such was the outcome of the battle fought in Africa between Hannibal and Scipio, the first time they had fought in combat against each other. Two thousand five hundred Romans were killed, somewhat more of Massinissa's men; twenty-five thousand of the enemy died, and eight thousand five hundred were taken prisoner.[19] Three hundred Iberians deserted to Scipio, and eight hundred Numidians deserted to Massinissa.

49. Before news of these events reached Rome or Carthage, the Carthaginians ordered Mago, who was still recruiting mercenaries among the Celts, to invade Italy, if he could, or sail back to Africa with the mercenaries. The

207

208

209

210

211

metum is only 100 miles or so from the town of Sicca where the battle probably took place (see above, n. 16).

[19] Livy 30.35, getting his figures from Polybius (15.14), reports fifteen hundred Romans killed, and more than twenty thousand Carthaginians killed and the same number captured.

APPIAN

τῶνδε τῶν γραμμάτων ἀλόντων καὶ ἐς Ῥώμην κομι-
σθέντων, στρατιὰν ἄλλην καὶ ἵππους καὶ ναῦς καὶ
212 χρήματα ἔπεμπον τῷ Σκιπίωνι. ὁ δὲ ἤδη τῇ Καρχηδόνι κατὰ μὲν τὴν γῆν ἐπέπεμπεν Ὀκτάουιον, ταῖς δὲ
213 ναυσὶν αὐτὸς ἐπέπλει. καὶ οἱ Καρχηδόνιοι τὴν ἧσσαν
Ἀννίβου πυθόμενοι πρέσβεις ἐπὶ κελητίου προσέπεμ-
πον τῷ Σκιπίωνι, ὧν ἡγοῦντο Ἄννων τε ὁ Μέγας λε-
γόμενος καὶ Ἀσρούβας ὁ Ἔριφος· οἳ τὸ κηρύκειον
ὑψηλὸν ἔστησαν ἐπὶ τῆς πρῴρας καὶ τὰς χεῖρας ὤρε-
214 γον ἐς τὸν Σκιπίωνα ἱκετῶν τρόπον. ὁ δὲ αὐτοὺς
ἐκέλευσεν ἥκειν ἐς τὸ στρατόπεδον καὶ ἐλθοῦσιν ἐφ᾽
ὑψηλοῦ προκαθήμενος ἐχρημάτιζεν. οἱ δὲ μετ᾽ οἰμωγῆς ἑαυτοὺς ἐρρίπτουν ἐς τὸ ἔδαφος, καὶ τῶν ὑπηρετῶν ἀνιστάντων καὶ λέγειν κελευόντων, ὅ τι θέλοιεν,
Ἀσρούβας ὁ Ἔριφος εἶπεν·

215   50. "Ἐμοὶ μὲν ἔστιν, ὦ Ῥωμαῖοι, καὶ Ἄννωνι τῷδε
καὶ ὅσοι Καρχηδονίων ἔμφρονες,[10] καθαρεύειν ἁμαρ-
τημάτων, ὧν ἡμῖν ἐπικαλεῖτε· τοὺς γὰρ πρέσβεις
ὑμῶν, ἐς οὓς ἐξήμαρτεν ἡ πατρὶς ἄκουσα ὑπὸ λιμοῦ,
216 περιεσώζομεν καὶ πρὸς ὑμᾶς ἐπέμπομεν. χρὴ δ᾽ ὑμᾶς
μηδὲ Καρχηδονίων καταγινώσκειν ἁπάντων, οἵ γε
τὴν εἰρήνην καὶ πρότερον ᾔτησαν καὶ λαβόντες προ-
217 θύμως ὤμνυον. εἰσὶ δ᾽ αἱ πόλεις ἐπὶ τὸ χεῖρον εὐεπί-
στρεπτοι, καὶ τὸ πρὸς χάριν αἰεὶ παρὰ τοῖς πλήθεσιν
ἐπικρατεῖ. ἃ καὶ ἡμεῖς ἐπάθομεν, οὔτε πεῖσαι δυνηθέντες τὸ πλῆθος οὔτ᾽ ἐπισχεῖν διὰ τοὺς ἐκεῖ μὲν διαβάλ-
λοντας ἡμᾶς, παρὰ δ᾽ ὑμῖν τὴν παρρησίαν ἀφῃρημέ-
218 νους. μὴ δὴ ἀπὸ τῆς ὑμετέρας εὐπειθείας ἢ εὐβουλίας,

80

Romans, when they intercepted this letter and brought it to the city, sent Scipio another army with horses, ships, and money. Scipio now dispatched Octavius to Carthage by land, while he himself sailed with the fleet. When the Carthaginians learned of Hannibal's defeat, they sent ambassadors ahead to Scipio on a yacht. Hanno the Great and Hasdrubal the Kid led the delegation. They placed the herald's staff high on the boat's prow, and stretched out their hands to Scipio as suppliants. Scipio ordered them to enter his camp, and he gave them audience presiding from a high rostrum when they came in. They threw themselves wailing on the ground, and when the attendants had raised them to their feet and told them to say what they wished, Hasdrubal the Kid spoke as follows:

50. "Men of Rome, I face the task, with Hanno here, and all sensible Carthaginians,[20] of clearing ourselves of the offenses of which you accuse us. For when our country mistreated your ambassadors under the constraint of hunger, we rescued them and sent them back to you. You should not condemn all Carthaginians, who had after all earlier asked for peace and when given it, swore an oath enthusiastically. Cities are easily persuaded to take the worse course of action, as whatever gives gratification always prevails with the common people. We too have had this experience, unable to persuade the masses or restrain them, because of those in the city who slandered us and prevented us speaking frankly with you. Do not, men of Rome, judge our affairs by the standards of your own dis-

----

[20] Other manuscripts have "all Carthaginians of good will."

[10] ἔμφρονες LP BJD; εὔφρονες V Exc

81

ὦ Ῥωμαῖοι, τὰ παρ' ἡμῖν κρίνετε, ἀλλ' εἴ τῳ καὶ τὸ
πεισθῆναι τοῖς ἐπιτρίβουσιν ἀδίκημα εἶναι δοκεῖ, τὸν
λιμὸν ὑπίδεσθε καὶ τὴν ἀνάγκην, ἣ γέγονεν ἡμῖν ὑπὸ
219 τοῦ πάθους. οὐ γὰρ δὴ τῶν αὐτῶν ἔργον ἑκούσιον ἦν
ἄρτι μὲν περὶ εἰρήνης παρακαλεῖν καὶ χρήματα τοσαῦτα διδόναι καὶ τῶν νεῶν τῶν μακρῶν πλὴν ὀλίγων
ἀφίστασθαι καὶ τὸ πολὺ τῆς ἀρχῆς ὑμῖν παριέναι
καὶ περὶ τῶνδε ὀμνύναι τε καὶ ὁρκοῦν πέμψαντας ἐς
Ῥώμην, ἔτι δ' ὄντων τῶν ἡμετέρων πρέσβεων παρ'
220 ὑμῖν ἑκόντας ἁμαρτεῖν. ἀλλὰ μάλιστα μὲν θεῶν τις
ἔβλαψε καὶ ὁ χειμὼν ὁ τὴν ἀγορὰν ὑμῶν ἐς Καρχηδόνα καταγαγών· ἐπὶ δὲ τῷ χειμῶνι ὁ λιμὸς ἡμᾶς
ἀφείλετο μὴ καλῶς ὑπὲρ τῶν ἀλλοτρίων φρονῆσαι,
πάντων ἐνδεεῖς ὄντας. οὐδὲ λογισμὸν αἰτεῖν ἄξιον
παρὰ πλήθους ἀσυντάκτου καὶ ἀτυχοῦντος.

221   51. "Εἰ δὲ καὶ ὡς ἀδικεῖν ὑμῖν δοκοῦμεν, οὐκ ἀτυ-
χεῖν, ὁμολογοῦμεν καὶ δι' αὐτὸ καὶ παρακαλοῦμεν.
ἔστι δὲ τῶν μὲν οὐδὲν ἁμαρτόντων δικαιολογία, τῶν
222 δ' ἁμαρτόντων παράκλησις. ἐφ' ᾗ ταχύτερός ἐστιν ὁ
τῶν εὐτυχούντων ἔλεος, τὰ ἀνθρώπεια ὑφορωμένων,
ὅταν αἴσθωνται διὰ τὰς αἰφνιδίους μεταβολὰς παρα-
223 καλοῦντας τοὺς ἐχθὲς ἀδικεῖν δυναμένους. οἷς καὶ ἡ
Καρχηδονίων πόλις, ἡ τῆς Λιβύης μεγίστη καὶ δυνα-
τωτάτη ναυσὶ καὶ χρήμασιν ὁμοῦ καὶ ἐλέφασιν καὶ
στρατῷ πεζῷ τε καὶ ἱππικῷ καὶ ὑπηκόοις πολλοῖς,
ἑπτακοσίοις ἔτεσιν ἀνθήσασα καὶ Λιβύης πάσης καὶ
ἄλλων ἐθνῶν καὶ νήσων καὶ θαλάσσης τοσῆσδε. ἄρ-
ξασα καὶ ὑμῖν αὐτοῖς ἐς ἀμφήριστον ἐπὶ πλεῖστον

cipline and good sense, but if anyone thinks it a crime to have been persuaded by those who would destroy us, do not forget the famine and the need our sufferings forced on us. For it cannot have been a voluntary action of the same people to have recently asked for peace, to have paid a great deal of money for it, to have surrendered all but a few of their warships and yielded to you most of their empire, to have sent a mission to Rome to exchange oaths on these matters, and then, when their ambassadors were still with you in Rome, to have willingly transgressed. It was undoubtedly one of the gods who deluded us, and the storm which drove your supplies into Carthage. And over and above the storm, it was hunger, when we had nothing, that robbed us of the ability to have decent regard for other people's belongings. It is not worthwhile demanding rational behavior from an undisciplined crowd down on its luck.

51. "But if you believe, even in spite of this, that we acted unjustly rather than as victims of fate, then we admit it and for that reason make our appeal to you. Vindication is for the innocent, supplication for the guilty. The successful are quicker to pity in the face of supplication, when they consider human affairs and see men forced by a sudden change in fortune to seek forgiveness, who only yesterday were in a position to do wrong. As, for example, Carthage, the greatest city in Africa, and the most powerful in ships and money, together with elephants and infantry and cavalry and its many subjects. It has flourished for seven hundred years, ruling all of Africa and other peoples and islands and a great expanse of sea. For a long time it was evenly matched with you yourselves, but now its hope

219

220

221

222

223

ἐλθοῦσα, νῦν οὐκ ἐν τῇ θαλάσσῃ καὶ ταῖς ναυσὶν οὐδ'
ἐν τοῖς ἐλέφασι καὶ ἵπποις οὐδ' ἐν τοῖς ὑπηκόοις, ὧν
πάντων ὑμῖν ἀφίσταται, τὴν ἐλπίδα τῆς σωτηρίας,
224   ἀλλ' ἐν αὐτοῖς ὑμῖν ἔχει τοῖς προπεπονθόσι κακῶς. ἃ
χρὴ θεωροῦντας ὑμᾶς καὶ τὴν ἐπ' αὐτοῖς νέμεσιν φυ-
λαττομένους μετριοπαθῶς χρῆσθαι ταῖς εὐπραξίαις
καὶ τῆς σφετέρας αὐτῶν, ὦ Ῥωμαῖοι, μεγαλοφρο-
σύνης καὶ τῆς Καρχηδονίων ποτὲ τύχης ἄξια πράσ-
σειν τάς τε τοῦ δαιμονίου μεταβολὰς ἀνεπιφθόνως ἐν
ταῖς ἡμετέραις συμφοραῖς διατίθεσθαι, ἵνα καὶ πρὸς
τοὺς θεοὺς ἀναμάρτητα ᾖ τὰ ὑμέτερα ὑμῖν καὶ πρὸς
ἀνθρώπους ἀξιέπαινα πάντας.

225   52. "Οὐ γὰρ δή, μὴ μετάθωνταί γε καὶ νῦν οἱ
Καρχηδόνιοι, δέος ἐστίν, οἳ τοσήνδε μετάνοιαν καὶ
δίκην τῆς πρὶν ἀγνωμοσύνης ὑφίστανται. ἔστιν δ'
ἀναμαρτησίας τοῖς μὲν σώφροσιν ἡ εὐβουλία φυ-
λακή, τοῖς δ' ἁμαρτοῦσι τὸ προπαθεῖν καὶ μεταγνῶ-
ναι. βεβαιοτέρους τε εἰκός ἐστιν τοὺς νενουθετημέ-
226   νους γε εἶναι τῶν ἀπειράτων. οὐδ' ἄξιον Καρχηδονίοις
ὑμᾶς ὠμότητα καὶ ἁμαρτίαν ἐπικαλοῦντας ταῦτα μι-
μεῖσθαι· τοῖς μὲν γὰρ ἀτυχοῦσιν ἑτέρων ἁμαρτη-
μάτων ἄρχουσιν ὑπὸ τῆς ἀπορίας αἱ συμφοραί, τοῖς
δ' εὖ πράσσουσιν ἐν ἐξουσίᾳ τὸ φιλάνθρωπόν ἐστιν.
227   οὐδ' εὐκλεὲς οὐδὲ συμφέρον ἐς τὴν ἀρχὴν ὑμῖν ἐστιν
πόλιν τοσήνδε καθαιρεῖν μᾶλλον ἢ περισῴζειν. ἐστὲ
δὲ ἀμείνονες μὲν ὑμεῖς τῶν ὑμετέρων συμφερόντων
κριταί, ἡμεῖς δ' ὑμῖν ἐς τὴν ἑαυτῶν σωτηρίαν δύο
ταῦτα μάλιστα φέρομεν ἐκ πάντων, τὸ τῆς Καρχηδο-

of safety lies not in the sea and ships, not in elephants and
horses, nor in its subjects, all of which it yields to you, but
in you, the very people who have just been so badly
treated. In considering these things, you must guard   224
against the divine retribution attaching to them, and use
your success with moderation to act worthily both of your
own magnanimity and of Carthage's former fate. You must
manage the divinity's changes wrought in our disaster
without reproach, to make your actions blameless before
the gods and praiseworthy in the eyes of all men.

52. "For, to be sure, you need have no fear that the   225
Carthaginians will change their mind even now, as they
have repented so fully and been punished so severely for
their former stupidity. It is sound judgment that protects
the wise against wrongdoing, but previous suffering and
repentance that does so for those who have committed
wrong. It is likely that those who have been rebuked will
be more reliable than those who have not had this experience. It would not be worthy of you to imitate the cruelty   226
and transgression of which you accuse the Carthaginians.
For the defeated, in the face of helplessness, their disasters give rise to new crimes, while for the victorious,
power gives rise to benevolence. It would be neither glori-   227
ous nor advantageous to your empire to destroy such a
great city as Carthage, rather than preserve it. You yourselves are the best judge of your own interests, but with
regard to our safety, we bring to your attention two things
above all, the once great reputation of the Carthaginian

νίων ἀρχῆς ποτε ἀξίωμα καὶ τὴν ὑμετέραν αὐτῶν ἐς
πάντα μετριοπάθειαν, ἢ μετὰ τῶν ὅπλων ἐς τοσοῦτον
228 ὑμᾶς ἐπῆρεν ἀρχῆς καὶ δυνάμεως. τίσιν δὲ συνθήκαις,
ἂν ἄρα διδῶτε τὴν εἰρήνην, χρησόμεθα περὶ αὐτῆς,
περισσὸν λέγειν τοὺς ἐφ᾽ ὑμῖν τὰ ἑαυτῶν τιθεμένους."

229   53. Τοσαῦτ᾽ εἰπὼν ὁ Ἔριφος ἐπέκλαυσεν. ὁ δὲ Σκιπίων μεταστησάμενος αὐτοὺς ἐβουλεύετο μετὰ τῶν
ἀρίστων ἐπὶ πολύ. ὡς δ᾽ ἔκρινεν, ἐσκαλέσας αὐτοὺς
230 ἔλεγεν ὧδε· "Ἐστὲ μὲν οὐδεμιᾶς συγγνώμης ἄξιοι,
πολλάκις ἐς σπονδὰς ἡμῶν ὑβρίσαντες καὶ τὰ τελευ-
ταῖα νῦν καὶ ἐς πρεσβείας ἁμαρτόντες οὕτω φανερῶς
καὶ ἀθεμίτως, ὡς μήτε ἐξαρνεῖσθαι μήτε ἀντιλέγειν,
231 ὅτι μὴ τῆς ἐσχάτης ἐστὲ τιμωρίας ἄξιοι. τί δὲ δεῖ
κατηγορεῖν τῶν ὁμολογούντων; ἐς ἱκεσίας καταφεύ-
γετε οἱ μηδ᾽ ὄνομα Ῥωμαίων ὑπολιπόντες ἄν, εἰ ὑμεῖς
232 ἐκρατήσατε. ἀλλ᾽ ἡμεῖς μὲν οὐδέποθ᾽ ὑμῖν ὅμοια
ποιήσομεν, ἐπεὶ καὶ τοὺς πρέσβεις ὑμῶν, ἔτι ὄντας
ἐν Ῥώμῃ, παρεσπονδηκότων ὑμῶν καὶ ἐς πρέσβεις
ἁμαρτόντων, ἥ τε πόλις ἀπέλυσε, κἀγὼ καταχθέντας
ἐς τὸ στρατόπεδον πρὸς ὑμᾶς ἤδη πολεμοῦντας ἀπέ-
233 πεμψα ἀπαθεῖς. χρὴ δ᾽ ὑμᾶς, καταγινώσκοντας αὐτῶν,
ὅ τι ἂν λάβητε, κέρδος ἡγεῖσθαι. λέγω δ᾽, ἅ μοι δοκεῖ,
καὶ ἡ σύγκλητος ἐπιψηφιεῖ, ἃ ἂν δοκιμάσῃ.

234   54. "Δίδομεν ὑμῖν τὴν εἰρήνην ἔτι καὶ νῦν, ὦ Καρχηδόνιοι, ἢν τάς τε ναῦς τὰς μακρὰς παραδιδῶτε Ῥωμαίοις χωρὶς δέκα μόνων καὶ τοὺς ἐλέφαντας, ὅσους
ἔχετε, καὶ ὅσα ἡρπάσατε πρώην ἢ τὴν τῶν ἀπολωλότων τιμήν, ἐμοῦ τὰ ἀμφίβολα κρίνοντος, καὶ αἰχμά-

empire, and your own moderation in all matters, which along with your arms has raised you to such a height of empire and power. As for the terms of the treaty, if you do in fact give us peace, it would be superfluous for us to discuss them, as we place our fate entirely in your power." 228

53. When he finished speaking, the Kid broke down in tears. Scipio dismissed Hanno and Hasdrubal, and consulted with his leading men for a long time. When he had made his decision, he recalled the Carthaginians and spoke as follows: "You do not deserve to be forgiven at all, considering how often you have abused our treaties, and now finally even outraged our ambassadors so openly and unlawfully that you can neither deny it nor provide an argument against why you deserve the death penalty. But what is the point of making accusations against those who admit what they have done? You take refuge in supplication, when you would not even have left the very name of Rome, if you had won. But we will never behave like you. When you broke the treaty and committed outrages against our representatives while your ambassadors were still in Rome, the city let them go. And when they were driven into my camp, I sent them back to you unharmed, even though you had resumed hostilities. Having condemned yourselves, you should consider anything you get as a gain. I will tell you what I think, and the senate will vote for what it approves. 229 230 231 232 233

54. "Even at this stage, men of Carthage, we grant you peace, if you agree to surrender all but ten of your warships, all the elephants in your possession, everything you have seized recently, or the value of what has been lost— I will resolve any disagreements—and all the prisoners 234

λωτα πάντα καὶ αὐτομόλους καὶ ὅσους Ἀννίβας ἐξ
235 Ἰταλίας ἤγαγεν. ταῦτα μὲν ἐν τριάκοντα ἡμέραις, ἀφ᾽
οὗ ἂν ἡ εἰρήνη κριθῇ· ἐν δ᾽ ἑξήκοντα ἡμέραις Μάγωνα χρὴ Λιγύων ἀποστῆναι καὶ τὰς φρουρὰς ὑμᾶς
ἐξαγαγεῖν ἐκ τῶν πόλεων, ὅσαι τῶν Φοινικίδων τάφρων ἐκτός εἰσι, καὶ ὅσα αὐτῶν ἔχετε ὅμηρα, ἀποδοῦναι καὶ ἐς Ῥώμην ἑκάστου ἔτους ἀναφέρειν Εὐβοϊκὰ
236 τάλαντα διακόσια ἐπὶ πεντήκοντα ἐνιαυτούς. καὶ μήτε
ξενολογεῖν ἀπὸ Κελτῶν ἢ Λιγύων ἔτι μήτε Μασσανάσσῃ μηδὲ ἄλλῳ Ῥωμαίων φίλῳ πολεμεῖν μηδὲ
στρατεύειν τινὰ Καρχηδονίων ἐπ᾽ ἐκείνους ἀπό γε τοῦ
κοινοῦ. τὴν δὲ πόλιν ὑμᾶς ἔχειν καὶ τὴν χώραν, ὅσην
ἐντὸς τῶν Φοινικίδων τάφρων εἴχετε ἐμοῦ διαπλέον-
237 τος ἐς Λιβύην. Ῥωμαίων τε εἶναι φίλους καὶ συμμάχους κατὰ γῆν καὶ κατὰ θάλασσαν, ἢν ἀρέσκῃ ταῦτα
τῇ βουλῇ. ἀρεσάντων δέ, Ῥωμαίους ἀναχωρεῖν ἐκ
238 Λιβύης πεντήκοντα καὶ ἑκατὸν ἡμέραις. ἀνοχὰς δὲ ἢν
ἐθέλητε λαβεῖν, ἔστε πρεσβεύσητε ἐς Ῥώμην, δώσετε
μὲν ἡμῖν αὐτίκα ὅμηρα πεντήκοντα καὶ ἑκατὸν παῖδας, οὓς ἂν αὐτὸς ἐπιλέξωμαι, δώσετε δὲ ἐς δαπάνην
τῇ στρατιᾷ τάλαντα ἄλλα χίλια καὶ ἀγοράν. καὶ γενομένων τῶν σπονδῶν ἀπολήψεσθε τὰ ὅμηρα."
239   55. Ταῦτα τοῦ Σκιπίωνος εἰπόντος οἱ μὲν πρέσβεις
ἔφερον ἐς Καρχηδόνα τοὺς λόγους, συνιόντος δὲ τοῦ
πλήθους ἐς ἐκκλησίαν ἐπὶ πολλὰς ἡμέρας τοῖς μὲν
ἀρίστοις ἐδόκει τὰ προτεινόμενα δέξασθαι καὶ μὴ
240 περί τινων ἀπειθοῦντας κινδυνεύειν περὶ ἁπάντων, τὸ
δ᾽ ἀγοραῖον πλῆθος, οὐ τὸ παρὸν δεινὸν ἐκλογιζόμε-

and deserters, and all the men Hannibal brought with him from Italy. This will take place within thirty days of the peace being declared. Within sixty days, Mago must return from Liguria, you must withdraw all your garrisons from towns outside the Phoenician Trenches, and you must return all hostages. Each year for the next fifty years you will have to pay two hundred Euboic talents to Rome. You will no longer be permitted to recruit mercenaries from the Celts or Ligurians, or attack Massinissa or any other friend of Rome, or by public authority allow any Carthaginian to fight against them. You may keep your city, and as much land as you had inside the Phoenician Trenches when I sailed to Africa. You are to be friends of the Romans by land and by sea, if the senate so wishes. When they give their consent, Rome will withdraw from Africa within one hundred and fifty days. If you want an armistice until you send representatives to Rome, you will immediately hand over as hostage some hundred and fifty children, whom I will choose. You will hand over another one thousand talents for the expenses of the army, and supplies as well. Once the treaty comes into effect, you will get the hostages back."

55. Such was the speech of Scipio. The Carthaginian representatives reported back to the city what he had said, and the people met to discuss it in the assembly for many days. The leading men thought it best to accept what had been offered, and not to risk everything by refusing to comply with particular conditions. The common people, on the other hand, focused their attention on the very

235

236

237

238

239

240

νοι μᾶλλον ἢ τὴν ἀφαίρεσιν ὧν ἔχουσιν, τοσήνδε
οὖσαν, ἠπείθουν καὶ ἠγανάκτουν, εἰ ἐν λιμῷ τὸν σῖτον
οἱ ἄρχοντες αἱροῦνται Ῥωμαίοις ἀντὶ τῶν πολιτῶν ἐς
τὰς ἀνοχὰς παρασχεῖν, ἐφ' ἕκαστόν τε αὐτῶν συν-
ιστάμενοι πᾶσιν ἠπείλουν τὰς οἰκίας αὐτῶν διαρπά-
241 σειν καὶ καταπρήσειν. τέλος δ' ἔγνωσαν Ἀννίβαν,
ἔχοντα μὲν ἤδη πεζοὺς ἑξακισχιλίους, ἱππέας δὲ πεντακοσίους, σταθμεύοντα δ' ἐν πόλει Μαρθαμά, σύμ-
βουλον ἐπὶ τοῖς παροῦσι καλεῖν. ὃ δ' ἧκε καὶ τῶν
μετρίων δεδιότων, μὴ φιλοπόλεμος ἀνὴρ ἐπιτρύψῃ τὸ
πλῆθος, πάνυ σεμνῶς ἐκέλευε τὴν εἰρήνην δέχεσθαι.
242 ὁ δὲ δῆμος καὶ τόνδε ὑπὸ ὀργῆς μανιώδους ἐβλασφή-
μει καὶ πᾶσιν ἠπείλει, μέχρι τῶν γνωρίμων τοὺς μὲν
ἐς Μασσανάσσην καταφυγεῖν, τοὺς δὲ ἐς αὐτοὺς Ῥωμαίους αὐτομολῆσαι, τῆς πόλεως ἀπογνόντας.
243   56. Οἱ δὲ Καρχηδόνιοι, πυθόμενοι σῖτον πολὺν ἐς
ἐμπόριόν τι ὑπ' Ἀννίβα σεσωρεῦσθαι, ὁλκάδας ἐπ'
αὐτὸν ἐξέπεμπον καὶ ναῦς μακράς, ἐγνωκότες, εἰ τὸν
σῖτον λάβοιεν, ἐκστρατεῦσαι καὶ ὑπομεῖναι πᾶν, ὅ τι
ἂν ἡ τύχη κρίνῃ, μᾶλλον ἢ Ῥωμαίοις δουλεύειν ἑκόν-
244 τες. ἐπεὶ δὲ ἄνεμός τε καὶ χειμὼν τὰς ναῦς συνέτρι-
ψαν, ἀπογνόντες ἁπάντων ἐμέμφοντο τοῖς θεοῖς ὡς
ἐπιβουλεύουσι καὶ συνετίθεντο τῷ Σκιπίωνι καὶ ἐπρεσβεύοντο ἐς Ῥώμην. καὶ ὁ Σκιπίων ἔπεμπε τοὺς συμ-
245 βουλεύσοντας κυροῦν τὰ συγκείμενα. λέγεται δὲ
τοῦτο ἐσηγήσασθαι τῇ τε πόλει συμφέρειν ὑπολαβὼν
καὶ πυθόμενος Γναῖον Κορνήλιον Λέντλον τὸν ὕπατον
ἐφεδρεύειν αὐτοῦ τῇ στρατηγίᾳ, τὴν δόξαν οὐκ ἐθέλων

substantial loss of resources rather than on the immediate danger, and rejected the treaty. They were annoyed that in the middle of a famine their rulers should decide to provide grain for the Romans instead of their own citizens during the ceasefire, and banding together against each one of them, they threatened to loot and burn all their houses. Finally, they decided to call on Hannibal for advice in the present situation. He was now quartered in the town of Marmatha, with six thousand infantry and five hundred cavalry. When he came, although reasonable people feared that such a warlike man might agitate the common people, he told them with all solemnity to accept the peace. But the people were now insanely angry and began to abuse him too and threaten everyone, until the leading citizens despaired of the city, and some fled for refuge to Massinissa, while others deserted to the Romans themselves.

56. As for the Carthaginians, they learned that Hannibal had stockpiled a large supply of grain in a certain market town, and sent off transports and warships to collect it, having decided that, if they could get the grain, they would march out and endure anything that fate might decide, rather than willingly become slaves of Rome. But when a wintry storm destroyed their ships, they lost heart completely, and blaming the gods for plotting against them, they gave their assent to Scipio, and sent a mission to Rome. Scipio also sent men to advise ratification of the treaty. He is said to have proposed this both because he thought it would be to Rome's advantage and because he had heard that the consul, Gnaeus Cornelius Lentulus, was waiting to take over his command, and he was not

APPIAN

ἑτέρου γενέσθαι. προσέταξε γοῦν λέγειν τοῖς ἀπιοῦσιν, ὅτι βραδυνόντων Ῥωμαίων αὐτὸς ἐφ᾽ ἑαυτοῦ
συνθήσεται.

246   57. Οἱ δὲ πάνυ μὲν ἥδοντο κεκρατηκότες πόλεως
τοσαύτης, ἢ πολλὰ καὶ δεινὰ πρότερον αὐτοὺς ἐδε-
δράκει καὶ τῶν ἐπὶ τῆς γῆς δευτέραν ἢ τρίτην εἶχεν
247   ἡγεμονίαν· οἱ σύμβουλοι δ᾽ ἐστασίαζον, οἱ μὲν ἔτι
σὺν ὀργῇ χαλεπαίνοντες τοῖς Καρχηδονίοις, οἱ δὲ
ἐλεοῦντες αὐτοὺς ἤδη καὶ ἀξιοῦντες ἐν ταῖς ἀλλο-
τρίαις συμφοραῖς τὸ σφέτερον εὐπρεπῶς διατίθεσθαι.
248   ὑπαναστὰς δέ τις τῶν Σκιπίωνος φίλων εἶπεν· "Οὐ
περὶ τῆς Καρχηδονίων σωτηρίας ἐστὶν ἡμῖν ἡ φρον-
τίς, ὦ ἄνδρες, ἀλλὰ περὶ τῆς Ῥωμαίων ἔς τε θεοὺς
πίστεως καὶ πρὸς ἀνδρῶν εὐφημίας, μὴ Καρχηδονίων
αὐτῶν ὠμότερα πράξωμεν, οἱ Καρχηδονίοις ὠμότητα
ἐπικαλοῦμεν, καὶ μετριοπαθείας ἀεὶ φροντίσαντες
249   ἐπὶ τῶν βραχυτέρων ἀμελήσωμεν ἐν τοῖς μείζοσιν· ἃ
μηδὲ λαθεῖν ἔνεστι διὰ τὸ μέγεθος, ἀλλ᾽ ἐς ἅπασαν
γῆν περιελεύσεται καὶ νῦν καὶ ὕστερον, ἢν πόλιν
περιώνυμον καὶ θαλασσοκράτορα ἀνέλωμεν, ἢ καὶ
νήσων ἦρξε πολλῶν καὶ θαλάσσης ὅλης καὶ Λιβύης
ὑπὲρ ἥμισυ ἔν τε τοῖς πρὸς ἡμᾶς αὐτοὺς ἀγῶσι πολλὰ
250   καὶ τύχης καὶ δυνάμεως ἔργα ἐπεδείξατο. οἷς ἔτι μὲν
φιλονεικοῦσιν ἐρίζειν ἔδει, πεσόντων δὲ φείδεσθαι,
καθὰ καὶ τῶν ἀθλητῶν οὐδεὶς τὸν πεσόντα ἔτι τύπτει
καὶ τῶν θηρίων τὰ πολλὰ φείδεται τῶν καταπεσόντων. καλὸν δ᾽ ἐν τοῖς εὐτυχήμασι νέμεσιν θεῶν φυ-

willing to let someone else get the glory.[21] At any rate, he instructed his emissaries to say that if Rome delayed, he would make a treaty on his own authority.

57. The Romans were extremely pleased to have vanquished such a powerful city, one that had inflicted many hardships on them in the past, and had held the second or third position as a world power.[22] But there was serious disagreement in the senate. Some senators were still very angry at the Carthaginians, others now pitied them and thought it right that they should behave with dignity in the face of other people's misfortunes. One of Scipio's associates rose to his feet and spoke as follows: "It is not the safety of Carthage we are considering, gentlemen, but Rome's faithfulness before the gods, and her good name among men. We accuse the Carthaginians of cruelty: let us not act with greater cruelty than them. In minor matters we always keep moderation in mind; let us not neglect it in matters of major importance. These things cannot escape notice, given their significance, and word will go around the whole world, now and for ever, if we destroy a famous city, once master of the seas, who ruled many islands, and all the sea and more than half of Africa. In its conflicts with us it has given frequent evidence of its success and power. When they were still eager rivals we had to contend with the Carthaginians; now that they have fallen we should spare them, just as no athlete hits an opponent when he is down, and most wild animals spare their fallen foes. In the midst of success it is good to guard

246

247

248

249

250

[21] Gnaeus Cornelius Lentulus was consul in 201 with P. Aelius Paetus.   [22] Appian is probably thinking of Macedon and Carthage as the next most powerful states after Rome.

APPIAN

251 λάσσεσθαι καὶ ἀνθρώπων φθόνον. εἰ δέ τις, ὅσα
ἔδρασαν ἡμᾶς, ἀκριβῶς ἐκλογίζεται, αὐτὸ μάλιστά
ἐστι τοῦτο τῆς τύχης τὸ φοβερώτατον, εἰ περὶ μόνης
ἄρτι σωτηρίας παρακαλοῦσιν οἱ πόσα καὶ πηλίκα
δεδυνημένοι δρᾶσαι καὶ οὐ πρὸ πολλοῦ περί τε Σικε-
252 λίας καὶ Ἰβηρίας καλῶς ἀγωνισάμενοι. ἀλλ᾽ ἐκείνων
μὲν δίκας ἔδοσαν, τῶν δὲ τελευταίων παραβάσεων
λιμὸν αἰτιῶνται, κακὸν ἀνθρώποις ἐπιπονώτατον, ὃ
πάντας ἐξαιρεῖν δύναται λογισμούς.

253 58. "Ἐγὼ δ᾽ οὐκ ἐρῶ μὲν οὐδὲν ὑπὲρ Καρχηδονίων
(οὐ γὰρ ἄξιον), οὐδ᾽ ἀγνοῶ καὶ πρότερον αὐτοὺς ἄλλας συνθήκας πρὸ τῶνδε παραβῆναι· ἃ δ᾽ ἐπὶ τοῖς
τοιούτοις ποιοῦντες οἱ πατέρες ἡμῶν ἐς τόδε τύχης
254 προῆλθον, εἰδότας ὑμᾶς ἀναμνήσω. τῶν γὰρ γειτόνων
ἡμῖν τῶνδε πάντων ἐν κύκλῳ πολλάκις ἀποστάντων
καὶ σπονδὰς συνεχῶς λυσάντων οὐ κατεφρόνησαν,
255 οὐ Λατίνων, οὐ Τυρρηνῶν, οὐ Σαβίνων. τούς τε αὖ
μετ᾽ ἐκείνους περιοικοῦντας ἡμῖν Αἰκανοὺς καὶ Οὐο-
λούσκους καὶ Καμπανοὺς καὶ ὅσα ἄλλα τῆς Ἰταλίας
256 ἐς σπονδὰς ὕβρισεν, εὐσταθῶς ἔφερον. καὶ τὸ Σαυνι-
τῶν γένος τρὶς μὲν φιλίας καὶ συνθηκῶν καταφρονῆ-
σαν, ἔτεσι δ᾽ ὀγδοήκοντα μεγίστους ἡμῖν πολέμους
πεπολεμηκὸς οὐκ ἀνέστησαν, οὐδὲ τοὺς ἄλλους, ὅσοι
257 Πύρρον προσηγάγοντο κατὰ τῆς Ἰταλίας. οὐδ᾽ ἡμεῖς,
τὰ ἔναγχος ταῦτα, τοὺς Ἰταλῶν Ἀννίβᾳ προσθεμέ-

23 Appian is referring to the three Samnite wars of the fourth
and third centuries BC, the last ending in 290. Pyrrhus was in-

94

against divine retribution and the envy of men. If one   251
makes a careful audit of the crimes they have committed
against us, it is in itself an extremely frightening demonstration of fate that the same people are simply asking for
deliverance, who in the past had the power to inflict such
frequent and extensive damage on us, and only recently
were competing nobly with us over Sicily and Iberia. For   252
that they have been punished. Their latest offenses they
blame on hunger, a misery human beings find most painful, and one that can rob all men of reason.

58. "For my part, I am not going to say anything on   253
behalf of the Carthaginians, as they do not deserve it. And
I am not ignoring the fact that they broke other treaties
before the present ones. But I am going to remind you,
well as you know it, that it is what our ancestors did in such
circumstances that has advanced us to our present good
fortune. Although on many occasions all the neighbors   254
encircling us revolted and repeatedly broke treaties, they
did not repudiate them, whether it was Latins, Etruscans,
or Sabines. And again, later, when the Aequi and Volsci   255
and Campanians and other Italians living around us violated their agreements, our fathers bore it calmly. They   256
did not annihilate the Samnite people, even though they
treated our friendship and treaties with contempt on three
occasions, and for eighty years conducted major wars
against us, nor did they wipe out those other states that
enlisted Pyrrhus on their side against Italy.[23] And, to take   257
recent events, we ourselves did not destroy those Italians

vited into Italy by the people of Tarentum, and remained there,
and in Sicily, from 280 to 275.

νους διεφθείραμεν, οὐδὲ Βρεττίους, οἳ μέχρι τέλους
αὐτῷ συνηγωνίσαντο, ἀλλὰ γῇ μόνῃ ζημιώσαντες
εἰάσαμεν ἔχειν τὰ ὑπόλοιπα, ὡς εὐσεβὲς ὁμοῦ καὶ ἐς
εὐτυχίαν ἡμῖν χρήσιμον μὴ ἀφανίζειν ἀνθρώπων
γένη μᾶλλον ἢ νουθετεῖν.

258   59. "Τί οὖν παθόντες ἐπὶ Καρχηδονίων ἀλλάξωμεν
τὴν φύσιν, ᾗ χρώμενοι μέχρι νῦν εὐτυχοῦμεν; ὅτι μεί-
ζων ἐστὶν ἡ πόλις αὕτη; δι' αὐτὸ μέντοι καὶ τοῦτο
μᾶλλον ἔτι φειδοῦς ἀξία. ἀλλ' ὅτι πολλάκις παρ-
εσπόνδησεν εἰς ἡμᾶς; καὶ γὰρ ἕτεροι καὶ σχεδὸν
259 ἅπαντες. ἀλλ' ὅτι μικρὰν νῦν ὑφίστανται τιμωρίαν;
ὧν νῆές τε πᾶσαι χωρὶς δέκα παραιροῦνται, καὶ τοὺς
ἐλέφαντας, οἷς ἰσχύουσι, παραδιδόασι καὶ τάλαντα
Εὐβοϊκὰ μύρια τελοῦσι καὶ πόλεων ἁπασῶν ἀφίσταν-
ται καὶ χώρας, ὅσης ἄρχουσιν ἐκτὸς τῶν Φοινικίδων
τάφρων, καὶ στρατολογεῖν αὐτοῖς ἀπηγόρευται, καὶ
ὅσα λιμώττοντες ἥρπασαν, ἀποδιδόασιν ἔτι λιμώττοντες, καὶ τῶν ἀμφιλόγων ἐστὶν αὐτοῖς Σκιπίων ὁ πο-
260 λεμήσας κριτής. ἐγὼ μὲν καὶ τοῦ μεγέθους τῶνδε καὶ
τοῦ πλήθους ἐπαινῶ τὸν Σκιπίωνα καὶ ὑμᾶς ἀξιῶ φεί-
σασθαι διὰ τὸν φθόνον καὶ τὴν τῶν ἀνθρωπείων με-
ταβολήν, οἷς εἰσιν ἔτι νῆες, πρὶν συνθώμεθα, πολλαὶ
καὶ πλῆθος ἐλεφάντων, καὶ Ἀννίβας στρατηγικώτα-
τος ἀνὴρ ἤδη στρατιὰν ἔχει, καὶ Μάγων ἐκ Κελτῶν
καὶ Λιγύων ἑτέρους ἄγει πολλούς, καὶ Οὐερμίνας ὁ
Σύφακος αὐτοῖς συμμαχεῖ καὶ ἄλλα Νομάδων ἔθνη,
261 δούλους τε ἔχουσι πολλούς. καὶ ἢν ἀπογνῶσι τὰ παρ'

who joined Hannibal, not even the Brutii who fought on his side until the very end: we merely confiscated some of their land, allowing them to keep the rest, in the belief that it was at the same time both righteous and conducive to our success to chastise rather than obliterate whole races of men.

59. "Why should our experiences at the hands of the Carthaginians lead us to change our nature, when we have been so successful until now by staying true to it? Is it because it is such a great city? But that is all the more reason why it is worth sparing. Is it because they have often broken their agreements with us? But so have others, indeed nearly everyone. Or is it because they are receiving such a light punishment? But they are losing all but ten of their ships; they have to give up their elephants, a great source of power to them; they have to pay ten thousand Euboic talents and withdraw from all towns and land under their control outside the Phoenician Trenches; they are forbidden from enlisting soldiers; whatever they seized when they were starving, they must give back, even though they are still starving; and the man who fought against them, Scipio, is to adjudicate disputed issues. For my own part, I praise Scipio for the severity and number of these conditions, and, keeping in mind envy and the changeability of human affairs, I ask you for mercy. Until we conclude an agreement, the Carthaginians still have many ships and a large force of elephants; Hannibal, a man of military genius, still has an army; Mago is bringing many new troops from the Celts and Ligurians; Verminas, the son of Syphax, is providing them with military assistance, along with other Numidian peoples; and they have a large number of slaves. If they give up on us in despair, they will

258

259

260

261

ἡμῶν, ἀφειδῶς ἅπασι χρήσονται. χαλεπώτερον δ᾽ οὐδὲν ἀφειδίας ἐν μάχαις, ἐν αἷς καὶ τὸ δαιμόνιον ἀνώ-
μαλον καὶ ἐπίφθονόν ἐστιν.

262   60. "Ἃ καὶ Σκιπίων ἔοικεν ὑφορώμενος ἐπιστεῖλαι
μὲν ἡμῖν τὴν ἑαυτοῦ γνώμην, ἐπειπεῖν δ᾽, ὅτι καὶ βραδυνόντων συνθήσεται. εἰκὸς δ᾽ ἐκεῖνον καὶ τάδε ἄμει-
νον ἡμῶν ἐκλογίζεσθαι καὶ πλέον ἔτι συνορᾶν, ὄντα
263   ἐπὶ τῶν ἔργων. λυπήσομέν τε ἀκυροῦντες αὐτοῦ τὴν
παραίνεσιν, ἄνδρα φιλόπολιν καὶ στρατηγὸν ἐξαίρετον, ὃς οὐδ᾽ ἐς Λιβύην ἡμᾶς ὁρμωμένους παρώξυνέ τε
καὶ στρατιὰν οὐ λαβὼν αὑτῷ συνεστήσατο καὶ τὰ
ἐκεῖ προήγαγεν ἡμῖν, ἐς ὅσον οὐκ ἠλπίζομεν. ὃ καὶ
θαυμάζειν ἄξιον, ὅτι ῥαθύμως ἔχοντες ἐν ἀρχῇ τοῦδε
264   τοῦ πολέμου νῦν ἔχετε φιλονείκως καὶ ἀμέτρως. εἰ δέ
τις ταῦτα μὲν ἡγεῖται καλῶς ἔχειν, δέδιε δέ, μὴ καὶ
νῦν τὰς σπονδὰς παραβῶσιν οἱ Καρχηδόνιοι, μάλιστα μὲν εἰκὸς αὐτοὺς ἤδη σπονδῶν φυλακῆς αἰσθά-
νεσθαι, πολλὰ ἐκ τῶν παραβάσεων παθόντας, καὶ
τὴν εὐσέβειαν ἐς τὸ μέλλον ποιήσεσθαι περὶ πολλοῦ,
ἐξ ἀσεβείας ἐς γόνυ πεσόντας· οὐκ ἔστι δὲ τῶν αὐτῶν
συμβούλων ἄρτι μὲν καταφρονεῖν τῶν Καρχηδονίων
ὡς οὐδὲν ἔτι ἰσχυόντων, δεδιέναι δ᾽ αὖθις ὡς ἀποστῆ-
265   ναι δυναμένους. ἡμῖν δὲ τὸ φυλάσσειν αὐτοὺς ἐς τὸ
μὴ πάλιν αὐξῆσαι τοῦ νῦν ἀνελεῖν εὐχερέστερόν ἐστι·
νῦν μὲν γὰρ ἐξ ἀπογνώσεως μαχέσονται, ὕστερον δ᾽
266   αἰεὶ δεδιότας τηρήσομεν. ἅλις δὲ κακῶν ἕξουσι καὶ
χωρὶς ἡμῶν, οἷς οἵ τε περίοικοι πάντες ἐπικείσονται,

use all these resources with abandon. And there is nothing more difficult to deal with in battle than recklessness; and in battle even the divinity is inconsistent and envious.

60. "It seems that Scipio too was apprehensive about this when he communicated his opinion to us, and added that, if we delayed, he would make an agreement himself. It is probable that his calculations on these matters are better than ours, and that he has a wider perspective on the situation, being, as he is, at the scene of the action. If we turn down his advice, we will be annoying a patriotic citizen and an outstanding general, who put us up to it when we were against attacking Africa, and levied an army himself when we would not give him one, and brought a level of success to our venture there far beyond our expectations. What is worthy of astonishment is how nonchalantly you behaved at the beginning of this war, but how determined and unrestrained you are now in pursuing it. If anyone believes that this is appropriate, but is afraid that the Carthaginians will now again break the treaty, I argue it is very likely that, because they have suffered so much from breaking their agreements, they now understand why they should keep them, and because they have been brought to their knees by dishonesty, they will in the future take great care to guard their integrity. The same senators cannot at one moment despise the Carthaginians as now powerless, and in the next express fear about their ability to revolt. And it will be easier to guard against them growing powerful again in the future than it will be to destroy them now. For now they will fight out of desperation, while in the future we will take care to keep them permanently in fear. And they will have enough trouble even without us. For all their neighbors are angry at the

262

263

264

265

266

δυσμεναίνοντες τῆς ποτε βίας, καὶ Μασσανάσσης,
ἀνὴρ πιστότατος ἡμῖν, ἐφεδρεύσει παρὼν αἰεί.

267   61. "Εἰ δ' ἄρα τις καὶ τῶνδε πάντων καταφρονεῖ,
ὅπως δ' αὐτὸς ἐκδέξεται τὴν Σκιπίωνος ἀρχήν, τὸ ἑαυτοῦ μόνον σκοπεῖ καὶ πιστεύει καὶ τὰ τῆς τύχης αὐτῷ
ἐς τέλος ἀπαντήσειν, τί καὶ χρησόμεθα τῇ πόλει λαβόντες αὐτήν, ἢν καὶ λάβωμεν; ἀνελοῦμεν ἄρδην, ὅτι
σῖτον ἡμῶν καὶ ναῦς ἥρπασαν· ἃ μετὰ πολλῶν ἄλλων
268   ἀξιοῦσιν ἀποδοῦναι. ἢ τοῦτο μὲν οὐ πράξομεν, νέμε-
σίν τε θεῶν φυλασσόμενοι καὶ ψόγον ἀνθρώπων,
Μασσανάσσῃ δ' ἔχειν δώσομεν; ἀλλ' εἰ καὶ φίλος
ἐστίν, οὐ χρὴ στερροποιεῖν οὐδ' ἐκεῖνον ἀμέτρως,
ἡγεῖσθαι δὲ τὴν ἔριν αὐτῶν τὴν ἐς ἀλλήλους τῷ
Ῥωμαίων κοινῷ συμφέρειν. ἀλλ' ἐς προσόδους τὴν
269   χώραν ἀνήσομεν; ἀλλ' ἡ φυλάξουσα στρατιὰ τὴν
πρόσοδον ἀναλώσει· πολλῆς γάρ, ὡς ἐν πολλοῖς
περιοίκοις καὶ πᾶσι βαρβάροις, δεησόμεθα. ἀλλ'
270   ἀποίκους πέμψομεν ἐς μέσους τοσούσδε Νομάδας; οἳ
τῶν μὲν βαρβάρων ἰσχυόντων ἀεὶ δεινὰ πείσονται, ἢν
δ' ἐπικρατήσωσιν αὐτῶν, ἐς τὸ μέλλον ἡμῖν ἔσονται
φοβεροὶ καὶ ἐπίφθονοι, χώραν τοσήνδε καὶ πολὺ
271   κρείττονα τῆς ἡμετέρας ἔχοντες. ἃ καὶ αὐτά μοι δοκεῖ
συνιδὼν ὁ Σκιπίων κελεύειν ἡμῖν δέχεσθαι τὰς Καρχηδονίων παρακλήσεις. πειθώμεθα οὖν καὶ τοῖς δεομένοις καὶ τῷ στρατηγῷ."

272   62. Ὁ μὲν οὕτως εἶπεν, Πούπλιος δὲ Κορνήλιος,
Κορνηλίου Λέντλου συγγενής, τοῦ τότε ὄντος ὑπάτου

violence done to them by the Carthaginians on former occasions and will bear down on them, and Massinissa, our most faithful friend, will always be there to keep watch on them.

61. "But if anyone has no interest in all these matters 267 and is concerned only for himself and how he might succeed to Scipio's command, confident that it will all work out well for him in the end, what are we going to do with Carthage when we have captured it—if indeed we do capture it? Are we going to raze it to the ground because they seized some of our grain and ships, which, along with many other items, they are asking to return? And if, in 268 guarding against divine retribution and the condemnation of men, we do not do this, will we give it to Massinissa to own? He may be our friend, but even him we should not make immoderately powerful; rather, we should regard the mutual rivalry of Massinissa and Carthage as to the advantage of the Roman state. Are we going to extract revenue from the country? But the army of occupation, 269 which would have to be a large one, given the many neighbors—all of them barbarians—would use up all the income. Are we going to establish colonies in the middle of so many Numidians? But if the barbarians dominate them, 270 they will always suffer badly, and if they master the barbarians, we will in the future have reason to fear and envy them, for having such an extensive territory and one much more powerful than our own. It seems to me that it was 271 because he understood these very issues that Scipio instructed us to accept the appeal of the Carthaginians. So, let us do what they and our general ask."

62. Publius Cornelius, a relative of the Cornelius Lentulus who was consul at the time, and who expected to 272

καὶ τὸν Σκιπίωνα διαδέξεσθαι προσδοκῶντος, ἀντέλε-
273 γεν οὕτως· "Τὸ μὲν συμφέρον ἐστὶ μόνον ἐν τοῖς πολέμοις, ὦ ἄνδρες, χρήσιμον· καὶ ὅσῳ δυνατὴν ἔτι καὶ
νῦν ἀποφαίνουσιν οὗτοι τὴν πόλιν, φυλάξασθαι χρὴ
τὴν ἀπιστίαν αὐτῆς μετὰ τῆς δυνάμεως καὶ τὴν ἰσχὺν
274 προανελεῖν, ἐπεὶ μὴ τὴν ἀπιστίαν δυνάμεθα. οὐδεὶς δ'
ἡμῖν καιρὸς ἐς τὸ λῦσαι τὸν ἀπὸ Καρχηδονίων φόβον
ἐπιτηδειότερός ἐστι τοῦ παρόντος, ἐν ᾧ πάντων εἰσὶν
ἀσθενεῖς καὶ ἄποροι, πρὶν αὖθις αὐτῶν ἐς ἑκάτερον
275 αὐξῆσαι. οὐ μέντοι καὶ τὸν τοῦ δικαίου λογισμὸν ἂν
περιφύγοιμι οὐδ' ἀμετρίας μοι δοκῶ δόξαν οἴσεσθαι
τὴν πόλιν ἐπὶ Καρχηδονίοις, οἳ παρὰ μὲν τὰς εὐπρα-
ξίας ἀδικοῦσι καὶ ἐνυβρίζουσιν ἐς ἅπαντας, ἐν δὲ
ταῖς συμφοραῖς παρακαλοῦσιν, ἂν δὲ τύχωσιν, εὐθὺς
276 ἐπὶ ταῖς συνθήκαις μετατίθενται. καὶ οὔτε σπονδῶν
ἐστιν αὐτοῖς αἰδὼς οὔτε λόγος ὅρκων· οὓς οὗτος ἀξιοῖ
περισῴζειν διὰ νέμεσιν θεῶν καὶ ἀνθρώπων φθόνον.
277 ἐγὼ δ' αὐτοὺς ἡγοῦμαι τοὺς θεοὺς ἐς τόδε τὴν Καρχηδόνα περιενεγκεῖν, ἵνα δῶσί ποτε δίκην τῆς ἀσεβείας, οἳ καὶ περὶ Σικελίαν καὶ Ἰβηρίαν καὶ Ἰταλίαν
καὶ ἐν αὐτῇ τῇ Λιβύῃ καὶ πρὸς ἡμᾶς καὶ πρὸς τοὺς
ἄλλους ἅπαντας αἰεὶ συνετίθεντο καὶ παρώρκουν καὶ
δεινὰ καὶ σχέτλια ἔδρων. ὧν τὰ ἀλλότρια ὑμῖν πρὸ
τῶν ἡμετέρων διέξειμι, ἵνα εἰδῆτε πάντας ἐφησθησο-
μένους Καρχηδονίοις, εἰ δίκην δοῖεν.
278   63. "Οὗτοι Ζακανθαίους, πόλιν Ἰβηρίας ἐπιφανῆ,

succeed Scipio, replied to this speech in the following manner:[24] "In wars, gentlemen, the only good thing is what works to your advantage. And, inasmuch as these men declare that Carthage is even still a powerful city, so should we take precautions against its duplicity and strength, by destroying its power, since we cannot destroy its duplicity. There is no more favorable opportunity to free ourselves from fear of Carthage than the present, when they lack all power and resources, and before they recover on both counts. It is not that I would want to ignore the consideration of justice, but I do not believe that Rome will get a reputation for lack of restraint against the Carthaginians, when they are people who in good times commit wrongs and violence against everyone, and when disaster strikes ask for mercy, and, when they get it, immediately go back on the agreements they have made. They have no shame in breaking treaties and attach no importance to oaths. And these are the people this man thinks we should save, to avoid divine retribution and the envy of men. It is my personal belief that the gods themselves have brought Carthage to their present predicament, in order to punish them finally for their impiety in making agreements and breaking their oaths, for committing acts of shocking wickedness, whether in Sicily, Iberia, Italy, or Africa itself. Let me list for you some of the experiences of other people before our own, to make sure you know that all people will gloat over the Carthaginians, if they are punished.

63. "These are the people who, for example, slaugh- 278

---

[24] P. Cornelius Lentulus had been praetor in 214. He governed Sicily from then until 212, but we hear no more of him.

σφίσι τε αὐτοῖς ἔνσπονδον καὶ φίλην ἡμῖν, ἡβηδὸν
ἔκτειναν οὐδὲν ἀδικοῦντας. οὗτοι Νουκερίαν ὑπήκοον
ἡμῶν ἐπὶ συνθήκῃ λαβόντες καὶ ὀμόσαντες σὺν δύο
ἱματίοις ἕκαστον ἀπολύσειν τὴν μὲν βουλὴν αὐτῶν ἐς
τὰ βαλανεῖα συνέκλεισαν καὶ ὑποκαίοντες τὰ βαλανεῖα ἀπέπνιξαν, τὸν δὲ δῆμον ἀπιόντα κατηκόντισαν.
Ἀχερρανῶν δὲ τὴν βουλὴν ἐν σπονδαῖς ἐς τὰ φρέατα
279 ἐνέβαλον καὶ τὰ φρέατα ἐπέχωσαν. Μάρκόν τε Κορνήλιον ὕπατον ἡμέτερον ὅρκοις ἀπατήσαντες ἤγαγον
μὲν ὡς ἐπισκεψόμενον αὐτῶν τὸν στρατηγὸν ἀρρω-
στοῦντα, συναρπάσαντες δ' ἀπήγαγον ἐς Λιβύην ἐκ
Σικελίας αἰχμάλωτον μετὰ δύο καὶ εἴκοσι νεῶν. ἔκτειναν δὲ καὶ Ῥῆγλον αἰκισάμενοι, στρατηγὸν ἕτερον
280 ἡμῶν, ὑπὸ εὐορκίας ἐπανελθόντα πρὸς αὐτούς. ὅσα δ'
Ἀννίβας ἢ πολεμῶν ἢ ἐνεδρεύων ἢ παρορκῶν ἔς τε
πόλεις καὶ στρατόπεδα ἡμῶν καὶ λήγων ἐς τοὺς συμμάχους ἔδρασε τοὺς αὐτοῦ, τάς τε πόλεις πορθῶν καὶ
τοὺς αὐτῷ συστρατευσαμένους κατακαίνων, μακρὸν
ἂν εἴη καταλέγειν, πλὴν ὅτι τετρακόσια ἡμῶν ἀνέ-
281 στησεν ἄστη. τοὺς δ' αἰχμαλώτους ἡμῶν τοὺς μὲν ἐς
τάφρους καὶ ποταμοὺς ἐμβαλόντες ὡς γεφύραις ἐπέ-
βαινον, τοὺς δὲ τοῖς ἐλέφασιν ὑπέβαλλον, τοὺς δ'
ἀλλήλοις μονομαχεῖν ἐκέλευον, ἀδελφοὺς ἀδελφοῖς
282 συνιστάντες καὶ πατέρας υἱοῖς. τὰ δ' ἔναγχος ταῦτα,

---

[25] Appian has the wrong member of the Cornelian family. It
was Cn. Cornelius Scipio Asina (the Ass), consul in 260 during

tered the entire adult population of Saguntum, a distinguished Iberian town and friend of ours, who had committed no wrong and with whom they themselves had a treaty. It was they who captured the town of Nuceria, one of our subjects, and made an agreement on oath to let the population go with just two cloaks. But they locked the senate up in the baths and suffocated them by raising the heat underneath, and the common people they shot down as they tried to get away. They made a treaty with the council of Acerra, but then threw the councilors into wells and blocked up the wells. They deceived our consul Marcus Cornelius with their oaths, taking him to visit their supposedly sick commander.[25] But then they grabbed him and took him off as a prisoner to Africa with twenty-two of our ships. They tortured and killed Regulus, another of our commanders, when he returned to Carthage in accordance with his oath.[26] It would take too long to recount in detail all the crimes Hannibal committed while fighting, laying traps, or swearing false oaths, and committed not just against our towns and armies, but finally even against his own allies, whose towns he destroyed and whose soldiers serving with him he killed. It is enough to say that he made desolate four hundred of our towns. He threw some of his Roman prisoners into ditches and rivers, walking over them like bridges; he had others crushed by elephants; and others again he ordered to fight against each other in single combat, pitting brother against brother, father against son. And recently, when they sent a peace

279

280

281

282

the First Punic War, who was ambushed and captured with his fleet in the Lipari islands.

[26] Appian tells the famous story above, at 3.11–4.15.

περὶ εἰρήνης ἐπρέσβευον ἐνταῦθα καὶ παρεκάλουν καὶ
ὤμνυον, καὶ οἱ πρέσβεις αὐτῶν ἔτι παρῆσαν, ἐν δὲ
Λιβύῃ τὰς ναῦς ἡμῶν διήρπαζον καὶ τοὺς στρατιώτας
κατέδεον. τοσοῦτον αὐτοῖς καὶ ἀνοίας διὰ τὴν ὠμότητα
περίεστι.

283   64. "Τούτοις οὖν τίς ἐστιν ἔλεος ἢ μετριοπάθεια
παρ' ἑτέρων, τοῖς οὐδὲν μέτριον οὐδ' ἥμερον ἐς οὐδέ-
νας εἰργασμένοις; τοῖς, ὥσπερ ἔφη Σκιπίων, εἰ ἐλά-
βοντο ἡμῶν, οὐδ' ἂν ὄνομα Ῥωμαίων ὑπολιποῦσιν;

284   ἀλλὰ πίστις ἐστὶ βέβαιος ἢ δεξιά. ποία; τίς σπονδή,
τίς ὅρκος, ὃν οὐκ ἐπάτησαν; τίς δὲ συνθήκη καὶ

285   χάρις, ἐς ἣν οὐχ ὕβρισαν; μὴ μιμησώμεθα, φησίν,
αὐτούς. τίνα γὰρ συνθήκην ἡμεῖς λύομεν, οἱ μήπω τι
συνθέμενοι; ἀλλὰ τὴν ὠμότητα, φησίν, αὐτῶν μὴ μιμησώμεθα. φίλους οὖν καὶ συμμάχους ποιησόμεθα

286   τοὺς ὠμοτάτους; οὐδέτερα τούτων ἄξια. ἀλλ' ἐπιτρε-
ψάτωσαν ἡμῖν αὐτοὺς νόμῳ νενικημένων, ὡς πολλοὶ
σφᾶς ἐπέτρεψαν, σκεψόμεθα δ' ἡμεῖς. καὶ ὅ τι ἂν δῶ-
μεν, εἴσονται χάριν, οὐχὶ συνθήκην νομίζοντες εἶναι.

287   διαφέρει δὲ τούτοιν ἑκάτερον ὧδε. μέχρι μὲν συντίθεν-
ται, παραβήσονται, καθάπερ καὶ πάλαι, πρόφασιν
αἰεί τινα τῶν συνθηκῶν φέροντες ὡς ἐν αὐταῖς ἠλατ-
τωμένοι· τὰ δ' ἀμφίλογα εὐπροφάσιστα· ὅταν δὲ
παραδῶσιν αὑτοὺς καὶ τὰ ὅπλα παρελώμεθα καὶ τὰ
σώματα ἐφ' ἡμῖν γένηται καὶ πεισθῶσιν, ὅτι μηδὲν
αὐτοῖς ἐστιν ἴδιον, τὰ μὲν φρονήματα αὐτῶν καταβή-
σεται, ἀγαπήσουσιν δ', ὅ τι ἂν παρ' ἡμῶν λάβωσιν

288   ὡς ἀλλότριον. εἰ μὲν οὖν Σκιπίωνι ἑτέρως δοκεῖ, τὰς

mission here, and were making appeals and swearing oaths, while their ambassadors were still in Rome, in Africa they were seizing our ships and arresting our soldiers. Such is the pitch of insanity to which their cruelty has led them.

64. "So, why should the Carthaginians get pity or forbearance from others, when they have shown no restraint or gentleness to them, and, as Scipio said, would have wiped out the very name of Rome, if they had got the better of us? But the right hand, he says, is a firm pledge. In what way? What treaty, what oath have they not trampled under foot? What agreement, what favor have they not abused? Let us not copy what they do, Scipio says. But what agreement are we going to break, when we have not made any yet? Let us not copy their savagery either, he says. Are we, then, to accept complete savages as our friends and allies? They deserve neither. Rather, let them surrender unconditionally to us, as is normal for the defeated, and as many have done before, and then we will consider what to do. Whatever we grant them, they will know is a favor, and not regard it as something we have agreed. These two approaches differ in the following way. On the one hand, so long as we negotiate agreements, they will break them as before, always presenting some excuse about the agreements disadvantaging them: disputed issues are a good source of excuses. On the other hand, when they surrender themselves, and we disarm them, and even their bodies belong to us, so that they know for sure they have nothing of their own, then their spirits will sink, and they will be happy with whatever they get from us, knowing it is does not belong to them. So, if Scipio thinks otherwise, you can compare his opinion and mine.

283

284

285

286

287

288

γνώμας ἔχετε συγκρίνειν· εἰ δὲ συνθήσεται Καρχηδονίοις χωρὶς ὑμῶν, τί καὶ ἐπέστελλεν ὑμῖν; ἐγὼ μὲν
γάρ, ὡς ὑμῖν κυρίοις οὖσι περὶ τῶνδε κρῖναι, τὴν
γνώμην εἶπον, ἣν νομίζω συνοίσειν τῇ πόλει."

289   65. Τοιαῦτα μὲν καὶ ὁ Πούπλιος εἶπεν· ἡ δὲ βουλὴ
κατὰ ἄνδρα παρ' ἑκάστου ψῆφον ᾔτει, καὶ ἐς τὴν Σκιπίωνος γνώμην αἱ πλείους συνέδραμον. ἐγίγνοντο οὖν
αἱ συνθῆκαι, τρίται αἵδε, Ῥωμαίοις καὶ Καρχηδονίοις
290   πρὸς ἀλλήλους. καὶ ὁ Σκιπίων ἐς αὐτὰς ἐδόκει μάλιστα τοὺς Ῥωμαίους ἐναγαγέσθαι, εἴτε τῶν εἰρημένων
οὕνεκα λογισμῶν, εἴτε ὡς ἀρκοῦν Ῥωμαίοις ἐς εὐτυχίαν τὸ μόνην ἀφελέσθαι Καρχηδονίους τὴν ἡγεμο-
νίαν· εἰσὶ γάρ, οἳ καὶ τόδε νομίζουσιν, αὐτὸν ἐς Ῥωμαίων σωφρονισμὸν ἐθελῆσαι γείτονα καὶ ἀντίπαλον
αὐτοῖς φόβον ἐς ἀεὶ καταλιπεῖν, ἵνα μή ποτε ἐξυβρί-
291   σειαν ἐν μεγέθει τύχης καὶ ἀμεριμνίᾳ. καὶ τόδε οὕτω
φρονῆσαι τὸν Σκιπίωνα οὐ πολὺ ὕστερον ἐξεῖπε τοῖς
Ῥωμαίοις Κάτων, ἐπιπλήττων παρωξυμμένοις κατὰ
292   Ῥόδου. ὁ δὲ Σκιπίων ταῦτα συνθέμενος ἐκ Λιβύης ἐς
τὴν Ἰταλίαν παντὶ τῷ στρατῷ διέπλει καὶ ἐς τὴν
Ῥώμην ἐσήλαυνε θριαμβεύων, ἐπιφανέστατα δὴ τῶν
πρὸ αὑτοῦ.

293   66. Καὶ ὁ τρόπος, ᾧ καὶ νῦν ἔτι χρώμενοι διατελοῦ-
σιν, ἐστὶ τοιόσδε. ἐστεφάνωνται μὲν ἅπαντες, ἡγοῦνται δὲ σαλπιγκταί τε καὶ λαφύρων ἅμαξαι, πύργοι τε

---

27 In 167, M. Porcius Cato (consul 195, censor 184) delivered
a speech advising Rome against declaring war on Rhodes, who

And if he is going to make a unilateral agreement with the Carthaginians, why did he send a message to you at all? On the assumption that you are the ones with the authority to make a decision on this matter, I have given you the opinion that I believe will benefit the city."

65. Such was the speech of Publius. The senate called 289 for an individual vote from all members, and the majority favored Scipio's view. So, for the third time, Rome and Carthage agreed terms. Scipio was thought to have pressed 290 the Romans into this policy particularly, either for the reasons already stated, or in the belief that it was sufficient for Roman prosperity to have deprived the Carthaginians of their political dominance. There are also those who believe that in order to promote Roman self-discipline, Scipio wanted to leave a neighbor as a permanent rival and source of fear to them, so that the extent of their success would never lead them into careless presumption. That 291 this was Scipio's intention, Cato claimed not long after, when he was rebuking the Romans for allowing themselves to be provoked against Rhodes.[27] As for Scipio, 292 when he had concluded the treaty, he sailed from Africa to Italy with his whole army, and marched into Rome in a triumph more splendid than held any before him.

66. The form of the triumph, which they continue to 293 use right up to the present day, is as follows. Everyone wears a crown. The trumpeters and wagons with the plun-

had annoyed Rome by offering to negotiate an end to Rome's war against Perseus, king of Macedon (the Third Macedonian War, 172–168). Fragments of the speech survive, as do extensive comments on it by Aulus Gellius (6.3), but there is no mention of Scipio.

APPIAN

παραφέρονται μιμήματα τῶν εἰλημμένων πόλεων καὶ
γραφαὶ καὶ σχήματα τῶν γεγονότων, εἶτα χρυσὸς καὶ
ἄργυρος ἀσήμαντός τε καὶ σεσημασμένος καὶ εἴ τι
τοιουτότροπον ἄλλο, καὶ στέφανοι, ὅσοις τὸν στρατηγὸν ἀρετῆς ἕνεκα ἀναδοῦσιν ἢ πόλεις ἢ σύμμαχοι ἢ
294 τὰ ὑπ᾽ αὐτῷ στρατόπεδα. βόες δ᾽ ἐπὶ τοῖσδε λευκοὶ
καὶ ἐλέφαντες ἦσαν ἐπὶ τοῖς βουσίν, καὶ Καρχηδονίων αὐτῶν καὶ Νομάδων, ὅσοι τῶν ἡγεμόνων ἐλήφθη-
295 σαν. αὐτοῦ δ᾽ ἡγοῦνται τοῦ στρατηγοῦ Ῥαβδοῦχοι
φοινικοῦς χιτῶνας ἐνδεδυκότες καὶ χορὸς κιθαριστῶν
τε καὶ τιτυριστῶν, ἐς μίμημα Τυρρηνικῆς πομπῆς,
περιεζωσμένοι τε καὶ στεφάνην χρυσῆν ἐπικείμενοι·
ἴσα τε βαίνουσιν ἐν τάξει μετὰ ᾠδῆς καὶ μετ᾽ ὀρχή-
σεως. Λυδοὺς αὐτοὺς καλοῦσιν, ὅτι, οἶμαι, Τυρρηνοὶ
296 Λυδῶν ἄποικοι. τούτων δέ τις ἐν μέσῳ, πορφύραν πο-
δήρη περικείμενος καὶ ψέλια καὶ στρεπτὰ ἀπὸ χρυσοῦ, σχηματίζεται ποικίλως ἐς γέλωτα ὡς ἐπορχού-
297 μενος τοῖς πολεμίοις. ἐπὶ δ᾽ αὐτῷ θυμιατηρίων πλῆθος
καὶ ὁ στρατηγὸς ἐπὶ τοῖς θυμιάμασιν, ἐφ᾽ ἅρματος
καταγεγραμμένου ποικίλως· ἔστεπται μὲν ἀπὸ χρυσοῦ καὶ λίθων πολυτίμων, ἔσταλται δ᾽ ἐς τὸν πάτριον
τρόπον πορφύραν, ἀστέρων χρυσῶν ἐνυφασμένων,
καὶ σκῆπτρον ἐξ ἐλέφαντος φέρει καὶ δάφνην, ἣν ἀεὶ
298 Ῥωμαῖοι νομίζουσι νίκης σύμβολον. ἐπιβαίνουσι δ᾽
αὐτῷ ἐπὶ τὸ ἅρμα παῖδές τε καὶ παρθένοι, καὶ ἐπὶ τῶν
παρηόρων ἑκατέρωθεν ἤθεοι συγγενεῖς. καὶ παρέπον-
ται ὅσοι παρὰ τὸν πόλεμον ἦσαν αὐτῷ γραμματεῖς τε
299 καὶ ὑπηρέται καὶ ὑπασπισταί. καὶ μετ᾽ ἐκείνους ἡ

110

der lead the way. Then towers representing the captured towns are carried in the procession, and drawings and images of events. Next, gold and silver coin and bullion, and anything else of this sort, and the crowns awarded to the general for his courage by towns, allies, or the armies under his command. White oxen come next, and addition- 294 ally in this case, elephants and the captured Carthaginian and Numidian leaders. Lictors wearing purple cloaks walk 295 in front of the general himself, and a troop of lyre players and pipers wearing belts and golden crowns, modeled after an Etruscan procession, and marching together in ranks while singing and dancing. They call them Lydians, in my opinion, because the Etruscans are colonists from Lydia. One of them in the middle, wearing an ankle-length 296 purple robe and armbands and torques of gold, makes all sorts of gestures to induce laughter as if dancing trium- phantly over the enemy. After him there is a crowd of in- 297 cense burners, then the general himself on an elaborately painted chariot. He has a golden crown set with precious stones, and is dressed, as is the Roman fashion, in a purple robe with golden stars woven into it, and he carries an ivory staff and a laurel branch, which the Romans always regard as a symbol of victory. With the general on the 298 chariot are young boys and girls, and riding escort horses on either side, unmarried youths related to him. In atten- dance too are all the secretaries and attendants and bat- men who were with him on campaign. After them comes 299

στρατιὰ κατά τε ἴλας καὶ τάξεις, ἐστεφανωμένη πᾶσα
καὶ δαφνηφοροῦσα· οἱ δὲ ἀριστεῖς καὶ τὰ ἀριστεῖα
ἐπίκεινται. καὶ τῶν ἀρχόντων οὓς μὲν ἐπαινοῦσιν,
οὓς δὲ σκώπτουσιν, οὓς δὲ ψέγουσιν· ἀφελὴς γὰρ ὁ
300 θρίαμβος καὶ ἐν ἐξουσίᾳ λέγειν, ὅ τι θέλοιεν. ἀφικό-
μενος δὲ ἐς τὸ Καπιτώλιον ὁ Σκιπίων τὴν μὲν πομπὴν
κατέπαυσεν, εἱστία δὲ τοὺς φίλους, ὥσπερ ἔθος ἐστίν,
ἐς τὸ ἱερόν.

301   67. Καὶ τέλος εἶχε Ῥωμαίοις ὁ δεύτερος πρὸς Καρχηδονίους πόλεμος, ἀρξάμενος ἀπὸ Ἰβηρίας, λήξας
δ᾿ ἐν Λιβύῃ ἐς τάσδε τὰς περὶ αὐτῆς Καρχηδόνος
σπονδάς. καὶ ὀλυμπιάδες ἐν τοῖς Ἕλλησιν ἦσαν
ἀμφὶ τὰς ἑκατὸν καὶ τεσσαράκοντα καὶ τέσσαρας.
302 Μασσανάσσης δὲ Καρχηδονίοις τε μηνίων καὶ Ῥωμαίοις θαρρῶν ἐπέβαινε γῇ πολλῇ τῶν Καρχηδονίων
ὡς γενομένῃ ποτὲ ἑαυτοῦ, καὶ οἱ Καρχηδόνιοι Ῥωμαίους παρεκάλουν σφίσι Μασσανάσσην συναλλάξαι. οἱ δ᾿ ἔπεμπον διαλλακτάς, οἷς εἴρητο συμπράσ-
303 σειν, ὅσα δύναιντο, Μασσανάσσῃ. οὕτω μὲν τὴν γῆν
ἀπετέμετο Καρχηδονίων ὁ Μασσανάσσης, καὶ συνθῆκαι Καρχηδονίοις καὶ πρὸς τόνδε ἐγένοντο, αἳ διέμειναν ἐς ἔτη πεντήκοντα, ἐν οἷς μάλιστα ἡ Καρχηδὼν εἰρηνεύουσα ὁμαλῶς ἐς μέγα δυνάμεως καὶ
εὐανδρίας ἦλθεν ἔκ τε πεδίων εὐκαρπίας καὶ θαλάσσης εὐκαιρίας.

304   68. Καὶ εὐθύς, οἷον ἐν ταῖς εὐτυχίαις γίγνεται, οἱ
μὲν ἐρρωμάιζον, οἱ δὲ ἐδημοκράτιζον, οἷς δ᾿ ἤρεσκε
305 Μασσανάσσης. ἡγοῦντο δὲ ἑκάστων οἱ καὶ δόξῃ καὶ

the army in companies and ranks, all of them with crowns and laurel branches, and the champions with their prizes for valor. The soldiers praise some of their officers, and make fun of, or abuse, others. For participants in the triumph are unrestricted and allowed to say whatever they like. When he arrived at the Capitol, Scipio brought the 300 procession to a conclusion, and entertained his associates to the customary feast in the temple.

67. So ended the second war between Rome and Car- 301 thage, which started in Iberia and finished in Africa with the agreement about Carthage itself discussed above. By Greek dating this was about the 144th Olympiad.[28] In his 302 anger at the Carthaginians, and confident of Roman support, Massinissa attacked a large section of Carthaginian territory, claiming that it once belonged to him. The Carthaginians appealed to Rome to reconcile Massinissa to them, but the Romans sent mediators with instructions to cooperate with Massinissa as much as possible. As a result, 303 Massinissa set about detaching Carthaginian land for himself, and a treaty was agreed between him and Carthage, which lasted for almost fifty years. In this time of unbroken peace, the power and population of Carthage in particular grew as a result of the fertility of its plain, and its strategic location by the sea.

68. Very soon, as happens when times are good, divi- 304 sions appeared: there was a Roman party, a democracy party and a pro-Massinissa group. Each had leaders of 305

[28] The 144th Olympiad ran from 204/3 to 201/0.

ἀρετῇ προύχοντες, τῶν μὲν Ῥωμαϊζόντων ὁ Μέγας
Ἄννων, τῶν δ᾽ αἱρουμένων τὰ Μασσανάσσου Ἀννίβας, ὁ Ψὰρ ἐπικαλούμενος, τῶν δὲ δημοκρατιζόντων
Ἀμίλχαρ, ᾧ Σαυνίτης ἐπώνυμον ἦν, καὶ Καρθάλων·
306 οἳ φυλάξαντες Ῥωμαίους τε Κελτίβηρσι πολεμοῦντας
καὶ Μασσανάσσην ἐπικουροῦντα υἱῷ πρὸς ἑτέρων
Ἰβήρων συγκεκλεισμένῳ πείθουσι τὸν Καρθάλωνα,
βοήθαρχον ὄντα καὶ ἐπὶ τῇδε τῇ ἀρχῇ τὴν χώραν
περιόντα, ἐπιθέσθαι τοῖς Μασσανάσσου σκηνουμέ-
307 νοις ἐν ἀμφιλόγῳ γῇ. ὁ δὲ καὶ ἔκτεινέν τινας αὐτῶν
καὶ λείαν περιήλασε καὶ τοὺς ἐν τοῖς ἀγροῖς Λίβυας
ἐπὶ τοὺς Νομάδας ἤγειρεν. ἄλλα τε πολλὰ αὐτοῖς
ἔργα πολέμων ἐς ἀλλήλους γίγνεται, μέχρι Ῥωμαίων
ἕτεροι πρέσβεις ἐπῆλθον ἐς διαλύσεις, οἷς ὁμοίως
308 εἴρητο Μασσανάσσῃ βοηθεῖν ἀδήλως. καὶ ἐβεβαίω-
σαν οἵδε τῷ Μασσανάσσῃ, ὅσα προειλήφει, μετὰ
τέχνης ὧδε. εἶπον μὲν οὐδὲν οὐδὲ ἤκουσαν, ἵνα μή τι
ὡς ἐν δίκῃ Μασσανάσσης ἐλασσοῖτο, ἐν μέσῳ δ᾽ ἀμφοῖν γενόμενοι τὰς χεῖρας διέστησαν· καὶ τοῦτο ἦν
309 αὐτοῖς κέλευσμα πρὸς ἀμφοτέρους ἐς διαλύσεις. οὐ
πολὺ δὲ ὕστερον ὁ Μασσανάσσης ἠμφισβήτει καὶ
τῶν λεγομένων μεγάλων πεδίων καὶ χώρας πεντήκοντα πόλεων, ἣν Τύσκαν προσαγορεύουσιν. ἐφ᾽ οἷς
πάλιν οἱ Καρχηδόνιοι κατέφυγον ἐπὶ Ῥωμαίους.
310   69. Οἱ δ᾽ ὑπέσχοντο μὲν αὐτοῖς καὶ τότε πρέσβεις
πέμψειν ἐς δίαιταν, διέτριψαν δέ, ἕως εἴκασαν πολλὰ
τῶν Καρχηδονίων διεφθάρθαι, καὶ τότε πρέσβεις

outstanding reputation and excellence. Hanno the Great was head of the Romanizing group, Hannibal surnamed "the Starling" led the supporters of Massinissa, and Hamilcar surnamed "the Samnite" and Carthalo led the democratic party. The democrats, observing the Romans fighting a Celtiberian war and Massinissa going to the aid of his son, who had been cut off by other Iberians, persuaded Carthalo to attack the forces of Massinissa encamped on disputed land. Carthalo was Boetharch, and in that role was traveling around the country.[29] He killed some of Massinissa's men and collected booty, and stirred up the African farmers against the Numidians. There were many other acts of war committed by both sides against each other, until eventually new Roman envoys arrived to negotiate a settlement. But, as before, they had been told to help Massinissa secretly, and they skillfully managed to secure for him what he had previously taken, in the following manner. They would neither say anything nor hear anything said, to avoid any setback for Massinissa in the dispute, but standing between the two sides, they held out their arms. This was their way of ordering both sides to resolve their dispute. Not long after, Massinissa laid claim to what is called "the Great Plains," and the region of fifty towns they call Tuska.[30] The Carthaginians again looked to Rome for help.

69. And on this occasion too, the Romans promised to send envoys to arbitrate. But they delayed until they estimated that the Carthaginian cause had been badly af-

[29] It is not clear what the functions of the Boetharch were, but Carthalo was clearly a senior Carthaginian official.

[30] Thugga, modern Dougga, is located in northwest Tunisia.

APPIAN

ἔπεμπον ἑτέρους τε καὶ Κάτωνα, οἳ εἰς τὴν ἀμφίλογον
γῆν ἀφικόμενοι ἠξίουν σφίσιν ἀμφοτέρους περὶ
311 ἁπάντων ἐπιτρέπειν. Μασσανάσσης μὲν οὖν, οἷα πλε-
ονεκτῶν καὶ Ῥωμαίοις αἰεὶ θαρρῶν, ἐπέτρεπεν, οἱ
Καρχηδόνιοι δ᾽ ὑπώπτευον, ἐπεὶ καὶ τοὺς πρότερον
ᾔδεσαν οὐκ εὖ δικάσαντας. ἔφασαν οὖν τὰς συνθήκας
τὰς ἐπὶ Σκιπίωνος οὐδὲν χρῄζειν δικῶν οὐδὲ διορθώ-
312 σεως, ὅσα μὴ ἐξ αὐτῶν παραβαίνεται μόνα. οἱ δ᾽ οὐκ
ἀνασχόμενοι περὶ μέρους δικάζειν ἐπανῄεσαν καὶ τὴν
χώραν περιεσκόπουν, ἀκριβῶς τε εἰργασμένην καὶ
κατασκευὰς μεγάλας ἔχουσαν. εἶδον δὲ καὶ τὴν πόλιν
εἰσελθόντες, ὅση τε τὴν δύναμιν ἦν, καὶ πλῆθος, ὅσον
ηὔξητο ἐκ τῆς οὐ πρὸ πολλοῦ κατὰ Σκιπίωνα δια-
313 φθορᾶς. ἐπανελθόντες τε ἐς Ῥώμην ἔφραζον οὐ ζήλου
μᾶλλον ἢ φόβου γέμειν αὐτοῖς τὰ Καρχηδονίων, πόλεως δυσμενοῦς τοσῆσδε καὶ γείτονος εὐχερῶς οὕτως
314 αὐξανομένης. καὶ ὁ Κάτων μάλιστα ἔλεγεν οὔ ποτε
Ῥωμαίοις βέβαιον οὐδὲ τὴν ἐλευθερίαν ἔσεσθαι, πρὶν
ἐξελεῖν Καρχηδόνα. ὧν ἡ βουλὴ πυνθανομένη ἔκρινε
μὲν πολεμεῖν, ἔτι δ᾽ ἔχρῃζε προφάσεων, καὶ τὴν κρί-
315 σιν ἀπόρρητον εἶχον. Κάτωνα δ᾽ ἐξ ἐκείνου φασὶν ἐν
τῇ βουλῇ συνεχεῖ γνώμῃ λέγειν, Καρχηδόνα μὴ εἶναι, Σκιπίωνα δὲ τὸν Νασικᾶν τὰ ἐναντία ἀξιοῦν,
Καρχηδόνα ἐᾶν, ἐς φόβον ἄρα καὶ τόνδε Ῥωμαίων
ἐκδιαιτωμένων ἤδη.
316 70. Καρχηδονίων δ᾽ οἱ δημοκρατίζοντες τοὺς τὰ

---

31 This was in 153.

fected. At that point they sent a new mission, one that included Cato.[31] When the envoys arrived in the disputed territory, they asked both sides to refer all issues to them. Massinissa, although claiming more than his due, was enduringly confident of Roman support, and agreed. The Carthaginians, on the other hand, were suspicious, as they knew the previous envoys had not given fair decisions. So, they said that the treaty negotiated in Scipio's time did not need lawsuits or punishment, except only for the transgressions being committed by them. The Roman delegates refused to arbitrate in a piecemeal fashion and withdrew. But they did reconnoiter the countryside carefully, noting how diligently it was cultivated and what substantial resources it had. They also entered the city of Carthage and saw how powerful it was, and how much its population had grown in the short time since its destruction at the hands of Scipio. On their return to Rome, the envoys said that Carthage filled them with fear rather than envy: it was a large and malevolent city, a neighbor, and one expanding effortlessly. Cato in particular said that Rome's freedom would never be secure until Carthage had been destroyed. When the senate heard this, they decided on war, but, still needing a pretext, kept their decision secret. They say that it was from this time that Cato began to express in the senate his unwavering conviction that Carthage should not exist. Scipio Nasica believed the opposite, that they should leave Carthage be, precisely to preserve the very fear that Rome was already losing as a way of life.[32]

70. The democratic party at Carthage then expelled

311

312

313

314

315

316

---

[32] P. Cornelius Scipio Nasica, consul in 162 and 155, was the son-in-law of Scipio Africanus, the conqueror of Hannibal.

Μασσανάσσου φρονοῦντας ἐξέβαλον, ἐς τεσσαράκοντα μάλιστα ὄντας, καὶ ψῆφον ἐπήνεγκαν φυγῆς
καὶ τὸν δῆμον ὥρκωσαν μήτε καταδέξεσθαί ποτε μήτε
317 ἀνέξεσθαι τῶν λεγόντων καταδέχεσθαι. οἱ δ' ἐξελαθέν-
τες ἐπὶ τὸν Μασσανάσσην κατέφυγον καὶ ἐξώτρυνον
ἐς πόλεμον. ὁ δὲ καὶ αὐτὸς οὕτως ἔχων ἔπεμπε τῶν
παίδων ἐς Καρχηδόνα Γολόσσην τε καὶ Μικύψαν,
ἀξιῶν καταδέχεσθαι τοὺς δι' αὐτὸν ἐξεληλαμένους.
318 τούτοις προσιοῦσι τὰς πύλας ὁ βοήθαρχος ἀπέκλεισε,
δείσας, μὴ τὸν δῆμον οἱ συγγενεῖς τῶν φευγόντων
καταδακρύσειαν. Γολόσσῃ δὲ καὶ ἐπανιόντι Ἀμίλχαρ
ὁ Σαυνίτης ἐπέθετο καί τινας μὲν ἔκτεινεν, αὐτὸν
319 δὲ ἐθορύβησεν. ἐφ' οἷς ὁ Μασσανάσσης προφάσεις
τάσδε ποιούμενος ἐπολιόρκει πόλιν Ὁρόσκοπα, καὶ
τῆσδε παρὰ τὰς συνθήκας ἐφιέμενος. οἱ δὲ Καρχηδόνιοι πεζοῖς μὲν δισμυρίοις καὶ πεντακισχιλίοις, ἱππεῦσι δὲ πολιτικοῖς τετρακοσίοις Ἀσρούβα τοῦ τότε
σφῶν βοηθάρχου στρατηγοῦντος ἐπὶ τὸν Μασσανάσ-
320 σην ἐστράτευον. καὶ πλησιάσασιν αὐτοῖς Ἄγασίς τε
καὶ Σούβας, ταξίαρχοι τοῦ Μασσανάσσου, διενεχθέν-
τες τι τοῖς παισὶ Μασσανάσσου, προσέδραμον ἐς
αὐτομολίαν ἱππέας ἄγοντες ἑξακισχιλίους, οἷς ἐπαρ-
θεὶς ὁ Ἀσρούβας μετεστρατοπέδευεν ἐγγυτέρω τοῦ
βασιλέως, καὶ ἐν ταῖς ἀκροβολίαις ἐπὶ κρεισσόνων
321 ἦν. ὁ δὲ Μασσανάσσης ἐνεδρεύων αὐτὸν ὑπεχώρει
κατ' ὀλίγον οἷα φεύγων, ἕως προσήγαγεν ἐς πεδίον
μέγα καὶ ἔρημον, οὗ πανταχόθεν ἦσαν λόφοι καὶ
ἀπόκρημνα καὶ ἀγορᾶς ἀπορία. τότε δ' ἐπιστρέψας

about forty of Massinissa's supporters, and passed a vote of exile on them, forcing the people to swear an oath that they would never take them back or even allow anyone to propose taking them back. The exiles made their way to Massinissa for protection and urged him to go to war. As he was minded to do so anyway, he sent two of his sons, Gulussa and Micipsa, to demand that the Carthaginians restore those they had banished because of him. When his representatives approached the gates of the city, the Boetharch prevented them from entering, afraid that the relatives of the exiles might move the common people to tearful sympathy. As he was withdrawing, Hamilcar "the Samnite" attacked him and killed some of his men and alarmed Gulussa himself. This gave Massinissa his excuse, and he began to lay siege to the town of Horoscopa, which he wanted even though this was contrary to the terms of the treaty. The Carthaginians, under the command of Hasdrubal, who was Boetharch at the time, now marched against Massinissa, with twenty-five thousand infantry and four hundred cavalry from the city. At the approach of the Carthaginians, two of Massinissa's officers, Asasis and Soubas, who were quarreling with Massinissa's sons about something, deserted to them with six thousand cavalry. Encouraged by this, Hasdrubal moved his camp nearer the king's and got the better of him in skirmishing. But Massinissa set a trap for him by falling back gradually, as if trying to escape, until he led him into a big, deserted plain with steep hills around and no food supply. Here

317

318

319

320

321

ἐστρατοπέδευεν ἐν τοῖς πεδινοῖς· ὁ δὲ Ἀσρούβας ἐς
τοὺς λόφους ὡς ὀχυρωτέρους ἀνέδραμεν.

322   71. Καὶ οἱ μὲν τῆς ἐπιούσης ἔμελλον ἐς χεῖρας
ἥξειν, Σκιπίων δ' ὁ νεώτερος, ὁ τὴν Καρχηδόνα ὕστερον ἑλών, ὑποστρατευόμενος τότε Λευκόλλῳ Κελτίβηρσι πολεμοῦντι, ἐς τὸν Μασσανάσσην ἀφικνεῖτο,
πεμφθεὶς ἐλέφαντας αἰτῆσαι, καὶ αὐτῷ Μασσανάσσης, τοῦ σώματος ὡς ἐς μάχην ἐπιμελούμενος, ἱππέας ἀπαντᾶν[11] ἔπεμψε καὶ τῶν παίδων τισὶν ἐκέλευεν
323   ἐλθόντα ὑποδέξασθαι. αὐτὸς δ' ἅμ' ἔῳ τὸν στρατὸν
ἐξέτασσεν, ὀγδοήκοντα μὲν καὶ ὀκτὼ γεγονὼς ἔτη,
ἱππέων δ' ἔτι καρτερῶς καὶ γυμνὸν τὸν ἵππον ἀνα-
βαίνων, ὡς ἔθος ἐστὶ Νομάσι, καὶ στρατηγῶν καὶ
324   μαχόμενος. εἰσὶ γὰρ Λιβύων οἱ Νομάδες εὐρωστότα-
τοι καὶ μακροβίων ὄντων μακροβιώτατοι. αἴτιον δ'
ἴσως ὅ τε χειμὼν οὐ πολὺ κρύος ἔχων, ὑφ' οὗ φθείρε-
ται πάντα, καὶ τὸ θέρος οὐ κατακαῖον ὥσπερ Αἰθίο-
325   πάς τε καὶ Ἰνδούς. διὸ καὶ τῶν θηρίων τὰ δυνατώτατα
ἥδε ἡ γῆ φέρει, καὶ οἱ ἄνδρες ἐν ὑπαίθρῳ καὶ πόνοις
εἰσὶν αἰεί. ὀλίγος τε ὁ οἶνος αὐτοῖς καὶ ἡ τροφὴ πᾶσιν
326   ἁπλῆ τε καὶ εὐτελής. ὁ μὲν δὴ Μασσανάσσης ἐπιβὰς
ἵππου διεκόσμει τὸν στρατόν, καὶ Ἀσρούβας ἀντε-
ξῆγε τὸν ἴδιον αὐτῷ, πολὺ πλῆθος· ἤδη γὰρ καὶ τῷδε
327   πολλοὶ προσεληλύθεισαν ἐκ τῆς χώρας. ὁ δὲ Σκιπίων
ἐθεᾶτο τὴν μάχην ἀφ' ὑψηλοῦ καθάπερ ἐκ θεάτρου.
ἔλεγέν τε πολλάκις ὕστερον, ἀγῶσι συνενεχθεὶς ποι-

_____
[11] ἀπαντᾶν edd: ἄπαντας codd.

Massinissa turned and made camp in the plain. Hasdrubal withdrew rapidly to the hills which he regarded as more secure.

71. They were about to join battle the following day when Scipio the Younger, the one who later captured Carthage, and who was at the time serving under Lucullus in his campaign against the Celtiberians, arrived at Massinissa's army having been sent there to ask for elephants.[33] Massinissa was getting his body ready for battle, but sent some cavalry to meet him, and ordered some of his sons to receive him when he arrived. He personally drew up his army for battle at dawn, for although he was eighty-eight years old, he was still a strong rider, going bareback in the Numidian way, whether actually fighting or conducting himself as commander in chief. Among Africans the Numidians are the most rugged and long-lived of a long-lived people. The reason may be that their winters are not very frosty—and frost kills everything—while their summers do not burn everything up as in Ethiopia and India. This is also the reason why Africa produces the most powerful wild animals, and why the men are always outside at work. Numidians do not drink much wine, and they all eat simply and frugally. When Massinissa marshaled his army from horseback, Hasdrubal led his force out to face them; it was a large army, bolstered by many now arriving off the land. Scipio watched the battle from a high point, as if he was in a theater. Later on, he often used to say that while

322

323

324

325

326

327

[33] For the campaigns of L. Licinius Lucullus (consul 151) in Iberia, where Scipio Aemilianus, who destroyed Carthage in 146, was one of his military tribunes, see *Ib.* 49.210–55.237.

κίλοις, οὔποτε ὧδε ἡσθῆναι· μόνον γὰρ ἔφη τόνδε τὸν
πόνον ἄφροντις ἰδεῖν, μυριάδας ἀνδρῶν συνιούσας ἐς
μάχην ἕνδεκα. ἔλεγέν τε σεμνύνων δύο πρὸ αὑτοῦ τὴν
τοιάνδε θέαν ἰδεῖν ἐν τῷ Τρωικῷ, τὸν Δία ἀπὸ τῆς
Ἴδης καὶ τὸν Ποσειδῶνα ἐκ Σαμοθράκης.

328   72. Γενομένης δὲ τῆς μάχης ἐς νύκτα ἀπ᾽ ἠοῦς καὶ
πολλῶν πεσόντων ἑκατέρωθεν ἔδοξεν ἐπὶ κρεισσόνων
ὁ Μασσανάσσης γενέσθαι. καὶ αὐτῷ ὑποστρέφοντι
ἀπὸ τοῦ ἔργου ὁ Σκιπίων ὤφθη. ὁ δὲ αὐτὸν οἷα φίλον
329 ἐκ πάππου περιεῖπε θεραπεύων. ὅπερ οἱ Καρχηδόνιοι
μαθόντες ἐδέοντο τοῦ Σκιπίωνος πρὸς Μασσανάσσην
σφᾶς συναλλάξαι. ὁ δὲ συνήγαγε μὲν αὐτούς, γιγνομένων δὲ προκλήσεων οἱ Καρχηδόνιοι τῷ Μασσανάσσῃ τὴν μὲν περὶ τὸ Ἐμπόριον γῆν ἔλεγον μεθή-
σειν καὶ ἀργυρίου τάλαντα δώσειν διακόσια αὐτίκα
καὶ ὀκτακόσια σὺν χρόνῳ, τοὺς δ᾽ αὐτομόλους αἰτοῦν-
τος οὐχ ὑπέστησαν οὐδ᾽ ἀκοῦσαι, ἀλλ᾽ ἄπρακτοι
330 διεκρίθησαν. καὶ Σκιπίων μὲν ἐς Ἰβηρίαν ἔχων τοὺς
ἐλέφαντας ἐπανῄει, Μασσανάσσης δέ, τὸν λόφον τῶν
πολεμίων περιταφρεύσας, ἐφύλασσε μηδεμίαν αὐτοῖς
ἀγορὰν ἐσφέρεσθαι. οὐδ᾽ ἄλλως ἐγγὺς ἦν οὐδέν, ἐπεὶ
καὶ αὐτῷ μόλις ἐκ μακροῦ σφόδρα ἐπιμόχθως ἐφέρετο
331 ὀλίγη. Ἀσρούβας δ᾽ εὐθὺς μὲν ἐδόκει δύνασθαι διεκ-

34 In Homer's *Iliad*, Zeus mostly operates and watches the
Trojan War from Mt. Ida in the Troad. Poseidon is said to be
watching the fighting from the island of Samothrace (Hom. *Il.*
13.11–16).

35 Scipio Aemilianus was adopted by P. Cornelius Scipio, the

he had participated in a variety of different battles, he never enjoyed one as much as this. For this was, he said, the only engagement in which he had nothing to worry about while watching one hundred and ten thousand men join battle. He would also claim rather grandiosely that only two people had seen such a spectacle before him, Zeus from Mt. Ida and Poseidon from Samothrace, both during the Trojan War.[34]

72. The battle lasted from dawn to dusk and although 328 many died on both sides, Massinissa seemed to be the victor. On the way back from the field of battle he spotted Scipio and greeted him assiduously as a family friend from the time of his grandfather.[35] When the Carthaginians 329 heard this, they asked Scipio to reconcile them with Massinissa. He brought the two sides together for negotiations, out of which a proposal arose that the Carthaginians would cede to Massinissa the land around Emporion and would pay him two hundred talents immediately and a further eight hundred talents later; they would not, however, agree even to listen to his demand for the return of deserters. And so the parties separated without making progress. While Scipio returned to Iberia with his ele- 330 phants, Massinissa dug a trench around the hill where the Carthaginians were camped, and made sure that no supplies got through to them. These were certainly not available in the vicinity, since even from far away only a small amount was being brought to him with extreme difficulty. Hasdrubal believed he could immediately break through 331

son of Hannibal's conqueror, the famous Scipio Africanus. Massinissa's exploits as a close friend of Africanus are recounted earlier in this book.

παῖσαι τοὺς πολεμίους ἐρρωμένῳ ἔτι καὶ ἀπαθεῖ τῷ
στρατῷ, ἀγορὰν δ᾽ ἔχων Μασσανάσσου πλείονα
προκαλεῖσθαι τὸν Μασσανάσσην ἐνόμιζε καὶ παρ-
έμενε, πυνθανόμενος ἅμα καὶ Ῥωμαίων ἐπιέναι πρέσβεις ἐς διαλύσεις. οἳ δ᾽ ἦλθον μέν, εἴρητο δ᾽ αὐτοῖς,
εἰ Μασσανάσσης ἐλασσοῖτο, λῦσαι τὴν διαφοράν, εἰ
δ᾽ ἐπὶ κρεισσόνων εἴη, καὶ παροξῦναι.

332   73. Οἱ μὲν δὴ τὸ ἑαυτῶν ἔπραξαν, ὁ δὲ λιμὸς
τὸν Ἀσρούβαν καὶ τοὺς Καρχηδονίους ἐξέτριβε· καὶ
τοῖς σώμασι πάντα ἔχοντες ἀσθενῶς βιάσασθαι μὲν
οὐκέτι τοὺς πολεμίους ἐδύναντο, τὰ δ᾽ ὑποζύγια πρῶτον, εἶτα τοὺς ἵππους ἐπὶ τοῖς ὑποζυγίοις ἔθυον καὶ
333   ἱμάντας ἑψοῦντες ἤσθιον. καὶ νόσων αὐτοὺς ἰδέαι πᾶσαι κατελάμβανον ἔκ τε πονηρίας τροφῶν καὶ ἀκινη-
σίας ἔργων καὶ ὥρας ἔτους· συνεκέκλειστο γὰρ ἐς ἓν
χωρίον, καὶ τόδε ὂν στρατόπεδον, ὄχλος ἀνθρώπων ἐν
334   Λιβύῃ θέρους. τῶν τε ξύλων αὐτοῖς ἐς τὴν ἕψησιν
ἐπιλειπόντων τὰ ὅπλα κατέκαιον. καὶ τῶν ἀποθνησκόντων οὐδεὶς οὔτ᾽ ἐξεφέρετο, Μασσανάσσου τὴν φυλακὴν οὐκ ἀνιέντος, οὔτ᾽ ἐξεκαίετο ξύλων ἀπορίᾳ. ὁ οὖν
φθόρος αὐτοῖς ἦν πολύς τε καὶ περιώδυνος, συνοῦσιν
335   ὀδωδόσι καὶ σηπομένοις σώμασι. τό τε πλεῖστον ἤδη
τοῦ στρατοῦ διέφθαρτο· καὶ τὸ ὑπόλοιπον οὐδεμίαν
σφίσιν ἐλπίδα σωτηρίας ὁρῶντες τοὺς αὐτομόλους
ὑπέστησαν ἐκδοῦναι τῷ Μασσανάσσῃ καὶ πεντακισ-
χίλια ἀργυρίου τάλαντα πεντήκοντα ἔτεσιν ἐσενεγκεῖν τούς τε φυγάδας σφῶν καταδέξασθαι παρὰ τὸ
ὅρκιον καὶ αὐτοὶ διὰ μιᾶς πύλης τοὺς ἐχθροὺς καθ᾽

the enemy lines, as his troops were still healthy and sound, but since he had more supplies than Massinissa, he thought the latter would offer battle, and so he held his position. At the same time he learned that Roman envoys were coming for negotiations. They did arrive, but with instructions to bring the conflict to an end if Massinissa was being beaten, and to spur him on if he was on top.

73. While they went about their business, famine began 332 to wear down Hasdrubal and the Carthaginians. They found themselves physically weakened and no longer able to force their way past the enemy. First, they slaughtered their baggage animals, then their horses, and then they boiled leather straps and ate them. All sorts of disease af- 333 fected them, due to their poor diet, a lack of exercise, and the season of the year. For they were cooped up in a single space, which was furthermore an army camp, a large crowd of men in the heat of an African summer. When 334 they ran out of firewood for cooking, they burned their shields. And with Massinissa keeping up his guard, they could not take the bodies of the dead away, or, in the absence of wood, burn them. So they suffered from a widespread and painful epidemic, amid stinking and rotting bodies. Most of the soldiers had already died; the remain- 335 der, seeing they had no hope of safety, agreed to surrender the deserters to Massinissa, to pay him five thousand talents of silver within fifty years, to take back their own exiles, in breach of their oath, and to exit by a single gate, one by one, making their way through the midst of the

APPIAN

ἕνα διεξελθεῖν διὰ ‹μέσου μετὰ› χιτωνίσκου μόνου.¹²

336 Γολόσσης δ᾽ αὐτοῖς ἀπιοῦσι, χαλεπαίνων τῆς οὐ πρὸ
πολλοῦ διώξεως, εἴτε συνειδότος τοῦ πατρός, εἴτε δι᾽
ἑαυτοῦ, Νομάδας ἱππέας ἐπέπεμψεν, οἳ οὐκ ἀμυνομέ-
νους, οὔτε ὅπλον ἔχοντας ἐς ἄμυναν οὔτε φυγεῖν ὑπ᾽

337 ἀσθενείας δυναμένους, ‹ἔκτειναν.›¹³ ἔκ τε μυριάδων
πέντε στρατοῦ καὶ ὀκτακισχιλίων ἀνδρῶν ὀλίγοι
πάμπαν ἐς Καρχηδόνα περιεσώθησαν καὶ σὺν αὐτοῖς
Ἀσρούβας τε ὁ στρατηγὸς καὶ ἕτεροι τῶν ἐπιφανῶν.

338 74. Τοιόσδε μὲν ὁ Μασσανάσσου καὶ Καρχηδονίων πόλεμος ἦν, ἐκδέχεται δ᾽ αὐτὸν ὁ τρίτος ἐν Λι-

339 βύῃ καὶ τελευταῖος Ῥωμαίων. καὶ Καρχηδόνιοι τῷ
Μασσανάσσου πταίσματι συμπεσόντες, ἀσθενεστά-
της ὑπ᾽ αὐτοῦ τῆς πόλεως γενομένης, αὐτόν τε Μασσανάσσην ἐδεδοίκεσαν, ἐγγὺς ἔτι ὄντα μετὰ πολλοῦ
στρατοῦ, καὶ Ῥωμαίους δυσμεναίνοντας αἰεὶ σφίσιν
καὶ πρόφασιν θησομένους τὰ ἐς τὸν Μασσανάσσην

340 γενόμενα. ὧν οὐδέτερον κακῶς ὑπενόουν· αὐτίκα γὰρ
οἱ Ῥωμαῖοι πυθόμενοι στρατὸν ἐπήγγελλον ἐς ὅλην
τὴν Ἰταλίαν, τὴν μὲν χρείαν οὐ λέγοντες, ὡς δ᾽ ἂν

341 ὀξέως ἔχοιεν ἐς τὰ παραγγελλόμενα χρῆσθαι. καὶ
οἱ Καρχηδόνιοι, νομίζοντες ἐκλύσειν τὴν πρόφασιν,
ἐπεκήρυσσον Ἀσρούβᾳ τε τῷ στρατηγήσαντι τοῦδε
τοῦ πρὸς Μασσανάσσην πολέμου καὶ Καρθάλωνι τῷ
βοηθάρχῳ καὶ εἴ τις ἄλλος ἐφῆπτο τοῦ ἔργου, θάνατον, ἐς ἐκείνους τὴν αἰτίαν τοῦ πολέμου περιφέροντες.

342 ἔς τε Ῥώμην πρέσβεις ἔπεμπον, οἳ κατηγόρουν μὲν

enemy wearing only a single tunic. Gulussa, however, who   336
was angry at the way he had been chased recently,[36] sent
Numidian cavalry against them as they left, either with his
father's knowledge, or on his own initiative, and killed
them in spite of meeting no resistance, since they had no
weapons to defend themselves and were too weak to flee.
From an army of fifty-eight thousand men only a very few   337
returned safely to Carthage, among them their general
Hasdrubal and other Carthaginian notables.

74. Such was the war between Massinissa and Car-   338
thage. It is followed by Rome's third and last war in Africa.
After the defeat inflicted by Massinissa, and the extreme   339
weakening of the city that resulted from it, the Carthaginians were apprehensive about Massinissa himself, who
remained nearby with a large army. They were also afraid
of the Romans, who persistently displayed ill will to them
and were always minded to make Massinissa's affairs the
excuse for it. They were right on both counts. For as soon   340
as the Romans learned of developments, they began to
recruit an army throughout Italy, not specifying its purpose, but to have for immediate use in executing orders.
Intending to make the Roman excuse redundant, the Car-   341
thaginians sentenced to death both Hasdrubal, the commander of the war against Massinissa, and the Boetharch,
Carthalo, and anyone else involved in the affair, placing
the blame for the war on them. They also sent ambassa-   342

---

[36] For the attack on him by Hamilcar "the Samnite," see
above, 70.317–18.

---

[12] μέσου μετὰ add. Goukowsky: σὺν χιτωνίσκῳ μόνῳ
Schweig: διὰ χιτωνίσκου μόνου V   [13] ἔκτειναν add. Schweig.

APPIAN

αὐτοῦ Μασσανάσσου, κατηγόρουν δὲ καὶ τῶνδε τῶν
ἀνδρῶν ὡς ἀμυναμένων αὐτὸν ὀξέως τε καὶ προπετῶς
καὶ τὴν πόλιν ἐς πρόφασιν ἔχθρας ἐμβαλόντων.
343 ὡς δέ τις τῶν βουλευτῶν τοὺς πρέσβεις ἤρετο, ὅπως
οὐκ ἐν ἀρχῇ τοῦ πολέμου τοὺς αἰτίους, ἀλλὰ μετὰ
τὴν ἧσσαν ἐξεκήρυξαν "Καὶ πρὸς ἡμᾶς οὐ πρότερον,
ἀλλὰ νῦν πρεσβεύεσθε," οἱ μὲν ἀποκρίσεως ἠπόρουν,
ἡ δὲ βουλὴ πάλαι διεγνωκυῖα πολεμῆσαι καὶ προφάσεις ἐρεσχηλοῦσα ὧδε ἀπεκρίνατο, Καρχηδονίους
344 οὔπω Ῥωμαίοις ἱκανῶς ἀπολογήσασθαι. πάλιν οὖν
ἀγωνιῶντες ἠρώτων, εἰ δοκοῦσιν ἁμαρτεῖν, τί παθόντες ἀπολύσονται τὸ ἔγκλημα. οἱ δὲ οὕτως ἔφασαν τῷ
345 ῥήματι· "Εἰ τὸ ἱκανὸν ποιήσετε Ῥωμαίοις." ζητούντων
δ' ἐκείνων, ὅ τι εἴη τὸ ἱκανόν, οἱ μὲν ᾤοντο Ῥωμαίους
ἐθέλειν τοῖς χρήμασιν προσεπιθεῖναι τοῖς ἐπὶ Σκιπίωνος ὡρισμένοις, οἱ δὲ Μασσανάσσῃ τῆς ἀμφιλόγου
346 γῆς μεταστῆναι. ἀποροῦντες οὖν πάλιν ἐς Ῥώμην
ἔπεμπον καὶ παρεκάλουν γνῶναι σαφῶς, ὅ τι ἐστὶν
αὐτοῖς τὸ ἱκανόν. οἱ δὲ αὖθις ἔφασαν εἰδέναι Καρχηδονίους καλῶς καὶ εἰπόντες ἀπέπεμψαν.

347   75. Οἱ μὲν δὴ φόβου καὶ ἀπορίας ἦσαν ἐν τούτῳ,
Ἰτύκη δέ, ἡ Λιβύης μεγίστη μετὰ Καρχηδόνα πόλις,
λιμένας τε ἔχουσα εὐόρμους καὶ στρατοπέδων κατα-
γωγὰς δαψιλεῖς, ἑξήκοντα σταδίους ἀπὸ Καρχηδόνος
ἀφεστῶσα καὶ καλῶς ἐς πόλεμον αὐτοῖς ἐπικειμένη,
τὰ Καρχηδονίων ἄρα καὶ αὐτὴ τότε ἀπογνοῦσα καὶ
τὸ πάλαι μῖσος ἐς αὐτοὺς ἐκφέρουσα ἐν καιρῷ, πρέσβεις ἐς Ῥώμην ἔπεμψεν, οἳ τὴν Ἰτύκην Ῥωμαίοις

128

dors to Rome, to complain about Massinissa himself, and about those men who, by precipitately and rashly driving him away, laid the city open to an accusation of hostility. When one of the senators asked the ambassadors why they 343 had condemned the guilty parties after they had been defeated and not at the beginning of the war, and why "you are sending an embassy to us now rather than earlier," they were unable to furnish an answer. The senate, who had long ago decided on war and were looking for any old excuse, answered that the Carthaginians had not yet defended themselves satisfactorily to the Romans. In great 344 distress, the Carthaginians asked again, if they were thought to have committed an offense, what they had to do to get the charge dismissed. "By giving satisfaction to Rome," was the phrase the senate gave in reply. When 345 they discussed what "satisfaction" meant, some thought that Rome wanted an additional sum of money added to the terms of the agreement made in Scipio's time, others that the disputed territory should be ceded to Massinissa. So, still at a loss, they sent to Rome again, asking to be told 346 clearly what they would regard as satisfaction. The Romans' response was to repeat that the Carthaginians knew perfectly well, and with these words dismissed them.

75. While fear and uncertainty thus affected the Car- 347 thaginians, the situation in Utica was as follows. It is the largest city in Africa after Carthage and has harbors with good moorings and plenty of places to embark armies. Sixty stades away from Carthage, it is well situated for war against the Carthaginians. Now recognizing, no doubt, the desperate situation of Carthage, and taking the opportunity to display their ancient animosity against it, the people of Utica sent envoys to turn their own city over to

348 ἐπέτρεπον. ἡ δὲ βουλή, καὶ τέως ἐς τὸν πόλεμον ὁρ-
μῶσά τε καὶ παρασκευαζομένη, πόλεως ὀχυρᾶς οὕτως
καὶ ἐπικαίρου προσγενομένης ἐξέφηνέ τε τὴν γνώμην
καὶ ἐς τὸ Καπιτώλιον, οὗπερ εἰώθασιν περὶ πολέμου
σκοπεῖν, συνελθοῦσα ἐψηφίσατο Καρχηδονίοις πολε-

349 μεῖν. στρατηγούς τε τοὺς ὑπάτους αὐτίκα ἐξέπεμπον,
ἐπὶ μὲν τοῦ πεζοῦ Μᾶρκον Μανίλιον, ἐπὶ δὲ τοῦ στόλου Λεύκιον Μάρκιον Κηνσωρῖνον, οἷς ἐν ἀπορρήτῳ
λέλεκτο μὴ ἀνασχεῖν τοῦ πολέμου, πρὶν Καρχηδόνα

350 κατασκάψαι. οἱ μὲν δὴ θύσαντες ἐς Σικελίαν ἔπλεον
ὡς ἐκεῖθεν εἰς τὴν Ἰτύκην διαβαλοῦντες, ναυσὶ δ᾽
ἐφέροντο πεντήκοντα μὲν πεντήρεσιν, ἑκατὸν δ᾽ ἡμι-
ολίαις, ἀφράκτοις δὲ καὶ κερκούροις καὶ στρογγύλοις

351 πολλοῖς. καὶ στρατὸν ἦγον ὀκτακισμυρίους πεζοὺς
καὶ ἱππέας ἐς τετρακισχιλίους, ἀρίστους ἅπαντας· ὡς
γὰρ ἐς ἐπιφανῆ στρατείαν καὶ πρόῦπτον ἐλπίδα πᾶς
τις ἀστῶν καὶ συμμάχων ὥρμα, καὶ πολλοὶ καὶ ἐθε-
λονταὶ παρήγγελλον ἐς τὸν κατάλογον.

352 76. Καρχηδονίοις δὲ προσέπεσεν ἥ τε κρίσις τοῦ
πολέμου καὶ τὸ ἔργον ὁμοῦ δι᾽ ἑνὸς ἀγγέλου· ὁ γὰρ
αὐτὸς ἔφερέν τε τὸ ψήφισμα τοῦ πολέμου καὶ τὰς

353 ναῦς ἐδήλου πλεῖν ἐπὶ σφᾶς. ἐκπλαγέντες οὖν ἀπε-
γίνωσκον αὐτῶν ἀπορίᾳ τε νεῶν καὶ ἀπωλείᾳ προσ-
φάτῳ τοσῆσδε νεότητος, οὐ συμμάχους ἔχοντες, οὐ
μισθοφόρους ἑτοίμους, οὐ σῖτον ἐς πολιορκίαν συν-
ενηνεγμένον, οὐκ ἄλλο οὐδέν, ὡς ἐν ἀκηρύκτῳ καὶ
ταχεῖ πολέμῳ, οὐδ᾽ αὐτοὶ διαρκεῖν δυνάμενοι Ῥωμαί-

354 οις τε καὶ Μασσανάσσῃ. πρέσβεις οὖν ἑτέρους ἐς

Rome. With the accession of such a strong and well positioned city, the senate, long since eager and preparing for war, now made its intention public by gathering in the Capitol, where they traditionally debate issues of war, and voted to declare war on Carthage. They immediately sent the consuls off as generals, Manius Manilius in command of the infantry, Lucius Marcius Censorinus of the fleet, and gave them secret orders not to stop fighting until Carthage had been razed to the ground.[37] After offering sacrifice, they sailed for Sicily, with the intention of crossing from there to Utica. They traveled in fifty quinqueremes, one hundred hemiolii and many undecked boats, light ships, and merchantmen. They led an army of eighty thousand infantry and about four thousand cavalry, all the very best troops. For every citizen and ally was eager to join such a distinguished expedition with such foreseeable results, and many volunteers enlisted too.

76. A single messenger brought news to Carthage both of the Roman decision to fight and its implementation. For the same man carried with him both the vote to declare war and news that the fleet was sailing against them. The Carthaginians were distraught and despaired of their situation: they lacked ships, they had recently suffered the loss of many of their young men, they had no allies or mercenaries to hand, they had collected no supplies for a siege, nor anything else for an unannounced and sudden war; they could not on their own hold out against a combination of Rome and Massinissa. So they sent another mission to

348

349

350

351

352

353

354

---

[37] Manius Manilius and L. Marcius Censorinus were the consuls of 149.

Ῥώμην ἔπεμπον αὐτοκράτορας, ὅπῃ δύναιντο, τὰ
παρόντα διαθέσθαι. οἷς ἡ σύγκλητος εἶπεν, ἐὰν τοῖς
ὑπάτοις ἔτι οὖσιν ἐν Σικελίᾳ, τριάκοντα ἡμερῶν
τῶνδε, οἱ Καρχηδόνιοι τριακοσίους τοὺς ἐνδοξοτάτους
σφῶν παῖδας ἐς ὁμηρείαν παράσχωσι καὶ τἆλλα
κατακούσωσιν αὐτῶν, ἕξειν Καρχηδόνα ἐλευθέραν τε
καὶ αὐτόνομον καὶ γῆν, ὅσην ἔχουσιν ἐν Λιβύῃ.
355 ταῦτα μὲν ἐς τὸ φανερὸν ἐψηφίσαντο καὶ τοῖς πρέσβεσιν ἔδωκαν ἐς Καρχηδόνα φέρειν τὸ δόγμα, ἐν
ἀπορρήτῳ δὲ τοῖς ὑπάτοις ἐπέστειλαν ἔχεσθαι τῶν
ἰδίᾳ σφίσιν ἐντεταλμένων.

356   77. Οἱ δὲ Καρχηδόνιοι τὴν μὲν γνώμην ὑπώπτευον,
οὐκ ἐπὶ συνθήκῃ βεβαίᾳ τὰ ὅμηρα παρέχοντες· οἷα
δ᾽ ἐν κινδύνῳ τοσῷδε τὰς ἐλπίδας, ἐν ᾧ μηδὲν ἐκ-
λείψουσι, τιθέμενοι, σπουδῇ προλαβόντες τὴν προ-
θεσμίαν τοὺς παῖδας ἦγον ἐς Σικελίαν, γονέων τε
αὐτοῖς ἐπικλαιόντων καὶ οἰκείων καὶ μάλιστα τῶν
μητέρων, αἳ σὺν ὀλολυγῇ μανιώδει τῶν τέκνων ἐξ-
ήπτοντο καὶ νεῶν τῶν φερουσῶν αὐτὰ καὶ στρατηγῶν
τῶν ἀγόντων ἀγκυρῶν τε ἐπελαμβάνοντο καὶ καλῴδια
διέσπων καὶ ναύταις συνεπλέκοντο καὶ τὸν πλοῦν
357 ἐκώλυον. εἰσὶ δ᾽, αἳ καὶ μέχρι πολλοῦ τῆς θαλάσσης
παρένεον, δεδακρυμέναι τε καὶ ἐς τὰ τέκνα ἀφορῶσαι.
358 αἱ δ᾽ ἐπὶ τῆς γῆς τὰς κόμας ἐτίλλοντο καὶ τὰ στέρνα
ἔκοπτον ὡς ἐπὶ πένθει· ἐδόκουν γὰρ ὄνομα μὲν ἐς εὐ-
πρέπειαν εἶναι τὴν ὁμηρείαν, ἔργῳ δὲ τῆς πόλεως ἔκδοσιν, ἐπ᾽ οὐδεμιᾷ συνθήκῃ τῶνδε τῶν παίδων διδο-
μένων. καὶ πολλαὶ καὶ τοῦτο ἐν ταῖς οἰμωγαῖς

Rome with the authority to settle the crisis in any way they could. The senate informed them that if, within thirty days, the Carthaginians provided three hundred children from their leading families as hostages to the consuls while they were still in Sicily, and agreed to the other demands made of them, they could retain Carthage as free and autonomous, as well as the territory they held in Africa. This was the decision of a public vote and they gave the 355 envoys the decree to take to Carthage. In secret, however, they instructed the consuls to follow the orders given to them in private.

77. The Carthaginians were suspicious of the Roman 356 decision, since they were providing the hostages without a valid agreement in place. But finding themselves in such great danger and placing their hopes in complete subservience, they were quick to bring the children to Sicily ahead of the deadline. Parents and relatives wept over them, especially their mothers, who with frenzied cries clung to their children, to the ships transporting them, to the commanders taking them away, and in their efforts to stop the ships sailing they even laid hold of the anchors, tried to pull at the ropes, and embraced the sailors. There were 357 even some who swam beside the ship far out to sea, weeping and trying to keep their children in view. Others on 358 land tore their hair and beat their breasts, as if in mourning for the dead. For they thought that because they had surrendered these children without an agreement, the word for handing over hostages was, in reality, just a euphemism for giving up the city. Many also predicted in

κατεμαντεύοντο τῇ πόλει, μηδὲν αὐτὴν ὀνήσειν τοὺς
359 παῖδας ἐκδιδομένους. ἐν μὲν δὴ τῇ Καρχηδόνι τῶν
ὁμήρων ἡ ἀναγωγὴ τοιάδε τις ἦν, ἐν δὲ τῇ Σικελίᾳ
παραλαβόντες αὐτὰ οἱ ὕπατοι διέπεμπον ἐς Ῥώμην
καὶ τοῖς Καρχηδονίοις ἔφασαν ἐς τὸ τέλος τοῦ πολέμου τὰ λοιπὰ ἐρεῖν ἐν Ἰτύκῃ.

360   78. Διαπλεύσαντές τε ἐς αὐτὴν ἐστρατοπέδευον, ὁ
μὲν πεζός, ἔνθα πάλαι τὸ Σκιπίωνος ἦν στρατόπεδον,
361 αἱ δὲ νῆες ἐν τοῖς λιμέσι τοῖς Ἰτυκαίων. ἀφικομένων
δὲ κἀκεῖ πρέσβεων ἐκ Καρχηδόνος οἱ μὲν ὕπατοι
προυκάθηντο ἐπὶ βήματος ὑψηλοῦ, ἡγεμόνων τε
σφίσι καὶ χιλιάρχων παρεστώτων, ἡ στρατιὰ δ᾽ ἑκατέρωθεν ἐπὶ μῆκος πολὺ ὅπλοις τε ἐπισήμοις ἐσκεύ-
αστο, καὶ τὰ σημεῖα ἔφερον ὀρθά, ἵνα οἱ πρέσβεις τὸ
362 πλῆθος ἐκ τούτων συμβάλοιεν. ἐπεὶ δ᾽ οἱ μὲν ὕπατοι
τῷ σαλπικτῇ προσέταξαν ὑποσημῆναι σιωπήν, ὁ δὲ
κῆρυξ ἀνεῖπεν τοὺς Καρχηδονίων πρέσβεις προσιέναι, οἳ μὲν εἰσήγοντο διὰ στρατοπέδου μακροῦ καὶ
τοῦ βήματος οὐ προσεπέλαζον, ἀλλὰ περισχοίνισμα
ἦν ἐν μέσῳ, οἱ δ᾽ ὕπατοι λέγειν αὐτοὺς ἐκέλευον, ὅ τι
363 χρήζοιεν. καὶ οἱ πρέσβεις ἔλεγον ἐλεεινὰ πολλὰ καὶ
ποικίλα συνθηκῶν τε πέρι τῶν σφίσι πρὸς Ῥωμαίους
γενομένων καὶ Καρχηδόνος αὐτῆς χρόνου καὶ πλήθους καὶ δυνάμεως καὶ ἀρχῆς τῆς ἐς πολὺ μεγίστης
364 ἐν γῇ καὶ θαλάσσῃ γενομένης. οὐκ ἐπὶ σεμνολογίᾳ δ᾽
ἔφασαν λέγειν· οὐ γὰρ εἶναι καιρὸν ἐν συμφοραῖς
σεμνολογίας, "Ἀλλ᾽ ἐς σωφρόνισμα ὑμῖν, ὦ Ῥωμαῖοι,
καὶ μετριοπάθειαν ἡ τῆς ἡμετέρας μεταβολῆς ὀξύτης

their lamentations that delivering up their children would be of no benefit to the city. This was the sort of thing that happened in Carthage when the hostages were shipped off. In Sicily, the consuls received them and sent them to Rome, and informed the Carthaginians that in relation to the end of the war, they would tell them the rest in Utica.   359

78. Here, after the crossing, the Romans set up their base, the infantry where Scipio had previously camped, the ships in the harbors of Utica. When Carthaginian envoys also arrived there, the consuls presided from a high podium, officers and military tribunes standing beside them, with the army deployed for a considerable distance on either side in shining armor and with standards held straight. The purpose of all this was to impress the ambassadors with the size of the Roman force. When the consuls ordered the trumpets to sound for silence, the herald told the Carthaginian ambassadors to come forward, and they were brought in through the large camp. They did not approach closely to the podium, which was in a roped-off section in the middle. The consuls ordered them to say what it was they wanted. The envoys spoke movingly on various matters to do with the agreements between Rome and Carthage, the antiquity of Carthage, its size and power, its empire, for long the greatest by land and sea. They said they were not boasting with these words—adversity was not the right time for boasting—"But to let the rapidity of our fall lead you, men of Rome, to self-control   360 361 362 363 364

ἔστω. κράτιστοι δέ, ὅσοι τοὺς πταίσαντας ἐλεοῦντες
τὸ σφέτερον εὔελπι ποιοῦνται τῷ μηδὲν ἐς ἄλλας τύ-
χας ἁμαρτεῖν.

365   79. "Καὶ τάδε μὲν ὑμῶν ἄξια καὶ τῆς ὑμετέρας
εὐσεβείας, ἣν προσποιεῖσθε μάλιστα ἀνθρώπων· εἰ δὲ
καὶ ἀνημέρων τετυχήκειμεν ἐχθρῶν, κόρος ἐστὶν ἀτυ-
χημάτων, ὅσα πεπόνθαμεν, οἳ τὴν ἡγεμονίαν τῆς τε
γῆς καὶ θαλάσσης ἀφῃρήμεθα καὶ τὰς ναῦς ὑμῖν
παρεδώκαμεν καὶ ἄλλας οὐκ ἐπικτώμεθα καὶ θήρας
καὶ κτήσεως ἐλεφάντων ἀπέστημεν καὶ ὅμηρα τὰ
κράτιστα καὶ πάλαι καὶ νῦν παρεδώκαμεν καὶ φόρους
366   τελοῦμεν εὐτάκτως, οἱ παρ' ἑτέρων αἰεὶ λαβόντες. καὶ
τάδε ἤρκεσε τοῖς πατράσιν ὑμῶν, οἷς ἐπολεμήσαμεν·
καὶ συνθήκας ἐπ' αὐτοῖς ἐγράψαντο ἡμῖν ὡς φίλοις τε
καὶ συμμάχοις, καὶ ὅρκος ἔστιν ἐν ταῖς συνθήκαις
367   ἀμφοῖν ὅμοιος. κἀκεῖνοι μὲν ἡμῖν, οἷς ἐπολεμήσαμεν,
πιστοὶ μετὰ ταῦτα ἐγένοντο· ὑμεῖς δ', οἷς οὐδὲ εἰς
χεῖρας ἤλθομεν, τί τῶνδε τῶν συνθηκῶν αἰτιώμενοι
παραβεβάσθαι τὸν πόλεμον τόνδε ὀξέως οὕτως ἐψη-
φίσασθέ τε καὶ ἀκηρύκτως ἐπηγάγετε ἡμῖν; πότερον
οὐ δίδομεν τοὺς φόρους; ἢ ναῦς ἔχομεν ἢ τοὺς ἐπιφθόνους ἐλέφαντας; ἢ οὐ πιστοὶ τὰ πρὸς ὑμᾶς ἐξ
ἐκείνου γεγόναμεν; ἢ οὐκ ἐλεεινοὶ τῶν πέντε μυριάδων
368   τῶν χθὲς ἀπολομένων ὑπὸ λιμοῦ; ἀλλὰ Μασσανάσσῃ
πεπολεμήκαμεν. πολλά γε πλεονεκτοῦντι· καὶ πάντα
δι' ὑμᾶς ἐφέρομεν. ἀπαύστως δ' ἔχων καὶ ἀθεμίστως
ἐς ἡμᾶς καὶ τὸ ἔδαφος, ἐν ᾧ καὶ ἐτράφη καὶ ἐπαι-
δεύθη, γῆν ἄλλην ἡμῶν ἀπέσπα περὶ τὸ Ἐμπόριον·

and moderation. The mightiest are those who pity the fallen and rest their own best hopes on not taking wrongful advantage of the fate of others.

79. "Such behavior is worthy of you and your piety, in 365 which you claim preeminence among men. Even if we had encountered savage enemies, we already have a surfeit of misfortunes in what we have suffered. We have been deprived of our leadership both by land and sea; we have handed over our ships to you and acquired no new ones; we have given up hunting for elephants and possessing them; we have surrendered to you our most noble people as hostages both now and previously; we have been paying you tribute regularly, we who always used to receive it from others. Your fathers, with whom we had been at war, 366 were satisfied with these things. They made a written treaty with us on these conditions, treating us as friends and allies, and the oath in the treaty was the same for both sides. And although we had been at war with them, these 367 men remained faithful thereafter. But you, with whom we have not even come to blows, what part of this treaty do you accuse us of breaking, that you have voted for war so swiftly and marched against us without even announcing it? Have we not been paying the tribute? Or, do we have any ships, or the hated elephants? Have we not been faithful to you since we made the treaty? Do you not pity the fifty thousand of us who died recently from hunger? But 368 we have made war on Massinissa. True, but he has greedily claimed much that does not belong to him, and we have put up with all this because of you. He has persisted in treating us unlawfully and the very ground on which he was raised and educated. He seized more of our land near

καὶ λαβὼν καὶ τήνδε ἐπέβαινεν ἑτέρας, μέχρι τὰς

369 συνθήκας ἡμῖν τὰς πρὸς ὑμᾶς συνέχεεν. εἰ τοῦτό ἐστιν ἡ τοῦδε τοῦ πολέμου πρόφασις, ἡμεῖς δὲ καὶ τοὺς ἀμυναμένους αὐτὸν ἐξεκηρύξαμεν καὶ πρὸς ὑμᾶς πρέσβεις ἐπέμψαμεν, οἳ περὶ τούτων ἀπελογοῦντο, καὶ ἑτέρους αὐτοκράτορας, ὅπῃ θέλετε, συνθέσθαι. τί οὖν ἔδει νεῶν καὶ στόλου καὶ στρατοῦ πρὸς ἄνδρας οὐχ ὁμολογοῦντας μὲν μὴ ἁμαρτεῖν, ἑαυτοὺς δὲ ὑμῖν

370 ἐπιτρέποντας; ὅτι δὲ οὐκ ἀπατῶντες ὑμᾶς οὐδὲ μικρολογούμενοι παθεῖν, ὅ τι ἂν ζημιῶτε, ταῦτα προυτείνομεν, ἐπιδέδεικται σαφῶς, ὅτε τοὺς ἀρίστους παῖδας ἐς ὁμηρείαν αἰτοῦσιν ὑμῖν εὐθύς, ὡς τὸ δόγμα ἐκέλευε, τὰς τριάκοντα προλαβόντες ἡμέρας ἀπεστείλαμεν. τοῦ δ' αὐτοῦ δόγματός ἐστιν, ἢν παράσχωμεν ὑμῖν τὰ ὅμηρα, τὴν Καρχηδόνα ἐλευθέραν ἐᾶν καὶ αὐτόνομον, κεκτημένη, ἃ ἔχομεν."

371 80. Οἱ μὲν δὴ πρέσβεις τοσαῦτα εἶπον, Κηνσωρῖνος δ' ὑπαναστὰς ἀντέλεξεν ὧδε· "Τὰς μὲν αἰτίας τοῦ πολέμου τί δεῖ λέγειν ὑμῖν, ὦ Καρχηδόνιοι, πρεσβεύσασιν ἐς Ῥώμην καὶ παρὰ τῆς συγκλήτου μαθοῦσιν; ὃ

372 δὲ ἐψεύσασθε περὶ ἡμῶν, τοῦθ' ὑμᾶς ἐλέγξω. καὶ γὰρ τὸ δόγμα δηλοῖ, καὶ ἡμεῖς ὑμῖν ἐν Σικελίᾳ προείπομεν τὰ ὅμηρα παραλαμβάνοντες, τὰ λοιπὰ τῶν δοξάντων

373 ἐπικελεύσειν ἐν Ἰτύκῃ. τῶν μὲν οὖν ὁμήρων τῆς τε ταχυτῆτος καὶ τῆς ἐπιλέξεως ἐπαινοῦμεν ὑμᾶς· τί δὲ ὅπλων δεῖ τοῖς εἰρηνεύουσι καθαρῶς; φέρετε· πάντα, ὅσα δημοσίᾳ τε καὶ ἰδίᾳ ἕκαστος ὑμῶν ἔχει, βέλη τε

374 καὶ καταπέλτας, ἡμῖν παράδοτε." ὁ μὲν οὕτως εἶπεν,

Emporium, and having got hold of that, attacked yet other territory, until he has dissolved our treaty with you. If this 369 is the excuse you are using to make war, we ourselves have even condemned the men who defended us against Massinissa, and have sent ambassadors to you to explain the situation; and we have sent other envoys with complete authority to make peace on whatever terms you want. So, why are ships, an expedition, and an army needed against men who, while they do not admit to wrongdoing, have turned themselves over to you? That we were not deceiv- 370 ing you in making these proposals, or playing down our readiness to submit to whatever punishment you imposed, was shown clearly when you demanded the children of our most noble families as hostages, and we sent them immediately, as the decree ordered, before the thirty day deadline. The same decree ordained that if we provided the hostages for you, Carthage would be left free and autonomous, retaining the territory we hold."

80. This was the speech of the Carthaginian ambassa- 371 dors. Censorinus stood and responded as follows: "Why do you need me to tell you the causes of the war, men of Carthage, when your ambassadors at Rome have been told them by the senate? But I want to refute the lie you have told about us. For the decree makes clear, and we our- 372 selves explained this to you before in Sicily when we received the hostages, that we would give you additional orders at Utica about the rest of what we decided. We 373 commend you for the speed with which you chose and sent the hostages. But why do you need weapons if you are serious about peace? Come on, now, hand over to us all your weapons held by anyone, in public or private ownership, missiles and catapults." That is what Censorinus said. 374

οἱ δὲ πρέσβεις ἔφασαν ἐθέλειν μὲν καὶ τοῖσδε ὑπακοῦσαι, ἀπορεῖν δέ, ὅπως Ἀσρούβαν, ᾧ θάνατον
ἐπεκήρυξαν, δύο μυριάδας ἀνδρῶν ἤδη συναγαγόντα
καὶ αὐτῇ Καρχηδόνι παραστρατοπεδεύοντα ἀμυνοῦν-
375 ται. εἰπόντων δὲ τῶν ὑπάτων, ὅτι Ῥωμαῖοι τούτων
ἐπιμελήσονται, οἱ μὲν καὶ ταῦτα δώσειν ὑπέσχοντο,
καὶ συμπεμφθέντες αὐτοῖς Κορνήλιός τε Σκιπίων ὁ
Νασικᾶς καὶ Γναῖος Κορνήλιος ὁ Ἱσπανὸς ἐπίκλησιν
παρελάμβανον εἴκοσι μυριάδας πανοπλιῶν καὶ βελῶν
καὶ ἀκοντίων πλῆθος ἄπειρον καὶ καταπέλτας ὀξυβε-
376 λεῖς τε καὶ λιθοβόλους εἰς δισχιλίους. καὶ φερομένων
αὐτῶν ἡ μὲν ὄψις ἦν λαμπρὰ καὶ παράλογος, ἁμαξῶν
τοσῶνδε ὑπ᾽ αὐτῶν τῶν πολεμίων ἀγομένων, οἱ δὲ
πρέσβεις εἵποντο αὐτοῖς καὶ ὅσοι τῆς γερουσίας ἢ
τῆς ἄλλης πόλεως ἄριστοι ἢ ἱερεῖς ἢ ἄλλως ἐπιφανεῖς
377 ἔμελλον τοὺς ὑπάτους ἐς ἐντροπὴν ἢ ἔλεον ἄξειν. ἐσαχθέντες δὲ αὐτῷ κόσμῳ τοῖς ὑπάτοις παρέστησαν.
καὶ ὁ Κηνσωρῖνος (ἦν γὰρ εἰπεῖν ἱκανώτερος τοῦ
συνάρχου) ἀναστὰς καὶ τότε καὶ σκυθρωπάσας ἐπὶ
πολὺ ἔλεξεν ὧδε·
378   81. "Τῆς μὲν εὐπειθείας ὑμᾶς, ὦ Καρχηδόνιοι, καὶ
προθυμίας τῆς μέχρι νῦν ἔς τε τὰ ὅμηρα καὶ τὰ ὅπλα
ἐπαινοῦμεν, χρὴ δ᾽ ἐν τοῖς ἀναγκαίοις βραχυλογεῖν.
ὑπόστητε γενναίως τὸ λοιπὸν τῆς συγκλήτου κέλευσμα. ἔκστητε τῆς Καρχηδόνος ἡμῖν καὶ ἀνοικίσασθε,
ὅπῃ θέλετε τῆς ὑμετέρας, ὀγδοήκοντα σταδίους ἀπὸ

---

38 P. Cornelius Scipio Nasica Serapio (consul 138) and Cn.

The Carthaginian ambassadors replied that they were willing to obey even this command, but that they did not know how they were going to defend themselves against Hasdrubal, whom they had sentenced to death, and who was camped outside Carthage itself with twenty thousand men he had already recruited. When the consuls said that they would deal with this matter, the envoys promised to give up the weapons too. Cornelius Scipio Nasica and Gnaeus Cornelius, surnamed Hispanus, were dispatched with the envoys, and collected two hundred thousand full sets of armor, countless numbers of missiles and javelins, and about two thousand catapults for firing bolts and stones.[38] It was a wonderful and strange sight to see their conveyance, so many wagons driven by the enemy themselves, followed by the ambassadors, and those who were intending to elicit either respect or pity from the consuls—leading members of the Carthaginian assembly and of the rest of the city, priests and other prominent figures. The ambassadors were brought in wearing full dress and stood before the consuls. Censorinus, because he was a better speaker than his fellow consul, rose on this occasion too and after glowering at them for a long time, spoke as follows:

81. "Men of Carthage, we applaud the zealous obedience you have shown up to now in the matter of the hostages and weapons, but in the face of necessity brevity is required. You must bear nobly the rest of the senate's command. Leave Carthage to us and move to wherever you like in your own territory, at a distance of eighty stades

375

376

377

378

Cornelius Scipio Hispanus (praetor 139) were probably military tribunes.

379 θαλάσσης· τήνδε γὰρ ἡμῖν ἔγνωσται κατασκάψαι." οἱ
δ᾽ ἔτι λέγοντος αὐτοῦ τὰς χεῖρας ἐς τὸν οὐρανὸν ἀν-
έσχον μετὰ βοῆς καὶ τοὺς θεοὺς ὡς ἠπατημένοι κατ-
εκάλουν πολλά τε καὶ δυσχερῆ κατὰ Ῥωμαίων ἐβλα-
σφήμουν, ἢ θανατῶντες ἢ ἔκφρονες ὄντες ἢ τοὺς
380 Ῥωμαίους ἐς μύσος πρέσβεων διερεθίζοντες. ἔς τε
τὴν γῆν σφᾶς ἐρρίπτουν καὶ χερσὶ καὶ κεφαλαῖς
αὐτὴν ἔτυπτον· οἱ δὲ καὶ τὰς ἐσθῆτας ἐπερρήγνυντο
καὶ τοῖς σώμασι τοῖς ἑαυτῶν ἐνύβριζον ὡς ὑπὸ ἀνοίας
ἐνηδρευμένοι. ἐπεὶ δέ ποτε αὐτοῖς ὁ οἶστρος ἔληξε,
σιωπὴ πολλὴ καὶ κατήφεια ἦν οἷα νεκρῶν κειμένων.
381 Ῥωμαῖοι δ᾽ ἐξεπλήσσοντο, καὶ οἱ ὕπατοι φέρειν αὐτοὺς ἐγνώκεσαν ὡς ἐπὶ ἀλλοκότῳ κελεύσματι, μέχρι
παύσαιντο ἀγανακτοῦντες, καλῶς εἰδότες, ὅτι τὰ μέγιστα δεινὰ αὐτίκα μὲν ἐς θρασύτητα ἐκπλήσσει, σὺν
382 χρόνῳ δὲ καταδουλοῖ τὴν τόλμαν ἡ ἀνάγκη. ὃ καὶ
τότε ἔπαθον οἱ Καρχηδόνιοι· παρὰ γὰρ τὴν σιωπὴν
ἁπτομένου σφῶν τοῦ κακοῦ μᾶλλον, ἀγανακτεῖν μὲν
ἔτι ἐπαύσαντο, ἀνέκλαιον δὲ καὶ κατεθρήνουν ἑαυτούς
τε καὶ παῖδας καὶ γυναῖκας ἐξ ὀνομάτων καὶ τὴν πατρίδα αὐτήν, ὡς ἐς ἄνθρωπον ἀκούουσαν λέγοντες
383 οἰκτρὰ καὶ πολλά. οἱ δὲ ἱερεῖς καὶ τὰ τῶν ἱερῶν
ὀνόματα καὶ τοὺς ἐν αὐτοῖς θεοὺς ἀνεκάλουν, ὡς παροῦσι κἀκείνοις προφέροντες τὴν ἀπώλειαν. ἦν τε παμ-
μιγὴς καὶ ἐλεεινὸς οἶκτος οἰμωζόντων ὁμοῦ τά τε
κοινὰ καὶ τὰ ἴδια, μέχρι καὶ Ῥωμαίους αὐτοῖς ἐπιδα-
κρῦσαι.

384 82. Τοὺς δὲ ὑπάτους ἐσῄει μὲν οἶκτος ἀνθρωπίνης

from the sea.[39] For we have decided to raze your city to the ground." Even as he was still speaking, the Carthaginians lifted their hands to heaven, shouting and appealing to the gods as victims of deceit, and repeatedly cursing the Romans malevolently. Either they wanted to die, or they were out of their mind, or they were trying to provoke the Romans into sacrilege against ambassadors. They threw themselves on the ground and hit it with their hands and heads. Some even tore their clothes and did violence to their own bodies, as if they had been ambushed by insanity. When the madness relented, there was complete silence and dejection, as if they were dead bodies. The Romans were astonished, and the consuls decided to be patient with them in view of the unwelcome command they had received, until their anger had subsided. For they were well aware that the greatest horrors can shock men into sudden desperation, while in time necessity subdues rashness. And that is what happened to the Carthaginians on this occasion. For in the silence they got a better grasp of their plight, and leaving aside their anger they began to weep and cry for themselves and for their children and wives, calling out their names, and for their country itself, as if it could hear them like a human being, as they recounted their many woes. The priests called on the names of the temples and their resident gods as if they were present, blaming them for their destruction. The grief was varied and pitiful as they lamented their situation both public and private, until even the Romans were moved to tears for them.

82. The consuls felt pity for the sudden change of for-

379

380

381

382

383

384

---

[39] Eighty stades is approximately nine miles.

143

μεταβολῆς, σκυθρωποὶ δ' ἀνέμενον καὶ τούτων κόρον
αὐτοῖς ἐγγενέσθαι. ὡς δὲ καὶ ὀδυρμῶν ἔληξαν, αὖθις
385 ἦν σιωπή. καὶ λόγον αὐτοῖς διδόντες, ὡς ἡ μὲν πόλις
ἐστὶν ἄνοπλος, ἔρημος, οὐ ναῦν, οὐ καταπέλτην, οὐ
βέλος, οὐ ξίφος ἔχουσα, οὐκ ἄνδρας οἰκείους ἱκανοὺς
ἀπομάχεσθαι, πέντε μυριάδων ἔναγχος διεφθαρμέ-
νων, ξενικὸν δὲ οὐδὲν ἔστιν ἢ φίλος ἢ σύμμαχος ἢ
καιρὸς ἐς ταῦτα, ἔχουσι δ' αὐτοῖς οἱ πολέμιοι καὶ τὰ
τέκνα καὶ τὰ ὅπλα καὶ τὴν χώραν καὶ περικάθηνται
τὸ ἄστυ ἔνοπλοι ναυσὶ καὶ πεζῷ καὶ μηχανήμασι καὶ
ἵπποις, Μασσανάσσης δ' ἐχθρὸς ἕτερος ἐν πλευραῖς,
θορύβου μὲν ἔτι καὶ ἀγανακτήσεως ἐπέσχον, ὡς οὐδὲν ἐν ταῖς συμφοραῖς ὠφελούντων, ἐς δὲ λόγους
αὖθις ἐτράποντο. καὶ Βάννων, ᾧ Τιγίλλας ἐπώνυμον
ἦν, ἐπιφανέστατος ὢν ἐν τοῖς τότε παροῦσιν, αἰτήσας
εἰπεῖν, ἔλεξεν·
386 83. "Εἰ μέν ἐστι καὶ τῶν πρότερον εἰρημένων ἔτι
πρὸς ὑμᾶς, ὦ Ῥωμαῖοι, λόγος, ἐροῦμεν, οὐχ ὡς δίκαια
προφέροντες (οὐ γάρ ἐστιν ἐν καιρῷ τοῖς ἀτυχοῦσιν
ἀντιλογία), ἀλλ' ἵνα μάθητε, ὡς οὐκ ἀπροφάσιστός
387 ἐστιν ὑμῖν ὁ ἔλεος ὁ ἐφ' ἡμῖν οὐδὲ ἄλογος. ἡμεῖς γὰρ
Λιβύης ἄρχοντες καὶ θαλάσσης ὅτι πλείστης περὶ
ἡγεμονίας ὑμῖν ἐπολεμήσαμεν· καὶ ταύτης ἀπέστημεν
ἐπὶ Σκιπίωνος, ὅτε τὰς ναῦς ὑμῖν παρέδομεν καὶ ἐλέφαντας, ὅσους εἴχομεν, καὶ φόρους ἐταξάμεθα δώσειν
388 καὶ δίδομεν ἐν καιρῷ. πρὸς οὖν θεῶν τῶν τότε ὀμω-
μοσμένων φείδεσθε μὲν ἡμῶν, φείδεσθε δὲ τῶν Σκιπίωνος ὅρκων, ὀμόσαντος ἔσεσθαι Ῥωμαίους Καρχη-

tune that affects mankind, but dourly waited for them to
have their fill of grief. When they finished weeping, silence
descended again. The Carthaginians gave thought to how   385
their city was unarmed and defenseless: they did not have
a ship, catapult, missile, or sword; with fifty thousand recently dead, they did not have enough of their own men to
defend themselves, and they had no mercenaries, friends
or allies, nor the opportunity to acquire them; the enemy
held their children, and their weapons, and their country;
their city was invested by an enemy armed with ships,
infantry, siege engines and horses, and yet another opponent, Massinissa, pressed on their flanks. Understanding
that in a crisis there was nothing to be gained from continuing with disruption and anger, they turned once again
to rational argument. Banno Tigillas, the most distinguished of their present company, asked for permission to
speak. This is what he said:

83. "If you still set any store by what we said before to   386
you, men of Rome, we will speak now, not to offer justifi-
cation—for it is never a good time for those facing misfortune to argue their case—but to tell you that there is nothing inexcusable or illogical about the pity you feel for us.
As rulers of Africa and most of the Mediterranean, it was   387
we who fought with you for supremacy. We were forced
to give this up in the time of Scipio, when we surrendered
to you all our ships and elephants, and agreed to pay tribute—which we pay punctually. Now, by the gods in whose   388
name oaths were sworn at the time, spare us and spare the
oaths of Scipio, who swore that the Romans and Cartha-

145

δονίοις συμμάχους καὶ φίλους. οὐδ' ἔστιν ἐς ταῦθ' ὅ
τι ἡμάρτομεν. οὐ ναῦς ἔχομεν, οὐκ ἐλέφαντας, οὐ τοὺς
φόρους ἐκλείπομεν, ἀλλὰ καὶ συνεμαχήσαμεν ὑμῖν

389 ἐπὶ τρεῖς βασιλέας. μηδέ τῳ παραστῇ καταγινώσκειν,
εἰ ταὐτὰ[14] καὶ πρῴην εἴπομεν, ὅτε τὰ ὅπλα ᾐτεῖτε· αἵ
τε γὰρ συμφοραὶ ποιοῦσι μακρολόγους, καὶ ἅμα συνθηκῶν οὐδὲν ἐν ταῖς ἱκεσίαις δυνατώτερον, οὐδ' ἔχομεν ἐς οὐδὲν ἕτερον ἀντὶ λόγων καταφυγεῖν, οἳ τὴν

390 δύναμιν ὑμῖν ἅπασαν ἐξέδομεν. τὰ μὲν δὴ πρότερα
τοιαῦτα, ὧν ὁ Σκιπίων ἐστὶν ἡμῖν, ὦ Ῥωμαῖοι, βεβαι-
ωτής· τῶν δὲ παρόντων ὑμεῖς, ὦ ὕπατοι, δημιουργοὶ
καὶ μάρτυρές ἐστε ἡμῖν. ὅμηρα ᾐτήσατε, καὶ τὰ
κράτιστα ἠγάγομεν ὑμῖν. ὅπλα ᾐτήσατε, καὶ πάντα
ἐλάβετε, ὧν οὐδὲ οἱ ληφθέντες ἐν ταῖς πολιορκίαις

391 ἑκόντες μεθίενται. ἐπιστεύσαμεν δὲ ἡμεῖς τῷ Ῥωμαίων ἤθει καὶ τρόπῳ· καὶ γὰρ ἡ σύγκλητος ἡμῖν
ἐπέστειλεν, καὶ ὑμεῖς, τὰ ὅμηρα αἰτοῦντες, ἔφατε τὴν

392 Καρχηδόνα αὐτόνομον ἐάσειν, εἰ λάβοιτε. εἰ δὲ προσέκειτο καὶ τὰ λοιπὰ ὑμῶν ἀνέξεσθαι κελευόντων, οὐκ
εἰκὸς ἦν ὑμᾶς ἐπὶ μὲν τοῖς ὁμήροις, αἰτήματι σαφεῖ,
τὴν πόλιν αὐτόνομον ἔσεσθαι προαγορεῦσαι, ἐν δὲ
προσθήκῃ τῶν ὁμήρων ποιεῖσθαι τὴν Καρχηδόνος
αὐτῆς κατασκαφήν, ἣν εἰ θέμις ὑμῖν ἐστιν ἀνελεῖν,
πῶς ἐλευθέραν ἔτι ἀφήσετε ἢ αὐτόνομον, ὡς ἐλέγετε;

393 84. "Τάδε μὲν εἴχομεν εἰπεῖν καὶ περὶ τῶν προτέρων
συνθηκῶν καὶ περὶ τῶν πρὸς ὑμᾶς γενομένων. εἰ δὲ
καὶ τούτων οὐκ ἀνέξεσθε, παρίεμεν ἅπαντα καί, ὃ τοῖς

ginians should be friends and allies. In this respect, we
have done nothing wrong. We do not have any ships or
elephants; we have not failed to pay the tribute; but we
have fought on your side against three kings. Let no one   389
think of taking offense at us for repeating what we said
before, when you demanded our weapons. For disaster
makes people talk too much, but at the same time, there
is no more powerful argument when making your case as
a suppliant than the terms of a treaty. And there is nothing
for us to have recourse to except words, since we have
handed all our power over to you. These were the earlier   390
terms, men of Rome, for which Scipio is our guarantor.
You, the consuls, are the ones who fashioned and witnessed the present conditions. You demanded hostages;
we brought you our best. You demanded weapons; you got
them all—and even those captured in sieges do not willingly give up their weapons. We have placed our trust in   391
the character and nature of the Romans. The senate informed us, and when demanding the hostages, you too
told us that, if you got them, you would leave Carthage
autonomous. If there was an additional condition ordering   392
us to put up with the rest of your demands, it was not
reasonable to expect that you would proclaim Carthage
autonomous, and at the same time make a clear demand,
in addition to the hostages, for its destruction. If it is your
right to destroy it, how will you leave it free and autonomous, as you said you would?

84. "This is all we can say about the earlier agreements   393
and those negotiated with you. If you cannot even bring
yourselves to listen to our case, we give up on everything

ἀτυχοῦσίν ἐστι λοιπόν, ὀδυρόμεθα καὶ δεόμεθα.

394 πολλὴ δ᾽ ἡ ἱκεσία δι᾽ ἀφθονίαν κακῶν· ὑπέρ τε γὰρ
πόλεως παρακαλοῦμεν ἀρχαίας, χρησμοῖς μετὰ θεῶν
συνῳκισμένης, καὶ ὑπὲρ δόξης ἐπὶ μέγα προελθούσης
καὶ ὀνόματος ἐπιφοιτήσαντος ἐπὶ τὴν γῆν ὅλην ὑπέρ
τε ἱερῶν τῶν ἐν αὐτῇ τοσῶνδε καὶ θεῶν οὐδὲν ἀδικούν-
των, οὓς μὴ πανηγύρεις ἀφέλησθε καὶ πομπὰς καὶ
ἑορτὰς μηδὲ τοὺς τάφους τὰ ἐναγίσματα, οὐδὲν ὑμῖν

395 ἔτι τῶν νεκρῶν ἐπιζημίων ὄντων. εἰ δὲ καὶ ἡμῶν ἐστιν
ἔλεος (φατὲ δὲ καὶ ἡμᾶς ἐλεεῖν, οἳ συγχωρεῖτε μετοι-
κίσασθαι), φείσασθε πολιτικῆς ἑστίας, φείσασθε
ἀγορᾶς, φείσασθε βουλαίας θεοῦ πάντων τε τῶν ἄλ-

396 λων, ὅσα τοῖς ἔτι ζῶσι τερπνὰ καὶ τίμια. τί γὰρ δὴ
καὶ δέος ἐστὶν ὑμῖν ἔτι Καρχηδόνος, οἳ καὶ τὰς ναῦς
ἔχετε ἡμῶν καὶ τὰ ὅπλα καὶ τοὺς ἐπιφθόνους ἐλέφαν-

397 τας; περὶ δὲ τῆς ἀνοικίσεως, εἴ τῳ δοκεῖ τοῦτο ἐς παρ-
ηγορίαν ἡμῖν προτίθεσθαι, ἔστι καὶ τόδε ἀμήχανον
ἀνδράσιν ἐς ἤπειρον ἀνοικίσασθαι θαλασσοβιώτοις,

398 ὧν ἄπειρον πλῆθος ἐργάζεται τὴν θάλασσαν. δίδομεν
δ᾽ ὑμῖν ἀντίδοσιν αἱρετωτέραν ἡμῖν καὶ εὐκλεεστέραν
ὑμῖν· τὴν μὲν πόλιν ἐᾶτε τὴν οὐδενὸς ὑμῖν αἰτίαν,
αὐτοὺς δὲ ἡμᾶς, οὓς ἀνοικίζετε, εἰ θέλετε, διαχρή-
σασθε. οὕτω γὰρ ἀνθρώποις δόξετε χαλεπαίνειν, οὐχ
ἱεροῖς καὶ θεοῖς καὶ τάφοις καὶ πόλει μηδὲν ἀδικούσῃ.

399 85. "Δόξης δ᾽ ἀγαθῆς καὶ εὐσεβοῦς ἐφίεσθε, ὦ
Ῥωμαῖοι, παρὰ πάντα ἔργα καὶ μετριοπάθειαν ἐν τοῖς
εὐτυχήμασιν ἐπαγγέλλεσθε καὶ τοῦθ᾽, οἷς ἂν αἰεὶ λά-

400 βητε, καταλογίζεσθε. μὴ δή, πρὸς Διὸς καὶ θεῶν, τῶν

else and take to weeping and begging, which is all that is
left for the unfortunate. The abundance of our troubles   394
gives plenty of scope for supplication. So, we appeal to you
on behalf of our ancient city founded in response to ora-
cles and with divine help; and on behalf of a glory that
advanced to greatness, of a name that spread over the
whole world, of the city's many temples and their gods who
have done no wrong. Do not deprive these gods of their
national gatherings, their processions, their festivals. And
as the dead no longer do you harm, do not deprive the
tombs of their offerings. If you have pity for us—and you   395
say that it is out of pity that you grant us the right to resettle elsewhere—spare the city's hearth, spare its place of
assembly, spare the goddess of our council, spare everything else that is pleasing and precious to those still living.
For how can you still be afraid of Carthage when you hold   396
our ships, our weapons, our hated elephants? And as for   397
the resettlement, if anyone thinks they are proposing this
as a consolation for us, it is also unworkable for shore-
dwelling men, a large number of whom earn their living
from the sea, to move to the country. We suggest to you   398
an exchange, more desirable for us and more glorious for
you: leave the city alone—it has done nothing to you—
and, instead of ordering us to move, please kill us. In this
way, you will appear to be visiting your anger on men
rather than temples, gods, tombs, and a city that has done
no wrong.

85. "You seek a reputation for goodness and piety in   399
everything you do, men of Rome, and you preach moderation in prosperity and you list the examples to everyone
you ever conquer. In the name of Zeus and the other gods,   400

τε ἄλλων καὶ ὅσοι Καρχηδόνα ἔτι ἔχουσί τε καὶ μή
ποτε μνησικακήσαιεν ὑμῖν μηδὲ παισὶν ὑμετέροις, μὴ
ἀγαθὴν δόξαν ὑμῶν αὐτῶν ἐν ἡμῖν πρώτοις δια-
βάλητε μηδὲ τοιῷδε ἔργῳ τὴν εὔκλειαν ὑμῶν κατα-
μιάνητε, χαλεπῷ μὲν ἐργασθῆναι, χαλεπῷ δὲ ἀκου-
σθῆναι παρά τε πρώτοις ὑμῖν ἐξ ἅπαντος τοῦ βίου
401 γενησομένῳ. πόλεμοι γὰρ πολλοὶ μὲν Ἕλλησιν ἐγένοντο καὶ βαρβάροις, πολλοὶ δὲ ὑμῖν, ὦ Ῥωμαῖοι,
πρὸς ἑτέρους· καὶ οὐδείς πω κατέσκαψε πόλιν χεῖράς
τε πρὸ μάχης καθιεῖσαν καὶ ὅπλα καὶ τέκνα παρα-
δοῦσαν καὶ εἴ τις ἔστιν εἰς ἀνθρώπους ἄλλη ζημία,
402 καὶ ταύτην παθεῖν ὑπομένουσαν. προφέροντες δ᾽ ὑμῖν
ὁρκίους θεοὺς καὶ τύχην ἀνθρωπείαν καὶ τὴν φοβε-
ρωτάτην τοῖς εὐτυχοῦσι Νέμεσιν δεόμεθα μήτε ἐς τὴν
ὑμετέραν εὐπραγίαν ὑμᾶς ὑβρίσαι μήτε τὰς ἡμετέρας
συμφορὰς ἐς ἀνήκεστον προαγαγεῖν, συγχωρῆσαι δ᾽,
εἰ μὴ δίδοτε τὴν πόλιν ἔχειν, ἔς γε τὴν σύγκλητον ἔτι
403 πρεσβεῦσαι περὶ αὐτῆς καὶ δεηθῆναι. βραχὺ δ᾽ ὁρᾶτε
τὸ διάστημα τοῦ χρόνου, βάσανον μὲν ἡμῖν φέρον
μακρὰν ἐν ὀλίγῳ διὰ τὴν τῶν ἐσομένων ἀμφιβολίαν·
ὑμῖν δὲ τὸ μὲν ἀσφαλὲς ἴσον, ἢ νῦν ἢ μετ᾽ ὀλίγον τὰ
δοκοῦντα δρᾶν, τὸ δ᾽ εὐσεβὲς καὶ φιλάνθρωπον ἐπι-
γίνεται."

404   86. Τοιαῦτα μὲν εἶπεν ὁ Βάννων, οἱ δὲ ὕπατοι δῆλοι
μὲν ἦσαν ἐσκυθρωπακότες παρὰ πάντα τὸν λόγον,
ὅτι μηδὲν ἐνδώσουσιν αὐτοῖς, παυσαμένου δὲ ὁ Κηνσωρῖνος ἔλεξεν· "Περὶ μὲν ὧν ἡ σύγκλητος προσέτα-
ξεν, τί δεῖ πολλάκις λέγειν; προσέταξε γάρ, καὶ χρὴ

particularly those who still inhabit Carthage—may they never bear a grudge against you or your children—do not, in your treatment of us, damage your own good reputation for the first time, and do not stain your good name with such a deed, dreadful to do, dreadful to hear about, for the first time in your entire existence. Greeks and barbarians 401 have fought many wars against each other, and you, men of Rome, have fought many against other peoples. But no one has ever razed a city to the ground that surrendered before combat was joined and handed over its weapons and children, and submitted to every other punishment devised against men. Calling your attention to the oaths 402 sworn by the gods, to human fortune, to Nemesis, whom the fortunate have most cause to fear, we beg you not to do violence to your own success or worsen our disasters so that they become impossible to bear: if you cannot let us keep our city, allow us to send another mission to the senate and make our appeal on its behalf. You can see that it 403 will only take a short time, but a time that will be torturously long for us, however short it is, because of the uncertainty of our future. But it is equally safe for you whether you carry out your decision now or after a little time, and it will add an element of piety and generosity."

86. This was the speech of Banno. It was, however, 404 clear from their sullen expression throughout his whole speech that the consuls would be making no concessions to the Carthaginians. When Banno had finished speaking, Censorinus replied: "What is the point of repeatedly talking about the senate's orders? They have issued their or-

APPIAN

γενέσθαι· οὐδὲ ἀναθέσθαι δυνάμεθα τὰ ἤδη κεκελευ-
405 σμένα γενέσθαι. ταῦτα δὲ εἰ μὲν ὡς ἐχθροῖς ἐπεκε-
λεύομεν, ἔδει μόνον εἰπεῖν καὶ ποιεῖν ἀναγκάζειν· ἐπεὶ
δὲ ἐπ᾽ ὠφελείᾳ κοινῇ, τάχα μέν τι καὶ ἡμῶν, τὸ δὲ
πλέον ὑμῶν, ὦ Καρχηδόνιοι, γίνεται, οὐκ ὀκνήσω καὶ
τοὺς λογισμοὺς ὑμῖν εἰπεῖν, ἢν δύνησθε πεισθῆναι
406 μᾶλλον ἢ βιασθῆναι. ἡ θάλασσα ὑμᾶς ἤδε, μεμνημέ-
νους τῆς ἐν αὐτῇ ποτε ἀρχῆς καὶ δυνάμεως, ἀδικεῖν
ἐπαίρει καὶ ἀπὸ τοῦδε ἐς συμφορὰς περιφέρει. Σικελίᾳ τε γὰρ δι᾽ αὐτὴν ἐπεχειρήσατε καὶ Σικελίαν
ἀπωλέσατε· ἔς τε Ἰβηρίαν διεπλεύσατε καὶ Ἰβηρίαν
407 ἀφήρησθε. ἔν τε ταῖς συνθήκαις ἐλῄζεσθε τοὺς ἐμπόρους καὶ τοὺς ἡμετέρους μάλιστα, ἵνα λανθάνοιτε,
κατεποντοῦτε, ἕως ἁλόντες ποινὴν ἡμῖν ἔδοτε Σαρδώ.
οὕτω καὶ Σαρδοῦς ἀφῃρέθητε διὰ τὴν θάλασσαν, ἣ
πέφυκε πείθειν ἅπαντας αἰεὶ τοῦ πλέονος ὀρέγεσθαι
διὰ τὴν ἐν αὐτῇ ταχυεργίαν.
408 87. "Ὃ καὶ Ἀθηναίους, ὅτε ἐγένοντο ναυτικοί, μάλιστα ηὔξησέ τε καὶ καθεῖλεν· ἔοικε γὰρ τὰ θαλάσσια
τοῖς ἐμπορικοῖς κέρδεσιν, ἃ καὶ τὴν αὔξησιν ἔχει καὶ
409 τὴν ἀπώλειαν ἀθρόαν. ἴστε γοῦν αὐτοὺς ἐκείνους, ὧν
ἐπεμνήσθην, ὅτι τὴν ἀρχὴν ἐπὶ τὸν Ἰόνιον ἐκτείνοντες
ἐς Σικελίαν οὐ πρὶν ἀπέστησαν τῆς πλεονεξίας, πρὶν
τὴν ἀρχὴν ἅπασαν ἀφαιρεθῆναι καὶ λιμένας καὶ ναῦς
παραδοῦναι τοῖς πολεμίοις καὶ φρουρὰν ἐνδέξασθαι
τῇ πόλει καὶ τὰ τείχη σφῶν αὐτοὶ τὰ μακρὰ καθελεῖν
410 καὶ σχεδὸν ἠπειρῶται τότε κἀκεῖνοι γενέσθαι. ὃ καὶ
διέσωσεν ἐπὶ πλεῖστον αὐτούς· εὐσταθέστερος γάρ, ὦ

152

ders, and they must be carried out. We do not even have the power to delay what has already been commanded. If we were issuing these demands to you as enemies, we would only have to state what they were and carry them out by force. But since, men of Carthage, we are dealing with the common good, ours perhaps to a certain extent, yours more so, I have no hesitation in telling you the rationale, if you can be persuaded rather than forced into compliance. Because it recalls for you the powerful empire you once enjoyed on it, it is this sea that inspires you to do wrong and from there carries you into disaster. Because of the sea you invaded Sicily and then lost Sicily. You sailed across to Iberia and Iberia was taken from you. With a treaty in place you practiced piracy against merchants, particularly our merchants, and to avoid detection, threw them overboard. Eventually you were caught, and handed Sardinia to us in recompense. So you lost Sardinia too because of the sea, which by its nature, that is, the speed with which operations can be carried out on it, always persuades all men to be greedy for more.

87. "This is what happened to the Athenians too, when they became a seafaring people: the sea strengthened them greatly and then destroyed them. For naval power is like the profits made by merchants: they bring both increased wealth and total bankruptcy. You are at any rate aware that the Athenians I have just mentioned, when they extended their empire over the Ionian sea to Sicily, could not restrain their greed until they lost their whole empire, gave up their harbors and ships to the enemy, accepted a garrison in Athens, tore down their long walls with their own hands and then virtually became an inland people. This is what saved them for such a long time. For life on

405

406

407

408

409

410

Καρχηδόνιοι, ὁ ἐν ἠπείρῳ βίος, γεωργίᾳ καὶ ἠρεμίᾳ
προσπονῶν· καὶ σμικρότερα μὲν ἴσως τὰ κέρδη, βε-
βαιότερα δὲ καὶ ἀκινδυνότερα καθάπαξ τὰ τῆς γεωρ-
411 γίας παρὰ τοὺς ἐμπόρους. ὅλως τέ μοι δοκεῖ πόλις ἡ
μὲν ἐν τῇ θαλάσσῃ ναῦς τις εἶναι μᾶλλον ἢ γῆ, πολὺν τὸν σάλον τῶν πραγμάτων ἔχουσα καὶ τὰς μετα-
βολάς, ἡ δὲ ἐν τῷ μεσογείῳ καρποῦσθαι τὸ ἀκίνδυνον
412 ὡς ἐν γῇ. διὰ τοῦτ' ἄρα καὶ τὰ πάλαι βασίλεια ὡς
ἐπίπαν ἦν ἐν μέσῳ, καὶ ἀπὸ τοῦδε μέγιστα ἐγένοντο
τὰ Μήδων καὶ Ἀσσυρίων καὶ Περσῶν καὶ ἑτέρων.

413   88. "Ἀλλὰ βασιλικῶν μὲν ὑποδειγμάτων παύομαι,
οὐδὲν ὑμῖν ἔτι διαφερόντων· ἐς δὲ τὴν ὑμετέραν Λιβύην ἀπίδετε, ὅσαι μεσόγειοι πόλεις ἀκινδύνως βι-
414 οῦσιν. ὧν ἧς ἂν ἐθέλητε, γείτονες ἔσεσθε, ἵνα τὴν
ἐρεθίζουσαν ὑμᾶς ὄψιν τε καὶ μνήμην ἀφῆτε τῶν νῦν
ἐνοχλούντων κακῶν, ὅταν ἐς τὴν θάλασσαν κενὴν
σκαφῶν ἀφορῶντες ἀναμιμνήσκησθε τοῦ πλήθους ὧν
εἴχετε νεῶν, καὶ λαφύρων ὅσων ἐφέρετε, καὶ ἐς οἵους
γε τοὺς λιμένας κατήγεσθε σοβαροὶ καὶ τὰ νεώρια
415 καὶ τὰ τῶν σκευῶν ταμεῖα ἐνεπίμπλατε. τί δὲ αἱ ἐν
τοῖς τείχεσιν ὑποδοχαὶ στρατοπέδων τε καὶ ἵππων καὶ
ἐλεφάντων; τί δὲ θησαυροὶ τούτοις παρῳκοδομημένοι;
τί ταῦτα μνημεῖα ὑμῖν ἐστιν; ἢ τί ἄλλο πλὴν ὀδύνη
καὶ ἐρέθισμα ἐπανελθεῖν ἐς αὐτά, εἴ ποτε δύναισθε;
πάθος ἐστὶν ἀνθρώπειον τοῖς μεμνημένοις τῆς ποτὲ
τύχης ἐλπίζειν τὴν τύχην ἐπανελεύσεσθαι, φάρμακον
δὲ κακῶν ἀκεστήριον λήθη, ἧς οὐκ ἔνι μετασχεῖν
416 ὑμῖν, ἢν μὴ τὴν ὄψιν ἀπόθησθε. καὶ τούτου σαφέστα-

the land is more stable, men of Carthage, with its quiet
agricultural labor. The gains of farming are perhaps
smaller, but sounder and altogether less dangerous than
those of merchants. Indeed, a city by the sea strikes me as   411
more like a sort of ship than land: it rides on the great swell
of affairs and is subject to sudden change, while an inland
city enjoys a harvest without danger, located as it is on solid
ground. This is, of course, why imperial capitals of old   412
were almost all inland, and why the Median, Assyrian,
Persian and other empires became very powerful.

88. "But I have said enough about imperial examples,   413
which are no longer relevant to you. Turn your eyes to your
own Africa and consider how many cities in the middle of
the country live without danger. You will have as neighbors   414
whichever of these you like, so that you get rid of the sight
that agitates you and forget the troubles that now disturb
you, whenever you look out over the shipless sea and re-
member the huge fleets you used to have, and the rich
plunder you used to carry off, and the great harbors where
you proudly came to land, and the dockyards and ware-
houses you filled. What is the point of accommodation for   415
soldiers, horses, and elephants? What is the point of the
magazines built along side them? What do these remind
you of? What else can they bring to mind but grief and a
stimulus to get them back if you possibly can? When we
recall our former good fortune, the human reaction is to
hope it will return. The drug that heals our troubles is
forgetfulness, but you cannot avail of it, if you do not put
away the sight of these things. The clearest proof of this is   416

τος ἔλεγχος, ὅτι πολλάκις συγγνώμης καὶ συνθηκῶν
τυχόντες παρεσπονδήσατε. εἰ μὲν οὖν ἔτι τῆς ἀρχῆς
ἐφίεσθε καὶ δυσμεναίνετε ἡμῖν ὡς ἀφῃρημένοι καὶ
καιροφυλακεῖτε, δεῖ τῆσδε τῆς πόλεως ὑμῖν καὶ λιμένων τοιῶνδε καὶ νεωρίων καὶ τειχῶν ἐς στρατοπέ-
417 δου τρόπον εἰργασμένων. καὶ τί ἔτι φειδόμεθα ἐχθρῶν
εἰλημμένων; εἰ δὲ τῆς μὲν ἀρχῆς ἀπέστητε καθαρῶς,
οὐ λόγῳ μᾶλλον ἢ γνώμῃ, μόνα δ' ἐξῄρησθε Λιβύης
ἃ ἔχετε, καὶ τάδε ἀποφασίστως συνέθεσθε ἡμῖν,
φέρετε καὶ ἔργῳ ταῦτ' ἐπιδείξατε, ἐς μὲν Λιβύην, ἣν
ἔχετε, ἀνοικισάμενοι, τῆς δὲ θαλάσσης ἐκστάντες, ἧς
ἀπέστητε.

418 89. "Μηδ' ὑποκρίνεσθε ἐλεεῖν ἱερὰ καὶ ἑστίας καὶ
ἀγορὰς καὶ τάφους· ὧν τάφοι μὲν ἔστων ἀκίνητοι, καὶ
ἐναγίζετε αὐτοῖς ἐπερχόμενοι καὶ τοῖς ἱεροῖς, θύειν εἰ
θέλετε, ἐπιόντες, τὰ δὲ λοιπὰ καθέλωμεν. οὐ γὰρ καὶ
419 νεωρίοις θύετε οὐδ' ἐναγίζετε τείχεσιν. ἑστίας δὲ καὶ
ἱερὰ ἄλλα καὶ ἀγορὰς ἔνι καὶ μετελθόντας ἐργάσα-
σθαι, καὶ ταχὺ κἀκεῖνα ὑμῖν ἔσται πάτρια, ᾧ λόγῳ
καὶ τὰ ἐν Τύρῳ καταλιπόντες ἠλλάξασθε Λιβύην τά
τε ἐπίκτητα ὑμῖν τότε γενόμενα νῦν πάτρια τίθεσθε.
420 βραχεῖ τε λόγῳ μάθοιτε ἄν, ὡς οὐχ ὑπὸ δυσμενείας,
ἀλλ' ἐπὶ βεβαίῳ τε ὁμονοίᾳ καὶ ἀμεριμνίᾳ κοινῇ τάδε
προστάσσομεν, εἰ ἀναμνησθείητε, ὅτι καὶ Ἄλβην
ἡμεῖς, οὐκ ἐχθράν, ἀλλὰ μητρόπολιν οὖσαν, οὐδὲ
δυσμεναίνοντες, ἀλλ' ὡς ἄποικοι προτιμῶντες, ἐπὶ
συμφέροντι κοινῷ μετῳκίσαμεν ἐς Ῥώμην, καὶ ἐλυσι-
421 τέλησεν ἀμφοτέροις. ἀλλ' εἰσὶ γὰρ ὑμῖν ἔτι χειρώ-

the regularity with which you broke treaties as often as you won forgiveness and peace terms. If you still hunger after empire and resent us for taking it away from you, if you are still waiting for the main chance, then you need this city, this great harbor and dockyards, these walls built like a military camp. But in that case, why should we continue to spare the enemy we have captured? If, on the other hand, you have entirely renounced empire and are not just saying it, but have decided it, and your choice is solely for what you possess in Africa, and you have made this agreement with us without equivocation, then come on and prove it by your actions: resettle in Africa, which you own, and move away from the sea, which you have rejected.   417

89. "And do not pretend to feel sorry for your temples, your hearths, your places of assembly, your graves. Your graves are to remain undisturbed: visit them and make offerings to the dead; enter your temples and sacrifice to the gods, if you want. The rest let us destroy. For you do not sacrifice to shipsheds, you do not make offerings to walls. You can build hearths and new temples and meeting places when you have moved, and they too will quickly become your ancestral possessions, in the same way as when you left Tyre and emigrated to Africa, what you acquired then you now regard as your ancestral possessions. In short, you will come to understand that we make this order not out of malice toward you, but to create a stable consensus and general freedom from worry. Perhaps you will recall how it was to our mutual benefit, when for the common good we moved the city of Alba to Rome. Alba was not our enemy, but our mother city, and we did not treat it with malice, but as its colonists, we honored it preeminently. But you still have many workers, you claim,   421

  418

  419

  420

νακτες πολλοὶ θαλασσοβίωτοι. καὶ τούτου πεφρον-
τίκαμεν, ὡς ἂν εὐκόλως ἐπιμιγνύοισθε τῇ θαλάσσῃ
καὶ τὴν τῶν ὡραίων διάθεσίν τε καὶ ἀντίληψιν ἔχοιτε
εὐμαρῆ· οὐ γὰρ μακρὰν ὑμᾶς ἀπὸ θαλάσσης, ἀλλ'
ὀγδοήκοντα σταδίους ἀναδραμεῖν κελεύομεν. ἡμεῖς δ'
οἱ ταῦτα προστάσσοντες ὑμῖν ἑκατὸν τῆς θαλάσσης
422 ἀπέχομεν. χωρίον δὲ ὑμῖν δίδομεν, ὃ θέλετε, ἐπιλέξα-
σθαι καὶ μετελθοῦσιν αὐτονόμοις εἶναι. τοῦτο δ'
ἐστίν, ὃ προυλέγομεν, αὐτόνομον ἐάσειν Καρχηδόνα,
εἰ πείθοιτο ἡμῖν· Καρχηδόνα γὰρ ὑμᾶς, οὐ τὸ ἔδαφος
ἡγούμεθα."

423   90. Τοσαῦτα δ' εἰπὼν ὁ Κηνσωρῖνος ἡσύχασε. καὶ
τῶν Καρχηδονίων ὑπ' ἐκπλήξεως οὐδὲν ἀποκριναμένων ἐπεῖπεν· "Ἃ μὲν ἔδει πείθοντα καὶ παρηγοροῦντα
εἰπεῖν, εἴρηται· τὸ δὲ πρόσταγμα τῆς βουλῆς δεῖ γενέσθαι καὶ αὐτίκα γενέσθαι. ἄπιτε οὖν· ἐστὲ γὰρ ἔτι
424 πρέσβεις." ὁ μὲν εἶπεν οὕτως, οἱ δ' ἐξωθούμενοι πρὸς
τῶν ὑπηρετῶν καὶ τὸ μέλλον ὑπὸ Καρχηδονίων ἔσεσθαι προορῶντες ᾔτησαν αὖθις εἰπεῖν. καὶ εἰσαχθέν-
τες ἔφασαν· "Τὸ μὲν ἀπαραίτητον τοῦ κελεύσματος
ὁρῶμεν· οὐ γὰρ οὐδὲ πρεσβεῦσαι δίδοτε ἐς Ῥώμην.
ἡμεῖς δ' ἐπανελεύσεσθαι μὲν πρὸς ὑμᾶς οὐκ ἐλπίζο-
μεν, ἀλλ' ὑπὸ Καρχηδονίων ἔτι λέγοντες ἀπολεῖσθαι·
425 δεόμεθα δ' ὑμῶν, οὐχ ὑπὲρ ἑαυτῶν (ἐσμὲν γὰρ πάντα
παθεῖν ἕτοιμοι), ἀλλ' ὑπὲρ αὐτῆς ἔτι Καρχηδόνος, εἰ
δύναιτο καταπλαγεῖσα τὰς συμφορὰς ὑποστῆναι·
περιστήσατε αὐτῇ τὰς ναῦς, ἕως ὁδεύοντες ἄπιμεν,
ἵνα καὶ θεωροῦντες καὶ ἀκούοντες ὧν προσετάξατε,

who make their living from the sea. This too we have thought about. To ensure that you have easy access to the sea and convenient facility for seasonal import and export, we are only ordering you to withdraw eighty stades from the sea, not a huge distance. We ourselves, who are placing this requirement on you, are one hundred stades from the coast. We give you the right to choose whatever place you want, and when you move there, to be autonomous. This is what we told you before, that if you obeyed our commands, we would leave Carthage autonomous. We believe that what constitutes Carthage is you, not the site." 422

90. Censorinus finished his speech, and remained silent. The Carthaginians were too shocked to reply, so Censorinus added the following: "Everything that needed to be said by way of persuasion or consolation has been said. The decree of the senate must be carried out, and carried out immediately. So, leave now: for you are still ambassadors." With these words, the ambassadors were removed by the attendants, but foreseeing the likely reaction of the Carthaginians, they asked permission to speak again. On being readmitted to the senate, they spoke as follows: "We can see that there is no way of evading your command, since you will not even let us send a mission to Rome. We do not expect to return to you again, but to die at the hands of the Carthaginians while we are still speaking. We ask you, not on our own account—for we are ready to pay the ultimate price—but still for Carthage itself, to see if the city might be terrorized into submitting to its misfortunes. Station your ships by the city while we journey back, so that by both hearing and seeing your orders, the Cartha- 423 424 425

ἐνέγκωσιν, ἂν ἄρα δύνωνται. ἐς τοῦτο δ᾽ ἡμῖν ἀνάγκης ἀφῖκται καὶ τύχης, ὡς αὐτοὶ παρακαλεῖν ὑμᾶς
426 τὰς ναῦς ἐπάγειν ἐπὶ τὴν πατρίδα." οἱ μὲν δὴ τοσαῦτα εἰπόντες ἀπήεσαν, καὶ ὁ Κηνσωρῖνος πεντήρεσιν εἴκοσι παραπλεύσας ἀνεκώχευε παρὰ τὴν πόλιν·
τῶν δὲ πρέσβεων οἱ μὲν ἐκ τῆς ὁδοῦ διεδίδρασκον, οἱ
δὲ πλέονες ἐπορεύοντο σιγῇ.

427   91. Καρχηδόνιοι δὲ οἱ μὲν ἀπὸ τῶν τειχῶν ἐς τοὺς
πρέσβεις, ὁπότε ἥξουσιν, ἀφεώρων καὶ βραδύνουσιν
αὐτοῖς ἤχθοντο καὶ τὰς κόμας ἐτίλλοντο· οἱ δ᾽ ὑπήντων ἔτι προσιοῦσιν, οὐκ ἀναμένοντες, ἀλλ᾽ ἐπειγόμε-
428 νοι μαθεῖν. σκυθρωποὺς δὲ ὁρῶντες ἐτύπτοντο τὰ
μέτωπα καὶ διηρώτων, οἱ μὲν ὁμοῦ πάντας, οἱ δ᾽ ἕκαστον, ὡς εἶχεν ἕκαστός τις φιλίας ἢ γνώσεως ἐς
αὐτόν, ἐπιστρέφων τε καὶ πυνθανόμενος. ὡς δὲ οὐδεὶς
429 ἀπεκρίνετο, ἀνῴμωζον ὡς ἐπ᾽ ὀλέθρῳ σαφεῖ. καὶ οἱ
ἐπὶ τοῦ τείχους ἀκούοντες συνανῴμωζον αὐτοῖς, οὐκ
εἰδότες μὲν οὐδέν, ὡς δ᾽ ἐπὶ σαφεῖ καὶ μεγάλῳ κακῷ.
περὶ δὲ τὰς πύλας ὀλίγου μὲν αὐτοὺς καὶ συνεπάτουν,
ἐπιπίπτοντες ἀθρόοι, ὀλίγου δὲ καὶ διέσπασαν, εἰ μὴ
τοσόνδε ἔφασαν, ὅτι χρὴ τῇ γερουσίᾳ πρότερον ἐντυ-
430 χεῖν. τότε γὰρ οἱ μὲν διίσταντο αὐτοῖς, οἱ δὲ καὶ ὡδοποίουν ἐπιθυμίᾳ τοῦ θᾶσσον μαθεῖν. ὡς δὲ ἐς τὸ βουλευτήριον εἰσῆλθον, ἡ μὲν γερουσία τοὺς ἄλλους
μετεστήσατο καὶ μόνοι συνήδρευον ἐφ᾽ ἑαυτῶν, τὸ δὲ
431 πλῆθος ἔξω περιειστήκεσαν. οἱ δὲ πρέσβεις ἀπήγ-
γελλον πρῶτα μὲν τὸ κέλευσμα τῶν ὑπάτων· καὶ
εὐθὺς ἦν βοὴ τῆς γερουσίας, καὶ ὁ δῆμος ἔξω συν-

160

ginians may find some way of being able to endure them. Fate has brought us to such an extremity of need, that we are actually inviting you to lead your ships against our country." After they had spoken, they left, and Censorinus sailed along side them with twenty quinqueremes, and then anchored off Carthage. Some of the envoys made their escape on the journey, but most traveled in silence. 426

91. There were those among the Carthaginians who watched out from the walls for the arrival of the ambassadors and, annoyed with them at the delay, began to tear their hair. Others went out to meet them as they were still approaching, unwilling to wait, and pressing to find out the news. When they saw their sullen expression, they beat their foreheads and began to question them both as a group, and individually when someone encountered a friend or relation, accosting him and asking for information. Receiving no answer, they groaned aloud at what they regarded as their certain destruction. The men on the walls heard this and groaned with them without knowing anything for sure, but assuming a clear and great calamity. At the gates the ambassadors were all but trodden under foot by the crowds pressing in on them, and only avoided being torn limb from limb by saying that they must first meet with the council of elders. At that point some stood back from them, and others even made a way through for them in their desire to learn the news more quickly. When they entered the council chamber, the elders removed all the others and convened a meeting of themselves alone, while the crowd stood around outside. First of all, the ambassadors reported the order of the consuls. Immediately there was a roar from the elders, and the people 427 428 429 430 431

ἐβόα. ὡς δὲ ἐπῆγον οἱ πρέσβεις, ὅσα ἀντέλεξαν δι-
καιολογούμενοι καὶ δεόμενοι καὶ ἐς Ῥώμην πρεσβεῦσαι παραιτούμενοι, αὖθις ἦν τῆς βουλῆς σιγὴ βαθεῖα,
τὸ τέλος μαθεῖν περιμενούσης, καὶ ὁ δῆμος αὐτῇ συν-
εσιώπα.

432   92. Ὡς δὲ ἔμαθον, ὅτι μηδὲ πρεσβεύειν ἐπέτρεψαν,
ἠλάλαξαν ἐξαίσιον ὀδυρόμενοι, καὶ ὁ δῆμος ἐσέδρα-
μεν ἐς αὐτούς. καὶ ἀπὸ τοῦδε ἦν οἶστρος ἄλογός τε
καὶ μανιώδης, οἷον ἐν τοῖς βακχείοις πάθεσί φασι
433   τὰς μαινάδας ἀλλόκοτα καινουργεῖν. οἱ μὲν τῶν βουλευτῶν τοὺς περὶ τῶν ὁμήρων ἐσηγησαμένους ὡς
ἐξάρχους τῆς ἐνέδρας ἠκίζοντο καὶ διέσπων, οἱ δὲ
τοὺς συμβουλεύσαντας περὶ τῶν ὅπλων. οἱ δὲ τοὺς
πρέσβεις κατέλευον ὡς κακῶν ἀγγέλους, οἱ δὲ καὶ
434   περιέσυρον ἀνὰ τὴν πόλιν. ἕτεροι δὲ τοὺς Ἰταλούς, οἳ
ἔτι παρ' αὐτοῖς ὡς ἐν αἰφνιδίῳ καὶ ἀκηρύκτῳ κακῷ
ἦσαν, ἐλυμαίνοντο ποικίλως, ἐπιλέγοντες ὁμήρων
435   πέρι καὶ ὅπλων καὶ ἀπάτης ἀμύνεσθαι. οἰμωγῆς τε
ἅμα καὶ ὀργῆς καὶ δέους καὶ ἀπειλῆς ἡ πόλις ἐνεπέ-
πληστο, καὶ ἐν ταῖς ὁδοῖς ἀνεκάλουν τὰ φίλτατα καὶ
ἐς τὰ ἱερὰ ὡς ἐς ἄσυλα κατέφευγον καὶ τοὺς θεοὺς
ὠνείδιζον ὡς οὐδὲ σφίσιν αὐτοῖς ἐπικουρῆσαι δυναμέ-
436   νους. ἕτεροι δὲ ἐς τὰς ὁπλοθήκας ἰόντες ἔκλαιον,
ὁρῶντες κενάς· οἱ δ' ἐς τὰ νεώρια καταθέοντες ὠδύ-
ροντο τὰς ναῦς ὡς ἀπίστοις ἀνδράσιν ἐκδεδομένας.
καὶ τὰ ὀνόματά τινες τῶν ἐλεφάντων ἀνεκάλουν ὡς ἔτι

outside roared with them. But when the ambassadors went on to explain what counter arguments they had made, remonstrating and begging and asking permission to send an embassy to Rome, there was again complete silence in the council while they waited to hear what happened in the end; and the people remained silent with them.

92. On learning that they were not even allowed to send an embassy, the elders let out an extraordinary wail of lamentation, and the people ran in among them. After this, there followed a frenzy of unutterable madness, such as happens in Bacchic experiences, where they say that the maenads devise perverse new rites. Some assaulted and tore apart those councilors who had proposed the motion about the hostages, regarding them as the men who led them into the trap. Others did the same to those who had given the advice about the weapons. Others stoned the ambassadors as bringers of bad news and dragged them through the city. Yet others committed various outrages on the Italians who were still in Carthage, caught as they were in a sudden and unannounced horror, adding that they would take revenge for the deception committed in relation to the hostages and weapons. The city was filled with wailing, as well as anger and fear and threats. In the streets people invoked everything that was most dear to them, took refuge in the temples on the assumption that they were inviolate, and reproached the gods for not even being able to help themselves. Others went into the armories and wept to see them empty. Others again ran to the dockyards, bitterly regretting that they had surrendered their ships to treacherous men. Some shouted out the names of their elephants, as if they were still there, and denounced

432

433

434

435

436

παρόντων τούς τε προγόνους καὶ σφᾶς αὐτοὺς ἐλοι-
δόρουν, ὡς δέον μήτε ναῦς μήτε ἐλέφαντας μήτε πόρους[15] μήτε τὰ ὅπλα παραδόντας ἀποθανεῖν σὺν τῇ
437 πατρίδι ὡπλισμένῃ. μάλιστα δ' αὐτοὺς ἐς ὀργὴν
ἀνέκαιον αἱ μητέρες αἱ τῶν ὁμήρων, οἷά τινες ἐκ τρα-
γῳδίας ἐρινύες ἐντυγχάνουσαι μετ' ὀλολυγῆς ἑκάστῳ
καὶ τὴν ἔκδοσιν τῶν παίδων προφέρουσαι καὶ τὴν
ἑαυτῶν ἀπόρρησιν· ἐπεγέλων τε αὐτοῖς ὡς θεῶν ἀμυ-
438 νομένων αὐτοὺς ἀντὶ τῶν παίδων. ὀλίγον δ' ὅσον ἐσω-
φρόνει, τὰς πύλας ἀπέκλειε καὶ τὸ τεῖχος λίθων ἀντὶ
καταπελτῶν ἐπλήρουν.

439   93. Ἡ δὲ βουλὴ πολεμεῖν μὲν ἐψηφίσατο αὐτῆς
ἡμέρας καὶ τοὺς δούλους ἐκήρυξεν ἐλευθέρους εἶναι,
στρατηγοὺς δὲ εἵλοντο τῶν μὲν ἔξω πράξεων Ἀσρούβαν, ᾧ θάνατος ἐπικήρυκτος ἦν, ἔχοντα δισμυρίων
ἤδη σύνοδον ἀνδρῶν· καί τις ἐξέτρεχεν αὐτοῦ δεησό-
μενος μὴ μνησικακῆσαι τῇ πατρίδι ἐν ἐσχάτῳ κινδύνου μηδέ, ὧν ὑπ' ἀνάγκης ἠδικήθη Ῥωμαίων δέει, νῦν
ἀναφέρειν. ἐντὸς δὲ τειχῶν ᾑρέθη στρατηγὸς ἕτερος
440 Ἀσρούβας, θυγατριδοῦς Μασσανάσσου. ἔπεμψαν δὲ
καὶ ἐς τοὺς ὑπάτους, αἰτοῦντες αὖθις ἡμερῶν τριάκοντα ἀνοχάς, ἵνα πρεσβεύσειαν ἐς Ῥώμην. ἀποτυ-
χόντες δὲ καὶ τότε, ἐπὶ θαυμαστῆς ἐγίγνοντο μεταβολῆς τε καὶ τόλμης ὁτιοῦν παθεῖν μᾶλλον ἢ τὴν πόλιν
441 ἐκλιπεῖν. ταχὺ δὲ καὶ θάρσους ἐκ τῆς μεταβολῆς
ἐπίμπλαντο. καὶ δημιουργεῖα μὲν τὰ δημόσια τεμένη
καὶ ἱερὰ πάντα καὶ εἴ τι ἄλλο εὐρύχωρον ἦν, ἐγένετο·
εἰργάζοντο δὲ ὁμοῦ ἄνδρες τε καὶ γυναῖκες ἡμέρας τε

both their ancestors and themselves for not dying, as they should have, with their country under arms, and not having handed over ships and elephants and revenues and weapons. But it was the mothers of the hostages who particularly inflamed their anger: like avenging furies from a tragedy they shrieked at everyone they met, accusing them of giving up their children in the face of their resistance, but also mocking them as victims of divine vengeance exacted on behalf of the children. The few who kept their self-control closed the gates and piled stones on the walls to replace the catapults.

437

438

93. The same day, the Carthaginian council voted to declare war and proclaimed the slaves free. To be generals, they chose Hasdrubal for operations outside the city. He had been condemned to death, but had already collected a force of twenty thousand men. A messenger hurried out to ask him not to bear any malice to the city in its extreme danger, or to bring up the wrongs done to him under force of necessity caused by fear of the Romans. As commander inside the walls of the city, they chose another Hasdrubal, a grandson of Massinissa. They sent a message to the consuls, asking again for a truce of thirty days, to enable them to send a mission to Rome. But when they were turned down on this occasion too, a remarkable change came over them in the form of a determination to put up with anything rather than abandon their city. As a result of this change they were soon filled with courage. All the public precincts and temples, and any other open space, were turned into workshops. Day and night, men

439

440

441

---

[15] πόρους Goukowsky: φόρους codd: ὁμήρους prop. Mend.

καὶ νυκτός, [μὴ]¹⁶ ἀναπαυόμενοι καὶ σῖτον αἱρούμενοι
παρὰ μέρος, ἐπὶ ὅρῳ τακτῷ, θυρεοὺς ἑκατὸν ἡμέρας
ἑκάστης καὶ ξίφη τριακόσια καὶ καταπελτικὰ βέλη
χίλια, σαύνια δὲ καὶ λόγχας πεντακοσίας καὶ καταπέλτας, ὅσους δυνηθεῖεν. ἐς δὲ τὰς ἐπιτάσεις αὐτῶν
ἀπέκειραν τὰς γυναῖκας τριχῶν ἑτέρων ἀπορίᾳ.

442   94. Καὶ οἱ μὲν ἐν τούτῳ σπουδῆς καὶ παρασκευῆς
ἦσαν, οἱ δ᾽ ὕπατοι τάχα μέν τι καὶ ὄκνῳ, μὴ εὐθὺς
ἐπιχειρεῖν ἐς ἔργον ἀλλόκοτον, ἅμα δὲ καὶ τὴν πόλιν
ἄνοπλον οὖσαν λήψεσθαι κατὰ κράτος, ὅτε θέλοιεν,
ἡγούμενοι, διέμελλον ἔτι καὶ ἐνδώσειν αὐτοὺς ἐνόμι-
ζον ἐκ τῆς ἀπορίας, οἷον ἐν τοῖς δυσχερέσι γίγνεσθαι
φιλεῖ, εὐθὺς μὲν ἀντιλέγειν, προϊόντος δὲ χρόνου καὶ
443   λογισμοῦ φόβον ἅπτεσθαι τῶν ἀπειθούντων. ἃ καὶ
τῶν Καρχηδονίων τις αὐτῶν, εἰκάσας σφῶν ἤδη τὸ
δέος ἅπτεσθαι, ἐτόλμησεν ὡς ἐπὶ δή τι ἄλλο παρελθὼν ἐς τὸ μέσον εἰπεῖν, ὅτι χρὴ τῶν κακῶν ἐπιλέγεσθαι τὰ μετριώτερα, ὄντας ἀνόπλους, οὕτω σαφῶς
444   εἰπὼν¹⁷ τὴν γνώμην ‹. . .› Μασσανάσσης δὲ ἤχθετο
Ῥωμαίοις καὶ ἔφερε βαρέως, ὅτι τὴν Καρχηδονίων
δύναμιν αὐτὸς ἐς γόνυ βαλὼν ἄλλους ἑώρα τῷ ἐπι-
γράμματι αὐτῆς ἐπιτρέχοντάς τε καὶ οὐ κοινώσαντας
αὐτῷ, πρὶν ἐπελθεῖν, ὡς ἐν τοῖς πάλαι πολέμοις
445   ἐποίουν. ὅμως δ᾽ αὐτοῦ τῶν ὑπάτων ἀποπειρωμένων

16 μὴ del Schweig.
17 εἰπόντα codd: εἰπὼν prop. Schweig.

166

and women worked together, with set times for taking turns to rest and eat. Every day they produced one hundred shields, three hundred swords, one thousand catapult bolts, five hundred javelins and spears, and as many catapults as they could manage. For the torsion springs, in the absence of any other fibers, women cut off their hair.

94. While the Carthaginians were energetically making their preparations, the consuls continually delayed, perhaps hesitating to carry out immediately an act of perversity, and at the same time believing that they could take the unarmed city by storm whenever they liked. They also thought that the Carthaginians would surrender for lack of supplies, as usually happens with desperate people, when initially there is resistance, but with the passage of time and the opportunity for rational thought, fear takes hold of those minded to disobey. A certain Carthaginian, suspecting that they had already been gripped by fear, dared to come forward in public, apparently on another matter, and say this, that since they had no weapons, they had to choose the lesser of the evils facing them—thus clearly stating his opinion ‹. . . ›[40] Massinissa, however, was annoyed with the Romans, taking it badly that while he himself was the one who had brought Carthaginian power to its knees, he had to watch others making off with the credit for it, and they did not even inform him before they invaded, as they had done in previous wars. Nevertheless, when the consuls tested him by asking for his

[40] Editors have suspected a lacuna in the text here, and the manuscripts would require one. Schweighäuser's reading, adopted here, does not necessitate one, although the sudden transition to Massinissa implies that something is missing.

442

443

444

445

APPIAN

καὶ καλούντων ἐπὶ συμμαχίαν ἔφη τὴν συμμαχίαν
πέμψειν, ὅταν αἴσθηται δεομένων. καὶ μετ᾽ οὐ πολὺ
πέμψας ἤρετο, εἴ τινος ἤδη δέονται. οἱ δὲ οὐ φέροντες
αὐτοῦ τὸ σοβαρόν, ἤδη δέ τι καὶ ἀπιστοῦντες ὡς δυσ-
μεναίνοντι ἀπεκρίναντο προσπέμψειν, ὅτε δεηθεῖεν.
446 περὶ δὲ ἀγορᾶς τῷ στρατῷ καὶ πάνυ ἐφρόντιζον, ἐκ
μόνης ἔχοντες Ἀδρυμητοῦ καὶ Λέπτεως καὶ Θάψου
καὶ Ἰτύκης καὶ Ἀχόλλης· τὰ γὰρ δὴ λοιπὰ Λιβύης ἦν
ἔτι πάντα ὑπὸ Ἀσρούβᾳ, ὅθεν ἐκεῖνος ἀγορὰν ἐς Καρχηδόνα ἔπεμπεν.
447   95. Ὀλίγων δ᾽ ἐς ταῦτα διατριφθεισῶν ἡμερῶν οἱ
μὲν ὕπατοι προσῄεσαν ἄμφω τῇ πόλει τῶν Καρχηδο-
448 νίων, ἐς μάχην ἐσκευασμένοι, καὶ ἐπεχείρουν. ἦν δὲ
ἡ πόλις ἐν μυχῷ κόλπου μεγίστου, χερρονήσῳ τι μάλιστα προσεοικυῖα· αὐχὴν γὰρ αὐτὴν ἀπὸ τῆς ἠπείρου
449 διεῖργεν, εὖρος ὢν πέντε καὶ εἴκοσι σταδίων. ἀπὸ δὲ
τοῦ αὐχένος ταινία στενὴ καὶ ἐπιμήκης, ἡμισταδίου
μάλιστα τὸ πλάτος, ἐπὶ δυσμὰς ἐχώρει, μέση λίμνης
τε καὶ τῆς θαλάσσης <. . .> ἁπλῷ τείχει περίκρημνα
ὄντα, τὰ δὲ πρὸς μεσημβρίαν ἐς ἤπειρον, ἔνθα καὶ ἡ
450 Βύρσα ἦν, ἐπὶ τοῦ αὐχένος, τριπλῷ τείχει. τούτων δ᾽
ἕκαστον ἦν ὕψος μὲν πηχῶν τριάκοντα, χωρὶς ἐπάλξεών τε καὶ πύργων, οἳ ἐκ διπλέθρου διαστήματος
αὐτοῖς τετρώροφοι περιέκειντο, βάθος δὲ ποδῶν τριάκοντα, διώροφον δ᾽ ἦν ἑκάστου τείχους τὸ ὕψος, καὶ

41 These were all coastal towns.
42 Schweighaüser suggested, surely correctly, that the lacuna

168

military assistance, he said he would send help whenever he thought they needed it. Shortly after, he sent off to ask them if they needed anything now. They did not like his impertinence, and already distrustful of him as someone ill-disposed, they answered that they would send for him when they needed him. But they were very anxious about   446 supplies for the army, which they were only getting from Hadrumetum, Leptis, Thapsus, Utica, and Acholla.[41] For Hasdrubal still held all the rest of Africa, and from here he sent supplies to Carthage.

95. Having spent a few days on this matter, the consuls   447 both marched against the city of Carthage prepared for battle, and began their attack. The city was located in the   448 innermost part of a very large bay, and closely resembled a peninsula. For an isthmus, twenty five stades wide, kept it separate from the mainland. From this isthmus a long   449 and narrow strip of land, about half a stade wide, extended westward, between a lagoon and the sea ‹. . .› with a single wall,[42] as it was very steep there, while toward the south and the mainland, where The Hide lay on the isthmus, with a triple wall. Each wall was thirty cubits high,   450 not counting the parapets and towers, which were four stories high and thirty feet deep, and were situated at intervals of two plethra all the way around.[43] In its elevation, every wall had two levels. Inside the wall, which was hol-

must contain something like, "‹The city was walled all round, on the sea side› with a single wall, as it was very steep there . . ."

[43] A cubit was originally the length of a forearm, from the elbow to the tip of the middle finger. Its exact length differed from one culture to another, but the Roman cubit was 1½ feet (44.4 cm.). A plethron was about 100 feet (30 m.).

ἐν αὐτῷ, κοίλῳ τε ὄντι καὶ στεγανῷ, κάτω μὲν ἐστάθμευον ἐλέφαντες τριακόσιοι, καὶ θησαυροὶ παρέκειντο
αὐτοῖς τῶν τροφῶν, ἱπποστάσια δ᾽ ὑπὲρ αὐτοὺς ἦν
τετρακισχιλίοις ἵπποις καὶ ταμεῖα χιλοῦ τε καὶ κριθῆς ἀνδράσιν τε καταγωγαί, πεζοῖς μὲν ἐς δισμυρίους, ἱππεῦσι δὲ ἐς τετρακισχιλίους. τοσήδε παρα-
σκευὴ πολέμου διετέτακτο σταθμεύειν ἐν τοῖς τείχεσι
451   μόνοις. γωνία δ᾽, ἢ παρὰ τὴν γλῶσσαν ἐκ τοῦδε τοῦ
τείχους ἐπὶ τοὺς λιμένας περιέκαμπτεν, ἀσθενὴς ἦν
μόνη καὶ ταπεινὴ καὶ ἠμέλητο ἐξ ἀρχῆς.

452   96. Οἱ δὲ λιμένες ἐς ἀλλήλους διεπλέοντο, καὶ
ἔσπλους ἐκ πελάγους ἐς αὐτοὺς ἦν εἰς εὖρος ποδῶν
ἑβδομήκοντα, ὃν ἁλύσεσιν ἀπέκλειον σιδηραῖς. ὁ μὲν
δὴ πρῶτος ἐμπόροις ἀνεῖτο, καὶ δείγματα[18] ἦν ἐν αὐτῷ
πυκνὰ καὶ ποικίλα· τοῦ δ᾽ ἐντὸς ἐν μέσῳ νῆσος ἦν,
καὶ κρηπῖσι μεγάλαις ἥ τε νῆσος καὶ ὁ λιμὴν διεί-
453   ληπτο. νεωρίων τε ἔγεμον αἱ κρηπῖδες αἵδε ἐς ναῦς
διακοσίας καὶ εἴκοσι πεποιημένων καὶ ταμιείων ἐπὶ
τοῖς νεωρίοις ἐς τριηριτικὰ σκεύη. κίονες δ᾽ ἑκάστου
νεωσοίκου προὖχον Ἰωνικοὶ δύο, ἐς εἰκόνα στοᾶς τὴν
454   ὄψιν τοῦ τε λιμένος καὶ τῆς νήσου περιφέροντες. ἐπὶ
δὲ τῆς νήσου σκηνὴ πεποίητο τῷ ναυάρχῳ, ὅθεν ἔδει
καὶ τὸν σαλπικτὴν σημαίνειν καὶ τὸν κήρυκα προλέ-
γειν καὶ τὸν ναύαρχον ἐφορᾶν. ἔκειτο δ᾽ ἡ νῆσος κατὰ
τὸν ἔσπλουν καὶ ἀνετέτατο ἰσχυρῶς, ἵνα ὅ τε ναύαρχος τὰ ἐκ πελάγους πάντα ἐφορᾷ καὶ τοῖς ἐπιπλέου-

[18] δείγματα Goukowsky: πείσματα codd.

170

lowed out and had a roof, the lower level accommodated three hundred elephants, with food stores for them alongside, and above them stabling for four thousand horses with barns for forage and barley. There were also quarters for troops, for about twenty thousand infantry and four thousand cavalrymen. Such was Carthage's military capacity for providing quarters in the walls alone. The angle   451 which bent around along the tongue of land from this wall to the harbors was low and the only weak spot; it had been neglected right from the beginning.

96. The harbors were connected to each other and   452 there was an entrance to them from the sea about seventy feet wide, which they could close off with iron chains. The first harbor, where there were crowded bazaars[44] of all sorts, was open to merchants. In the middle of the inner harbor was an island, and both the island and the harbor were provided at intervals with long quays. The quays   453 were full of slipways designed for two hundred and twenty ships, and there were storerooms above them for the triremes' equipment. Two Ionic columns stood in front of each shipshed, which made the harbor and island look like a continuous portico. A command post had been erected   454 on the island for the commander of the fleet, and from here the trumpets were supposed to give signals, the herald to proclaim orders and the commander to oversee operations. The island lay opposite the entrance to the harbor, and rose to a considerable height, enabling the commander of the fleet to observe everything that was happening out at sea, while those approaching by sea

[44] The manuscripts read "many cables/ropes of all sorts."

455 σιν ἀφανὴς ᾖ τῶν ἔνδον ἡ ὄψις ἡ ἀκριβής. οὐ μὴν
οὐδὲ τοῖς ἐσπλεύσασιν ἐμπόροις εὐθὺς ἦν τὰ νεώρια
σύνοπτα· τεῖχός τε γὰρ αὐτοῖς διπλοῦν περιέκειτο καὶ
πύλαι, αἳ τοὺς ἐμπόρους ἀπὸ τοῦ πρώτου λιμένος ἐς
τὴν πόλιν ἐσέφερον, οὐ διερχομένους τὰ νεώρια.

456   97. Οὕτω μὲν εἶχεν ἡ πόλις ἡ Καρχηδονίων ἡ τότε,
οἱ δ᾽ ὕπατοι διελόμενοι τὸ ἔργον ᾔεσαν ἐπὶ τοὺς πολεμίους, Μανίλιος μὲν ἀπὸ τῆς ἠπείρου κατὰ τὸν αὐ-
χένα, ἐγχώσων τε τὴν τάφρον καὶ βραχὺ ἐπιτείχισμα
τι[19] ἐπ᾽ αὐτῇ βιασόμενος καὶ ἐπ᾽ ἐκείνῳ τὰ ὑψηλὰ
τείχη· Κηνσωρῖνος δὲ κλίμακας ἔκ τε γῆς καὶ νεῶν
457 ἐπέφερε κατὰ τὴν εὐτελῆ τοῦ τείχους γωνίαν. ἄμφω
δ᾽ ὡς ἀνόπλων κατεφρόνουν, ἕως ἐντυχόντες ὅπλοις τε
καινοῖς καὶ ἀνδρῶν προθυμίᾳ παραλόγῳ κατεπλάγησαν καὶ ὑπεχώρουν. καὶ εὐθὺς αὐτοῖς τοῦτο πρῶτον
ἀντεκεκρούκει, ἐλπίσασιν ἀμαχεὶ λήψεσθαι τὴν πό-
458 λιν. ὡς δὲ καὶ αὖθις ἐπεχείρουν καὶ αὖθις ἀπετύγχανον, τὰ μὲν τῶν Καρχηδονίων φρονήματα ἐπήρτο, οἱ
δ᾽ ὕπατοι δεδιότες Ἀσρούβαν ὄπισθεν σφῶν ὑπὲρ τὴν
λίμνην οὐκ ἐκ μακροῦ διαστήματος ἐστρατοπεδευμέ-
νον ὠχύρουν καὶ αὐτοὶ δύο στρατόπεδα, Κηνσωρῖνος
μὲν ἐπὶ τῆς λίμνης ὑπὸ τοῖς τείχεσι τῶν πολεμίων,
459 Μανίλιος δ᾽ ἐν τῷ αὐχένι τῆς ἐς τὴν ἤπειρον ὁδοῦ. ὡς
δὲ αὐτοῖς ἐγήγερτο τὰ στρατόπεδα, ὁ Κηνσωρῖνος ἐπὶ
ὕλῃ ἐς μηχανὰς διέπλευσεν διὰ τῆς λίμνης· καὶ ἀπ-
έβαλεν ὑλοτόμων ἐς πεντακοσίους ἄνδρας ὅπλα τε
πολλά, Ἱμίλκωνος αἰφνίδιον αὐτῷ, τοῦ Καρχηδονίων
ἱππάρχου, προσπεσόντος, ᾧ Φαμέας ἐπώνυμον ἦν.

could get no clear view of what was happening inside the
harbor. The naval dockyards were not even immediately   455
visible to merchants who sailed in. For a double wall surrounded them, and there were gates which enabled the
merchants to get from the first harbor to the city without
going by way of the docks.

97. Such was the city of Carthage at that time. The   456
consuls divided the task facing them and made their way
against the enemy. Manilius approached from the mainland along the isthmus, intending to fill in the ditch, force
his way over a sort of low defensive wall overlooking it and
from there take the high walls. From both the land and
ships, Censorinus brought ladders up against the low section of the wall. Both of them underestimated the enemy,   457
assuming they had no weapons; but when they encountered new armaments and an unexpected enthusiasm in
the defenders, they were astonished and withdrew. Having expected to capture the city without a fight, they had
been checked at the very first attempt. A second attempt   458
and second failure raised the spirits of the Carthaginians,
while the consuls were uneasy about Hasdrubal, who had
encamped no great distance behind them on the other
side of the lagoon. They were fortifying two camps, Censorinus beside the lake under the enemy walls, Manilius
on the isthmus where the road led to the mainland. When   459
they had erected the camps, Censorinus crossed the lagoon to collect timber for siege engines, but Himilco, who
had the surname Phameas, the Carthaginian cavalry commander, fell on him suddenly, and he lost about five hundred men in the woodcutting operation. He did, however,

---

[19] τι Goukowsky: τὸ codd.

κομίσας δ' ὅμως τινὰ ὕλην μηχανὰς ἐποίησεν καὶ
460 κλίμακας. καὶ πάλιν ἐπεχείρουν ἄμφω τῇ πόλει καὶ
ἀπετύγχανον ὁμοίως. Μανίλιος μὲν οὖν μικρὸν ἔτι
προσκαμὼν καὶ μόλις τι τοῦ προτειχίσματος καταβαλὼν ἀπέγνω μηδὲ ἐπιχειρεῖν ἔτι ταύτῃ·

461   98. Κηνσωρῖνος δὲ χώσας τι τῆς λίμνης παρὰ τὴν
ταινίαν, ἵνα εὐρυτέρα εἴη, δύο μηχανὰς κριοφόρους
ἐπῆγε μεγάλας, τὴν μὲν ὠθουμένην ἑξακισχιλίοις πεζοῖς, ἡγουμένων τῶν χιλιάρχων, τὴν δὲ ὑπὸ τῶν ἐρε-
462 τῶν, ἡγουμένων καὶ τοῖσδε ναυάρχων. φιλονεικίας δ',
ὡς ἐν ἴσῳ καὶ ὁμοίῳ ἔργῳ, τοῖς τε ὑπηρέταις καὶ τοῖς
ἄρχουσιν αὐτῶν γενομένης συνέπεσέ τι τοῦ τείχους,
καὶ τὰ ἐντὸς ἤδη κατεφαίνετο. Καρχηδόνιοι δὲ καὶ ὡς
αὐτοὺς ἀπωσάμενοι τὰ πεσόντα νυκτὸς ᾠκοδόμουν.
463 οὐκ ἀρκούσης δ' ἐς τὸ ἔργον αὐτοῖς τῆς νυκτός, δεδιότες περὶ τῷ ἤδη γεγονότι, μὴ καὶ τοῦτο μεθ' ἡμέραν
αἱ Ῥωμαίων μηχαναὶ νεότευκτον καὶ ὑγρὸν ἔτι κατα-
βάλοιεν, ἐξέδραμον ἐπὶ τὰ μηχανήματα τῶν πολεμίων, οἱ μὲν σὺν ὅπλοις, οἱ δὲ γυμνοὶ λαμπάδας ἠμ-
μένας ἔχοντες, καὶ ἐνέπρησαν μὲν οὐχ ὅλα (οὐ γὰρ
ἔφθασαν Ῥωμαίων ἐπιδραμόντων), ἀχρεῖα δ' ὅλα
464 ποιήσαντες ἀνεχώρουν. ἅμα δ' ἡμέρᾳ Ῥωμαίοις ἐπέ-
πεσεν ὁρμὴ διὰ τοῦ πεσόντος οὔπω τελέως ἐγηγερμέ-
νου βιάσασθαι καὶ ἐσδραμεῖν· καὶ γάρ τι πεδίον
ἐντὸς ἐφαίνετο εὐφυὲς ἐς μάχην, ἐν ᾧ τοὺς ἐνόπλους
ἔστησαν οἱ Καρχηδόνιοι κατὰ μετώπου, τοὺς δ' ἀνόπλους αὐτοῖς ἐπέταξαν σὺν λίθοις ὀπίσω καὶ ξύλοις

collect some wood, and built some siege engines and ladders. Both consuls then made another attack on the city, but were equally unsuccessful. Manilius put his hand to the task for a little longer, and although he managed with difficulty to knock down a part of the outworks, he gave up on making any further attacks at this location.   460

98. Censorinus filled in part of the lagoon along the tongue of land, to make it broader, and then brought up two huge battering rams, one pushed along by six thousand infantrymen under the command of the military tribunes, the other by the rowers, led by their naval officers. Competition involving both the men and the officers developed between the two groups, engaged as they were on a similar and equally important task, and they knocked down part of the wall, now revealing the interior of the city. But even so, the Carthaginians beat them off, and during the night began to rebuild what had been knocked down. As the night was not long enough for the job, and fearing that during the day the Roman siege engines would destroy the work they had already done, as it was newly built and still wet, they made a sortie, some armed, others unarmed but carrying lit torches, to attack the enemy siege engines, and set fire to them, although the Romans counterattacked before they could burn them completely. Having rendered them totally unusable, the Carthaginians withdrew. Next day, the Roman impulse was to force their way in by overrunning the part of the wall that had been knocked down, but not yet fully repaired. For a flat space could be seen inside ideal for fighting, where the Carthaginians awaited the rush of the attackers, having stationed armed men there at the front, and behind them men who did not have weapons but did   461   462   463   464

175

ἑτέρους τε πολλοὺς διαθέντες ἐπὶ τῶν περικειμένων
οἰκιῶν ἀνέμενον τοὺς ἐπερχομένους ἐσδραμεῖν. οἱ δ'
ἔτι μᾶλλον ἠρεθίζοντο ὡς ὑπὸ γυμνῶν ἀνδρῶν κατα-
465 φρονούμενοι καὶ θρασέως ἐπεπήδων. Σκιπίων δέ, ὃς
μετ' ὀλίγον εἷλεν Καρχηδόνα καὶ παρὰ τοῦτο Ἀφρι-
κανὸς ἐπεκλήθη, χιλιαρχῶν τότε ᾤκνει καὶ τοὺς ἑαυτοῦ λόχους ἐς πολλὰ διελὼν καὶ στήσας ἐκ διαστήματος ἐπὶ τοῦ τειχίου κατιέναι μὲν εἰς τὴν πόλιν
οὐκ εἴα, τοὺς δὲ ἐσελθόντας ἐξωθουμένους ὑπὸ τῶν
Καρχηδονίων πάντοθεν αὐτοῖς ἐπιπεσόντων ὑπεδέ-
χετο καὶ περιέσῳζεν. καὶ τοῦτο πρῶτον αὐτὸν ἐπὶ δόξης ἐποίησεν, εὐβουλότερον τοῦ στρατηγοῦ φανέντα.

466   99. Κυνὸς δ' ἦν ἐπιτολή, καὶ τὸ Κηνσωρίνου στρατόπεδον ἐνόσει, σταθμεῦον ἐπὶ λίμνῃ σταθεροῦ καὶ
βαρέος ὕδατος καὶ ὑπὸ τείχεσι μεγίστοις, οὐ κατα-
πνεόμενον ἐκ τῆς θαλάσσης. ὅθεν ὁ Κηνσωρῖνος ἐς
τὴν θάλασσαν ἀπὸ τῆς λίμνης μετεστρατοπέδευσεν.
467 καὶ οἱ Καρχηδόνιοι, ὅτε γίγνοιτο πνεῦμα ἐς τοὺς Ῥωμαίους ἐπίφορον, σκάφας φρυγάνων καὶ στυππίου
εἷλκον ὑπὸ τοῖς τείχεσιν, οὐ καθορώμενοι τοῖς πολεμίοις, ἀπὸ κάλων· εἰ δὲ ἐπικάμπτοντες ἔμελλον
γενήσεσθαι καταφανεῖς, θεῖον αὐταῖς καὶ πίσσαν ἐπι-
χέοντες ἀνέτεινον τὰ ἱστία καὶ πλήσαντες ἀνέμου πῦρ
ἐνέβαλον ἐς τὰ σκάφη. τὰ δὲ τῷ τε ἀνέμῳ καὶ τῇ
ῥοπῇ τοῦ πυρὸς ἐς τὰς Ῥωμαίων ναῦς ἐωθεῖτο καὶ

have stones and wooden clubs; and they had put many
others on the roofs of surrounding houses. The Romans
were even more annoyed to think that they were the object
of contempt for unarmed men, and rushed at them
overconfidently. But Scipio, who shortly afterward cap-   465
tured Carthage and was awarded the additional name,
Africanus, for this service, was at the time a military tribune and held back: dividing his centuries into many
separate groups, he positioned them at intervals on the
walls and refused to let them go down into the city. The
Roman troops entering the city were beaten back by the
Carthaginians, who fell on them from all sides, but Scipio
took them in and saved them. This was the first boost to
his reputation, as he had shown himself more prudent
than the commanding officer.

99. With the rising of the dog star,[45] sickness began to   466
affect Censorinus' camp, as it was located beside a stag-
nant lagoon of polluted water, under very high walls where
sea breezes could not reach. For this reason Censorinus
moved his camp from the lagoon to the sea. But when the   467
wind blew toward the Romans, the Carthaginians would
use ropes to pull small boats filled with tow and firewood
along under the walls, where they could not be overlooked
by the enemy. At the point where they turned and were
just about to be visible, they poured on brimstone and
pitch, raised the sails and when the wind filled them, set
fire to the boats. The wind and momentum of the fire
drove them into the Roman ships, damaging them and

[45] The dog star, Sirius, rises (in the sense that it becomes visible on the horizon before the rising sun makes it invisible—its
heliacal rising) about July 28.

468 ἐλυμαίνετο καὶ ὀλίγου τὸν στόλον κατέφλεξεν. μετὰ
δὲ οὐ πολὺ Κηνσωρῖνος μὲν ἐς Ῥώμην ᾤχετο ἀρχαι-
ρεσιάσων, οἱ δὲ Καρχηδόνιοι τῷ Μανιλίῳ θρασύτε-
ρον ἐπέκειντο· καὶ νυκτός, οἳ μὲν ὅπλα ἔχοντες, οἳ δὲ
γυμνοί, σανίδας φέροντες ἐπετίθεσαν τῇ κατὰ σφᾶς
τάφρῳ τοῦ Μανιλίου, καὶ τὸ χαράκωμα διέσπων.
469 ἀπορουμένων δὲ ὡς ἐν νυκτὶ τῶν ἔνδον ὁ Σκιπίων ἐξέ-
δραμεν σὺν ἱππεῦσιν ἐκ τοῦ στρατοπέδου κατὰ πύλας
ἄλλας, ἔνθα οὐδεὶς πόλεμος, καὶ περιδραμὼν τοὺς
Καρχηδονίους κατεφόβησεν. οἱ δὲ ἀνεχώρουν ἐς τὴν
πόλιν. καὶ δεύτερον ὁ Σκιπίων ἐδόκει τῷδε τῷ ἔργῳ
περισῶσαι Ῥωμαίους, ἐν νυκτὶ θορυβουμένους.

470   100. Ὁ δὲ Μανίλιος τὸ μὲν στρατόπεδον ἔτι μᾶλλον
ὠχύρου, τεῖχός τε ἀντὶ χάρακος αὐτῷ περιτιθεὶς καὶ
ἐπίνειον φρούριον ἐγείρων ἐπὶ τῆς θαλάσσης διὰ τὴν
καταπλέουσαν ἀγοράν· τραπεὶς δ' ἐς τὰ μεσόγαια μυρίοις πεζοῖς καὶ ἱππεῦσι δισχιλίοις τὴν χώραν ἐπόρθει, ξυλευόμενός τε καὶ χορτολογῶν καὶ ἀγορὰν συλ-
λέγων· ἡγεῖτο δ' ἀεὶ τῶν προνομευόντων χιλίαρχος
471 ἕτερος παρ' ἕτερον. καὶ Φαμέας, ὁ ἵππαρχος ὁ τῶν
Λιβύων, νέος τε ὢν ἔτι καὶ θρασύτερος ἐς μάχας, καὶ
ἵπποις χρώμενος σμικροῖς καὶ ταχέσι καὶ ποηφαγοῦ-
σιν, ὅτε μηδὲν εἴη, καὶ φέρουσι δίψος, εἰ δεήσειε, καὶ
λιμόν, ὑποκρυπτόμενος ἐν λόχμαις ἢ φάραγξιν, ὅπῃ
τι ἀμελούμενον ἴδοι, ἐφίπτατο ἐξ ἀφανοῦς ὥς τις αἰε-
τὸς καὶ λυμηνάμενος ἀπεπήδα· ὅτε δὲ Σκιπίων ἄρχοι,
472 οὐδαμοῦ οὐδ' ἐπεφαίνετο. ὁ γάρ τοι Σκιπίων ἀεὶ συν-
τεταγμένους ἦγε τοὺς πεζοὺς καὶ τοὺς ἱππέας τῶν

almost burning the whole fleet. Not long after, while Cen- 468
sorinus went off to Rome to preside over the elections,
the Carthaginians began to beleaguer Manilius more daringly.
One night, a force of armed and unarmed men brought
planks to bridge the ditch Manilius had constructed
against them, and started tearing down the palisade. The 469
men inside got into difficulties, as happens at night, but
Scipio escaped from the camp with some horsemen by
another gate, where there was no fighting, and riding
around to the front, caused alarm among the Carthaginians who withdrew into the city. So for a second time
Scipio appeared with his action to have rescued the Romans, this time from their confusion in the dark.

100. Manilius strengthened his camp still further by 470
building a wall around it instead of a palisade and estab-
lishing a naval fort by the sea to protect his incoming
supplies. Turning his attention inland, he ravaged the
country with ten thousand infantry and two thousand cavalry, while collecting wood, fodder and food; the military
tribunes took turns in command of the foraging parties.
Phameas, commander of the African cavalry, still a young 471
man and very keen to fight, used small, fast horses who ate
grass when there was nothing else and could go without
food and water when necessary. Hiding in the thickets and
gullies, he would observe where the Romans were not
paying attention, and fly down on them unnoticed like an
eagle, before inflicting casualties and turning away again.
But whenever Scipio was in command, Phameas was no- 472
where to be seen, as Scipio always kept his infantry in
battle order and made sure the cavalry remained mounted.

ἵππων ἐπιβεβηκότας· ἔν τε ταῖς προνομαῖς οὐ πρὶν
διέλυε τὴν σύνταξιν ἢ τὸ πεδίον, ὃ ἔμελλεν θεριεῖν,
ἱππεῦσι καὶ ὁπλίταις περιλάβοι· καὶ τότε κυκλῶν
αὐτὸς ἑτέραις ἴλαις ἱππέων αἰεὶ περιῄει καὶ τῶν θερι-
ζόντων τὸν ἀποσκιδνάμενον ἢ ἐξιόντα τοῦ κύκλου
πικρῶς ἐκόλαζεν.

473   101. Ὅθεν οἱ Φαμέας οὐκ ἐπεχείρει μόνῳ. καὶ
γιγνομένου τοῦδε συνεχῶς τὸ μὲν κλέος ηὔξετο τῷ
Σκιπίωνι, οἱ δ᾽ ἕτεροι χιλίαρχοι κατὰ φθόνον ἐλογο-
ποίουν ξενίαν ἐκ πατέρων εἶναι Φαμέᾳ πρὸς Σκιπίωνα,
474 τὸν τοῦδε πάππον. Λιβύων δὲ τοῖς ἐς πύργους καὶ
φρούρια, ἃ πολλὰ ἦν ἐν τῇ χώρᾳ, καταφεύγουσιν οἱ
μὲν ἄλλοι χιλίαρχοι σπενδόμενοι καὶ μεθιέντες ἐπε-
τίθεντο ἀπιοῦσιν, ὁ δὲ Σκιπίων ἐς τὰ οἴκοι παρέπεμπεν, καὶ ἀπὸ τοῦδε οὐ πρὶν ἢ Σκιπίωνα ἀφικέσθαι
475 συνετίθετο οὐδείς. τοσαύτη δόξα αὐτοῦ ἀνδρείας τε
πέρι καὶ πίστεως καὶ παρὰ τοῖς ἰδίοις δι᾽ ὀλίγου γε-
476 γένητο καὶ παρὰ τοῖς πολεμίοις. ἐπανελθόντων δ᾽
αὐτῶν ἀπὸ τῆς προνομῆς ἐς τὸ στρατόπεδον οἱ Καρχηδόνιοι νυκτὸς ἐπέθεντο τῷ ἐπινείῳ· καὶ θόρυβος ἦν
ποικίλος, συνεπηχούντων ἐς ἔκπληξιν τῶν ἐν ἄστει
477 Καρχηδονίων. ὁ μὲν οὖν Μανίλιος τὸν στρατὸν ἔνδον
συνεῖχεν ὡς ἐν ἀγνοίᾳ τοῦ κακοῦ· ὁ δὲ Σκιπίων ἱππέων ἴλας δέκα λαβὼν ἐπῆγε μετὰ δάδων ἡμμένων,
προειπὼν διὰ τὴν νύκτα μὴ συμπλέκεσθαι, περιτρέ-
χειν δὲ σὺν τῷ πυρὶ καὶ τὸ πλῆθος ἐπιφαίνειν καὶ
φόβον ἐμπεσουμένων παρέχειν αἰεί, μέχρι ταρασσό-
μενοι διχόθεν οἱ Καρχηδόνιοι κατεπλάγησαν καὶ ἐς

While foraging, he never broke formation until he had posted cavalry and infantrymen all around the area he was going to harvest. At that point, he himself would always circle around with other cavalry squadrons, and impose heavy penalties on any of the harvesters who fell behind or went outside the circle.

101. For this reason Scipio was the only one Phameas would not attack, and as this happened repeatedly, Scipio's reputation grew, while the other military tribunes made up a story out of jealousy that Phameas and Scipio were ancestral guest friends since the time of Scipio's grandfather. Certain Africans had taken refuge in towers and forts of which there were many on the land. The other tribunes would make terms with these men to let them go free, and then attack them as they left, but Scipio would accompany them to their homes. As a result of this, no one would make an agreement before Scipio arrived. To such an extent had his reputation for courage and good faith grown in a short time among both his own men and the enemy. When the Romans returned to camp from the foraging expedition, the Carthaginians made a night attack on their naval fort, which caused widespread confusion, the inhabitants of the city exacerbating the consternation by shouting at the same time. So Manilius kept his army inside the fort, in apparent ignorance of the trouble. But Scipio took command of ten troops of cavalry and gave them lit torches, with orders not to engage with the enemy because of the dark, but to ride around with their torches giving the impression that they were numerous and instilling fear the whole time that they would attack. Eventually the Carthaginians, harassed on both sides, were panicked into

473

474

475

476

477

APPIAN

478 τὴν πόλιν ἐσέφυγον. καὶ τόδε τοῖς Σκιπίωνος κατορ-
θώμασιν προσεγίγνετο. ἦν τε διὰ στόματος ἐπὶ πᾶσιν
ἔργοις ὡς μόνος ἄξιος Παύλου τε τοῦ πατρός, τοῦ
Μακεδόνας ἑλόντος, καὶ τῶν Σκιπιώνων, ἐς οὓς κατὰ
θέσιν ἀνείληπτο.

479 102. Μανιλίου δὲ ἐς Νέφεριν ὁδεύοντος ἐπὶ Ἀσρούβαν ἐδυσχέραινεν ὁ Σκιπίων, ὁρῶν πάντα ἀπόκρημνα
καὶ φάραγγας καὶ λόχμας καὶ τὰ ὑψηλὰ προειλημ-
μένα. ὡς δ᾽ ἀπὸ σταδίων τριῶν ἐγίγνοντο τοῦ Ἀσρούβα καὶ ἔς τι ῥεῦμα καταβάντας ἐχρῆν ἀναβαίνειν
ἐπὶ τὸν Ἀσρούβαν, ἐνέκειτο δὴ τότε καὶ συνεβούλευε
στραφῆναι ὡς ἄλλου καιροῦ καὶ μηχανῆς ἄλλης ἐπὶ
480 τὸν Ἀσρούβαν δεομένους. ἀντιλεγόντων δὲ κατὰ
ζῆλον αὐτοῦ τῶν ἑτέρων χιλιάρχων καὶ μαλακίαν καὶ
οὐκ εὐβουλίαν ἡγουμένων, εἰ τοὺς πολεμίους ἰδόντες
ἀναχωρήσουσιν, ἐν ᾧ καὶ καταφρονοῦντες φεύγουσιν
ἐπικείσονται, δεύτερα τούτων ἠξίου στρατόπεδον πρὸ
τοῦ Ῥεύματος ἐγεῖραι, ἵν᾽, εἰ βιασθεῖεν, ἔχοιεν ἀνα-
χώρησιν, οὐκ ὄντος αὐτοῖς νῦν οὐδ᾽ ὅποι καταφεύ-
481 γοιεν. οἱ δὲ καὶ τοῦτο ἐγέλων, καὶ τὸ ξίφος τις ἠπείλη-
σεν ἀπορρίψειν, εἰ μὴ Μανίλιος, ἀλλὰ Σκιπίων ἄρχοι.
διέβαινεν οὖν ὁ Μανίλιος, οὐδὲ τἆλλα ὢν ἐμπειρο-
πόλεμος, καὶ αὐτῷ περάσαντι ὁ Ἀσρούβας ἀπήντα,
482 φόνος τε ἦν πολὺς ἐξ ἑκατέρων. καὶ ὁ Ἀσρούβας,
ἀναδραμὼν ἐς τὸ φρούριον, ἔνθα μηδὲν παθεῖν ἐδύνατο, ἐφήδρευεν ἀπιοῦσιν ἐπιθέσθαι. οἱ δὲ σὺν μετα-
νοίᾳ τῶν γεγονότων ἀπεχώρουν, ἄχρι μὲν ἐπὶ τὸ

182

taking refuge back inside the city. This too was added to   478
the list of Scipio's successes. On the back of all these
deeds, men spoke of him as the only one worthy of his
father—Paullus, the conqueror of Macedonia—and of the
Scipios into whose family he had been adopted.[46]

102. When Manilius made an expedition to Nepheris   479
to attack Hasdrubal, Scipio had misgivings because he
could see all the cliffs and gullies and thickets, and that
the enemy had already occupied the high ground. At a
distance of three stades from Hasdrubal, they came down
to a river from which they had to climb to face him. Scipio
urgently advised Manilius at the time to turn back, saying
that they needed another opportunity and another way of
attacking Hasdrubal. The other tribunes argued against   480
him out of jealousy, maintaining that it would be cowardice rather than wise counsel if they withdrew after coming
within sight of the enemy, who would attack them con-
temptuously for fleeing. As a second best proposal, Scipio
thought they should build a camp in front of the stream,
so that if forced to yield they would have a refuge, whereas
at the moment they had nowhere to escape to. They   481
laughed at this too, one of them even threatening to throw
his sword away, if Scipio were to be in command rather
than Manilius. So Manilius, who was not at all experienced
in warfare, crossed the stream, and Hasdrubal came to
join battle with him. There was heavy slaughter on both
sides, until Hasdrubal retired into his fort, where nothing   482
could happen to him and he could watch for an opportunity to attack the Romans as they withdrew. The latter
regretted their actions, but fell back in good order as far

[46] For Scipio's adoption, see above, note 35.

ρεῦμα ἐν τάξει· δυσπόρου δ' ὄντος τοῦ ποταμοῦ καὶ
διαβάσεων ὀλίγων τε καὶ δυσχερῶν ἐς ἀταξίαν δι-
483 ηροῦντο ὑπ' ἀνάγκης. καὶ ὁ Ἀσρούβας καθορῶν ἐπέκειτο λαμπρῶς τότε μάλιστα καὶ πλῆθος ἔκτεινεν οὐδ'
ἀμυνομένων, ἀλλὰ φευγόντων. ἔπεσον δὲ καὶ τῶν χιλιάρχων τρεῖς, οἳ τὸν στρατηγὸν μάλιστα ἐπεπείκε-
σαν ἐς τὴν μάχην.

484   103. Ὁ δὲ Σκιπίων τριακοσίους ἱππέας, οὓς εἶχεν
ἀμφ' αὑτὸν καὶ ὅσους ἄλλους συναγαγεῖν ἔφθασεν,
διελὼν ἐς δύο τοῖς ἐχθροῖς ἐπῆγε σὺν δρόμῳ πολλῷ,
παρὰ μέρος ἀκοντίζοντάς τε καὶ εὐθὺς ἀποχωροῦντας,
εἶτ' αὖθις ἐπιόντας καὶ πάλιν εὐθὺς ἀποπηδῶντας·
οὕτω γὰρ εἴρητο αὐτοῖς, τοὺς ἡμίσεας αἰεὶ παρὰ
μέρος ἐπιέναι καὶ ἀκοντίσαντας ἀπελαύνειν, ὥσπερ ἐν
485 κύκλῳ περιόντας. γιγνομένου δὲ τοῦδε πυκνοῦ καὶ
διαστήματος οὐδενὸς ὄντος οἱ μὲν Λίβυες ἐβάλλοντο
συνεχῶς καὶ ἐπιστρέφοντες ἐς τὸν Σκιπίωνα ἧσσον
τοῖς περῶσιν ἐπέκειντο, οἳ δ' ἔφθασαν διελθεῖν τὸ
ρεῦμα. καὶ ὁ Σκιπίων ἐπ' αὐτοῖς ἀφίππευσεν βαλλό-
486 μενός τε καὶ χαλεπῶς. σπεῖραι δ' ἐν ἀρχῇ τοῦδε τοῦ
πόνου τέσσαρες ἀποσχισθεῖσαι τοῦ ρεύματος ὑπὸ
τῶν πολεμίων ἔς τινα λόφον ἀνέδραμον· καὶ αὐτὰς ὁ
Ἀσρούβας περιεκάθητο, ἀγνοούντων ἔτι Ῥωμαίων,
487 ἕως ἐστάθμευσαν. ἐπεὶ δ' ἔμαθον, ἠπόρουν, καὶ τοῖς
μὲν ἐδόκει φεύγειν καὶ μὴ κινδυνεύειν ἅπασι δι' ὀλίγους, ὁ δὲ Σκιπίων ἐδίδασκεν ἀρχομένων μὲν ἔργων
εὐβουλίᾳ χρῆσθαι, κινδυνευόντων δὲ ἀνδρῶν τοσῶνδε
488 καὶ σημείων τόλμῃ παραβόλῳ. αὐτὸς δ' ἐπιλεξάμενος

184

as the river. Since this was difficult to cross—the fords were few and not easy to negotiate—they were forced to separate and break rank. Looking down on this, Hasdrubal chose this exact moment to launch a brilliant attack. He killed a large number of them, who did not even defend themselves but fled. Among the dead were three of the military tribunes who had been particularly responsible for persuading the general to fight. 483

103. Scipio now took three hundred cavalry he had with him and as many more as he could collect before dividing them into two groups and leading frequent charges against the enemy, taking turns to launch volleys of missiles and immediately retreat, then attacking again and immediately hurrying back. For he had given orders that half of them should constantly be attacking in turn, throwing their javelins and riding back, as if going round in a circle. As the attack was continuous with no intervals, the Africans were under constant fire, and turning to face Scipio, pressed their attack on those crossing the river less vigorously, giving the latter time to cross. Scipio rode off after them under heavy attack. At the beginning of the engagement, four Roman cohorts had been cut off by the enemy on the other side of the river, where they had retreated to a hill and were surrounded by Hasdrubal. The Romans were not aware of this until they were in quarters. When they learned of it, they did not know what to do. Some thought they should retreat and not risk everyone for the sake of a few, but Scipio advised that, when you begin an enterprise good counsel is required, but with so many men and standards in danger, reckless daring was needed. So he himself chose some cavalry units, and said 484 485 486 487 488

τινας ἱππέων ἴλας, ἐπανοίσειν ἔφη ἐκείνους ἢ χαίρων
αὐτοῖς συναπολεῖσθαι. δύο τε ἡμερῶν σιτία φέρων
εὐθὺς ὤδευε, δεδιότος πάνυ τοῦ στρατοῦ, μὴ οὐδ᾽
489 αὐτὸς ἐπανέλθοι. ὡς δ᾽ ἦκεν ἐπὶ τὸν λόφον, ἔνθα ἦσαν
οἱ πολιορκούμενοι, τὸν μὲν ἄντικρυς αὐτοῦ δρόμῳ
κατέλαβεν, καὶ μία τοὺς δύο χαράδρα διεῖργεν, οἱ δὲ
Λίβυες τότε μάλιστα ἐπέκειντο τοῖς πολιορκουμένοις
καὶ πρὸς αὐτοὺς[20] ἐνενεύκεσαν, ὡς οὔπω δυναμένου
490 τοῦ Σκιπίωνος ἐπικουρεῖν ἐξ ὁδοιπορίας συντόνου. ὁ
δὲ Σκιπίων, ὡς εἶδε τὰς πέζας τῶν δύο λόφων τὴν
χαράδραν περιιούσας, τὸν καιρὸν οὐ μεθῆκεν, ἀλλὰ
περιέδραμε δι᾽ αὐτῶν ὑπὲρ τοὺς πολεμίους. οἱ δ᾽ ἤδη
κυκλούμενοι διέφευγον ἀκόσμως, μεθιέντος αὐτοὺς
ἀπιέναι τοῦ Σκιπίωνος ἀδεῶς, πολὺ πλείονας ὄντας.

491   104. Οὕτω μὲν δὴ καὶ τούσδε ὁ Σκιπίων περιέσωσεν
ἐν ἀπογνώσει γενομένους. καὶ αὐτὸν ἡ στρατιὰ μακρόθεν ἰδοῦσα ἐξ ἀέλπτου περισεσωσμένον τε καὶ
περισώσαντα τοὺς ἑταίρους[21] μέγα ἠλάλαξαν ἡδόμε-
νοι καὶ δαιμόνιον αὐτῷ συλλαμβάνειν ἐδόξαζον, ὃ καὶ
τῷ πάππῳ Σκιπίωνι προσημαίνειν ἐδόκει τὰ μέλ-
492 λοντα. ὁ μὲν δὴ Μανίλιος ἀνεζεύγνυεν ἐς τὸ πρὸς
τῇ πόλει στρατόπεδον, πολλὴν τίσιν ὑποσχὼν τοῦ
μὴ πεισθῆναι Σκιπίωνι τῆς στρατείας ἀποτρέποντι·
ἀχθομένων δὲ πάντων ἐπὶ τῇ τῶν πεσόντων ἀταφίᾳ,
καὶ μάλιστα ἐπὶ τοῖς χιλιάρχοις, ὁ Σκιπίων τινὰ λύσας αἰχμάλωτα ἔπεμψε πρὸς Ἀσρούβαν καὶ παρῄνει
493 θάψαι τοὺς χιλιάρχους. ὁ δ᾽ ἐρευνησάμενος τὰ νεκρὰ
καὶ ἀπὸ τῆς σφραγῖδος εὑρών (χρυσοφοροῦσι γὰρ

that he would either bring the beleaguered men back or
happily die with them. With two days' supplies he immediately set off on the road, while the army was extremely
anxious that he himself might not even get back. When he
reached the hill where the men were under siege, he immediately rushed to occupy the one right in front of him,
which was separated from the other one by a single ravine.
The Africans now pressed the besieged Romans particularly hard, and had turned on them in the belief that Scipio
was not yet in a position to help them after his forced
march. But Scipio, when he saw that the base of the two
hills followed the line of the ravine, wasted no time in
hurrying round the hills above the enemy. They were now
surrounded and fled in disorder, but Scipio let them go
with impunity, as they greatly outnumbered his men.

104. So Scipio rescued these men too from the desperate situation in which they had found themselves. When
the army saw from a distance that he had unexpectedly
saved himself and his companions, they shouted out loud
in pleasure, and began to believe that a divinity was helping Scipio, the same one that apparently revealed the future for his grandfather Scipio. Manilius, however, withdrew to his camp by the city, having paid a heavy price for
not listening to Scipio when he tried to divert him from
the expedition. Since everyone was distressed that the
dead had not been buried, especially the military tribunes,
Scipio set free one of the prisoners and sent him to Hasdrubal urging him to bury the tribunes. Hasdrubal went
in search of their bodies and identified them by means of

489

490

491

492

493

20 αὐτοὺς V: αὐτοὺς recentiores
21 ἑταίρους V: ἑτέρους rell.

τῶν στρατευομένων οἱ χιλίαρχοι, τῶν ἐλαττόνων σι-
δηροφορούντων), ἔθαψεν αὐτούς, εἴτε τὸ ἔργον ἀνθρώπειον καὶ κοινὸν ἐν τοῖς πολέμοις ἡγούμενος, εἴτε
τὴν Σκιπίωνος δόξαν ἤδη δεδιώς τε καὶ θεραπεύων.

494 Ῥωμαίοις δ' ἀναζευγνύουσι μὲν ἀπὸ τοῦ Ἀσρούβα
ἐπέκειτο Φαμέας, διὰ τὸ πταῖσμα θορυβουμένοις· ἐσι-
οῦσι δὲ οἱ Καρχηδόνιοι, τῆς πόλεως ἐκδραμόντες,
ὑπήντων καί τινα καὶ τῶν σκευοφόρων διέφθειραν.

495 105. Ἐν τούτῳ δὲ καὶ ἡ σύγκλητος ἐς τὸ στρατόπεδον ἔπεμπε τοὺς εἰσομένους καὶ μεταδώσοντας
αὐτῇ τὰ ἀκριβέστατα, ἐφ' ὧν ὅ τε Μανίλιος καὶ τὸ
συνέδριον καὶ οἱ λοιποὶ τῶν χιλιάρχων, ἐσβεσμένου
τοῦ φθόνου διὰ τὴν εὐπραγίαν, ἐμαρτύρουν τῷ Σκιπίωνι καὶ ὁ στρατὸς ἅπας καὶ τὰ ἔργα ἐπ' ἐκείνοις,
ὥστ' ἐπανελθόντες οἱ πρέσβεις διεθρόησαν ἐς ἅπαντας τὴν ἐμπειρίαν καὶ ἐπίτευξιν τοῦ Σκιπίωνος καὶ
496 τῆς στρατιᾶς τὴν ἐς αὐτὸν ὁρμήν. ἡ δὲ βουλὴ τούτοις
μὲν ἔχαιρεν, πολλῶν δὲ γεγενημένων πταισμάτων ἐς
Μασσανάσσην ἔπεμπε καὶ παρεκάλει συμμαχεῖν
497 αὐτὸν ἐρρωμένως ἐπὶ Καρχηδόνα. ὃ δ' ὑπὸ μὲν τῶν
πρέσβεων οὐ κατελήφθη, κάμνων δὲ γήρᾳ καὶ νόσῳ
καὶ παῖδας ἔχων νόθους μὲν πλείονας, οἷς ἐδεδώρητο
πολλά, γνησίους δὲ τρεῖς, οὐδὲν ἀλλήλοις τὰ ἔργα
ἐοικότας, ἐκάλει τὸν Σκιπίωνα κατὰ φιλίαν αὐτοῦ τε
καὶ τοῦ πάππου σύμβουλόν οἱ περὶ τῶν τέκνων καὶ
498 τῆς ἀρχῆς ἐσόμενον. ὃ δὲ ᾔει μὲν αὐτίκα, μικρὸν δὲ
πρὶν ἐλθεῖν ὁ Μασσανάσσης ἀποψύχων ἐπέσκηψε

their signet rings: for among serving soldiers, tribunes have gold rings, the other ranks iron ones. Whether he regarded it as the sort of humane act that is common in war, or, already in deference to Scipio's reputation, was doing him a favor, he gave the tribunes due burial. While the Romans were withdrawing from the engagement with Hasdrubal, and in a state of confusion because of the reverse they suffered, Phameas attacked them; and as they approached their camp the Carthaginians made a sortie from the city to meet them, killing some of their pack animals. 494

105. While this was happening, the senate sent a mission to the army to get and report back to them the most accurate information available. Jealousy of Scipio had been extinguished by his successes, and Manilius and his advisory council and the other military tribunes now reported favorably on him, and the whole army and its achievements also served as witness, with the result that when the envoys returned to Rome they spread the word to everyone about Scipio's experience and success and the army's enthusiasm for him. The senate was pleased at the news, but in view of the many reverses the Romans had suffered, they sent an embassy to Massinissa inviting him to give vigorous military assistance to them against Carthage. But the ambassadors failed to meet with him. Exhausted by old age and sickness, and with numerous illegitimate sons, to whom he had given generously, and three legitimate ones, very different from each other in their abilities, he had invited Scipio out of his friendship with both him and his grandfather to advise him about his children and kingdom. Scipio went immediately, but shortly before he arrived, Massinissa died, having instructed his 495 496 497 498

τοῖς παισὶ πείθεσθαι τοῦ Σκιπίωνος, ὡς ἂν αὐτοῖς
διαιρῇ τὰ ὄντα.

499   106. Καὶ ὁ μὲν τοῦτ᾽ εἰπὼν ἐτελεύτησεν, ἀνὴρ ἐς
πάντα ἐπιτυχής, ᾧ τὴν μὲν ἀρχὴν τὴν πατρῴαν θεὸς
ἔδωκεν, ἀφαιρεθέντι πρὸς Καρχηδονίων καὶ Σύφακος,
ἀναλαβεῖν καὶ προαγαγεῖν ἐπὶ μέγιστον, ἀπὸ Μαυρουσίων τῶν παρ᾽ ὠκεανῷ μέχρι τῆς Κυρηναίων ἀρχῆς ἐς τὰ μεσόγαια, ἡμερῶσαι δὲ γῆν πολλήν, τὰ
πολλὰ τῶν Νομάδων ποηφαγούντων διὰ τὸ ἀγεώργη-
τον, θησαυρούς τε μεγάλους χρημάτων καταλιπεῖν
καὶ στρατιὰν πολλὴν γεγυμνασμένην, τῶν δ᾽ ἐχθρῶν
Σύφακα μὲν αἰχμάλωτον ἑλεῖν αὐτοχειρί, Καρχηδόνι
δ᾽ αἴτιον τῆς ἀναστάσεως γενέσθαι, πάμπαν ἀσθενῆ
500   Ῥωμαίοις ὑπολιπόντα. ἔφυ δὲ καὶ τὸ σῶμα μέγας τε
καὶ εὔρωστος ἐς γῆρας πολὺ καὶ μάχης ἐπειρᾶτο μέχρι τοῦ θανάτου ἵππου τε χωρὶς ἀναβολέως ἐπέβαινε.
καὶ μεγίστῳ δὴ τῷδε τεκμηριώσω μάλιστά τὴν εὐρω-
στίαν αὐτοῦ· πολλῶν γὰρ αὐτῷ παίδων γιγνομένων
τε καὶ ἀποθνησκόντων οὔποτε μὲν ἦσαν αὐτῷ μείους
τῶν δέκα, τετραετὲς δὲ παιδίον ἐνενηκοντούτης ὢν
501   ἀπέλιπεν. ὁ μὲν δὴ Μασσανάσσης ὧδε χρόνου τε καὶ
σώματος ἔχων ἐτεθνήκει, Σκιπίων δὲ τοῖς μὲν νόθοις
αὐτοῦ παισὶ προσέθηκεν ἑτέρας δωρεάς, τοῖς δὲ γνη-
σίοις τοὺς μὲν θησαυροὺς καὶ φόρους καὶ τὸ ὄνομα
502   τῆς βασιλείας κοινὸν ἀπέφηνεν, τὰ δ᾽ ἄλλα διέκρινεν,
ὡς ἔμελλεν ἁρμόσειν πρὸς ὃ ἐβούλετο ἕκαστος, Μι-
κίψῃ μέν, ὃς πρεσβύτατος ὢν εἰρηνικώτατος ἦν, Κίρ-
την ἐξαίρετον ἔχειν καὶ τὰ βασίλεια τὰ ἐν αὐτῇ, Γο-

sons to accept whatever division of the estate Scipio made among them.

106. With these words he died, a man blessed by fortune in everything. His ancestral kingdom, which had been taken from him by Syphax and the Carthaginians, the gods allowed him to recover and extend on a very large scale, from Mauretania on the Ocean to the kingdom of Cyrene in the interior. He cultivated a great deal of land, most of the Numidians being herb eaters for lack of agricultural skills. He left a great sum of money in the treasury and a large well-trained army. Of his enemies he personally took Syphax prisoner, and was responsible for the destruction of Carthage, having left it utterly weak and exposed to the Romans. He was a tall man and vigorous into extreme old age, with experience of fighting right up to his death, and the ability to mount his horse without the assistance of a groom. The greatest witness to his vitality I can provide was that while he had many children who died, there were never fewer than ten of them alive, and at his death at the age of ninety he left one aged four. Such was Massinissa's life and physical character at the time of his death. Scipio bestowed other gifts on his illegitimate sons, and declared that the legitimate sons should share the treasures, the revenues, and the royal title. The rest he divided up in a way that would best suit the wishes of each one. Micipsa, the eldest and a man of most peaceable disposition, was assigned the city of Cirta and its palace.

499

500

501

502

λόσσῃ δέ, στρατιωτικῷ τε ὄντι καὶ δευτέρῳ καθ᾿
ἡλικίαν, πολέμου τε καὶ εἰρήνης εἶναι κυρίῳ, Μαστα-
νάβᾳ δέ, ὃς νεώτατος ὢν ἤσκει δικαιοσύνην, δικάζειν
τοῖς ὑπηκόοις τὰ ἀμφίλογα.

503   107. Οὕτω μὲν ὁ Σκιπίων τὴν ἀρχὴν καὶ περιουσίαν
Μασσανάσσου διεῖλε τοῖς παισὶ καὶ Γολόσσην εὐθὺς
ἐς συμμαχίαν ἐπήγετο· ὁ δὲ τὰς Φαμέου μάλιστα
ἐνέδρας, αἳ πολλὰ Ῥωμαίους ἐλύπουν, ἐρευνώμενος
504   ἀνέστελλεν. ἐν δέ τινι χειμασίᾳ Σκιπίων καὶ Φαμέας
ἀντιπαρώδευον ἀλλήλοις, μέσην ἔχοντες ἄβατον χαράδραν καὶ οὐδὲν ἐς ἀλλήλους δυνάμενοι. δεδιὼς δ᾿ ὁ
Σκιπίων, μή τις ἐνέδρα κατὰ τὸ πρόσθεν εἴη, προϊὼν
κατεσκέπτετο σὺν τρισὶ φίλοις. καὶ αὐτὸν ὁ Φαμέας
505   ἰδὼν ἀντιπροῄει μεθ᾿ ἑνὸς φίλου. ἐλπίσας δ᾿ αὐτὸν ὁ
Σκιπίων εἰπεῖν τι θέλειν ἐξίππευσε μεθ᾿ ἑνὸς καὶ ὅδε
φίλου. καὶ ὡς ἤδη κατακούειν ἐδύναντο ἀλλήλων,
506   πρότερος εἶπεν ὁ Σκιπίων· "Ὁρᾷς, ὦ Φαμέα, τὰ Καρχηδονίων οἷ προελήλυθεν· τί δὴ τῆς ἰδίας σωτηρίας
οὐ προνοεῖς, εἰ μὴ τῆς κοινῆς δύνασαι;" ὁ δέ, "Τίς
ἐστιν," ἔφη, "Μοι σωτηρία, Καρχηδονίων μὲν οὕτως
ἐχόντων, Ῥωμαίων δ᾿ ὑπ᾿ ἐμοῦ κακὰ πολλὰ πεπον-
θότων;" καὶ ὁ Σκιπίων "Ἐγγυῶμαί σοί," φησιν, "Εἰ
πιστὸς ἐγὼ καὶ ἀξιόχρεως, καὶ σωτηρίαν καὶ συγγνώμην παρὰ Ῥωμαίων καὶ χάριν ἔσεσθαι." ὁ δ᾿ ἐπή-
νεσε μὲν ὡς ἀξιοπιστότατον ἐκ πάντων, "Κρινῶ," δ᾿
ἔφη· "Κἂν δυνατὸν ἡγῶμαι, φανερὸν ἔσται σοι."

507   108. Καὶ οἳ μὲν ἐπὶ τούτους διεκρίθησαν, ὃ δὲ Μανίλιος, αἰδούμενος τὴν δυσπραξίαν τὴν ἐς Ἀσρούβαν

Gulussa, the next eldest, a military man, was put in charge of matters of war and peace. The youngest, Mastanabal, was a keen student of justice, and was given the task of adjudicating disputes among subjects.

107. This was how Scipio divided Massinissa's kingdom and estate among his sons. He immediately enlisted Gulussa as an ally. The latter made a particular search for the hiding places of Phameas, from where he had inflicted much damage on the Romans, and put a check on his activities. One winter's day, Scipio and Phameas encountered each other on the march, but with an uncrossable ravine between them and no possibility of attacking each other. Scipio was afraid there might be an ambush up ahead and advanced to reconnoiter with three companions. Seeing him do this, Phameas went forward along beside him, but with one companion. Scipio assumed that Phameas wanted to say something to him and so rode on with just one companion. When they were within hearing distance of each other, Scipio spoke first. "You can see, Phameas, what Carthaginian affairs have come to. As you can't do anything about your country's safety, why don't you look out for your own?" Phameas replied, "What sort of safety can I have, when the Carthaginians are in such difficulties, and the Romans have suffered so badly at my hands?" "If you believe I am a man of good faith and trustworthy," said Scipio, "I will guarantee that Rome will grant you safety, forgiveness, and gratitude." Phameas commended him as the most dependable of all men, but said, "I will assess the situation, and if I think your proposal possible, it will be made clear to you."

108. They then went their separate ways. Manilius, embarrassed by the failure he had suffered against Has-

503

504

505

506

507

αὑτῷ γενομένην, αὖθις ἐς Νέφεριν ἐστράτευε, πεντε-
508 καίδεκα ἡμερῶν τροφὰς ἐπαγόμενος. πλησιάσας δ'
ἔθετο χάρακα καὶ ὠχύρου καὶ ἐτάφρευεν, καθὰ Σκιπίων ἐν τῇ προτέρᾳ στρατείᾳ παρήγγειλεν. οὐδὲν δὲ
ἀνύων ἐν αἰδοῖ μείζονι ἐγίγνετο καὶ φόβῳ τοῦ πάλιν
509 αὐτοῖς ἀπιοῦσιν τὸν Ἀσρούβαν ἐπιθέσθαι. καὶ ὁ μὲν
ἐν τῷδε ἦν ἀπορίας, ἐπιστολὴν δέ τις ἐκ τοῦ Γολόσσου στρατοῦ ἔφερεν τῷ Σκιπίωνι. ὁ δ', ὡς εἶχε, σεση-
510 μασμένην ἐπέδειξε τῷ στρατηγῷ. καὶ λύσαντες εὗρον·
"Ἐς τήνδε τὴν ἡμέραν ἐγὼ μὲν τόδε τὸ χωρίον κατα-
λήψομαι· σὺ δ' ἐλθὲ μεθ' ὅσων βούλει, καὶ τοῖς προ-
φύλαξιν εἰπὲ δέχεσθαι τὸν νυκτὸς ἀφικνούμενον." ἡ
μὲν ἐπιστολὴ χωρὶς ὀνομάτων τοιάδ' ἐδήλου, συνῆκε
511 δὲ ὁ Σκιπίων εἶναι παρὰ Φαμέου. καὶ ὁ Μανίλιος ἐδεδοίκει μὲν περὶ τῷ Σκιπίωνι, μή τις ἀπάτη παρ' ἀνδρὸς γένοιτο πιθανωτάτου πάντων ἐς ἐνέδρας· εὔελπιν
δ' αὐτὸν ὁρῶν ἔπεμπεν, ἐπιτρέψας περὶ μὲν τῆς σωτηρίας δοῦναι πίστιν ἀσφαλῆ τῷ Φαμέᾳ, χάριν δὲ μὴ
ὁρίζειν, ἀλλ' ἐπαγγέλλεσθαι Ῥωμαίους τὰ πρέποντα
512 ποιήσειν. οὐ μὴν ἐδέησεν οὐδ' ἐπαγγελίας· ὁ γάρ τοι
Φαμέας, ὡς ἧκεν εἰς τὸ συγκείμενον, περὶ μὲν τῆς
σωτηρίας ἔφη πιστεύειν δεξιουμένῳ Σκιπίωνι, τὰς
513 δὲ χάριτας Ῥωμαίοις ἐπιτρέπειν. ταῦτα δ' εἰπὼν
ἐξέτασσε τῆς ἐπιούσης ἐς μάχην καὶ προπηδήσας
μετὰ τῶν ἰλάρχων ἐς τὸ μεσαίχμιον ὡς ἐπί τινα σκέψιν ἑτέραν εἶπεν· "Εἰ μὲν ἔστιν ἔτι τῇ πατρίδι βοηθεῖν, ἕτοιμός εἰμι μεθ' ὑμῶν· εἰ δ' ἔχει τὰ ἐκείνης, ὡς
ἔχει, ἐμοὶ μὲν δοκεῖ τῆς ἰδίας σωτηρίας προνοεῖν, καὶ

drubal, now led another expedition to Nepheris, taking with him fifteen days' of supplies. When he got near, he built a palisade and fortified it with a ditch, as Scipio had advised on the previous expedition, but he achieved nothing and was even more embarrassed; and he was worried that Hasdrubal would attack them again as they retreated. While he was in such difficulties, someone in Gulussa's army brought Scipio a letter. The messenger immediately showed it, sealed as it was, to Scipio, and opening it, they found the following message: "On such and such a day I will seize such and such a place. You go there with as many men as you like, and tell your sentries to let in a man who arrives by night." Such was the content of the letter. It mentioned no names, but Scipio understood it was from Phameas. Manilius was afraid on Scipio's behalf that he might be led into a trap by the deceit of one of the most convincing of all men, but seeing how optimistic he was, he sent him off with instructions to give Phameas a firm guarantee about his personal safety, but not to say anything definite about a reward; he was to promise that the Romans would do what was fitting. But Phameas required no promise. For when he came to the appointed place, he said that with respect to his safety he trusted the pledge of Scipio's right hand, while the rewards he would leave up to the Romans. That is what he said, and next day he arrayed his army for battle. Advancing with his officers into the space between the battle lines, as if making another reconnaissance, he spoke to them: "If there is still some way of helping our country, I am ready to do it with you. But if the situation is as it is now, it seems to me right to look after one's own safety. I have received a pledge for

508

509

510

511

512

513

πίστιν ἔλαβον ἐπί τε ἐμαυτῷ καὶ ὅσους πείσαιμι
ὑμῶν. καιρὸς δὲ καὶ ὑμᾶς ἐπιλέγεσθαι τὰ συνοί-
514 σοντα." ὃ μὲν οὕτως εἶπεν, τῶν δ' ἰλάρχων οἱ μὲν σὺν
τοῖς αὑτῶν ηὐτομόλησαν, καὶ ἐγένοντο πάντες εἰς
διακοσίους καὶ δισχιλίους ἱππέας· τοὺς δ' Ἄννων
κατεκώλυσεν, ᾧ Λεῦκος ἦν ἐπίκλησις.

515   109. Ἐπανιόντι δὲ τῷ Σκιπίωνι μετὰ τοῦ Φαμέου ὁ
στρατὸς ἀπήντα καὶ τὸν Σκιπίωνα εὐφήμουν ὡς ἐπὶ
θριάμβῳ. Μανίλιος δ', ὑπερηδόμενός τε καὶ οὐκέτι
τὴν ἐπάνοδον αἰσχρὰν ἐπὶ τῷδε ἡγούμενος οὐδ' Ἀσρούβαν ἕψεσθαι προσδοκῶν καταπεπληγμένον, ἀνεζεύγνυεν αὐτίκα δι' ἔνδειαν, ἑπτακαιδεκάτην ἡμέραν
ἀντὶ πεντεκαίδεκα ἔχων. τρισὶ δ' ἄλλαις ἐχρῆν κακο-
516 παθοῦντα ἐπανελθεῖν. ὁ οὖν Σκιπίων, τόν τε Φαμέαν
καὶ Γολόσσην καὶ τοὺς ὑφ' ἑκατέρῳ λαβὼν ἱππέας,
προσλαβὼν δέ τινας καὶ τῶν Ἰταλικῶν, ἐς πεδίον
ἠπείχθη τὸ καλούμενον Μέγα Βάραθρον καὶ πολλὴν
ἐξ αὐτοῦ λείαν τε καὶ ἀγορὰν ἧκε φέρων τῷ στρατῷ
517 περὶ Τύνητα. Μανίλιος δέ, πυθόμενός οἱ διάδοχον
ἐπιέναι Καλπούρνιον Πίσωνα, προέπεμπεν ἐς Ῥώμην
Σκιπίωνα μετὰ Φαμέου· καὶ ὁ στρατὸς ἐπὶ τὴν ναῦν
καταθέοντες εὐφήμουν τὸν Σκιπίωνα καὶ ηὔχοντο
ὕπατον ἐς Λιβύην ἐπανελθεῖν ὡς μόνον αἱρήσοντα
Καρχηδόνα. θεόληπτος γάρ τις αὐτοῖς ἥδε ἡ δόξα
ἐνέπιπτεν, Σκιπίωνα μόνον αἱρήσειν Καρχηδόνα· καὶ
518 πολλοὶ ταῦτα τοῖς οἰκείοις ἐς Ῥώμην ἐπέστελλον. ἡ
δὲ βουλὴ Σκιπίωνα μὲν ἐπῄνει, Φαμέαν δ' ἐτίμησαν

myself and for as many of you as I can persuade to agree. It is time for you too to consider your own advantage." After he had spoken, some of his officers deserted with 514 their men, in all about two thousand two hundred cavalry-men. The others were prevented from doing so by Hanno, surnamed "the Mullet."[47]

109. As Scipio was returning with Phameas, the army 515 went out to meet him and shouted their approval as if at a triumphal procession. Manilius was extremely pleased, and after this success no longer considered his retreat embarrassing or was afraid the astonished Hasdrubal would chase him. But breaking camp immediately for lack of supplies—it was the seventeenth day rather than the fifteenth—he had to endure three more days of misery on the return journey. So, Scipio took Phameas and Gulussa 516 and the cavalry under the command of each, adding a few Italians, and having launched an attack into a plain known as the Great Depression, returned to the army at Tyneta with a large amount of plunder and provisions. When Ma- 517 nilius heard that his successor, Calpurnius Piso, was com-ing, he sent Scipio ahead to Rome with Phameas.[48] The soldiers ran down to the ship praising Scipio and praying that he would return to Africa as consul, in the belief that he alone could capture Carthage. For this apparently di-vinely inspired notion had got into them that only Scipio would take Carthage, and many of them sent word of this to their relatives in Rome. The senate praised Scipio, and 518

[47] Or, Hanno "the White." The Greek word for "white" and for the name of the fish is the same (with different accentuation).

[48] L. Calpurnius Piso Caesoninus was consul in 148 with Sp. Postumius Albinus Magnus.

ἀλουργίδι καὶ ἐπιπορπήματι χρυσέῳ καὶ ἵππῳ χρυ-
σοφαλάρῳ καὶ πανοπλίᾳ καὶ ἀργυρίου δραχμαῖς
μυρίαις, ἔδωκαν δὲ καὶ μνῶν ἑκατὸν ἀργύρωμα καὶ
σκηνὴν καὶ κατασκευὴν ἐντελῆ. καὶ ἐπήλπισαν περὶ
πλειόνων, εἰ τὰ λοιπὰ τοῦ πολέμου συνεκπονήσειεν
αὐτοῖς. ὁ δ᾽ ὑποσχόμενος ἐς Λιβύην διέπλευσεν ἐς τὸ
Ῥωμαίων στρατόπεδον.

519   110. Ἧκεν δὲ Καλπούρνιος Πίσων ὁ ὕπατος ἅμα
ἦρι, καὶ σὺν αὐτῷ Λεύκιος Μαγκῖνος ἐπὶ τὴν ναυαρ-
χίαν· οἱ Καρχηδονίοις μὲν οὐκ ἐπεχείρουν, οὐδὲ Ἀσρούβᾳ, τὰς δὲ πόλεις ἐπιόντες Ἀσπίδος μὲν ἀπετύγχανον, ἐκ γῆς καὶ θαλάσσης ἀποπειράσαντες, ἑτέραν
δ᾽ ἐγγὺς εἷλεν ὁ Πίσων καὶ διήρπαζεν, αἰτιωμένην ἐπὶ
520   συνθήκαις αὐτῷ προσελθεῖν. ἀπὸ δὲ ταύτης ἐς Ἱππάγρετα μετῆλθεν, ἣ μεγάλη τε ἦν καὶ τείχεσι καὶ ἀκροπόλει καὶ λιμέσι καὶ νεωρίοις ὑπ᾽ Ἀγαθοκλέους, τοῦ
Σικελιωτῶν τυράννου, κατεσκεύαστο καλῶς, μέση δ᾽
οὖσα Καρχηδόνος καὶ Ἰτύκης τὴν ἀγορὰν ἐλῄστευεν
τὴν Ῥωμαίοις διαπλέουσαν· ὅθεν καὶ πάνυ ἐπλούτουν.
521   καὶ ὁ Καλπούρνιος ἀμύνασθαί τε αὐτοὺς ἐπενόει καὶ
τό γε κέρδος ἀφελέσθαι. ἀλλ᾽ ὁ μέν, τὸ θέρος ὅλον
ἐφεδρεύων, οὐκ ἤνυεν, δὶς δὲ ἐκδραμόντες οἱ Ἱππα-
γρέτιοι, Καρχηδονίων αὐτοῖς συμμαχούντων, τὰς μηχανὰς αὐτοῦ κατέπρησαν.

---

49 L. Hostilius Mancinus became consul in 145. Livy (*Per.* 51)
calls him a legate, but his exact status in Africa is not clear. He
may have been praetor at the time.

honored Phameas with a purple robe, a golden cloak, a gold-caparisoned horse, a suit of armor and ten thousand silver drachmas. They also gave him one hundred minas of silver plate and a fully furnished tent, and said he could expect more, if he spent the rest of the war working hard on their side. He undertook to do so and then crossed to Africa, to the Roman camp.

110. With the coming of spring the consul, Calpurnius Piso, arrived, and with him Lucius Mancinus as commander of the fleet.[49] They did not attack Carthage or Hasdrubal, but moved against the towns. They made an unsuccessful attempt by land and sea against Aspis,[50] but Piso captured another town nearby and plundered it, although the inhabitants made the accusation that they had approached him to negotiate a treaty. From there he moved to Hippagreta. This was a big town which the Sicilian tyrant Agathocles had adorned with walls, a harbor, an acropolis, and dockyards. It was situated between Carthage and Utica and had grown very rich from raiding the Roman supply ships.[51] Calpurnius intended to punish them, or at least to deprive them of their gains, but after spending the whole summer besieging them, he achieved nothing. Indeed on two occasions the people of Hippagreta, with the Carthaginians assisting them, made a sortie and burned his siege engines.

519

520

521

[50] Aspis is the modern coastal town of Kelibia, just over sixty-two miles east of Carthage.

[51] Appian is presumably referring to Hippou Acra, modern Bizerte, which lies north of Utica, not between Utica and Carthage. For Agathocles, see above, note 8.

522   111. Καὶ ὃ μέν, ἄπρακτος ἐς Ἰτύκην ἐπανελθών,
ἐχείμαζεν· οἱ Καρχηδόνιοι δέ, ἐπειδή σφισι καὶ τὸ
Ἀσρούβα στρατόπεδον ἀπαθὲς ἦν καὶ αὐτοὶ κρείτ-
τους ἐν τῇ μάχῃ γεγένηντο Πίσωνος ἀμφὶ τὰ Ἱππάγρετα Βιθύας τε αὐτοῖς ὁ Νομὰς μετὰ ὀκτακοσίων
ἱππέων ἀπὸ Γολόσσου προσκεχωρήκει καὶ Μικύψην
καὶ Μαστανάβαν, τοὺς Μασσανάσσου παῖδας, ἑώρων
ὑπισχνουμένους μὲν αἰεὶ Ῥωμαίοις ὅπλα καὶ χρήματα,
βραδύνοντας δὲ καὶ περιορωμένους ἄρα τὸ μέλλον,
ἐπήρθησαν τοῖς φρονήμασι καὶ Λιβύην ἀδεῶς ἐπῄεσαν, κρατυνόμενοί τε τὴν χώραν καὶ πολλὰ ὑβρι-
στικὰ ἐν ταῖς πόλεσι κατὰ Ῥωμαίων ἐκκλησιάζοντες.
523   ἔς τε τὴν ἀνανδρίαν αὐτῶν προύφερον τὰ ἐς Νέφεριν
αὐτοῖς δὶς γενόμενα καὶ ὅσα ἔναγχος ἐς Ἱππάγρετα,
καὶ τὸ αὐτῆς Καρχηδόνος, ἀνόπλου τε οὔσης καὶ
524   ἀφράκτου, μὴ δεδυνῆσθαι κατασχεῖν. ἔπεμπον δὲ καὶ
ἐς Μικύψην καὶ Μαστανάβαν καὶ ἐς τοὺς αὐτονόμους
Μαυρουσίων, παρακαλοῦντες ὁμοῦ καὶ διδάσκοντες,
ὅτι καὶ σφίσι μεθ᾽ αὑτοὺς ἐπιχειρήσουσι Ῥωμαῖοι.
525   ἔστελλον δὲ καὶ ἐς Μακεδονίαν ἄλλους πρὸς τὸν νο-
μιζόμενον υἱὸν εἶναι Περσέως, πολεμοῦντα Ῥωμαίοις,
καὶ ἀνέπειθον ἔχεσθαι τοῦ πολέμου καρτερῶς, ὡς οὐκ
ἐλλειψόντων αὐτῷ χρημάτων καὶ νεῶν ἀπὸ Καρχηδόνος. ὅλως τε μικρὸν οὐδὲν ἔτι ἐφρόνουν ὁπλισάμενοι,
ἀλλὰ θυμῷ καὶ τόλμῃ καὶ παρασκευῇ κατὰ μικρὸν

---

52 Andriscus, a pretender to the Macedonian throne, claimed
to be a son of the Macedonian king Perseus, who had been de-

111. He returned to spend the winter in Utica without   522
achieving anything. Neither the Carthaginians nor Hasdrubal's army had suffered any losses; they had gotten the
better of Piso in the battle at Hippagreta; Bithyas the Numidian had deserted to them from Gulussa with eight
hundred cavalry; and they noted that Micipsa and Mastanabal, the sons of Massinissa, while constantly promising
weapons and money to the Romans, were delaying and
waiting to see what would happen. In view of this, the
confidence of the Carthaginians rose and they began to
range over Africa without fear, strengthening their position on the land and violently denouncing the Romans at
public meetings in the towns. As evidence of Roman cow-   523
ardice they cited the two reverses inflicted on them at
Nepheris, and the recent one at Hippogreta, and the situation at Carthage itself, which the Romans had been
unable to capture, in spite of it being unarmed and unprotected. They also sent embassies to Micipsa and Mas-   524
tanabal, and to those of the Moors who were autonomous,
calling on them simultaneously for help, and explaining
that the Romans would attack them too after the Carthaginians. And they sent other messengers to Macedon, to   525
the self-styled son of Perseus, who was at war with Rome,
to convince him to persevere with the war resolutely, as
there would be no shortage of money and ships for him
from Carthage.[52] Now that they were armed, their ambi-
tions were no longer in any way limited, but they were
growing little by little in spirit, daring, and military re-

feated by Rome in 168. Andriscus' war against Rome, the Fourth
Macedonian War, ended in his defeat in 148.

526 ηὔξοντο. ἐπῆρτο δ᾽ ἐν μέρει καὶ Ἀσρούβας, ὁ κατὰ
τὴν χώραν στρατηγός, τῷ δὶς κρατῆσαι Μανιλίου·
τήν τε τῆς πόλεως στρατηγίαν προσλαβεῖν ἐπειγόμενος Ἀσρούβαν, τὸν ἄρχοντα αὐτῆς, ἀδελφιδοῦν ὄντα
Γολόσσου, διέβαλλε τῇ βουλῇ τὰ Καρχηδονίων Γο-
527 λόσσῃ προδιδόναι. καὶ τοῦ λόγου προτεθέντος ἐς μέσον ὃ μὲν ἠπορεῖτο ὡς ἐπ᾽ ἀδοκήτῳ, οἳ δὲ τύπτοντες
αὐτὸν τοῖς ὑποβάθροις κατέβαλον.

528   112. Ἐς δὲ Ῥώμην ἐξαγγελλομένης τῆς τε Πίσωνος
ἀπραξίας καὶ Καρχηδονίων παρασκευῆς ὁ δῆμος
ἤχθετο καὶ ἐδεδοίκει αὐξομένου πολέμου μεγάλου τε
καὶ ἀδιαλλάκτου καὶ γείτονος· οὐ γάρ τινα διάλυσιν
529 προσεδόκων, ἄπιστα πρότεροι κελεύσαντες. τῶν δ᾽ οὐ
πρὸ πολλοῦ Σκιπίωνος ἔργων, ἐν Λιβύῃ χιλιαρχοῦν-
τος ἔτι, μεμνημένοι καὶ παραβάλλοντες αὐτὰ τοῖς
παροῦσιν τῶν τε ἐπεσταλμένων σφίσιν ὑπὸ τῶν ἐκ
στρατοπέδου φίλων καὶ οἰκείων ἀναφέροντες ὥρ-
530 μηντο ὕπατον ἐς Καρχηδόνα πέμπειν Σκιπίωνα. ἐνει-
στήκει δ᾽ ἀρχαιρέσια, καὶ ὁ Σκιπίων (οὐ γάρ πω δι᾽
ἡλικίαν αὐτῷ συνεχώρουν ὑπατεύειν οἱ νόμοι) ἀγορανομίαν μετῄει, καὶ ὁ δῆμος αὐτὸν ὕπατον ᾑρεῖτο.
531 παρανόμου δ᾽ ὄντος καὶ τῶν ὑπάτων προφερόντων
αὐτοῖς τὸν νόμον ἐλιπάρουν καὶ ἐνέκειντο καὶ ἐκεκράγεσαν ἐκ τῶν Τυλλίου καὶ Ῥωμύλου νόμων τὸν δῆμον
εἶναι κύριον τῶν ἀρχαιρεσίων καὶ τῶν περὶ αὐτῶν
532 νόμων ἀκυροῦν ἢ κυροῦν, ὃν ἐθέλοιεν. τέλος δὲ τῶν
δημάρχων τις ἔφη τοὺς ὑπάτους ἀφαιρήσεσθαι τὴν

sources. Hasdrubal too, the commander in the country, 526
was in turn encouraged by his two victories over Manilius.
Keen to acquire command of the city as well, he began
to discredit Hasdrubal, the city commander, who was a
nephew of Gulussa, by accusing him of betraying Carthage
to Gulussa. When the charge was made in public, Has- 527
drubal was not expecting it and did not know how to re-
spond, and they beat him to death with their benches.

112. When Piso's failure and the preparations of the 528
Carthaginians were made known at Rome, the people
were annoyed and anxious about the intensification of this
great and intractable war against a neighbor. For they had
no expectation of a settlement, as they had been the first
to make duplicitous demands. Recalling Scipio's recent 529
achievements while still a military tribune in Africa, and
comparing them with the present situation, and citing too
the letters sent to them by friends and relatives from the
army, they became very keen to send Scipio to Carthage
as consul. The elections were approaching, and Scipio was 530
standing for the aedileship, as the laws did not yet allow
him to be consul on account of his age.[53] But the people
elected him consul, even though this was illegal. When the 531
consuls quoted the law to them, they begged and bullied
and exclaimed that according to the laws dating from the
time of Tullius and Romulus, the people had authority
over the elections, and could repeal or confirm whatever
laws relating to the elections they liked. In the end, one of 532
the tribunes of the people said that he would remove the

[53] By the *lex Villia Annalis*, the minimum age for the consulship was forty-two. Scipio was born in 185/4, and thus only thirty-
seven. See also *Ib.* 84.364.

χειροτονίαν, εἰ μὴ συνθοῖντο τῷ δήμῳ. καὶ ἡ βουλὴ τοῖς δημάρχοις ἐπέθετο λῦσαι τὸν νόμον τόνδε καὶ μετὰ ἔτος ἓν αὖθις ἀναγράψαι, οἷόν τι καὶ Λακεδαιμόνιοι, λύοντες ἐν χρείᾳ τὴν ἀτιμίαν τῶν ἁλόντων περὶ Πύλον, ἔφασαν· "Κοιμάσθων οἱ νόμοι τήμερον."

533 οὕτω μὲν ὁ Σκιπίων, ἀγορανομίαν μετιών, ᾕρητο ὕπατος, καὶ αὐτὸν ὁ σύναρχος Δροῦσος περὶ Λιβύης πρὸς αὐτὸν ἐκέλευε διακληροῦσθαι, μέχρι τις τῶν δημάρχων εἰσηγήσατο τῆσδε τῆς στρατηγίας τὴν κρίσιν τοῦ δήμου γενέσθαι· καὶ ὁ δῆμος εἵλετο τὸν Σκι-

534 πίωνα. ἐδόθη δ' αὐτῷ στρατὸς ἐκ μὲν καταλόγου, ὅσος ἦν ἀντὶ τῶν ἀπολωλότων, ἐθελοντὰς δ' ἄγειν, ὅσους πείσειε παρὰ τῶν συμμάχων, καὶ ἐς βασιλέας καὶ πόλεις, ὅσας δοκιμάσειε, πέμπειν, τὸν Ῥωμαίων δῆμον ταῖς ἐπιστολαῖς ἐπιγράφοντα. καὶ ἔστιν οὓς ἔλαβεν οὕτω παρά τε πόλεων καὶ βασιλέων.

535 113. Ὁ μὲν δὴ τάδε διοικησάμενος ἐς Σικελίαν καὶ ἀπὸ Σικελίας ἐς Ἰτύκην ἔπλει· Καλπούρνιος δὲ Πίσων ἐπολιόρκει τὰ μεσόγαια, καὶ Μαγκῖνος, ἐφορμῶν Καρχηδόνι, μέρος τι τοῦ τείχους ἀμελούμενον ἰδών, οὗ κρημνοὶ προύκειντο συνεχεῖς καὶ δύσβατοι, καὶ παρ' αὐτὸ ἦν καὶ ἀμελούμενον, ἤλπισε λαθὼν κλίμα-

536 κας ἐποίσειν ἐπὶ τὸ τεῖχος. καὶ προσέθηκε μέν, καὶ

---

54 Spartan law required that any soldier displaying cowardice in battle be cast out from society, but when that involved too many men for Sparta to lose, so the story suggests, the laws had to be temporarily suspended (i.e., allowed to sleep for a day). Appian refers to the Peloponnesian War, and the shocking surrender in

holding of elections from the jurisdiction of the consuls, unless they supported the people. The senate then told the tribunes to repeal this law and reenact it a year later. It was like when the Spartans were forced to exempt those captured at Pylos from the loss of civic rights, and said, "let the laws sleep today."[54] In this way Scipio, while standing for the aedileship, was elected consul. When Drusus, his fellow consul,[55] invited him to draw lots with him concerning the assignment of Africa, eventually one of the tribunes proposed that the people should make the decision about this command; and the people chose Scipio. He was given permission to conscript as many troops as had been killed, and as many volunteers from the allies as he could persuade to join up, and to send letters, signing them in the name of the Roman people, to as many kings and cities as he decided. And he did get some volunteers from the cities and kings in this way.

113. After making these arrangements he sailed to Sicily and from there to Utica. Calpurnius Piso was besieging parts of the interior, while Mancinus was moored off Carthage. Observing a neglected part of the wall located over a line of cliffs very difficult to climb—this was the reason it had been neglected—Mancinus hoped to bring up ladders against the wall without being noticed. When he had

533

534

535

536

424 to Athenian forces of some three hundred Spartan soldiers on the island of Sphacteria near Pylos (Thuc. 4.38–41). As these men were lost to Sparta anyway, Plutarch's version (*Ages.* 30) is more convincing: he attributes the saying to the Spartan king Agesilaus, after the Spartan defeat at the battle of Leuctra in 371, during which a large number of Spartan soldiers had thrown down their shields.   55 C. Livius Drusus.

APPIAN

τινες τῶν στρατιωτῶν ἀνῆλθον εὐτόλμως· οἱ Καρχηδόνιοι δ', ὀλίγων ἔτι ὄντων καταφρονήσαντες, ἀνέῳξαν πύλην ἐς τοὺς κρημνοὺς ἐκφέρουσαν καὶ ἐπὶ τοὺς
Ῥωμαίους ἐξέδραμον. καὶ αὐτοὺς οἱ Ῥωμαῖοι τρεψά-
μενοί τε καὶ διώκοντες ἐς τὴν πόλιν διὰ τῆς πύλης
537 συνεσέδραμον. βοῆς δ' ὡς ἐπὶ νίκῃ γενομένης ὅ τε
Μαγκῖνος, ἐκφερόμενος ὑπὸ τῆς ἡδονῆς καὶ τὰ ἄλλα
ταχὺς ὢν καὶ κουφόνους, καὶ ὁ ἄλλος ὅμιλος ἅμα τῷ
Μαγκίνῳ, τὰς ναῦς ἀφέντες, ἐς τὸ τεῖχος ἐβοηδρόμουν
538 ἄνοπλοί τε καὶ γυμνοί. ἤδη δὲ τοῦ θεοῦ περὶ δείλην
ἑσπέραν ὄντος ἐχυρόν τι πρὸς τῷ τείχει καταλαβόν-
τες ἡσύχαζον. τροφῶν δ' ἀπορῶν ὁ Μαγκῖνος ἐκάλει
Πίσωνα καὶ τοὺς Ἰτυκαίων ἄρχοντας ἐπικουρεῖν αὐτῷ
κινδυνεύοντι καὶ τροφὰς φέρειν κατὰ σπουδήν.

539   114. Καὶ ὁ μὲν ἔμελλεν ἅμ' ἕῳ πρὸς τῶν Καρχηδονίων ἐξωθούμενος ἐς τοὺς κρημνοὺς συντριβήσεσθαι,
Σκιπίων δ' ἑσπέρας ἐς Ἰτύκην κατήγετο καὶ περὶ μέ-
σας νύκτας ἐντυχὼν οἷς ὁ Μαγκῖνος ἔγραφε, τόν τε
σαλπικτὴν ἐκέλευεν εὐθὺς ἐπὶ πόλεμον ἠχεῖν καὶ τοὺς
κήρυκας συγκαλεῖν ἐπὶ θάλασσαν, ὅσοι συνεληλύθε-
σαν ἐξ Ἰταλίας αὐτῷ, καὶ τοὺς ἡβῶντας Ἰτυκαίων·
ὅσοι δ' ὑπερήλικες, ἀγορὰν ἐς τὰς τριήρεις κατα-
540 φέρειν. αἰχμάλωτά τε Καρχηδονίων τινὰ λύσας ἀφῆκεν ἐξαγγέλλειν αὐτοῖς ἐπιπλεῖν Σκιπίωνα. ἔς τε τὸν
Πίσωνα ἱππέας ἄλλους ἐπ' ἄλλοις ἔπεμπε, καλῶν
αὐτὸν κατὰ τάχος. καὶ αὐτὸς ἐσχάτης φυλακῆς ἀνήγετο κελεύσας, ὅταν πλησιάζωσιν, ὀρθοὺς ἐπὶ τῶν
καταστρωμάτων ἑστάναι τοῦ πλέονα τὴν ὄψιν ἐμποι-

done this, some of the soldiers bravely began to climb up. The Carthaginians thought little of what were still only small numbers of the enemy, and opened a gate leading out to the cliffs to make a sortie against the Romans. The Romans beat them back, and chasing them into the city ran in along side them through the gate. They cried out as if they had won, and Mancinus, carried away by elation—he was generally flighty and reckless—joined the rest of the ranks, whether unarmed or lightly armed, in leaving the ships to bring assistance to those at the wall. With the sun god now going down in the late evening, they took up a strong position against the wall, and rested. Lacking supplies, Mancinus called on Piso and the magistrates of Utica to help him in this dangerous situation and bring food quickly.

114. For at dawn he was likely to be pushed out by the Carthaginians and pulverized on the rocks. Scipio landed at Utica in the evening, and about midnight met with those who had received the written message from Mancinus. He immediately ordered the trumpeter to give the signal for battle, and the heralds to summon to the shore all those who had come from Italy with him, as well as the young men of Utica. Those beyond military age he told to bring provisions to the warships. He also released some Carthaginian prisoners and sent them off to announce to the Carthaginians that Scipio was sailing against them. To Piso he dispatched one cavalryman after another, calling on him to come quickly. During the last watch he himself set sail, with orders to his men that when they were approaching the city they should stand up on deck to create an

537

538

539

540

541 εἶν τοῖς πολεμίοις. ὃ μὲν δὴ τάδε ἔπρασσεν, ὁ δὲ
Μαγκῖνος, ἅμ᾽ ἕῳ τῶν Καρχηδονίων αὐτῷ πανταχόθεν ἐπιπιπτόντων, πεντακοσίους μέν, οὓς μόνους
εἶχεν ἐνόπλους, περιέστησε τοῖς γυμνοῖς, τρισχιλίοις
οὖσι, τιτρωσκόμενος δὲ δι᾽ ἐκείνων καὶ συνωθούμενος
ἐπὶ τὸ τεῖχος ἤδη κατεκρημνίζετο, καὶ αἱ νῆες ὤφθη-
542 σαν αἱ τοῦ Σκιπίωνος, ῥοθίῳ τε φοβερῷ καταπλέουσαι καὶ μεσταὶ πανταχόθεν ὁπλιτῶν ἐφεστώτων,
Καρχηδονίοις μὲν ᾐσθημένοις διὰ τῶν αἰχμαλώτων
οὐκ ἀνέλπιστοι, Ῥωμαίοις δ᾽ ἀγνοοῦσιν ἀδόκητον
σωτηρίαν φέρουσαι· μικρὸν γὰρ ὑποχωρησάντων τῶν
Καρχηδονίων ὁ Σκιπίων τοὺς κινδυνεύοντας ἐς αὐτὰς
543 ἀνέλαβεν. καὶ Μαγκῖνον μὲν ἐς Ῥώμην αὐτίκα ἔπεμψε
(καὶ γὰρ ἧκεν αὐτῷ Σερρανὸς ἐπὶ τὴν ναυαρχίαν διά-
δοχος), αὐτὸς δ᾽ οὐ μακρὰν τῆς Καρχηδόνος ἐστρα-
544 τοπέδευεν. οἱ δὲ Καρχηδόνιοι, τῶν τειχῶν ἐς πέντε
σταδίους προελθόντες, ἀντήγειραν αὐτῷ χάρακα, καὶ
αὐτοῖς ἐς τόνδε τὸν χάρακα ἀφίκοντο Ἀσρούβας τε,
ὁ στρατηγὸς ὁ τῆς χώρας, καὶ Βιθύας ὁ ἵππαρχος,
ἑξακισχιλίους πεζοὺς ἄγοντες καὶ ἱππέας ἐς χιλίους,
χρόνῳ καὶ μελέτῃ γεγυμνασμένους.
545   115. Ὁ δὲ Σκιπίων οὐδὲν εὔκοσμον ἐν τοῖς στρα-
τιώταις ὁρῶν οὐδὲ τεταγμένον, ἀλλ᾽ ἐς ἀργίαν καὶ
πλεονεξίαν καὶ ἁρπαγὰς ὑπὸ τοῦ Πίσωνος ἐπιτετραμ-
μένους ἄλλο τε πλῆθος αὐτοῖς συνόντας ἀγοραῖον, οἳ
τῆς λείας χάριν ἑπόμενοι τοῖς θρασυτέροις συνεξέ-

impression among the enemy of greater numbers. While 541
Scipio was occupied with this, at dawn the Carthaginians
attacked Mancinus from all directions. He only had five
hundred armed men and he stationed them around the
three thousand who did not have arms. Wounded and
forced back by the Carthaginians to the wall, he was just
about to be pushed over the cliffs, when Scipio's ships
hove into view, putting in to land through the fearful waves 542
and packed everywhere with armed men standing up. The
Carthaginians had been told of this by the prisoners and
so were not surprised when they saw it, but to the Romans
it brought unexpected salvation: for when the Carthaginians drew back a short distance, Scipio took the men from
their dangerous position on to the ships. Immediately af- 543
ter, he sent Mancinus to Rome (for Serranus had arrived
to succeed him as commander of the fleet),[56] while he
himself set up camp close to Carthage. The Carthaginians 544
advanced about five stades from the walls and built a palisade opposite him, and they were joined at this palisade
by Hasdrubal the commander of the land forces and
Bithyas the cavalry commander, bringing with them an
experienced and well trained force of about six thousand
infantry and one thousand cavalry.

115. Scipio could see that his troops were neither well 545
disciplined nor well drilled, and had been given over by
Piso to laziness, greed, and looting. A large number of
traders attended them, and for the sake of booty followed
the more rash soldiers and went on unsanctioned raiding

[56] Perhaps the Sex. Atilius Serranus who became consul in
136. Like Mancinus before him, it is not clear if he was a legate
or a praetor.

APPIAN

τρέχον ἐπὶ τὰς ἁρπαγάς, ἄνευ παραγγέλματος ἰοῦσιν, τοῦ νόμου λειποστρατιώτην ἐν τοῖς πολέμοις ἡγουμένου τὸν ἀποχωροῦντα πορρωτέρω σάλπιγγος ἀκοῆς, ὅσα τε πταίσειαν οὗτοι, πάντα ἐς τὸν στρατηγὸν ἀναφερόμενα καί, ὅσα διαρπάσειαν, ἑτέρας ἔριδος αὐτοῖς καὶ κακῶν γιγνόμενα ἀρχάς· πολλοὶ γὰρ καὶ συσκήνων κατεφρόνουν διὰ τὰ κέρδη καὶ ἐς ἀνόμους πληγὰς καὶ τραύματα καὶ ἀνδροφονίας ἐχώρουν· ὧν αἰσθόμενος ὁ Σκιπίων καὶ ἐλπίζων οὔποτε κρατήσειν τῶν πολεμίων, εἰ μὴ τῶν ἰδίων κρατήσειε, συνήγαγεν ἐς ἐκκλησίαν αὐτοὺς καὶ ἐπὶ βῆμα ὑψηλὸν ἀναβὰς ἐπέπληξεν ὧδε·

547   116. "Ἐγώ, μεθ' ὑμῶν, ὦ ἄνδρες, ὑπὸ Μανιλίῳ τῷ στρατηγῷ τασσόμενος, τῆς εὐπειθείας ἐν ὑμῖν μάρτυσιν ἔδωκα πεῖραν, ἣν νῦν ὑμᾶς αἰτῶ στρατηγῶν, κολάσαι μὲν ἐς ἔσχατον ἔχων ἐξουσίαν τοὺς ἀπειθοῦντας, ὠφέλιμον δ' ἡγούμενος προαγορεῦσαι. ἴστε δέ, ἃ πράττετε· καὶ τί με δεῖ λέγειν, ἃ αἰσχύνομαι; ληστεύετε μᾶλλον ἢ πολεμεῖτε καὶ διαδιδράσκετε, οὐ στρατοπεδεύετε· καὶ πανηγυρίζουσιν ὑπὸ τῶν κερδῶν, οὐ πολιορκοῦσιν ἐοίκατε· καὶ τρυφᾶν ἐθέλετε πολεμοῦντες ἔτι, οὐ νενικηκότες. τοιγάρτοι τὰ τῶν πολεμίων ἐξ ἀέλπτου καὶ βραχέος, οὓς κατέλιπον, ἐς τοσοῦτον ἐπῆρται δυνάμεως, καὶ ἡμῖν ὁ πόνος ἐκ τῆσδε τῆς ῥᾳστώνης γέγονε χαλεπώτερος. τὰς δ' αἰτίας εἰ μὲν ἐν ὑμῖν οὔσας ἑώρων, εὐθὺς ἂν ἐκόλαζον· ἐπεὶ δ' ἀνατίθημι ἑτέρῳ, νῦν μὲν ὑμᾶς ἀφίημι τῶν μέχρι νῦν γεγονότων. ἥκω δὲ οὐ ληστεύσων

546

548

549

550

expeditions with them, even though the law defined a deserter as anyone who went beyond where they could hear the trumpet in time of war. Scipio also saw that all the reverses these men experienced were being blamed on their general, and that all the plunder they took was the cause of fresh wrangling and trouble among them. For 546 many despised their own comrades because of the desire for gain, and resorted to illegal fighting, assault, and even murder. Seeing all this, and realizing that he had no hope of mastering the enemy if he could not control his own men, Scipio summoned them to an assembly, and mounting a high rostrum, he rebuked them in the following manner:

116. "When I myself served with you, men, under Ma- 547 nilius' command, you witnessed the proof I gave of my obedience. Now that I am in command, I require your obedience. Although I have the power to punish with death those who do not obey orders, I think it useful to make a statement first. You know what you have been do- 548 ing. What need is there for me to talk about things I am ashamed to mention? You are more like bandits than warriors. You tear around the countryside rather than stay in camp. Your profits have made you more like men celebrating a holiday than conducting a siege. You want to have an easy life when you are still at war and haven't won the victory. This is the reason why the enemy, from the hope- 549 lessly weak position in which I left them, have been raised to such a height of power, and why your laziness has made our task more difficult. If I thought the blame lay with you, I would punish you immediately. But since I attribute it to someone else, I am now absolving you of blame for what has happened till now. For my part, however, I have not 550

ἔγωγε, ἀλλὰ νικήσων οὐδὲ χρηματιούμενος πρὸ τῆς
νίκης, ἀλλὰ τοὺς ἐχθροὺς πρῶτον ἐξεργασόμενος.
ἄπιτε πάντες ἐκ τοῦ στρατοπέδου τήμερον, ὅσοι μὴ
στρατεύεσθε, χωρὶς τῶν ἐπιτραπησομένων ὑπ᾽ ἐμοῦ
551 μένειν. τοῖς δ᾽ ἐξιοῦσιν οὐδ᾽ ἐπανελθεῖν δίδωμι, πλὴν
εἴ τις ἀγορὰν φέροι, καὶ ταύτην στρατιωτικήν τε καὶ
ψιλήν. ἔσται δὲ καὶ τούτοις χρόνος ὡρισμένος, ἐν ᾧ
τὰ ὄντα διαθήσονται, καὶ τῆς πράσεως αὐτῶν ἐγὼ καὶ
552 ὁ ταμίας ἐπιμελησόμεθα. καὶ τάδε μὲν εἰρήσθω τοῖς
περισσοῖς, ὑμῖν δὲ τοῖς ἐστρατευμένοις ἐν ἔστω
παράγγελμα κοινὸν ἐπὶ πᾶσιν ἔργοις ὁ ἐμὸς τρόπος
καὶ πόνος· πρὸς γὰρ τόδε κατευθύνοντες αὑτοὺς οὔτε
προθυμίας ἁμαρτήσεσθε οὔτε χάριτος ἀτυχήσετε.
553 χρὴ δὲ νῦν μὲν πονεῖν, ἐν ᾧ κινδυνεύομεν, τὰ δὲ κέρδη
καὶ τὴν τρυφὴν ἐς τὸν πρέποντα καιρὸν ἀναθέσθαι.
ταῦτ᾽ ἐγὼ προστάσσω καὶ ὁ νόμος, καὶ τοῖς μὲν εὐ-
πειθῶς ἔχουσιν οἴσει πολλὴν ἀγαθῶν ἀμοιβήν, τοῖς
δ᾽ ἀπειθοῦσι μετάνοιαν."
554   117. Ὁ μὲν δὴ Σκιπίων ταῦτ᾽ εἶπε, καὶ εὐθὺς
ἀπήλαυνε τὸ πλῆθος ἀνδρῶν ἀχρείων καὶ σὺν αὐτοῖς,
ὅσα περιττὰ καὶ μάταια καὶ τρυφερὰ ἦν. καθαροῦ
δὲ τοῦ στρατοῦ γενομένου καὶ περιδεοῦς καὶ ἐς τὰ
παραγγελλόμενα ὀξέος ἀπεπείραζε τῶν καλουμένων
555 Μεγάρων νυκτὸς μιᾶς διχῇ λανθάνων. χωρίον δ᾽
ἐστὶν εὐμέγεθες ἐν τῇ πόλει τὰ Μέγαρα, τῷ τείχει
παρεζευγμένον· ἐς ὃ τῇ μὲν ἑτέρους περιέπεμπε, τῇ δ᾽
αὐτὸς σὺν πελέκεσι καὶ κλίμαξι καὶ μοχλοῖς ἐβάδιζε
σταδίους εἴκοσιν ἀψοφητί, μετὰ σιγῆς βαθυτάτης.

come to carry out robberies, but to win victory, nor to make money before the victory, but to destroy the enemy first. I order all nonmilitary personnel to leave the camp today, apart from those who have been given my permission to stay. Those leaving I will not allow to return, unless 551 they are bringing supplies, and simple military fare at that. There will be a set time for them to dispose of their goods, and I and my quaestor will administer the sale of them. So 552 much for the noncombatants. As for you soldiers, let there be a single order applicable to all tasks: copy my way of living and hard work. If you apply yourselves to this one order, you will not lack eagerness and you will get your rewards. We have to work hard now, while we are in dan- 553 ger, and postpone profit and luxury to the proper time. These are my orders and this is the law: it will bring substantial returns to those who obey; those who do not, will regret it."

117. After giving this speech, Scipio immediately ex- 554 pelled from the camp the large number of unserviceable men, and with them everything that was superfluous, nonfunctional, or fancy. When the army had been purged, deferred to him fully, and carried out orders with precision, he made a surprise attack one night from two directions on what was called The Palace. This is a 555 large area of Carthage bordering the city wall. While he sent one group round to one side, he himself advanced noiselessly in the deepest silence on the other side for twenty stades with axes and ladders and crowbars.

556 αἰσθήσεως δ' ἄνωθεν, ὅτε μάλιστ' ἐπλησίαζε, καὶ
βοῆς ἀπὸ τειχῶν γενομένης ἀντεβόησεν αὐτός τε
πρῶτος καὶ ὁ στρατὸς αὐτοῦ καὶ οἱ ἐπὶ θάτερα ἀπεσταλμένοι μέγιστον, ὡς τῷδε πρώτῳ τοὺς Καρχηδονίους καταπλαγῆναι, τοσούτων ἐχθρῶν ἐν πλευραῖς
557 ἄφνω νυκτὸς ἐπιγενομένων. κατὰ μὲν οὖν τὸ τεῖχος
οὐδέν, καίπερ ἐπιχειρῶν, ἤνυεν, ἐς δέ τινος ἰδιώτου
πύργον ἔρημον, ἐκτὸς ὄντα τοῦ τείχους καὶ τὸ ὕψος
ἴσον ὄντα τῷ τείχει, νεανίας ἀνεβίβασεν εὐτόλμους,
οἳ τοὺς ἐπὶ τῶν τειχῶν ἀκοντίοις ἀνέστελλον ξύλα τε
καὶ σανίδας ἐς τὸ διάστημα ἐπιθέντες καὶ δι' αὐτῶν
ἐς τὰ τείχη διαδραμόντες καθήλαντο ἐς τὰ Μέγαρα
558 καὶ πυλίδα κόψαντες ἐδέχοντο τὸν Σκιπίωνα. ὁ δὲ
ἐσῆλθε μὲν σὺν ἀνδράσι τετρακισχιλίοις, καὶ φυγὴ
ταχεῖα τῶν Καρχηδονίων ἐς τὴν Βύρσαν ἦν, ὡς τῆς
ἄλλης πόλεως ἁλούσης. βοή τε ἐγίγνετο ποικίλη καὶ
τινων αἰχμαλωσία καὶ θόρυβος, ὡς καὶ τοὺς ἔξω
στρατοπεδεύοντας ἐκλιπεῖν τὸ χαράκωμα καὶ ἐς τὴν
559 Βύρσαν ὁμοῦ τοῖς ἄλλοις ἀναδραμεῖν. ὁ δὲ Σκιπίων
(τὸ γὰρ χωρίον, τὰ Μέγαρα, ἐλαχανεύετο καὶ φυτῶν
ὡραίων ἔγεμεν αἱμασιαῖς τε καὶ θριγκοῖς βάτου καὶ
ἄλλης ἀκάνθης καὶ ὀχετοῖς βαθέος ὕδατος ποικίλοις
τε καὶ σκολιοῖς κατάπλεων ἦν) ἔδεισε, μὴ ἄβατον καὶ
δυσχερὲς ᾖ στρατῷ διώκοντι, ἐν ἀγνωσίᾳ μάλιστα
διόδων, καί τις ἐν νυκτὶ ἐνέδρα γένοιτο. ἀνεζεύγνυε
δή.

560 118. Καὶ γενομένης ἡμέρας ὁ Ἀσρούβας, χαλεπῶς
ἔχων τῆς ἐς τὰ Μέγαρα ἐπιχειρήσεως, ὅσα Ῥωμαίων

When they were very close, they were spotted from above, and a cry went up from the walls. First he himself and then his army raised a counter cry, as loud as possible, and then those who had been sent around to the other side, so that the Carthaginians were alarmed for the first time now by suddenly finding so many of the enemy on their flanks at night. But Scipio made no progress against the wall, in spite of his efforts. He did, however, send some daring young men up a deserted tower belonging to a private citizen which was of the same height as the city wall. These men pushed back those on the wall with their javelins, and bridging the gap with logs and planks, they ran across onto the walls and jumped down into The Palace, where they cut through a gate and admitted Scipio. He entered with four thousand of his men, while the Carthaginians fled quickly to The Hide, in the belief that the rest of the city had been captured. Some prisoners were taken and there was all sorts of shouting and confusion, with the result that the Carthaginians encamped outside the city abandoned their palisade and ran to The Hide along with the others. The Palace quarter was planted as a kitchen garden and was full of seasonal plants, and there were walls everywhere, and fences of brambles and other thorns, and deep water channels winding around haphazardly. Scipio was afraid it would be difficult and dangerous terrain for an army pursuing the enemy, particularly as they did not know the routes across it; he also feared there might be a night ambush. So he withdrew.

118. At dawn, Hasdrubal, in his anger at the attack on The Palace, led the Roman prisoners he had onto the wall,

556

557

558

559

560

εἶχεν αἰχμάλωτα, ἐπὶ τὸ τεῖχος ἀγαγών, ὅθεν εὐ-
σύνοπτα Ῥωμαίοις ἔμελλε τὰ δρώμενα ἔσεσθαι, τῶν
μὲν ὀφθαλμοὺς ἢ γλώττας ἢ νεῦρα ἢ αἰδοῖα σιδηρίοις
ἐξεῖλκε καμπύλοις, τῶν δ᾽ ὑπέτεμνε τὰ πέλματα καὶ
τοὺς δακτύλους ἐξέκοπτεν ἢ τὸ δέρμα τοῦ λοιποῦ
σώματος ἀπέσπα καὶ πάντας ἔμπνους ἔτι κατεκρήμνι-
ζεν, ἀδιάλλακτα τοῖς Καρχηδονίοις τὰ ἐς Ῥωμαίους
561 ἐπινοῶν. καὶ ὁ μὲν αὐτοὺς οὕτως ἠρέθιζε τὴν σωτηρίαν ἔχειν ἐν μόνῃ τῇ μάχῃ, περιέστη δ᾽ αὐτῷ ἐς τὸ
ἐναντίον ὧν ἐπενόει· ὑπὸ γὰρ συνειδότος οἱ Καρχηδόνιοι τῶνδε τῶν ἀθεμίστων ἔργων περιδεεῖς ἀντὶ
προθύμων ἐγίγνοντο καὶ τὸν Ἀσρούβαν ὡς καὶ τὴν
συγγνώμην σφῶν ἀφῃρημένον ἐμίσουν· καὶ μάλισθ᾽
ἡ βουλὴ αὐτοῦ κατεβόα ὡς ὠμὰ καὶ ὑπερήφανα δε-
562 δρακότος ἐν συμφοραῖς οἰκείαις τοσαῖσδε. ὁ δὲ καὶ
τῶν βουλευτῶν τινας ἔκτεινε συλλαμβάνων καὶ ἐς
πάντα ὢν ἤδη περιδεὴς ἐς τυραννίδα μᾶλλον ἢ στρατηγίαν περιῆλθεν, ὡς ἐν τῷδε μόνῳ τὸ ἀσφαλὲς ἕξων,
εἰ φοβερὸς αὐτοῖς εἴη καὶ δι᾽ αὐτὸ καὶ δυσεπιχείρη-
τος.

563   119. Ὁ δὲ Σκιπίων τὸν μὲν χάρακα τῶν ἐχθρῶν, ὃν
τῇ προτέρᾳ κατελελοίπεσαν ἐς τὸ ἄστυ φεύγοντες,
ἐνέπρησεν, ὅλου δὲ τοῦ ἰσθμοῦ κρατῶν διετάφρευεν
αὐτὸν ἐκ θαλάσσης ἐπὶ θάλασσαν, ἀπέχων τῶν πολεμίων ὅσον ὁρμὴν βέλους. οἱ δὲ ἐπέκειντο, καὶ ἦν
αὐτῷ τὸ ἔργον ἐπὶ σταδίους τοῦ μετώπου πέντε καὶ
564 εἴκοσιν ἐργαζομένῳ τε ὁμοῦ καὶ μαχομένῳ. ὡς δὲ
αὐτῷ τοῦτ᾽ ἐξετετέλεστο, ἑτέραν ὤρυσσε τάφρον ἴσην,

from where the Romans could easily see what he was about to do. With some of them he used iron hooks to remove their eyes, or tongues, or sinews or genitals; with others he sliced away the soles of their feet, or cut off their fingers, or tore the skin from the rest of their body. All of them he threw off the cliffs while they were still alive. His intention was to make impossible any reconciliation between Rome and Carthage, and thus incite his men to 561 think that their only hope of safety was to fight; but it had quite the opposite effect to what he intended. For the Carthaginians, now complicit in these lawless deeds, became very nervous rather than enthusiastic, and began to hate Hasdrubal for depriving them even of the possibility of pardon. Their council in particular denounced him for such savage and brutal actions in the middle of a great domestic disaster. But he even arrested and executed 562 some of the council members, and made himself an object of such general fear that he ended up more tyrant than military commander, believing that he would only be safe if he terrorized them and for that reason made it difficult to attack him.

119. Scipio then burned down the enemy's palisade, 563 which they had abandoned the previous day when making their escape into the city, and now master of the whole isthmus, he began to dig a ditch across it from one shore to the other, keeping only a spear's throw away from the enemy. They pressed him hard, and he found it difficult along a front of over twenty-five stades to work and fight at the same time. When he had completed this, he dug 564

οὐ πολὺ τῆς προτέρας διασχών, ἐς τὴν ἤπειρον
ἀφορῶσαν. δύο τε ἐπικαρσίας αὐταῖς ἑτέρας περιθείς,
ὡς γενέσθαι τὸ ὅλον ὄρυγμα τετράγωνον, ἐσταύρωσε
565 πάντα ξύλοις ὀξέσι. καὶ ἐπὶ τοῖς σταυροῖς τὰς μὲν
ἄλλας τάφρους ἐχαράκωσε, τῇ δ᾽ ἐς τὴν Καρχηδόνα
ὁρώσῃ καὶ τεῖχος παρῳκοδόμησεν ἐπὶ τοὺς πέντε
καὶ εἴκοσι σταδίους, ὕψος μὲν δυώδεκα ποδῶν χωρὶς
ἐπάλξεών τε καὶ πύργων, οἳ ἐκ διαστήματος ἐπέκειντο
τῷ τείχει, τὸ δὲ βάθος ἐφ᾽ ἥμισυ μάλιστα τοῦ ὕψους·
ὁ δ᾽ ἐν μέσῳ πύργος ὑψηλότατός τε ἦν, καὶ ἐπ᾽ αὐτοῦ
ξύλινος ἐπέκειτο τετρώροφος, ὅθεν καθεώρα τὰ γιγνό-
566 μενα ἐν τῇ πόλει. ταῦτα δ᾽ ἡμέραις εἴκοσι καὶ νυξὶν
ἐργασάμενος ὅλῳ τῷ στρατῷ πονοῦντι καὶ παραλλὰξ
ἐργαζομένῳ τε καὶ πολεμοῦντι καὶ σῖτον ἢ ὕπνον αἱ-
ρουμένῳ τὴν στρατιὰν ἐσήγαγεν ἐς τόδε τὸ χαράκωμα.
567 120. Καὶ ἦν αὐτῷ τοῦτο στρατόπεδόν τε ὁμοῦ καὶ
κατὰ τῶν ἐχθρῶν ἐπιτείχισμα ἐπίμηκες, ὅθεν ὁρμώ-
μενος τὴν ἀγορὰν ἀφῃρεῖτο Καρχηδονίους, ὅσῃ κατὰ
γῆν αὐτοῖς ἐφέρετο· ὅτι γὰρ μὴ τῷδε τῷ αὐχένι μόνῳ,
568 τὰ λοιπὰ ἡ Καρχηδὼν περίκλυστος ἦν. καὶ τοῦτο
πρῶτον αὐτοῖς καὶ μάλιστα ἐγίγνετο λιμοῦ καὶ κακῶν
αἴτιον· ἅτε γὰρ τοῦ πλήθους παντὸς ἐκ τῶν ἀγρῶν ἐς
τὴν πόλιν ἀνοικισαμένου, οὔτε προϊόντες ποι διὰ τὴν
πολιορκίαν, οὔτε ξένων ἐμπόρων διὰ τὸν πόλεμον θαμινὰ ἐπιόντων, μόνῃ τῇ τῆς Λιβύης ἀγορᾷ χρώμενοι,
μικρὰ μέν ποτε καὶ διὰ θαλάσσης, ὅτε ὡραῖον εἴη, τὰ
πλέονα δὲ κατὰ τὴν γῆν ἐπεκομίζοντο, ἀφῃρημένοι δὲ
τότε τὴν ἐκ τῆς γῆς κομιδὴν ἐπιπόνως ᾔσθοντο τοῦ

another ditch of the same length not far from the previous one, but facing the mainland. He then added two more at right angles to them, so that the whole excavation formed a square, and he fenced it all round with sharp stakes. In addition to the stakes, he also built a palisade behind the ditches, and a wall on the side facing Carthage twenty-five stades long. This wall was twelve feet high, excluding the parapets and towers which lay at intervals on top of it, and it was about half as wide as it was high. The tower in the middle was the highest, and constructed on top of it was another wooden tower four stories high, from which Scipio could look down on what was going on in the city. When he had completed these works in twenty days and nights, with the whole army working on the task, taking turns in building, fighting, eating, and sleeping, he led the troops into this stockade.

120. This was a camp for Scipio, but at the same time a very long fortification against the enemy. Using it as a base, Scipio deprived the Carthaginians of the supplies being brought in to them from the land. For, with the exception only of this neck of land, the rest of Carthage was surrounded by water. And this was the first and foremost cause of famine and trouble for them. For, as the entire population had moved from the fields into the city, and because of the siege had nowhere to go, while foreign merchants rarely came on account of the war, the only supplies they had available came from Africa. Occasionally a small amount came by sea, when the weather allowed, but most was transported by land. Having now lost this land route, the Carthaginians began to feel the terri-

569 λιμοῦ. Βιθύας δέ, ὅσπερ ἵππαρχος ἦν αὐτοῖς καὶ ἐπέ-
πεμπτο ἐπὶ σῖτον ἐκ πολλοῦ, προσελθεῖν μὲν ἢ βιάσασθαι τὸ χαράκωμα τοῦ Σκιπίωνος οὐκ ἐτόλμα,
περιφέρων δὲ τὴν ἀγορὰν ἐς τὰ πόρρω διὰ μακροῦ
ναυσὶν ἐσέπεμπεν, ἐφορμουσῶν μὲν τῇ Καρχηδόνι
νεῶν τοῦ Σκιπίωνος· ἀλλ' οὔτε διηνεκῶς οὔτε πυκναὶ
συνειστήκεσαν, ὡς ἐν ἀλιμένῳ καὶ περικρήμνῳ θαλάσσῃ, παρά τε τὴν πόλιν αὐτὴν οὐκ ἐδύναντο ἀνα-
κωχεύειν, τῶν Καρχηδονίων τοῖς τείχεσιν ἐφεστώτων
καὶ τοῦ κύματος ἐκεῖ μάλιστα διὰ τὰς πέτρας ταρασ-
570 σομένου. ὅθεν αἱ φορτίδες αἱ Βιθύου καὶ εἴ τις ἄλλος
ἔμπορος ὑπὸ κέρδους ἐθελοκινδύνως ἠπείγετο, φυ-
λάσσοντες ἄνεμον ἐκ πόντου πολὺν πεπετασμένοις
τοῖς ἱστίοις διέθεον, ἀδυνάτων οὐσῶν ἔτι τῶν τριήρων
ὁλκάδας, φερομένας ἱστίῳ καὶ πνεύματι, διώκειν.
571 σπανίως μὲν οὖν ἐγίγνετο καὶ μόνον, ὅτε βίαιον εἴη
πνεῦμα ἐκ πόντου· καὶ ταῦτα δ', ὅσα φέροιεν αἱ νῆες,
Ἀσρούβας τρισμυρίοις ἀνδράσι μόνοις διένεμεν, οὓς
ἐς μάχην ἐπείλεκτο, καὶ τοῦ ἄλλου πλήθους κατεφρό-
νει· ὅθεν ἐμόχθουν μάλιστα ὑπὸ τοῦ λιμοῦ.

572   121. Καὶ ὁ Σκιπίων αἰσθανόμενος ἐπενόει τὸν
ἔσπλουν αὐτοῖς τοῦ λιμένος, ἐς δύσιν τε ἀφορῶντα
καὶ οὐ πάνυ πόρρω τῆς γῆς ὄντα, ἀποκλεῖσαι. χῶμα
οὖν ἐς τὴν θάλασσαν ἔχου μακρόν, ἀρχόμενος μὲν
ἀπὸ τῆς ταινίας, ἣ μεταξὺ τῆς λίμνης οὖσα καὶ τῆς
θαλάσσης Γλῶσσα ἐκαλεῖτο, προϊὼν δ' ἐς τὸ πέλα-
573 γος καὶ εὐθύνων ἐπὶ τὸν ἔσπλουν. ἔχου δὲ λίθοις τε
μεγάλοις καὶ πυκνοῖς, ἵνα μὴ ὑπὸ τοῦ κλύδωνος δια-

ble effects of hunger. Bithyas, their commander of cavalry, 569
who had long ago been sent to get food, did not dare to
approach Scipio's fort or try to force his way past it, but
carrying the supplies a considerable distance the long way
round, he sent them in by ship. Although Scipio's ships
were blockading Carthage, they did not keep station continuously or close together, as there was no harbor and the
sea was full of reefs, and they were unable to ride at anchor
near the city itself, with the Carthaginians manning the
walls and the sea there being particularly rough because
of the rocks. For these reasons Bithyas' transport ships, 570
and an occasional merchant driven by hope of profit to risk
danger willingly, would wait for a strong breeze off the sea,
and setting full sail, run the blockade, as triremes were not
capable of chasing merchantmen sailing downwind. But 571
this happened rarely and only when the wind blew hard
off the sea. And the supplies that came in by ship Hasdrubal distributed only to the thirty thousand soldiers he
had selected for battle: the rest of the population he ignored, and so they suffered particularly from hunger.

121. When Scipio saw what was happening, he planned 572
to close off their entrance to the harbor, which faced west
and was not very far from the shore. So he began to build
a long mole into the sea, starting from the strip of land
known as The Tongue, which lay between the harbor and
the sea, and extending it straight out into the sea toward
the harbor entrance. He built it up with big, heavy stones, 573
so that it would not be washed away by the waves. The

221

φέροιντο. καὶ πλάτος τοῦ χώματος τὸ μὲν ἄνω τεσσάρων καὶ εἴκοσι ποδῶν, τὸ δ' ἐς τὸν βυθὸν καὶ
574 τετραπλάσιον ἦν. τοῖς δὲ Καρχηδονίοις ἀρχομένου
μὲν τοῦδε τοῦ ἔργου καταφρόνησις ἦν ὡς χρονίου τε
καὶ μακροῦ καὶ ἴσως ἀδυνάτου· προϊόντος δὲ σὺν
ἐπείξει τοσοῦδε στρατοῦ, μήτε ἡμέραν ἐκλείποντος
ἐπὶ τοῖς ἔργοις μήτε νύκτα, ἔδεισαν καὶ στόμα ἕτερον
ἐπὶ θάτερα τοῦ λιμένος ὤρυσσον ἐς μέσον τὸ πέλαγος, οἱ μηδὲν χῶμα προελθεῖν ἐδύνατο ὑπὸ βάθους τε
575 καὶ πνευμάτων ἀγριωτέρων. διώρυσσον δ' ἅμα γυ-
ναιξὶ καὶ παισίν, ἔνδοθεν ἀρχόμενοι καὶ πάνυ λανθά-
νοντες· ἅμα δὲ καὶ ναῦς ἐξ ὕλης παλαιᾶς ἐναυπήγουν,
πεντήρεις τε καὶ τριήρεις, οὐδὲν ὑπολείποντες εὐψυ-
576 χίας τε καὶ τόλμης. οὕτω δ' ἅπαντα ἐπέκρυπτον, ὡς
μηδὲ τοὺς αἰχμαλώτους ἔχειν τι τῷ Σκιπίωνι σαφὲς
εἰπεῖν, ἀλλὰ κτύπον μὲν ἐν τοῖς λιμέσιν ἡμέρας τε καὶ
νυκτὸς εἶναι πολὺν ἀπαύστως, τὴν δὲ χρείαν οὐκ εἰδέναι, μέχρι γε δὴ πάντων ἑτοίμων γενομένων οἱ
Καρχηδόνιοι τὸ στόμα ἀνέῳξαν περὶ ἔω καὶ ναυσὶ
πεντήκοντα μὲν τριηριτικαῖς, κερκούροις δὲ καὶ μυ-
οπάρωσι καὶ ἄλλοις βραχυτέροις πολλοῖς ἐξέπλεον,
ἐς κατάπληξιν ἐσκευασμένοι φοβερῶς.

577   122. Ῥωμαίους δὲ τό τε στόμα ἄφνω γενόμενον καὶ
ὁ στόλος ἐπὶ τῷ στόματι ἐς τοσόνδε κατέπληξεν, ὡς
τοὺς Καρχηδονίους, εἰ αὐτίκα ταῖς ναυσὶ ταῖς Ῥωμαίων ἐπέθεντο, ἠμελημέναις τε ὡς ἐν τειχομαχίᾳ καὶ
οὐδενὸς ναύτου παρόντος οὐδ' ἐρέτου, ὅλου ἂν τοῦ
578 ναυστάθμου κρατῆσαι. νῦν οὖν (ἁλῶναι γὰρ ἔδει

mole was twenty-four feet wide at the top and four times that at the bottom. When the work on it began, the Carthaginians were disdainful as they believed it would take a long time, and was a big project and perhaps impossible to complete. But with so many Roman soldiers urgently pressing ahead, and not stopping from the task by day or night, the Carthaginians became uneasy, and began to excavate another way out to the open sea on the other side of the harbor, where no mole could reach because the water was too deep and the winds too strong. Women and children also took part in the digging operations which they began inside the harbor and completely out of sight. At the same time they began to construct ships, quinqueremes, and triremes from old timbers, a task in which they showed no lack of resolute courage. In this way they kept everything secret so that not even the prisoners had any clear information for Scipio, but could only tell him that there was loud and nonstop noise in the harbors day and night, the cause of which they did not know. Eventually, when everything was ready, the Carthaginians opened their entrance about dawn, and sailed out through it with fifty triremes, and with ketches, skiffs and many other smaller boats, all fitted out frighteningly to create consternation.

122. The sudden appearance of the new entrance, and a fleet at its mouth, astounded the Romans to such an extent that, if the Carthaginians had immediately attacked the Roman ships, which had been neglected since the fighting was at the walls and no sailors or rowers were present, they would have taken possession of the whole fleet. But as it was (for Carthage was destined to fall), they

574

575

576

577

578

Καρχηδόνα) τότε μὲν ἐς μόνην ἐπίδειξιν ἐπέπλευσαν
καὶ σοβαρῶς ἐπιτωθάσαντες ἀνέστρεφον, τρίτῃ δὲ
ἡμέρᾳ μετὰ τοῦτο ἐς ναυμαχίαν καθίσταντο· καὶ οἱ
Ῥωμαῖοι τάς τε ναῦς καὶ τἆλλα εὐτρεπισάμενοι
579 ἀντανήγοντο. βοῆς δὲ καὶ παρακελεύσεως ἑκατέρωθεν
γενομένης καὶ προθυμίας ἐρετῶν τε καὶ κυβερνητῶν
καὶ τῶν ἐπιβατῶν, ὡς ἐν τῷδε λοιπῷ Καρχηδονίοις
μὲν τῆς σωτηρίας οὔσης, Ῥωμαίοις δὲ τῆς νίκης ἐν-
τελοῦς, πληγαί τε πολλαὶ καὶ τραύματα ποικίλα ἐγί-
580 γνετο παρ᾽ ἀμφοῖν μέχρι μέσης ἡμέρας. ἐν δὲ τῷ
πόνῳ τὰ σκάφη τῶν Λιβύων τὰ σμικρὰ ταῖς Ῥωμαϊ-
καῖς ναυσί, μεγάλαις οὔσαις, ἐς τοὺς ταρσοὺς ὑπο-
τρέχοντα διετίτρη πρύμνας καὶ ἐξέκοπτε πηδάλια καὶ
κώπας καὶ ἄλλα πολλὰ καὶ ποικίλα ἐλύπει, εὐμαρῶς
581 τε ὑποφεύγοντα καὶ εὐμαρῶς ἐπιπλέοντα. ἀκρίτου δ᾽
ἔτι τῆς ναυμαχίας οὔσης καὶ τῆς ἡμέρας ἐς δείλην
τρεπομένης ἔδοξε τοῖς Καρχηδονίοις ὑποχωρεῖν, οὔ τι
κατὰ ἧτταν, ἀλλ᾽ ἐς τὴν ἐπιοῦσαν ὑπερτιθεμένοις.

582   123. Καὶ αὐτῶν τὰ σκάφη τὰ βραχύτερα πρού-
φευγε καὶ τὸν ἔσπλουν προλαβόντα ἐς ἄλληλα ὠθεῖτο
ὑπὸ πλήθους καὶ τὸ στόμα βύζην ἀπέκλειεν. ὅθεν αἱ
μείζους ἐπανιοῦσαι τὸν ἔσπλουν ἀφῄρηντο καὶ εἰς τὸ
χῶμα κατέφυγον, ὃ πρὸ τοῦ τείχους εὐρύχωρον ἐμπόροις ἐς διάθεσιν φορτίων ἐγεγένητο ἐκ πολλοῦ· καὶ
παρατείχισμα ἐπ᾽ αὐτοῦ βραχὺ ἐν τῷδε τῷ πολέμῳ
πεποίητο, ἵνα μὴ ὡς ἐν εὐρυχώρῳ στρατοπεδεύσειάν
583 ποτε οἱ πολέμιοι. ἐς μὲν δὴ τόδε τὸ χῶμα αἱ νῆες αἱ
τῶν Καρχηδονίων ἀπορίᾳ λιμένος καταφυγοῦσαι με-

sailed now merely to make a display: after mocking the
Romans insultingly, they returned to base. Three days
later, however, they arrayed themselves for a battle at sea,
and the Romans set sail to meet them, having readied
their ships and everything else. There were shouts of en-   579
couragement on both sides and great enthusiasm from the
rowers, helmsmen, and marines, since in this last encounter lay safety for the Carthaginians and total victory for the
Romans. Until the middle of the day many blows were
given and all sorts of wounds sustained by both sides. In   580
the course of the battle the small African skiffs would run
in under the oars of the big Roman ships and hole them
in the prow, or break off rudders and oars and inflict all
sorts of damage, retreating and sailing to the attack with
ease. While the battle was still undecided, but the day   581
moving toward evening, the Carthaginians decided to
withdraw, not because they were beaten, but to postpone
the battle until the following day.

123. Their smaller boats led the withdrawal, but when   582
they occupied the entrance, there were so many of them
that they started to collide with each other and completely
blocked the mouth of the harbor. As a result the bigger
ships were prevented from using the entrance, and took
refuge at the wide quay that had been built a long time
in front of the city wall for merchants to offload
their goods. A small defense wall had been built on the
quay during this war, to prevent the enemy ever establish-
ing a camp on the broad space it offered. When the Car-   583
thaginian ships retreated to this quay, for lack of a harbor,

APPIAN

τωπηδὸν ὡρμίσαντο· καὶ τοὺς ἐχθροὺς ἐπιπλέοντας οἱ
μὲν ἀπ᾿ αὐτῶν τῶν νεῶν, οἱ δ᾿ ἀπὸ τοῦ χώματος, οἱ
584 δ᾿ ἐκ τοῦ διατειχίσματος ἀπεμάχοντο. Ῥωμαίοις δ᾿ ὁ
μὲν ἐπίπλους ἦν ῥᾴδιος καὶ τὸ μάχεσθαι ναυσὶν
ἑστώσαις εὐμαρές, αἱ δ᾿ ἀναχωρήσεις δι᾿ ἀναστροφὴν
τῶν νεῶν, μακρῶν οὐσῶν, βραδεῖαί τε καὶ δυσχερεῖς
ἐγίγνοντο· ὅθεν ἀντέπασχον ἐν τῷδε τὰ ὅμοια (ὅτε
γὰρ ἐπιστρέφοιεν, ἐπλήσσοντο ὑπὸ τῶν Καρχηδο-
585 νίων ἐπιπλεόντων), μέχρι νῆες Σιδητῶν πέντε, αἱ φι-
λίᾳ Σκιπίωνος εἵποντο, τὰς μὲν ἀγκύρας καθῆκαν ἐκ
πολλοῦ διαστήματος ἐς τὸ πέλαγος, ἁψάμεναι δ᾿ ἀπ᾿
αὐτῶν κάλους μακροὺς εἰρεσίᾳ τοῖς Καρχηδονίοις
ἐπέπλεον καί, ὅτε ἐγχρίμψειαν, ὑπεχώρουν, τοὺς κάλους ἐπισπώμεναι κατὰ πρύμναν, αὖθίς τε ῥοθίῳ
586 καταπλέουσαι πάλιν ἀνήγοντο κατὰ πρύμναν. τότε
γὰρ ὁ στόλος ἅπας, τὸν νοῦν τῶν Σιδητῶν ὁρῶντές τε
καὶ μιμούμενοι, πολλὰ τοὺς ἐχθροὺς ἔβλαπτον. καὶ τὸ
ἔργον ἐς νύκτα ἐτελεύτα, καὶ ἐς τὴν πόλιν διέφυγον
αἱ τῶν Καρχηδονίων νῆες, ὅσαι γε ἔτι ἦσαν ὑπόλοι-
ποι.

587 124. Σκιπίων δὲ γενομένης ἡμέρας ἐπεχείρει τῷ
χώματι· καὶ γὰρ ἦν εὔκαιρον ἐπιτείχισμα τοῦ λιμένος. κριοῖς οὖν τὸ παρατείχισμα τύπτων καὶ μη-
588 χανήματα πολλὰ ἐπάγων μέρος αὐτοῦ κατέβαλεν. οἱ
δὲ Καρχηδόνιοι, καίπερ ὑπὸ λιμοῦ καὶ κακώσεως ποι-
κίλης ἐνοχλούμενοι, νυκτὸς ἐξέδραμον ἐπὶ τὰ Ῥωμαίων μηχανήματα, οὐ κατὰ γῆν (οὐ γὰρ ἦν δίοδος)
οὐδὲ ναυσὶν (ἁλιτενὴς γὰρ ἦν ἡ θάλασσα), ἀλλὰ γυ-

226

they moored with their prows facing out. As the enemy sailed in to attack, men from the ships and others from the quay and the defense wall fought them off. For the Romans, attack was easy, and it is a simple matter to engage stationary ships, but it was a slow and difficult process to go back, as the ships were long and had to be turned around. While executing this maneuver, therefore, they suffered as much damage as they inflicted. For whenever they turned around, they were hit by the attacking Carthaginian ships. Eventually, five ships from Side,[57] who were with Scipio out of friendship, dropped their anchors some distance out to sea, and after tying long ropes to them, rowed their way in against the Carthaginians and when they had delivered their attack, withdrew, stern first, by pulling on the ropes. And sailing in again on the waves, they put to sea again stern first. At this point, the whole fleet, seeing the good sense of the Sidetans and copying it, did a great deal of damage to the enemy. The engagement ended with the onset of night, and the Carthaginian ships, or those that were still left, took refuge in the city.

124. At daybreak Scipio attacked the quay, as it offered a strategic stronghold for command of the harbor. By ramming the defensive wall and bringing many siege engines against it, he breached a part of it. The Carthaginians, although burdened by hunger and various other sufferings, made a sortie during the night against the Roman siege engines. They did not go by land (for there was no way through) nor on ships (for the sea was too shallow),

584

585

586

587

588

---

[57] Side was in Pamhylia, on the southwest coast of Turkey.

μνοὶ δᾷδας ἔφερον, οὐχ ἡμμένας, ἵνα μὴ μακρόθεν
589 εἶεν καταφανεῖς· ἐς δὲ τὴν θάλασσαν ἐμβάντες, ᾗ μή
τις ἂν προσεδόκησεν, οἱ μὲν ἄχρι τῶν μαστῶν βρε-
χόμενοι διεβάδιζον, οἱ δὲ καὶ διένεον, ἕως ἐπὶ τὰ μηχανήματα ἐλθόντες ἐξῆψαν τὸ πῦρ καὶ κατάφωροι
γενόμενοι πολλὰ μὲν ἔπαθον, ἅτε γυμνοὶ τιτρωσκόμε-
590 νοι, πολλὰ δ' ἀντέδρασαν ὑπὸ τόλμης· οἳ καὶ τὰς ἀκί-
δας τῶν βελῶν καὶ τὰς αἰχμὰς ἐν στέρνοις καὶ ὄψεσι
φέροντες οὐκ ἀνίεσαν, ὥσπερ θηρία ταῖς πληγαῖς
ἐγκείμενοι, μέχρι τὰ μηχανήματα ἐνέπρησαν καὶ τοὺς
591 Ῥωμαίους ἐτρέψαντο θορυβουμένους. ἔκπληξίς τε καὶ
τάραχος ἦν ἀνὰ ὅλον τὸ στρατόπεδον καὶ φόβος, οἷος
οὐ πρίν, ὑπὸ μανίας γυμνῶν πολεμίων, ὥστε δείσας
ὁ Σκιπίων μετὰ ἱππέων ἔξω περιέθει καὶ τοὺς οἰκείους,
592 εἰ μὴ λήξαιεν τῆς φυγῆς, ἐκέλευε βάλλειν. ἔστι δὲ οὓς
ἔβαλε καὶ ἀπέκτεινεν, ἕως οἱ πλείους συνεώσθησαν ἐς
τὸ στρατόπεδον ὑπὸ ἀνάγκης καὶ διενυκτέρευσαν ἔνοπλοι, τὴν ἀπόγνωσιν τῶν ἐχθρῶν δεδιότες. οἱ δέ, τὰς
μηχανὰς ἐμπρήσαντες, ἐξένεον αὖθις ἐς τὰ οἰκεῖα.
593 125. Ἅμα δ' ἡμέρᾳ Καρχηδόνιοι μέν, οὐκ ἐνοχλου-
σῶν σφᾶς ἔτι μηχανῶν πολεμίων, τὸ διαπεπτωκὸς
τοῦ διατειχίσματος ᾠκοδόμουν καὶ πύργους ἐν αὐτῷ
πολλοὺς ἐποίουν ἐκ διαστήματος, Ῥωμαῖοι δ', ἑτέρας
ἐργασάμενοι μηχανάς, χώματα ἤγειρον ἀντιμέτωπα
τοῖς πύργοις δᾷδά τε συγκεκομμένην καὶ θεῖον ἐν
κώθωσι καὶ πίσσαν ἐπ' αὐτοὺς ἐσφενδόνων καὶ ἔστιν
οὓς τῶν πύργων ἐνεπίμπρασαν καὶ τοὺς Καρχηδονίους φεύγοντας ἐδίωκον. ὀλισθηρὸς δ' ἦν ὁ δρόμος

but naked and carrying torches they had not yet lit to avoid being visible from far away. Entering the sea where no one would have expected, they made the crossing, some wading through the water up to their chest, others swimming, and when they came up to the engines they lit the torches. They could now be seen and as they were unprotected they suffered heavy injuries, but retaliated bravely. Taking barbed arrows and spearheads in the chest and face, they did not relax their effort, but even with the blows raining down, they pressed on like wild animals until they set fire to the engines and threw the Romans back in confusion. The whole camp was filled with shock and confusion, and a level of fear they had not felt before, at the frenzy of a naked enemy, so that, in alarm, Scipio rode around outside with some cavalrymen and ordered them to shoot down their own men if they did not stop fleeing. And there were some he shot and killed, until the majority were forcibly rounded up into the camp. They spent the night under arms in fear of the enemy's desperation. Having burned the siege engines, the Carthaginians swam back to their own lines.

125. At dawn, since they were no longer troubled by the Roman engines, the Carthaginians repaired the breach in the cross-wall and built a large number of towers on it at intervals. The Romans began to construct new siege engines and to form mounds opposite the towers, and they used slings to throw burning torches and containers filled with brimstone and pitch against the enemy. They set fire to some of the towers and put the Carthaginians to flight, but although they gave chase to the fugitives, the ground underfoot was slippery with the large quantities of con-

589

590

591

592

593

APPIAN

ὑφ' αἵματος πεπηγότος ὑπογύου τε καὶ πολλοῦ, ὥστε
594 τῶν φευγόντων ἀπελίποντο ἄκοντες. ὁ δὲ Σκιπίων τοῦ
χώματος ὅλου κατασχὼν ἀπετάφρευεν αὐτὸ καὶ τεῖχος ἤγειρεν ἐκ πλίνθων, οὔτε κολοβώτερον τοῦ τῶν
595 πολεμίων οὔτ' ἐκ μακροῦ διαστήματος ἀπ' αὐτῶν. ὡς
δ' ἐξείργαστο αὐτῷ καὶ τὸ τεῖχος, τετρακισχιλίους ἐς
αὐτὸ ἔπεμψεν, ἐπαφιέναι τοῖς ἐχθροῖς βέλη τε καὶ
ἀκόντια σὺν καταφρονήσει. οἱ δὲ ἰσομέτωποι γενόμενοι ἔβαλλον αὐτοὺς ἐπιτυχῶς. καὶ τὸ θέρος ἐς ταῦτα
ἀναλώθη.
596   126. Χειμῶνος δ' ἀρχομένου τὴν ἐν τῇ χώρᾳ τῶν
Καρχηδονίων δύναμίν τε καὶ συμμάχους ὁ Σκιπίων
ἔγνω προκαθελεῖν, ὅθεν αὐτοῖς ἀγορὰ διεπέμπετο.
περιπέμψας οὖν ἑτέρωσε ἑτέρους, αὐτὸς ἐς Νέφεριν
ἐπὶ Διογένη, τὸν μετὰ Ἀσρούβαν φρουροῦντα τὴν Νέφεριν, ἠπείγετο διὰ τῆς λίμνης καὶ Γάιον Λαίλιον
597 κατὰ γῆν περιέπεμπεν. ὡς δὲ ἀφίκετο, δύο σταδίους
ἀποσχὼν τοῦ Διογένους ἐστρατοπέδευε καὶ Γολόσσην καταλιπὼν ἐγχειρεῖν ἀπαύστως τῷ Διογένει αὐτὸς ἐπὶ Καρχηδόνος ἠπείγετο· ὅθεν ἐς Νέφερίν τε καὶ
Καρχηδόνα διετρόχαζεν, αἰεὶ τὰ γιγνόμενα ἐφορῶν.
598 δύο δὲ τοῦ Διογένους μεσοπυργίων καταπεσόντων
ἧκεν ὁ Σκιπίων καὶ χιλίους ἐπιλέκτους ὄπισθεν τοῦ
Διογένους ἐνεδρεύσας ἑτέροις ἐκ μετώπου τρισχιλίοις, ἀριστίνδην καὶ τοῖσδε ἐπιλεγομένοις, ἐπέβαινεν
ἐπὶ τὰ πεπτωκότα τῶν μεσοπυργίων, οὐκ ἀθρόους

gealed blood that had been shed recently, and they reluctantly left off their pursuit of the enemy. Scipio now had 594 control of the whole quay, and after digging a protective ditch, began to build a brick wall no smaller than that of the enemy and not very far away from them. When he had 595 finished the wall, he sent four thousand men onto it to fire their missiles and javelins with impunity against the enemy. As they were at the same height, they were successful in hitting their targets. This action marked the end of the summer.

126. At the beginning of winter, Scipio decided to destroy Carthaginian power and their allies inland, from 596 where supplies were being sent to them. Dispatching his men in different directions, he himself hurried to Nepheris against Diogenes, who succeeded Hasdrubal in command of the garrison; Scipio went across the lagoon while he sent Gaius Laelius around by land.[58] When he got there, 597 he made camp two stades away from Diogenes. Leaving Gulussa to press home the attack against Diogenes relentlessly, he himself hurried back to Carthage, and thereafter rode to and fro between the two places to have permanent oversight of what was happening. When two sections of 598 Diogenes' wall between towers had been breached, Scipio came up and, after placing one thousand specially chosen men in ambush at Diogenes' rear, he launched a frontal attack on the sections of wall that had been knocked down between towers, with another three thousand men also specially selected for their bravery. He did not, however, send massed ranks into the attack, but separate units fol-

[58] C. Laelius was one of Scipio's legates. He reached the consulship in 140.

APPIAN

ἀναβιβάζων, ἀλλὰ κατὰ μέρη πυκνοὺς ἐπ' ἀλλήλοις,
ἵνα μηδὲ βιασθέντες οἱ πρῶτοι φυγεῖν δύναιντο διὰ
599 τοὺς ἑπομένους. πολλῆς δὲ βοῆς οὔσης καὶ πόνου καὶ
τῶν Λιβύων ἐς ταῦτ' ἐπεστραμμένων οἱ χίλιοι, καθάπερ αὐτοῖς προείρητο, οὐδενὸς ἐς αὐτοὺς ἀποβλέπον-
τος οὐδ' ὑπονοοῦντος ἐνέπεσον ἐς τὸ χαράκωμα εὐ-
600 τόλμως καὶ διέσπων αὐτὸ καὶ ὑπερέβαινον. καὶ τῶν
πρώτων ἔνδον γενομένων αἴσθησις ἐγίγνετο ταχεῖα,
καὶ ἔφευγον οἱ Λίβυες, οὐχ ὅσους ἑώρων, ἀλλὰ πολὺ
601 πλείονας ἡγούμενοι τοὺς ἐσελθόντας εἶναι. Γολόσσης
δ' αὐτοῖς ἐπιτρέχων σὺν Νομάσι πολλοῖς καὶ ἐλέφασι
πολὺν εἰργάζετο φόνον, ὡς ἀπολέσθαι μὲν ἐς ἑπτα-
κισμυρίους σὺν τοῖς ἀχρείοις, ἁλῶναι δ' ἐς μυρίους,
602 διαφυγεῖν δ' ἀμφὶ τοὺς τετρακισχιλίους. ἑάλω δὲ καὶ
ἡ πόλις ἡ Νέφερις ἐπὶ τῷ στρατοπέδῳ, δύο καὶ εἴκοσιν ἡμέραις ἄλλαις πολιορκηθεῖσα πρὸς τοῦ Σκιπίω-
603 νος πάνυ κακοπαθῶς ἐν χειμῶνι καὶ ψυχρῷ χωρίῳ. τὸ
δὲ ἔργον τόδε μάλιστα συνήνεγκεν ἐς τὴν τῆς Καρχηδόνος ἅλωσιν· ἥδε γὰρ ἡ στρατιὰ τὴν ἀγορὰν
αὐτοῖς διεπόρθμευεν, καὶ ἐς τόδε τὸ στρατόπεδον οἱ
Λίβυες ἀφορῶντες ἐθάρρουν. τότε δ' αὐτοῦ ληφθέντος
καὶ τὰ λοιπὰ τῆς Λιβύης χωρία τοῖς στρατηγοῖς Σκι-
604 πίωνος προσεχώρει ἢ οὐ δυσχερῶς ἐλαμβάνετο. ἥ τε
ἀγορὰ τοὺς Καρχηδονίους ἐπέλιπε, καὶ οὐδὲν οὔτ' ἐκ
Λιβύης, ἀλλοτρίας ἤδη γενομένης, οὔτ' ἀλλαχόθεν
αὐτοῖς καταπλεῖν ἐδύνατο διά τε τὸν πόλεμον αὐτὸν
καὶ τὴν ὥραν χειμέριον οὖσαν.

605   127. Ἀρχομένου δ' ἔαρος ὁ μὲν Σκιπίων ἐπεχείρει

232

lowing closely on each other, so that even if the first ones were forced back, they could not flee because of the ones behind them. There was a great deal of shouting and distress, and when the attention of the Africans was focused on this, the one thousand men, with nobody looking in their direction or suspecting their presence, did as they were ordered and made a daring attack on the palisade, which they tore apart and climbed over. As soon as the first ones were inside, their presence was quickly noted and the Africans fled, in the belief that there were far more intruders than they had seen. Gulussa ran them down with a large force of Numidian cavalry and elephants, and inflicted great slaughter, killing nearly seventy thousand of them, including civilians. About ten thousand were captured and approximately four thousand escaped. Not just the camp, but the town of Nepheris too was captured after a siege of another twenty-two days conducted by Scipio in severe wintery conditions and a bitterly cold location. This achievement contributed significantly to the capture of Carthage, for the army at Nepheris had been bringing them supplies, and the Africans were confident as long as they saw this camp. Now, with its capture, the remaining African strongholds surrendered to Scipio's generals or were seized without difficulty. Carthage's supplies of food began to run out; nothing came from Africa, which had become hostile; and both the war itself and the winter season made it impossible to sail to Carthage from anywhere else.

127. At the beginning of spring, Scipio attacked The

599
600
601
602
603
604
605

τῇ τε Βύρσῃ καὶ τῶν λιμένων τῷ καλουμένῳ Κώθωνι,
ὁ δὲ Ἀσρούβας νυκτὸς ἐνεπίμπρη τὸ μέρος τοῦ Κώθω-
606 νος τὸ τετράγωνον. ἐλπίσαντος δ᾽ ἔτι τὸν Σκιπίωνα
ἐπιθήσεσθαι καὶ πρὸς τόδε τῶν Καρχηδονίων ἐπεστραμμένων, ἔλαθε Λαίλιος ἐπὶ θάτερα τοῦ Κώθωνος
607 ἐς τὸ περιφερὲς αὐτοῦ μέρος ἀνελθών. βοῆς δ᾽ ὡς ἐπὶ
νίκῃ γενομένης οἱ μὲν ἔδεισαν, οἱ δὲ πανταχόθεν ἤδη
καταφρονοῦντες ἐβιάζοντο τὴν ἀνάβασιν, ξύλα καὶ
μηχανήματα καὶ σανίδας ἐπὶ τὰ διαστήματα διατιθέν-
τες, ἀσθενῶν τὰ σώματα τῶν φυλάκων ὑπὸ τοῦ λιμοῦ
608 γεγονότων καὶ ταῖς γνώμαις ἀπαγορευόντων. ληφθέντος δὲ τοῦ περὶ τὸν Κώθωνα τείχους τὴν ἀγοράν, ἐγγὺς οὖσαν, ὁ Σκιπίων κατέλαβεν. οὐδέν τε ὡς ἐν
ἑσπέρᾳ πλέον ἔτι δυνάμενος ἐν τοῖς ὅπλοις διενυκτέ-
609 ρευσε μεθ᾽ ἁπάντων. ἀρχομένης δὲ τῆς ἡμέρας ἑτέρους ἀκμῆτας ἐκάλει τετρακισχιλίους, οἳ ἐσιόντες
ἱερὸν Ἀπόλλωνος, οὗ τό τε ἄγαλμα κατάχρυσον ἦν
καὶ δῶμα αὐτῷ χρυσήλατον ἀπὸ χιλίων ταλάντων
σταθμοῦ περιέκειτο, ἐσύλων καὶ ταῖς μαχαίραις ἔκοπτον, ἀμελήσαντες τῶν ἐφεστώτων, ἕως ἐμερίσαντο
καὶ ἐπὶ τὸ ἔργον ἐτράποντο.

610 128. Σκιπίωνι δ᾽ ἦν μὲν ἐπὶ τὴν Βύρσαν ἡ σπουδή·
τὸ γὰρ ὀχυρώτατον τῆς πόλεως ἦν, καὶ οἱ πλέονες
ἐς αὐτὴν συνεπεφεύγεσαν. τριῶν δ᾽ οὐσῶν ἀπὸ τῆς
ἀγορᾶς ἀνόδων ἐς αὐτήν, οἰκίαι πυκναὶ καὶ ἐξώροφοι
πανταχόθεν ἦσαν· ὅθεν οἱ Ῥωμαῖοι βαλλόμενοι τὰς
πρώτας τῶν οἰκιῶν κατέλαβον καὶ ἀπ᾽ αὐτῶν ἠμύ-
611 νοντο τοὺς ἐπὶ τῶν πλησίον. ὅτε δ᾽ αὐτῶν κρατήσειαν,

Hide and the harbor known as The Cup, the square-shaped part of which Hasdrubal set fire to one night. Still 606 expecting Scipio to attack here, and while the attention of the Carthaginians was focused there, Laelius secretly moved to the other side and went up to the round-shaped part of The Cup. When his men let out a shout as if they 607 had won, the Carthaginians became alarmed, while the Romans recklessly forced their way up into the harbor on all sides, filling the gap between the walls with timber, siege engines and planks, and facing guards who were physically weakened by lack of food, and had given up in spirit. Having taken the wall around The Cup, Scipio then 608 seized the neighboring forum, and, unable to do any more because it was evening, spent the night under arms with his whole force. In the morning, he called up another four 609 thousand fresh troops, who entered the temple of Apollo, where there was a gilded statue of the god and shrine of beaten gold weighing one thousand talents. They plundered all this by cutting it up with daggers, and ignored their officers until they had divided it up among themselves. They then returned to their military duty.

128. Scipio now directed his keenest effort against The 610 Hide, for it was the strongest part of the city, and the majority of inhabitants had taken refuge there. There were three streets leading up to The Hide from the forum with six-story houses packed closely on both sides of the streets. Although the Romans were attacked by missiles from these houses, they captured the first ones and used these to attack the defenders of the next ones. When they 611

APPIAN

ξύλα καὶ σανίδας τοῖς διαστήμασι τῶν στενωπῶν
612 ἐπιτιθέντες διέβαινον ὡς ἐπὶ γεφυρῶν. καὶ ὅδε μὲν ὁ
πόλεμος ἦν ἐπὶ τῶν τεγῶν ἄνω, ἕτερος δ' ἐν τοῖς στε-
νωποῖς κατὰ τοὺς ἀπαντῶντας. στόνου δὲ καὶ οἰμωγῆς καὶ βοῆς πάντα καὶ ποικίλων παθῶν ἐνεπίμπλατο,
κτεινομένων τε ἐν χερσὶ καὶ ζώντων ἔτι ῥιπτουμένων
ἄνωθεν ἀπὸ τῶν τεγῶν ἐς τὸ ἔδαφος καὶ φερομένων
613 ἐνίων ἐπὶ δόρατα ὀρθὰ ἢ αἰχμὰς ἄλλας ἢ ξίφη. ἐνεπίμπρη δ' οὐδὲν οὐδεὶς πω διὰ τοὺς ἐπὶ τῶν τεγῶν,
ἕως ἐπὶ τὴν Βύρσαν ἦκεν ὁ Σκιπίων· καὶ τότε τοὺς
τρεῖς ὁμοῦ στενωποὺς ἐνεπίμπρη καὶ τὸ ἀεὶ πιμπρά-
μενον ἑτέροις ὁδοποιεῖν ἐκέλευεν, ἵνα εὐμαρῶς ὁ
στρατὸς ἀλλασσόμενος διαθέοι.

614   129. Ἄλλη δ' ἦν ἐκ τοῦδε ὄψις ἑτέρων κακῶν, τοῦ
μὲν πυρὸς ἐπιφλέγοντος πάντα καὶ καταφέροντος,
τῶν δὲ ἀνδρῶν τὰ οἰκοδομήματα οὐ διαιρούντων ἐς
615 ὀλίγον, ἀλλ' ἀθρόα βιαζομένων ἀνατρέπειν. ὅ τε γὰρ
κτύπος ἐκ τοῦδε πολὺ πλείων ἐγίγνετο, καὶ μετὰ τῶν
λίθων ἐξέπιπτον ἐς τὸ μέσον ἀθρόοι νεκροὶ ζῶντές τε
ἕτεροι, πρεσβῦται μάλιστα καὶ παιδία καὶ γύναια,
ὅσα τοῖς μυχοῖς τῶν οἰκιῶν ἐκέκρυπτο, οἳ μὲν καὶ
τραύματα φέροντες, οἳ δ' ἡμίφλεκτοι, φωνὰς ἀηδεῖς
616 ἀφιέντες. ἕτεροι δ', ὡς ἀπὸ τοσοῦδε ὕψους μετὰ λίθων
καὶ ξύλων καὶ πυρὸς ὠθούμενοι καὶ καταπίπτοντες, ἐς
πολλὰ σχήματα κακῶν διεσπῶντο ῥηγνύμενοί τε καὶ
617 καταρασσόμενοι. καὶ οὐδ' ἐς τέλος αὐτοῖς ταῦτα ἀπέ-
χρη· λιθολόγοι γάρ, ὅσοι πελέκεσι καὶ ἀξίναις καὶ
κοντοῖς τὰ πίπτοντα μετέβαλλόν τε καὶ ὡδοποίουν

236

had gotten the better of the defenders, they put wooden planks across the narrow gaps between the houses and crossed over as if they were on bridges. So this battle took place high up at roof level, and there was another down below in the narrow lanes where the combatants encountered each other. The whole place was filled with groans and cries and shouting and various ordeals, some dying in hand-to-hand fighting, others thrown still alive from high up on the roofs down to the ground where some landed on upright spears and swords or other sharp objects. No one made any use at all of fire because of the men on the roofs, until Scipio reached The Hide. Only then did he set fire to the three narrow streets at the same time, and ordered others to keep a path open through the fire as it continued to burn, so that the troops could run easily back and forth along the path.

129. These scenes were followed by the sight of new torments, when the fire spread and consumed everything, and the men did not destroy the buildings piecemeal, but were forced to tear them all down together. The noise grew much louder as a result, and piles of bodies fell together among the masonry, along with others still alive, particularly old men, women, and children, who had hidden in the inmost parts of their homes, some wounded, others half-burned, uttering awful sounds. Yet others, pushed and falling from such a great height amid the stones and timbers and flames, were torn apart into many terrible shapes, broken and crushed. And this was not even the end of their miseries. For the masons who were clearing the fallen debris with axes, mattocks, and pikes,

612

613

614

615

616

617

τοῖς διαθέουσιν, οἱ μὲν τοῖς πελέκεσι καὶ ταῖς ἀξίναις,
οἳ δὲ ταῖς χηλαῖς τῶν κοντῶν, τούς τε νεκροὺς καὶ
τοὺς ἔτι ζῶντας ἐς τὰ τῆς γῆς κοῖλα μετέβαλλον ὡς
ξύλα καὶ λίθους ἐπισύροντες ἢ ἀνατρέποντες τῷ σι-
618 δήρῳ, ἤν τε ἄνθρωπος ἀναπλήρωμα βόθρου. μετα-
βαλλόμενοι δ᾽ οἱ μὲν ἐς κεφαλὰς ἐφέροντο, καὶ τὰ
σκέλη σφῶν ὑπερίσχοντα τῆς γῆς ἤσπαιρον ἐπὶ
πλεῖστον· οἳ δ᾽ ἐς μὲν τοὺς πόδας ἔπιπτον κάτω καὶ
ταῖς κεφαλαῖς ὑπερεῖχον ὑπὲρ τὸ ἔδαφος, ἵπποι δ᾽
αὐτοὺς διαθέοντες ἐς τὰς ὄψεις ἢ τὸν ἐγκέφαλον
ἐκόλαπτον, οὐχ ἑκόντων τῶν ἐποχουμένων, ἀλλ᾽ ὑπὸ
σπουδῆς, ἐπεὶ οὐδ᾽ οἱ λιθολόγοι ταῦτ᾽ ἔδρων ἑκόντες·
619 ἀλλ᾽ ὁ τοῦ πολέμου πόνος καὶ ἡ δόξα τῆς νίκης
⟨τῆς⟩[22] ἐγγὺς καὶ ἡ τοῦ στρατοῦ σπουδὴ καὶ κήρυκες
ὁμοῦ καὶ σαλπικταὶ πάντα θορυβοῦντες χιλίαρχοί τε
καὶ λοχαγοὶ μετὰ τῶν τάξεων ἐναλλασσόμενοι καὶ
διαθέοντες ἔνθους ἅπαντας ἐποίουν καὶ ἀμελεῖς τῶν
ὁρωμένων ὑπὸ σπουδῆς.

620   130. Καὶ ταῦτα πονουμένων ἐδαπανήθησαν ἓξ
ἡμέραι τε καὶ νύκτες, τῆς μὲν στρατιᾶς ἐναλλασσο-
μένης, ἵνα μὴ κάμοιεν ὑπ᾽ ἀγρυπνίας καὶ κόπου καὶ
φόνου καὶ ὄψεως ἀηδοῦς, Σκιπίωνος δ᾽ ἀπαύστως ἐφε-
στῶτος ἢ διαθέοντος ἄυπνου καὶ σῖτον οὕτως ἐπὶ
τῶν ἔργων αἱρουμένου, μέχρι κάμνων καὶ παρειμένος
621 ἐκαθέζετο ἐφ᾽ ὑψηλοῦ, τὰ γιγνόμενα ἐφορῶν. πολλῶν
δ᾽ ἔτι πορθουμένων καὶ τοῦ κακοῦ μακροτάτου δοκοῦν-
τος ἔσεσθαι, προσέφυγον ἑβδόμης ἡμέρας αὐτῷ τινες
ἐστεμμένοι στέμματα Ἀσκληπίεια· τόδε γὰρ ἦν τὸ

and making a path for those rushing through, swept both corpses and still living bodies together into holes in the ground, some using the axes and mattocks, others the hooks of the pikes, dragging them along and turning them over with the iron implements as if they were pieces of wood or stones: in this way human beings were used as filling for potholes. Some were thrown in together head 618 first, their legs sticking out above ground and twitching for a long time. Others fell in feet first, with their head above ground, and horses ran over them, trampling their face or skull with their hooves, not because the riders intended to, but in their hurry. Nor did the masons act intentionally either. But the stress of war, the prospect of approaching 619 victory, the fervor of the soldiers, together with the general clamor caused by heralds and trumpeters, the tribunes and centurions running everywhere and relieving troops with their units—all this made everyone frenetic and, due to their haste, inattentive to what they were witnessing.

130. Six days and nights were spent in this struggle, 620 with the soldiers being relieved regularly, so that they were not worn out by lack of sleep, fatigue, killing, or the appalling sights. Scipio, however, was on his feet continuously and hurried around taking no rest and eating at his post when he could, until exhausted and yielding to fatigue, he sat on high ground where he could look down on what was happening. There was still much havoc being 621 wreaked and it seemed as if the suffering would last a very long time, but on the seventh day some Carthaginians wreathed with the garlands of Asclepius took refuge with

---

[22] $\tau\hat{\eta}s$ add. Goukowsky: $o\mathring{v}\sigma\eta s$ prop. Mend.

ἱερὸν ἐν ἀκροπόλει μάλιστα τῶν ἄλλων ἐπιφανὲς καὶ
πλούσιον, ὅθεν οἶδε τὰς ἱκετηρίας λαβόντες ἐδέοντο
τοῦ Σκιπίωνος περὶ μόνης συνθέσθαι σωτηρίας τοῖς
ἐθέλουσιν ἐπὶ τῷδε τῆς Βύρσης ἐξιέναι. ὁ δὲ ἐδίδου,
622 χωρὶς αὐτομόλων. καὶ ἐξῄεσαν αὐτίκα μυριάδες πέντε
ἀνδρῶν ἅμα καὶ γυναικῶν, ἀνοιχθέντος αὐτοῖς στενοῦ
διατειχίσματος. καὶ οὗτοι μὲν ἐφυλάσσοντο, ὅσοι δ'
αὐτόμολοι Ῥωμαίων ἦσαν, ἀμφὶ τοὺς ἐνακοσίους μάλιστα, ἀπογνόντες αὐτῶν ἐς τὸ Ἀσκληπιεῖον ἀνέδρα-
μον μετὰ Ἀσρούβα καὶ τῆς γυναικὸς τῆς Ἀσρούβα
623 καὶ δύο παίδων ἀρρένων. ὅθεν εὐμαρῶς ἀεὶ ἐμάχοντο,
καίπερ ὄντες ὀλίγοι, διὰ τὸ ὕψος τοῦ τεμένους καὶ τὸ
ἀπόκρημνον, ἐς ὃ καὶ παρὰ τὴν εἰρήνην διὰ βαθμῶν
624 ἑξήκοντα ἀνέβαινον. ὡς δὲ ὅ τε λιμὸς αὐτοὺς καθῄρει
καὶ ἡ ἀγρυπνία καὶ ὁ φόβος καὶ ὁ πόνος, τοῦ κακοῦ
προσπελάζοντος, τὸ μὲν τέμενος ἐξέλιπον, ἐς δὲ τὸν
νεὼν αὐτοῦ καὶ τὸ τέγος ἀνέτρεχον.

625 131. Κἀν τούτῳ λαθὼν ὁ Ἀσρούβας ἔφυγε πρὸς τὸν
Σκιπίωνα μετὰ θαλλῶν· καὶ αὐτὸν ὁ Σκιπίων ἐκάθισε
πρὸ ποδῶν ἑαυτοῦ καὶ τοῖς αὐτομόλοις ἐπεδείκνυεν. οἱ
δ', ὡς εἶδον, ᾔτησαν ἡσυχίαν σφίσι γενέσθαι καὶ γενομένης Ἀσρούβᾳ μὲν ἐλοιδορήσαντο πολλὰ καὶ ποικίλα, τὸν δὲ νεὼν ἐνέπρησάν τε καὶ κατεκαύθησαν.
626 τὴν δὲ γυναῖκα τὴν Ἀσρούβα λέγουσιν, ἁπτομένου
τοῦ πυρός, ἀντικρὺ τοῦ Σκιπίωνος γενομένην κατα-
κοσμήσασθαί τε, ὡς ἐν συμφοραῖς ἐδύνατο, καὶ
παραστησαμένην τὰ τέκνα εἰπεῖν ἐς ἐπήκοον τοῦ Σκι-
πίωνος· "Σοὶ μὲν οὐ νέμεσις ἐκ θεῶν, ὦ Ῥωμαῖε· ἐπὶ

Scipio. The temple of Asclepius was by far the richest and most famous of those on the acropolis. Taking the suppliant's olive branches from here, these men begged Scipio to agree to guarantee only the safety of those who were willing to leave The Hide on this condition. He granted the request, but excluded deserters. Immediately, a narrow gate was opened for them in the wall, and fifty thousand men and women came out. They were put under guard, while all the Roman deserters, about nine hundred of them, despairing of their situation, withdrew to the temple of Asclepius with Hasdrubal and his wife and their two sons. Here, although there were not many of them, they easily continued the fight because of the high and steep location of the sanctuary, which in peacetime was reached by a flight of sixty steps. But when they were overcome by hunger, lack of sleep, fear, and battle weariness, and facing a grim end, they left the sanctuary and fled into the temple and onto its roof.

131. Meanwhile Hasdrubal secretly fled to Scipio with an olive branch. Scipio made him sit at his feet and displayed him to the deserters. On seeing him, they asked for silence, and when it was granted, berated him with many insults of all sorts; they then set fire to the temple and died in the flames. They say that, once the fire was lit, Hasdrubal's wife placed herself right opposite Scipio, having dressed as best she could in her misfortune and positioned her children at her side, and spoke in the hearing of Scipio as follows: "For you, Roman, there will be no retribution

622

623

624

625

626

γὰρ πολεμίαν ἐστράτευσας· Ἀσρούβαν δὲ τόνδε, πατρίδος τε καὶ ἱερῶν καὶ ἐμοῦ καὶ τέκνων προδότην
γενόμενον, οἵ τε Καρχηδόνος δαίμονες ἀμύναιντο καὶ
627   σὺ μετὰ τῶν δαιμόνων." εἶτ᾽ ἐς τὸν Ἀσρούβαν ἐπι-
στρέψασα εἶπεν· "Ὦ μιαρὲ καὶ ἄπιστε καὶ μαλα-
κώτατε ἀνδρῶν, ἐμὲ μὲν καὶ τοὺς ἐμοὺς παῖδας τόδε
τὸ πῦρ θάψει· σὺ δὲ τίνα κοσμήσεις θρίαμβον, ὁ τῆς
μεγάλης Καρχηδόνος ἡγεμών; τίνα δ᾽ οὐ δώσεις
δίκην τῷδε, ᾧ παρακαθέζῃ;" τοσαῦτ᾽ ὀνειδίσασα κατ-
έσφαξε τοὺς παῖδας καὶ ἐς τὸ πῦρ αὐτούς τε καὶ ἑαυ-
τὴν ἐπέρριψεν.

628   132. Ὧδε μέν φασι τὴν Ἀσρούβα γυναῖκα, ὡς
αὐτὸν ἐχρῆν Ἀσρούβαν, εἰποῦσαν ἀποθανεῖν· ὁ δὲ
Σκιπίων, πόλιν ὁρῶν ἑπτακοσίοις ἔτεσιν ἀνθήσασαν
ἀπὸ τοῦ συνοικισμοῦ καὶ γῆς τοσῆσδε καὶ νήσων καὶ
θαλάσσης ἐπάρξασαν ὅπλων τε καὶ νεῶν καὶ ἐλεφάντων καὶ χρημάτων εὐπορήσασαν ἴσα ταῖς ἀρχαῖς
ταῖς μεγίσταις, τόλμῃ δὲ καὶ προθυμίᾳ πολὺ δια-
σχοῦσαν, ἥ γε καὶ ναῦς καὶ ὅπλα πάντα περιῃρημένη
τρισὶν ὅμως ἔτεσιν ἀντέσχε πολέμῳ τοσῷδε καὶ λιμῷ,
τότε ἄρδην τελευτῶσαν ἐς πανωλεθρίαν ἐσχάτην, λέγεται μὲν δακρῦσαι καὶ φανερὸς γενέσθαι κλαίων
629   ὑπὲρ πολεμίων, ἐπὶ πολὺ δ᾽ ἔννους ἐφ᾽ ἑαυτοῦ γενό-
μενός τε καὶ συνιδών, ὅτι καὶ πόλεις καὶ ἔθνη καὶ
ἀρχὰς ἁπάσας δεῖ μεταβαλεῖν ὥσπερ ἀνθρώπους
δαίμονα καὶ τοῦτ᾽ ἔπαθε μὲν Ἴλιον, εὐτυχής ποτε
πόλις, ἔπαθε δὲ ἡ Ἀσσυρίων καὶ Μήδων καὶ Περσῶν
ἐπ᾽ ἐκείνοις ἀρχὴ μεγίστη γενομένη καὶ ἡ μάλιστα

from the gods, as you have fought against the land of your enemy. But may the spirits of Carthage, and you with them, take vengeance on this man, Hasdrubal, who has betrayed his country and temples, and me and my children." Then turning to Hasdrubal, she said: "Foul, faith- 627 less, and most cowardly of men, this fire will provide the funeral rites for me and my children. But you, the leader of great Carthage, what triumph will you adorn? What penalty will you not have to pay to the man at whose feet you sit?" Having reviled him in this manner, she slew her children and threw them and herself into the fire.

132. With these words, so it is said, the wife of Has- 628 drubal died, as Hasdrubal himself should have done. Scipio, looking on a city that had flourished for seven hundred years from its founding, a city that had ruled such a large territory with islands and ocean, a city equally well supplied with weapons, ships, elephants, and money as the greatest of empires, but far exceeding them in courage and willpower, seeing that they endured such a great war and famine for three years after being deprived of their fleet and entire armament, a city now coming to an end in total and final destruction—seeing all this, Scipio is said to have wept and publicly lamented the fate of his enemy. Going off for a long time to think by himself, and recogniz- 629 ing that a divinity inevitably brings about the fall of cities, nations, and all empires just as of men, and that this is what happened to Troy, once a city blessed by good fortune, and to the empires of the Assyrians and the Medes, and to what became the greatest empire after them, the Persians, and the Macedonians too, the most recent to distinguish them-

ἔναγχος ἐκλάμψασα, ἡ Μακεδόνων, εἰπεῖν, ἐς Πολύ-
βιον τὸν λογοποιὸν ἀποβλέψαντα, εἴτε ἑκών, εἴτε προ-
φυγόντος αὐτὸν τοῦδε τοῦ ἔπους·

Ἔσσεται ἦμαρ, ὅταν ποτ᾽ ὀλώλῃ Ἴλιος ἱρὴ
καὶ Πρίαμος καὶ λαὸς ἐυμμελίω Πριάμοιο.

630 Πολυβίου δ᾽ αὐτὸν ἐρομένου σὺν παρρησίᾳ (καὶ γὰρ
ἦν αὐτοῦ καὶ διδάσκαλος), ὅ τι βούλοιτο ὁ λόγος,
φασὶν οὐ φυλαξάμενον ὀνομάσαι τὴν πατρίδα σαφῶς, ὑπὲρ ἧς ἄρα, ἐς τἀνθρώπεια ἀφορῶν, ἐδεδίει.

631 133. Καὶ τάδε μὲν Πολύβιος αὐτὸς ἀκούσας συγ-
γράφει· Σκιπίων δ᾽, ἐπεὶ κατέσκαπτο Καρχηδών, ἐπὶ
μέν τινα ἡμερῶν ἀριθμὸν ἐπέτρεψεν τῇ στρατιᾷ διαρ-
πάζειν, ὅσα μὴ χρυσὸς ἢ ἄργυρος ἢ ἀναθήματα ἦν,
μετὰ δὲ τοῦτ᾽ ἀριστεῖα πολλὰ διαδοὺς ἅπασι, χωρὶς
τῶν ἐς τὸ Ἀπολλώνιον ἁμαρτόντων, ναῦν μὲν ὀξυ-
τάτην κοσμήσας λαφύροις ἄγγελον τῆς νίκης ἔστει-
λεν ἐς Ῥώμην, ἐς δὲ Σικελίαν περιέπεμπεν, ὅσα
Καρχηδόνιοι σφῶν ἀναθήματα κοινὰ πολεμοῦντες
ἔλαβον, ἐλθόντας ἐπιγινώσκειν καὶ κομίζεσθαι· ὃ καὶ
μάλιστα αὐτὸν ἐδημαγώγησεν ὡς μετὰ τοῦ δυνατοῦ
632 φιλάνθρωπον. ἀποδόμενος δὲ τὴν λείαν τὴν περισσὴν
ὅπλα καὶ μηχανήματα καὶ ναῦς ἀχρήστους Ἄρει καὶ
Ἀθηνᾷ διαζωσάμενος αὐτὸς ἔκαιεν κατὰ τὰ πάτρια.

---

59 Polybius' history of Rome's rise to world power in the third
and second centuries (in forty books, but imperfectly preserved
after the first five books) ends in 146, with the destruction of

selves brilliantly, he turned to the historian Polybius and spoke the following words, either intentionally or because they escaped his lips:

> The day will come when sacred Ilium will perish,
> and Priam, and the people of Priam with his ashen
>   spear.

When Polybius asked him directly—for he was also his teacher—what he meant by this, they say that he did not hesitate to name his own country specifically, on whose behalf he was, to be sure, fearful when he looked on the affairs of men. 630

133. Polybius himself actually heard this, and wrote it down.[59] When Carthage had been destroyed, Scipio allowed the army a certain number of days to plunder anything except gold, silver, or votive offerings. He then awarded numerous prizes to all who had displayed exceptional courage, except those who had committed sacrilege against the temple of Apollo, and, decking out a very fast ship with spoils, he sent it to Rome to announce the victory. He also sent a message to Sicily to tell them that, if they came and identified public offerings that the Carthaginians had taken from them while at war, they could get them back. All this made him particularly popular, identifying him as a man both powerful and humane. Having sold the superfluous booty, he arrayed himself for sacrifice and, in accordance with ancestral custom, made a burnt offering to Ares and Athena of the weapons, siege engines, and unserviceable ships. 631 632

both Carthage and Corinth. The quotation is from Homer, *Iliad* 6.448–49.

633   134. Οἱ δ' ἐν ἄστει, ὡσαύτως τὴν ναῦν ἰδόντες καὶ
τῆς νίκης περὶ δείλην ἑσπέραν πυθόμενοι, ἐς τὰς
ὁδοὺς ἐξεπήδων καὶ διενυκτέρευον μετ' ἀλλήλων, ἡδό-
μενοι καὶ συμπλεκόμενοι ὡς ἄρτι μὲν ἐλεύθεροι φό-
βων γεγονότες, ἄρτι δ' ἄρχοντες ἑτέρων ἀσφαλῶς,
ἄρτι δὲ βέβαιον τὴν πόλιν ἔχοντες καὶ νενικηκότες
634 οἵαν οὔτινα πρότερον ἄλλην. πολλὰ μὲν γὰρ αὐτοῖς
συνῄδεσαν ἔργα λαμπρά, πολλὰ δὲ τοῖς πατράσιν ἔς
τε Μακεδόνας καὶ Ἴβηρας καὶ ἐς Ἀντίοχον τὸν Μέγαν ἔναγχος καὶ περὶ αὐτὴν Ἰταλίαν· πόλεμον δ' οὐδένα ἄλλον οὕτως ἐπὶ θύραις ἐπίφοβον αὐτοῖς ᾔδεσαν, διά τε ἀνδρείαν καὶ φρόνημα καὶ τόλμαν ἐχθρῶν
635 καὶ ἀπιστίαν σφίσιν ἐπικίνδυνον γενόμενον. ἀνέφε-
ρον δὲ καὶ ὧν ἔπαθον ὑπὸ Καρχηδονίων ἔν τε Σικελίᾳ
καὶ Ἰβηρίᾳ καὶ περὶ αὐτὴν Ἰταλίαν ἑκκαίδεκα ἔτεσιν,
Ἀννίβου τετρακόσια ἐμπρήσαντος ἄστη καὶ μυριάδας ἀνδρῶν τριάκοντα ἐν μόναις μάχαις ἀνελόντος
ἐπί τε τὴν Ῥώμην πολλάκις ἐλάσαντος καὶ ἐς ἔσχα-
636 τον κινδύνου συναγαγόντος. ὧν ἐνθυμούμενοι μάλιστα ἐξίσταντο περὶ τῆς νίκης ἐς ἀπιστίαν αὐτῆς καὶ
αὖθις ἀνεπυνθάνοντο ἀλλήλων, εἰ τῷ ὄντι Καρχηδὼν
κατέσκαπται· ἐλεσχήνευόν τε δι' ὅλης νυκτός, ὅπως
μὲν αὐτῶν τὰ ὅπλα περιῃρέθη καὶ ὅπως αὐτίκα παρὰ
δόξαν ἐκτήναντο ἕτερα, ὅπως δὲ τὰς ναῦς ἀφῃρέθη-
σαν καὶ στόλον ἐπήξαντο πάλιν ἐξ ὕλης παλαιᾶς τό
τε στόμα τοῦ λιμένος ὡς ἀπεκλείσθη καὶ στόμα ὡς
637 ὠρύξαντο ἕτερον ὀλίγαις ἡμέραις. καὶ τὸ τῶν τειχῶν
ὕψος αὐτοῖς διὰ στόματος ἦν καὶ τὰ τῶν λίθων με-

134. When the people of Rome saw the ship and 633
learned of the victory late in the afternoon, they poured
into the streets and passed the night together, delightedly
embracing each other, like men who had only just been
freed from fear, their rule over others only just made safe,
their city only just secured, and like winners of a victory
such as no other before. They exchanged many stories 634
about their own brilliant achievements, many about the
achievements of their ancestors against the Macedonians,
the Iberians, and recently against Antiochus the Great,
and in Italy itself. But they knew of no other war at their
own gates that had terrified them so much, such had been
the courage, determination and daring of the enemy, as
well as the treachery that had proved so dangerous. And 635
they recalled how they had suffered at the hands of the
Carthaginians in both Sicily and Iberia, and in Italy itself
for sixteen years, when Hannibal had destroyed four hundred towns by fire and had killed three hundred thousand
men in battle alone, marching on Rome a number of times
and subjecting it to the most extreme danger. Thinking on 636
these events, they were so excited at the victory that they
almost did not believe it, and kept asking each other if
Carthage really had been destroyed. And so they chatted
throughout the night, about how the Carthaginians had
been deprived of their weapons, but had immediately and
unexpectedly acquired new ones, about how they had lost
their ships but had constructed a new fleet from old timber, about how the mouth of their harbor had been closed
off, but they had dug a new one in a few days. They dis- 637
cussed the height of the walls and the size of the stones

247

γέθη καὶ τὸ πῦρ, ὃ πολλάκις ταῖς μηχαναῖς ἐπήνεγκαν. ὅλως τε τὸν πόλεμον ὡς ὁρῶντες ἄρτι γιγνόμενον ἀλλήλοις διετύπουν καὶ ἐς τὰς φαντασίας τῶν
λεγομένων τῷ σχήματι τοῦ σώματος συνεφέροντο.
καὶ τὸν Σκιπίωνα ὁρᾶν ἐδόκουν ἐπὶ κλιμάκων, ἐπὶ
νεῶν, ἐν πύλαις, ἐν μάχαις, πανταχοῦ διαθέοντα.

638   135. Οὕτω μὲν οἱ Ῥωμαῖοι διενυκτέρευσαν, ἅμα δ᾽
ἡμέρᾳ θυσίαι τε καὶ πομπαὶ τοῖς θεοῖς ἐγίγνοντο
κατὰ φυλὴν καὶ ἀγῶνες ἐπὶ τούτοις καὶ θέαι ποικίλαι.
639   δέκα δὲ σφῶν αὐτῶν ἡ βουλὴ τοὺς ἀρίστους ἔπεμπε
διαθησομένους Λιβύην μετὰ Σκιπίωνος ἐς τὸ Ῥωμαίων συμφέρον· οἳ Καρχηδόνος μὲν εἴ τι περίλοιπον
ἔτι ἦν, ἔκριναν κατασκάψαι Σκιπίωνα καὶ οἰκεῖν
αὐτὴν ἀπεῖπον ἅπασι καὶ ἐπηράσαντο, μάλιστα περὶ
τῆς Βύρσης, εἴ τις οἰκήσειεν αὐτὴν ἢ τὰ καλούμενα
640   Μέγαρα· ἐπιβαίνειν δ᾽ οὐκ ἀπεῖπον. ὅσαι δὲ πόλεις
συμμεμαχήκεσαν τοῖς πολεμίοις ἐπιμόνως, ἔδοξε
καθελεῖν ἁπάσας· καὶ ὅσαι Ῥωμαίοις βεβοηθήκεσαν,
χώραν ἔδωκαν ἑκάστῃ τῆς δορικτήτου, καὶ πρῶτον
μάλιστα Ἰτυκαίοις τὴν μέχρι Καρχηδόνος αὐτῆς καὶ
641   Ἱππῶνος ἐπὶ θάτερα. τοῖς δὲ λοιποῖς φόρον ὥρισαν
ἐπὶ τῇ γῇ καὶ ἐπὶ τοῖς σώμασιν, ἀνδρὶ καὶ γυναικὶ
ὁμοίως. καὶ στρατηγὸν ἐτήσιον αὐτοῖς ἐκ Ῥώμης ἐπι-
642   πέμπειν ἔκριναν. οἳ μὲν δὴ ταῦτα προστάξαντες ἀπέπλεον ἐς Ῥώμην, ὁ δὲ Σκιπίων ἐποίει τὰ δόξαντα καὶ
θυσίας ἐτέλει καὶ ἀγῶνας ἐπὶ τῇ νίκῃ. ὡς δὲ αὐτῷ
πάντα ἐξετετέλεστο, διαπλεύσας ἐπιφανέστατα δὴ
πάντων διεθριάμβευε πολύχρυσον θρίαμβον, ἀγαλ-

and how often the siege engines had been set on fire. In short, they described the war for each other as if they were seeing it happen right then, mimicking with their body language what was being said. And they imagined themselves seeing Scipio on the ladders, on the ships, at the gates, in combat, moving everywhere with speed.

135. This was how the Romans spent the night. The next day, organized by tribe, they sacrificed and conducted processions in honor of the gods, and there were also games and spectacles of different sorts. The senate sent ten of their best men to Africa to cooperate with Scipio in making the most advantageous arrangements for Rome. They decided that, if there was anything at all left of Carthage, Scipio was to destroy it, and they banned anyone from living there, placing a particular curse on anyone trying to settle in The Hide, or the place called The Palace. But they did not ban entry. All towns that had persisted in fighting on the enemy side they decided to destroy. To each of the towns that had helped Rome they granted land won in the war, first and foremost Utica, which received the territory extending to Carthage itself on one side and to Hippo on the other. The commissioners imposed a tribute on the rest of the population, men and women alike, both a land tax and a poll tax, and decided to send an annual governor there from Rome. Having made these arrangements, they sailed for Rome, while Scipio put their decisions into effect, and performed sacrifices and celebrated games to mark the victory. When he had finished all his work, he crossed to Rome, where he celebrated the most splendid triumph of all. It was heavy with gold, and crowded with all the statues and offerings

638

639

640

641

642

APPIAN

μάτων τε γέμοντα καὶ ἀναθημάτων, ὅσα Καρχηδόνιοι
χρόνῳ πολλῷ καὶ συνεχέσι νίκαις ἐκ πάσης γῆς
643 συνενηνόχεσαν ἐς Λιβύην. τότε δ' ἦν, ὅτε καὶ κατὰ
Μακεδόνων, ἁλόντος Ἀνδρίσκου τοῦ Ψευδοφιλίππου,
τρίτος ἤγετο θρίαμβος καὶ κατὰ τῆς Ἑλλάδος πρῶτος
ὑπὸ Μομμίου. καὶ ἦν ταῦτα ἀμφὶ τὰς ἑξήκοντα καὶ
ἑκατὸν ὀλυμπιάδας.

644 136. Χρόνῳ δ' ὕστερον, Γαΐου Γράκχου δημαρχοῦν-
τος ἐν Ῥώμῃ καὶ στάσεων οὐσῶν ἐξ ἀπορίας, ἔδοξε
κληρούχους ἐς Λιβύην πέμπειν ἑξακισχιλίους, δια-
γραφομένων δ' ἀμφὶ τὴν Καρχηδόνα τῶν θεμελίων
645 λύκοι τὰ θεμέλια ἀθρόα διέσπασαν καὶ συνέχεαν. καὶ
τότε μὲν ἀνέσχεν ἡ βουλὴ τοῦ συνοικισμοῦ· χρόνῳ
δὲ αὖθις, ὁπότε Γάιος Καῖσαρ, ὁ καὶ δικτάτωρ ὕστερον αὐτοῖς διηνεκὴς γενόμενος, Πομπήιον ἐς Αἴγυπτον ἐδίωκεν καὶ τοὺς Πομπηίου φίλους ἐς Λιβύην
ἀπ' Αἰγύπτου, λέγεται, τῇ Καρχηδόνι παραστρατοπε-
δεύων, ὑπ' ἐνυπνίου στρατὸν πολὺν ἰδὼν κλαίοντα
ἐνοχληθῆναι καὶ αὐτίκα ἑαυτῷ ἐς μνήμην ὑπογράψα-
646 σθαι Καρχηδόνα συνοικίζειν. καὶ μετ' οὐ πολὺ τῶν
ἀπόρων αὐτὸν ἐς Ῥώμην <ἐπανελθόντα>²³ περὶ γῆς
παρακαλούντων συνέτασσεν ὡς πέμψων τοὺς μὲν ἐς

²³ ἐπανελθόντα add. Schweig.

⁶⁰ A characteristically vague chronological statement by Appian. The 160th Olympiad ran from 141/0 to 138/7, but L. Mummius, who defeated the Achaeans and destroyed Corinth, held his

that the Carthaginians had collected in Africa from all over the world in their long years of uninterrupted victory. This was also the time when, after the capture of Andriscus, the false Philip, a third triumph was celebrated against Macedon, and when Mummius celebrated the first triumph against Greece. This happened in about the 160th Olympiad.[60]   643

136. Later on, when Gaius Gracchus was tribune of the people at Rome, and food shortages were causing riots, it was decided to send six thousand colonists to Africa.[61] But when the foundation markers for the settlement were being laid out near Carthage, wolves tore them apart completely and destroyed them. At the time the senate abandoned the attempt to found a settlement. Later again, however, there is a story that Gaius Caesar, who subsequently became dictator for life at Rome, when he was pursuing Pompey to Egypt, and then his partisans from Egypt to Africa, was disturbed by a dream while camped at Carthage, in which he saw a large army weeping. He immediately wrote a memorandum for himself to colonize Carthage. A short time later, when he returned to Rome, the poor asked him for land, and he issued instructions for   644   645   646

triumph over the Greeks in the year of his consulship, 146 (in the 158th Olympiad), the same year in which Q. Caecilius Metellus Macedonicus defeated Andriscus and celebrated a triumph against the Macedonians.

[61] C. Sempronius Gracchus was one of the tribunes of the people in the years 123 and 122. His extensive program of legislation included the establishment of a colony at Carthage, named Iunonia. It did not succeed at that time.

APPIAN

647 τὴν Καρχηδόνα, τοὺς δ' ἐς Κόρινθον. ἀλλ' ὅδε μὲν
θᾶσσον ἀνῃρέθη πρὸς ἐχθρῶν ἐν τῷ Ῥωμαίων βου-
λευτηρίῳ, ὁ δ' ἐκείνου παῖς Ἰούλιος Καῖσαρ, ὁ Σεβαστὸς ἐπίκλησιν, ἐντυχὼν ἄρα ταῖς ὑπογραφαῖς τοῦ
πατρός, συνῴκισε τὴν νῦν Καρχηδόνα, ἀγχοτάτω μάλιστα ἐκείνης, φυλαξάμενος τῆς πάλαι τὸ ἐπάρατον.
οἰκήτοράς τε Ῥωμαίους μὲν αὐτὸν τρισχιλίους μάλιστα πυνθάνομαι, τοὺς δὲ λοιποὺς ἐκ τῶν περιοίκων
648 συναγαγεῖν. ὧδε μὲν Λιβύης τῆς ὑπὸ Καρχηδονίοις
Ῥωμαῖοι κατέσχον καὶ Καρχηδόνα κατέσκαψάν τε
καὶ συνῴκισαν αὖθις μετὰ ἔτη τῆς κατασκαφῆς ἑκατὸν καὶ δύο.

some of them to be sent to Carthage, others to Corinth, but was soon assassinated by his enemies in the Roman   647 senate. His son, Julius Caesar, surnamed Augustus,[62] however, came across his father's memorandum and founded the present city of Carthage, very close to the old city, but taking care to avoid the land on which a curse had been placed before. My information is that he brought three thousand settlers from Rome and the rest from the surrounding areas. This is how Rome came into possession of   648 that part of Africa ruled by the Carthaginians, razed Carthage to the ground, and refounded it, one hundred and two years after they had destroyed it.[63]

[62] The emperor Augustus.

[63] With this dating, 45/44 BC, Appian seems to believe that the resettlement of Carthage took place in the time of Julius Caesar, rather than of the emperor Augustus.

VIII

ΕΚ ΤΗΣ ΝΟΜΑΔΙΚΗΣ

1. Ὅτι Βομίλχαρ κατηγορούμενος ἔφυγε πρὸ δίκης, καὶ Ἰογόρθας σὺν αὐτῷ, τοῦτο δὴ τὸ περιφερόμενον ἐς τοὺς δωροδοκοῦντας εἰπών, ὅτι Ῥωμαίων ἡ πόλις ἐστὶν ὠνία πᾶσα, εἴ τις ὠνητὴς αὐτῆς εὑρεθείη. (Exc. de sent. 21, p. 70 Boissevain)

2. Ὅτι Μέτελλος ἀνεζεύγνυεν ἐς Λιβύην τὴν ὑπὸ Ῥωμαίοις αἰτίαν ἔχων παρὰ τῷ στρατῷ βραδυτῆτος ἐς τοὺς πολεμίους καὶ ἐπὶ σφίσιν ὠμότητος· σφόδρα γὰρ τοὺς ἁμαρτάνοντας ἐκόλαζεν. (Exc. de virt. 32, p. 231 Roos)

3. Ὅτι Μέτελλος Βαγαίων ἀνήρει τὴν βουλὴν ὅλην ὡς τὴν φρουρὰν προδόντας Ἰογόρθᾳ, καὶ τὸν φρού-

---

[1] The Numidian Book appears to be an appendix to the African Book, or the term "Numidian" perhaps functions as a sort of subtitle of the African Book. It is a not a separate book. See above, Lib. n. 1.

[2] The story is reported in Sallust (Jug. 32–35). While in Rome under promise of safe passage, Jugurtha had a rival murdered by Bomilcar, who was charged with the crime. Jugurtha got Bomilcar

BOOK VIII
PART 2

FROM THE NUMIDIAN BOOK[1]

1. When Bomilcar had charges brought against him, he took to flight before the trial. With him went Jugurtha, who made that now widely circulated saying about those who take bribes, namely, that the whole city of Rome was for sale, if only a buyer for it could be found.[2] (*Exc. de sent.* 21, p. 70 Boissevain)

2. On returning to that part of Africa under Roman control, Metellus was accused by his soldiers of being slow to engage the enemy, and cruel in the treatment of his own men. For he inflicted severe punishments on those who committed offenses.[3] (*Exc. de virt.* 32, p. 231 Roos)

3. Metellus executed every member of the council of Vacca for betraying the garrison to Jugurtha.[4] In addition

out of the city and was then forced to leave himself. On leaving the city he was reported to have said, *urbem venalem et mature perituram, si emptorem invenerit* (the city was for sale and soon to perish, if it could find a buyer).

[3] As consul in 109, Q. Caecilius Metellus Numidicus took over command of the war against the African prince Jugurtha (112–106), but he was pushed aside by Gaius Marius in 107.

[4] Vacca is the modern town of Béja in Tunisia, just over sixty-two miles west of Tunis.

ραρχον Τουρπίλιον, ἄνδρα Ῥωμαῖον οὐκ ἀνυπόπτως
ἑαυτὸν ἐγχειρίσαντα τοῖς πολεμίοις, ἐπαπκέτεινε τῇ
βουλῇ. Θρᾷκας δὲ καὶ Λίγυας αὐτομόλους λαβὼν
παρὰ Ἰογόρθα, τῶν μὲν τὰς χεῖρας ἀπέτεμνε, τοὺς δὲ
ἐς τὴν γῆν μέχρι γαστρὸς κατώρυσσε, καὶ περιτο-
ξεύων ἢ ἐσακοντίζων ἔτι ἐμπνέουσι πῦρ ἐπετίθει.[1]
(*Exc. de virt.* 33, p. 231 Roos)

4. Ὅτι τοῦ Μαρίου ἐς Κίρταν ἀφικομένου πρέσβεις
Βόκχου παρῆσαν, οἳ πεμφθῆναί τινας ἐς λόγους
Βόκχῳ παρεκάλουν. καὶ ἐπέμφθησαν Αὖλός τε Μάλλιος ὁ πρεσβευτὴς καὶ Κορνήλιος Σύλλας ὁ ταμίας,
οἷς ὁ Βόκχος ἔφη Ῥωμαίοις πολεμῆσαι διὰ Μάριον·
γῆν γὰρ ἦν αὐτὸς Ἰογόρθαν ἀφείλετο, πρὸς Μαρίου
2 νῦν ἀφῃρῆσθαι. Βόκχος μὲν δὴ ταῦτα ἐνεκάλει, Μάλλιος δ᾽ ἔφη τὴν γῆν τήνδε Ῥωμαίους ἀφελέσθαι Σύφακα πολέμου νόμῳ καὶ δοῦναι Μασσανάσσῃ δω-
ρεάν, διδόναι δὲ Ῥωμαίους τὰς δωρεὰς ἔχειν τοῖς
3 λαβοῦσιν ἕως ἂν τῇ βουλῇ καὶ τῷ δήμῳ δοκῇ. οὐ μὴν
ἀλόγως μεταγνῶναι· Μασσανάσσην τε γὰρ ἀποθανεῖν, καὶ τοὺς Μασσανάσσου παῖδας Ἰογόρθαν κατα-

---

[1] ἐπετίθει Goukowsky; ὑποτίθει P

---

[5] T. Turpilius Silanus somehow avoided the massacre of the
rest of the garrison he commanded, but he was executed afterward: Sall. *Jug.* 66–69. He cannot have been a Roman citizen:
Roman citizens were not liable to summary execution. Sallust says
he had Latin rights.

to the council, he also executed the garrison commander, Turpilius, a Roman citizen, who had surrendered to the enemy in suspicious circumstances.[5] When he received Thracian and Ligurian deserters from Jugurtha, Metellus cut off the hands of some of them, and buried others in the ground up to their stomach, and after shooting arrows and throwing javelins at them, he set fire to them while they were still alive. (*Exc. de virt.* 33, p. 231 Roos)

4. When Marius arrived at Cirta, envoys of Bocchus met him and they invited him to send representatives for discussions with Bocchus. So Marius sent Aulus Manlius, his legate, and Cornelius Sulla, his quaestor.[6] Bocchus told them that he was at war with Rome because of Marius. For the very territory he himself had taken from Jugurtha had now been taken from him by Marius. This at any rate was Bocchus' complaint. But Manlius said that Rome had confiscated this territory from Syphax by right of arms, and they had given it as a gift to Massinissa.[7] Rome gives such gifts, however, he continued, for the recipients to keep only as long as the senate and people decide. And it was not without good reason that they changed their mind. For Massinissa was dead, and Jugurtha, by murdering his

---

[6] This was in 106, the year after the quaestorship of L. Cornelius Sulla, the future dictator. We hear nothing of A. Manlius besides his service under Marius in the war against Jugurtha. Bocchus was king of Mauretania and an ally of Jugurtha, until he betrayed him to Sulla.

[7] Appian tells the story of Syphax in *Lib.* 10.36–28.121.

καίνοντα Ῥωμαίοις πολέμιον γενέσθαι. οὐκ οὖν ἔτι
εἶναι δίκαιον οὔτε τὸν πολέμιον ἔχειν δωρεὰν "Ἦν
ἔδομεν φίλῳ, οὔτε δὲ δοκεῖν Ἰογόρθαν ἀφαιρεῖσθαι
τὰ Ῥωμαίων." καὶ Μάλλιος μὲν τάδε περὶ τῆς γῆς
ἔλεξεν. (Exc. de leg. gent. 28, p. 558 de Boor)

5. Ὅτι ὁ Βόκχος ἑτέρους ἔπεμψε πρέσβεις, οἳ Μαρίου μὲν ἔμελλον περὶ εἰρήνης δεήσεσθαι, Σύλλα δὲ
ἵνα συμπράξειεν ἐς τὰς διαλύσεις. λῃστευθέντας δ' ἐν
ὁδῷ τοὺς πρέσβεις τούσδε ὁ Σύλλας ὑπεδέξατο <. . .>
καὶ ξενίζων² μέχρι Μάριον ἀπὸ Γαιτούλων ἐπανελθεῖν. παρῄνει δὲ Βόκχον διδάσκειν ὅτι χρὴ Σύλλα
2 πείθεσθαι περὶ ἁπάντων. ἐνδιδοὺς οὖν ἤδη πρὸς τὴν
τοῦ Ἰογόρθα προδοσίαν ὁ Βόκχος, ἐς μὲν ὑπόκρισιν
ἐπ' ἄλλον στρατὸν περιέπεμπεν ἐς Αἰθίοπας τοὺς
γείτονας, οἳ ἐπὶ ἑσπέραν ἀπὸ τῶν ἑῴων Αἰθιόπων δι-
ήκουσιν ἐς τὸ Μαυρούσιον ὄρος ὃ καλοῦσιν Ἄτλαντα,
Μάριον δ' ἠξίου Σύλλαν οἱ πέμψαι συνελθεῖν ἐς λό-
3 γους. καὶ Μάριος μὲν ἔπεμπε τὸν Σύλλαν, Ἄψαρα δὲ
Ἰογόρθα φίλον, ἐν Βόκχου καταλελειμμένον ἐφορᾶν
τὰ γιγνόμενα, αὐτός τε Βόκχος καὶ Μαγδάλσης φίλος
Βόκχου, καί τις ἐξελεύθερος ἀνδρὸς Καρχηδονίου,
Κορνήλιος, ἐνήδρευσαν ὧδε.³ (Exc. de leg. gent. 29,
p. 559 de Boor)

² ξενίζει prop. Schweig.
³ ζήτει ἐν τῷ περὶ ἐπιβουλῶν post ὧδε codd.

⸻

8 Appian means Massinissa's grandsons. Micipsa inherited
Massinissa's kingdom and in turn left it to his two legitimate

sons, had made himself an enemy of Rome.[8] Hence, it was no longer right either for the enemy to keep possession of a gift, "which we gave to a friend, or for you to think you could take away from Jugurtha land that belongs to Rome." That is what Manlius said about this territory. (*Exc. de leg. gent.* 28, p. 558 de Boor)

5. Bocchus sent a new mission intending to ask Marius for peace, and to win Sulla's cooperation in reaching a settlement. His envoys were attacked by bandits on the way, but Sulla welcomed them ‹. . .› and entertained them until Marius got back from Gaetulia.[9] Marius advised them to instruct Bocchus that it was necessary to obey Sulla in all matters. Bocchus was already inclined to the 2 idea of betraying Jugurtha, and now, pretending to be recruiting another army, he sent word around to the neighboring Aethiopians (Aethiopia stretches westward from its eastern inhabitants to what they call Mt. Atlas in Mauretania), and asked Marius to send Sulla to him for discussions. Marius did send Sulla, while Bocchus himself, along 3 with Magdalses, an associate of his, and a Carthaginian freedman named Cornelius, set a trap, in the following manner, for Jugurtha's courtier Apsara, who had been left in Bocchus' company to keep an eye on what was happening.[10] (*Exc. de leg. gent.* 29, p. 559 de Boor)

sons, Adherbal and Hiempsal, and his illegitimate son Jugurtha. Jugurtha killed his two-half brothers.

[9] There seems to be something missing from the text in this sentence.

[10] The manuscripts continue "look in the *Excerpts on Conspiracies*," thus indicating that the rest of the account was to be found in this now lost collection of excerpts.

IX

ΕΚ ΤΗΣ ΜΑΚΕΔΟΝΙΚΗΣ

1. Ὅτι ἐνῆγε τοὺς Ῥωμαίους τὰ Σιβύλλεια εἰς τὸν Φιλίππου πόλεμον. ἔστι δὲ ταῦτα·

αὐχοῦντες βασιλεῦσι Μακηδόνες Ἀργεάδησιν,
ὑμῖν κοιρανέων ἀγαθὸν καὶ πῆμα Φίλιππος.
ἤτοι ὁ μὲν πρότερος πόλεσιν λαοῖσί τ᾽ ἄνακτας
θήσει, ὁ δ᾽ ὁπλότερος τιμὴν ἀπὸ πᾶσαν ὀλέσσει,
δμηθεὶς δ᾽ ἑσπερίοισιν ὑπ᾽ ἀνδράσιν ἐνθάδ᾽
ὀλεῖται.

(*Exc. de sent.* 22, p. 70 Boissevain)

2. Ὅτι Ῥωμαῖοι τοῦ Φιλίππου τοῦ Μακεδόνος [τοῦ πολεμήσαντος αὐτοῖς][1] πέρι πάμπαν ἐπολυπραγμό-νουν οὐδέν, οὐδὲ σφίσιν ἐνθύμιος ἦν ὅλως πονουμένης ἔτι τῆς Ἰταλίας ὑπὸ Ἀννίβου [τοῦ Καρχηδονίων

---

[1] τοῦ πολεμήσαντος αὐτοῖς del. Goukowsky ut glossema

---

[1] The place of this fragment is uncertain. Goukowsky argues reasonably that with its reference to Macedonian history stretching back to Philip II, the father of Alexander the Great, it may

BOOK IX
PART 1

FROM THE MACEDONIAN BOOK

1.[1] The Sibylline Books induced the Romans to go to war against Philip, with the following lines:[2] "The Macedonians boast of their royal Argive ancestors, but Philip's rule will bring both good and suffering to you. The older one will establish rulers for cities and peoples, the younger will lose all honor, and die here, vanquished by men from the west." (*Exc. de sent.* 22, p. 70 Boissevain)

2. The Romans paid no attention at all to Philip of Macedon [who went to war with them.][3] Indeed, he did not even enter their thoughts, as Italy was still suffering at the hands of Hannibal [the Carthaginian general] and they

have come from the preface of the book. Alternatively, with its reference to the Second Macedonian War, it could go after fragment 4. It does not make much sense as fragment 2, where it is usually placed.

[2] The Second Macedonian War (200–197). Philip V ruled Macedon from 221 to 179.   [3] This was the so-called First Macedonian War (214–205), a period of hostility, but indecisive engagements, between Rome and Philip V. The description of Philip as "the man who went to war with the Romans" looks like a scribal gloss, as does the identification of Hannibal as "the Carthaginian general" in the next sentence.

στρατηγοῦ]² καὶ αὐτοὶ μεγάλοις στρατοῖς Λιβύην καὶ
Καρχηδόνα καὶ Ἰβηρίαν περικαθήμενοι, καὶ καθιστά-
2 μενοι Σικελίαν. αὐτὸς δὲ Φίλιππος ἀρχῆς ἐπιθυμίᾳ
μείζονος, οὐδέν τι προπαθών, ἔπεμπε πρὸς Ἀννίβαν
ἐς τὴν Ἰταλίαν πρέσβεις, ὧν ἡγεῖτο Ξενοφάνης, ὑπισχνούμενος αὐτῷ συμμαχήσειν ἐπὶ τὴν Ἰταλίαν, εἰ
κἀκεῖνος αὐτῷ σύνθοιτο κατεργάσασθαι τὴν Ἑλλάδα.
3 συμβάντος δ᾽ ἐς ταῦτα τοῦ Ἀννίβου καὶ ἐπὶ τῇ συνθήκῃ ὁμόσαντος, πρέσβεις τε ἀντιπέμψαντος ἐπὶ τοὺς
ὅρκους τοῦ Φιλίππου, Ῥωμαίων τριήρης ἔλαβε τοὺς
ἑκατέρων πρέσβεις ἀναπλέοντας, καὶ ἐς Ῥώμην
ἐκόμισεν. ἐφ᾽ ᾧ Φίλιππος ἀγανακτῶν Κερκύρᾳ προσέβαλεν, ἣ Ῥωμαίοις συνεμάχει. (Exc. de leg. gent. 30,
p. 559 de Boor)

3. Ὅτι Πτολεμαίου τοῦ βασιλεύοντος Αἰγύπτου
πρέσβεις, καὶ σὺν αὐτοῖς ἕτεροι παρά τε Χίων καὶ
Μιτυληναίων καὶ Ἀμυνάνδρου τοῦ Ἀθαμάνων βασιλέως, δίς, ἔνθα περ οἱ Αἰτωλοὶ τὰς πόλεις ἐπισκεψο-
μένας ἐκάλουν, συνῆλθον ἐπὶ διαλλαγῇ Ῥωμαίων καὶ
Αἰτωλῶν καὶ Φιλίππου. Σουλπικίου δ᾽ εἰπόντος οὐκ
εἶναι κυρίου περὶ τῆς εἰρήνης τι κρῖναι, καὶ ἐς τὴν
βουλὴν κρύφα ἐπιστέλλοντος ὅτι Ῥωμαίοις συμφέρει
2 πολεμεῖν Αἰτωλοὺς Φιλίππῳ, ἡ μὲν βουλὴ τὰς συνθήκας ἐκώλυσε, καὶ τοῖς Αἰτωλοῖς ἔπεμπε συμμαχίαν
πεζοὺς μυρίους καὶ ἱππέας χιλίους, μεθ᾽ ὧν οἱ Αἰτωλοὶ κατέλαβον Ἀμβρακίαν, ἣν οὐ πολὺ ὕστερον

---

² τοῦ Καρχηδονίων στρατηγοῦ del. Goukowsky ut glossema

had large armies of occupation in Africa, Carthage, and
Iberia, and were restoring order in Sicily. Wishing to ex- 2
tend his kingdom, but having no earlier grievance, he took
it on himself to send a mission, headed by Xenophanes,
to Hannibal in Italy, promising him military assistance
against Italy, if he would help Philip conquer Greece.
Hannibal agreed to these terms and after swearing an oath 3
to uphold the treaty, he sent envoys back to receive Philip's
oath. A Roman trireme, however, captured both sets of
ambassadors as they were returning, and took them to
Rome. Philip was annoyed at this, and attacked Corcyra,
which was an ally of Rome. (*Exc. de leg. gent.* 30, p. 559
de Boor)

3. Ambassadors of king Ptolemy of Egypt,[4] and with
them others from Chios, Mytilene, and Amynander king
of the Athamanes, met on two occasions where the Aetolians customarily invited their towns for discussions, to
bring about a settlement between Rome, Aetolia, and
Philip. When Sulpicius[5] said that he did not have the authority to make a decision in the matter of peace, and secretly wrote to the senate telling them that it was to Rome's
advantage for the Aetolians to be at war with Philip, the 2
senate prevented an agreement being made and sent ten
thousand infantry and one thousand cavalry to help the
Aetolians, who used them to capture Ambracia, although

[4] Ptolemy IV Philopator ("Father-loving"), king of Egypt from
221 to 205.
[5] P. Sulpicius Galba Maximus served in Greece from the year
of his first consulship in 211 until 206.

APPIAN

3 αὐτῶν Φίλιππος ἀποπλευσάντων ἀνέλαβεν. οἱ δὲ πρέσβεις αὖθις συνῆλθον, καὶ πολλὰ φανερῶς ἔλεγον,
ὅτι Φίλιππος καὶ Αἰτωλοὶ διαφερόμενοι τοὺς Ἕλληνας ἐς δουλείαν Ῥωμαίοις ὑποβάλλουσιν, ἐθίζοντες
αὐτοὺς τῆς Ἑλλάδος θαμινὰ πειρᾶσθαι. ἐφ᾿ οἷς ὁ μὲν
Σουλπίκιος ἀντιλέξων ἀνίστατο, τὸ δὲ πλῆθος οὐκ
ἤκουσεν, ἀλλ᾿ ἐκεκράγεσαν τοὺς πρέσβεις εὖ λέγειν.
4 καὶ τέλος Αἰτωλοί τε πρῶτοι κατὰ σφᾶς, ἄνευ Ῥωμαίων, Φιλίππῳ συνέβησαν, καὶ πρέσβεις αὐτοῦ Φιλίππου καὶ Ῥωμαίων ἐπὶ διαλλαγαῖς ἀφίκοντο ἐς
Ῥώμην. καὶ ἐγένοντο συνθῆκαι Ῥωμαίοις καὶ Φιλίππῳ, μηδετέρους ἀδικεῖν τοὺς ἑκατέρωθεν φίλους. ἐς
μὲν δὴ τοῦτ᾿ ἔληξεν ἡ Φιλίππου καὶ Ῥωμαίων ἐς ἀλλήλους πεῖρα πρώτη, καὶ τὰς συνθήκας οὐδέτεροι
βεβαίους, οὐδ᾿ ἀπ᾿ εὐνοίας, ἐδόκουν πεποιῆσθαι. (Exc.
de leg. gent. 31, p. 560 de Boor)

4. Ὅτι μετ᾿ οὐ πολὺ Φίλιππος μὲν τῶν ὑπηκόων
τοῖς ἐπὶ θαλάσσης στόλον ἐπαγγείλας, Σάμον καὶ
Χίον εἷλε, καὶ μέρος τῆς Ἀττάλου γῆς ἐπόρθησε, καὶ
αὐτῆς ἀπεπείρασε Περγάμου, μὴ φειδόμενος ἱερῶν ἢ
τάφων, τήν τε Ῥοδίων περαίαν ἐδῄου διαλλακτήρων
οἱ γεγονότων, καὶ ἑτέρῳ μέρει στρατοῦ τὴν Ἀττικὴν
ἐλυμαίνετο καὶ τὰς Ἀθήνας ἐπολιόρκει, ὡς οὐδὲν
τῶνδε Ῥωμαίοις προσηκόντων. λόγος τε ἦν ὅτι Φίλιππος καὶ Ἀντίοχος ὁ Σύρων βασιλεὺς ὑπόσχοιντο ἀλλήλοις, Ἀντιόχῳ μὲν ὁ Φίλιππος συστρατεύσειν ἐπί
τε Αἴγυπτον καὶ ἐπὶ Κύπρον, ὧν τότε ἦρχεν ἔτι παῖς

264

they sailed away shortly after and Philip recovered it. When the ambassadors met again, they issued a number 3 of clear statements to the effect that the dispute between Philip and the Aetolians was beginning to enslave the Greeks to Rome, as it was acclimatizing the Romans to make frequent interventions in Greece. Sulpicius stood to reply to this, but the crowd refused to listen, and shouted that the ambassadors were right in what they were saying. In the end, the Aetolians took the initiative and unilater- 4 ally, without Roman input, made peace with Philip, while Philip's own envoys and those of the Romans went to Rome to arrange a settlement. Peace between Philip and Rome was made on condition that neither side would wrong the friends of the other. This was the end of the first trial of strength between Philip and Rome, but neither side believed that the treaty was stable or founded on goodwill.[6] (*Exc. de leg. gent.* 31, p. 560 de Boor)

4. Shortly after, Philip ordered up a fleet from his coastal subjects, captured Samos and Chios, and ravaged part of Attalus' territory, where he even made an attack on Pergamum itself, sparing neither temples nor graves.[7] He also pillaged Rhodian territory on the mainland (they had been peace mediators for him), and with another division of his army he laid waste to Attica and besieged the city of Athens: these places, he maintained, had nothing to do with Rome. There was a story circulating that Philip and Antiochus, the Syrian king, had made promises to each other that Philip would send military assistance to help Antiochus against Egypt and Cyprus, which were ruled

[6] The Peace of Phoinice was signed in 205.
[7] Philip V's aggressions are dated to 201.

ὧν Πτολεμαῖος ὁ τέταρτος [ᾧ φιλοπάτωρ ἐπώνυμον
ἦν]³ Φιλίππῳ δ᾽ Ἀντίοχος ἐπὶ Κυρήνην καὶ τὰς Κυ-
2 κλάδας νήσους καὶ Ἰωνίαν. καὶ τήνδε τὴν δόξαν,
ἐκταράσσουσαν ἅπαντας Ῥόδιοι μὲν Ῥωμαίοις ἐμή-
νυσαν, ἐπὶ δὲ τοῖς Ῥοδίων Ἀθηναίων πρέσβεις ᾐτιῶ-
ντο Φίλιππον τῆς πολιορκίας. καὶ Αἰτωλοὶ μεταγιγνώσκοντες κατηγόρουν ὡς καὶ περὶ σφᾶς ἀπίστου
γεγονότος, ἠξίουν τε αὖθις ἐς τοὺς Ῥωμαίων συμμάχους ἐγγραφῆναι. Ῥωμαῖοι δ᾽ Αἰτωλοῖς ἐμέμψαντο
τῆς οὐ πρὸ πολλοῦ μεταβολῆς, πρέσβεις δ᾽ ἐς τοὺς
βασιλέας ἔπεμπον, οἳ προηγόρευον αὐτοῖς Ἀντίοχον
μὲν Αἰγύπτῳ μὴ ἐπιχειρεῖν, Φίλιππον δὲ μηδὲν ἐς
Ῥοδίους ἢ Ἀθηναίους ἢ Ἄτταλον ἢ ἐς ἄλλον τινὰ
3 Ῥωμαίων φίλον ἁμαρτάνειν. τούτοις ὁ Φίλιππος ἀπεκρίνατο Ῥωμαίοις ἕξειν καλῶς, ἂν ἐμμένωσιν ᾗ
συνέθεντο πρὸς αὐτὸν εἰρήνῃ. οὕτω μὲν αἱ γενόμεναι
σπονδαὶ ἐλέλυντο, καὶ στρατιὰ Ῥωμαίων ἐς τὴν Ἑλλάδα ἠπείγετο, στρατηγοῦντος Ποπλίου καὶ ναυαρ-
χοῦντος Λευκίου. (Exc. de leg. gent. 32, p. 560 de Boor)

5. Ὅτι ὁ Φίλιππος ὁ Μακεδόνων βασιλεὺς τῷ Φλα-
μινίνῳ ἐς λόγους ᾔει, συναγόντων αὐτοὺς Ἠπειρωτῶν

³ ᾧ φιλοπάτωρ ἐπώνυμον ἦν del. Goukowsky ut glossema

---

8 This is a mistake: the child-king Ptolemy V Epiphanes had
succeeded his father, Ptolemy IV, in 205. But Appian came from
Alexandria and knew the Ptolemaic history of his own country
well. The mistake is more likely to have been that of a scribe in-

at the time by Ptolemy IV [surnamed Philopator] who was still a boy;[8] and Antiochus would help Philip against Cyrene,[9] the Cycladic islands, and Ionia. This rumor was worrying everybody, and the Rhodians reported it to Rome. After the Rhodians, Athenian ambassadors complained about Philip's siege of Athens. Then came the Aetolians, who accused Philip of bad faith toward them; they had changed their mind about him, and now asked to be listed again among Rome's allies. The Romans were critical of the Aetolians for their recent defection, but sent ambassadors to the kings, telling Antiochus to keep his hands off Egypt, and Philip to refrain from any offense against Rhodes, Athens, Attalus, or any other friend of Rome. Philip responded by saying that it would be a good idea if the Romans observed the terms of the peace treaty they had agreed with him. In this way the treaty that had been agreed was dissolved. A Roman army hurried to Greece, with Publius commanding the land troops and Lucius the navy.[10] (*Exc. de leg. gent.* 32, p. 560 de Boor)

5. Philip, king of Macedon, was engaged in discussions with Flamininus, the ambassadors of Epirus hav-

2

3

correctly explaining which Ptolemy his text was referring to. See Goukowsky (*Syr.*, p. lxxxiv). The Seleucid king Antiochus III ruled from 223 to 187.

[9] There is no other evidence for Philip coveting Cyrene. Polybius (3.2.8) mentions Caria as one of Philip's targets, and, as Goukowsky (*Ill.*, 189n36) surmises, "Cyrene" is probably a scribal error for "Caria."

[10] P. Sulpicius Galba Maximus was consul for the second time in 200 and was assigned the war against Philip. He arrived in Greece late in 200. Lucius Apustius Fullo was a legate of Sulpicius.

πρέσβεων. ὡς δὲ ὁ Φλαμινῖνος Φίλιππον ἐκέλευσεν
ἐκστῆναι τῆς Ἑλλάδος οὐ Ῥωμαίοις ἀλλὰ ταῖς πόλεσιν αὐταῖς, καὶ τὰς βλάβας ταῖς προειρημέναις ἀπο-
δοθῆναι, ὁ μὲν Φίλιππος τὰ μὲν <. . .> (Exc. de sent.
23, p. 70 Boissevain)

6. Ποιμὴν ὑπέσχετο στρατὸν εὔζωνον ἄξειν ὁδὸν
ἀτριβῆ τρισὶν ἡμέραις. (Suda, ε 3453)

7. Ὅτι Λεύκιος Κοΐντιος ἐς τὸν τῶν Ἀχαιῶν σύλ-
λογον ἀπέστειλε πρέσβεις, οἳ μετὰ Ἀθηναίων καὶ
Ῥοδίων ἔπειθον αὐτοὺς μεταθέσθαι πρὸς σφᾶς ἀπὸ
τοῦ Φιλίππου, διεπρεσβεύετο δὲ καὶ Φίλιππος αἰτῶν
βοήθειαν ὡς συμμάχους. οἱ δὲ ἐνοχλούμενοι μὲν
οἰκείῳ καὶ γείτονι πολέμῳ Νάβιδος τοῦ Λακεδαιμο-
νίων τυράννου, διεστῶτες δὲ ταῖς γνώμαις ἠπόρουν,
καὶ οἱ πλείονες ἡροῦντο τὰ Φιλίππου καὶ ἀπεστρέ-
φοντο Ῥωμαίους διά τινα ἐς τὴν Ἑλλάδα Σουλπικίου
τοῦ στρατηγοῦ παρανομήματα. ἐγκειμένων δὲ βιαίως
τῶν ῥωμαϊζόντων, οἱ πολλοὶ τῆς ἐκκλησίας ἀπεχώρουν δυσχεραίνοντες, καὶ οἱ λοιποὶ διὰ τὴν ὀλιγότητα
ἐκβιασθέντες συνέθεντο τῷ Λευκίῳ, καὶ εὐθὺς ἠκο-
λούθουν ἐπὶ Κόρινθον μηχανήματα φέροντες. (Exc. de
leg. Rom. 11, p. 72 de Boor)

8. Ὅτι Φλαμινῖνος αὖθις συνῆλθεν ἐς λόγους Φι-

---

11 T. Quinctius Flamininus took over command of the war
against Philip V while consul in 198 and defeated him at the
battle of Cynoscephalae in 197.

ing brought them together.[11] When Flamininus ordered Philip to withdraw from Greece, not for the benefit of the Romans, but for that of the Greek towns themselves, and to pay for the damage he had caused the aforementioned towns, Philip ‹. . .› (*Exc. de sent.* 23, p. 70 Boissevain)

6. A shepherd promised to take a lightly armed force by an unused track in three days.[12] (*Suda*, ε 3453)

7. Lucius Quinctius sent representatives to the Achaean League, who joined the Athenians and Rhodians in trying to persuade the League to abandon Philip and come over to the Roman side.[13] Philip also made a diplomatic approach to them, asking for their help as allies. But the Achaeans were preoccupied with their own war against their neighbor Nabis, tyrant of Sparta, and, being divided in their opinions, did not know what to do. The majority favored Philip and rejected Rome, because of some crimes Sulpicius had committed against Greece when he was in command. But when the partisans of Rome pressed their case violently, most Achaeans left the assembly in disgust, and the remainder, because there were so few of them, were forced into making an agreement with Lucius,[14] and immediately accompanied him to Corinth bringing siege engines with them. (*Exc. de leg. Rom.* 11, p. 72 de Boor)

8. Flamininus and Philip reopened negotiations on the

[12] The story of a shepherd leading a Roman force behind the Macedonian army in the campaign of 198 is reported in detail by Livy (32.11).

[13] L. Quinctius Flamininus, brother of Titus, was one of his legates in the Second Macedonian War. He became consul in 192.

[14] Livy (32.23.1–3) says they postponed making an agreement with Rome until they could send an embassy there.

APPIAN

λίππῳ κατὰ τὸν Μηλιέα κόλπον, ἔνθα κατηγορούντων
τοῦ Φιλίππου Ῥοδίων καὶ Αἰτωλῶν καὶ Ἀμυνάνδρου
τοῦ Ἀθαμᾶνος ἐκέλευσε Φίλιππον ἐξάγειν τὰς φρουρὰς ἐκ τῆς Φωκίδος, καὶ πρέσβεις ἐς Ῥώμην ἀμφο-
2 τέρους ἀποστεῖλαι. γενομένων δὲ τούτων, οἱ μὲν Ἕλληνες ἐν τῇ βουλῇ τῇ Ῥωμαίων ἠξίουν τὸν Φίλιππον
ἐξαγαγεῖν ἐκ τῆς Ἑλλάδος τὰς τρεῖς φρουρὰς ἃς
αὐτὸς πέδας ἐκάλει τῆς Ἑλλάδος, τὴν μὲν ἐν Χαλκίδι
Βοιωτοῖς καὶ Εὐβοεῦσι καὶ Λοκροῖς ἐπικειμένην, τὴν
δὲ ἐν Κορίνθῳ καθάπερ πύλαις τὴν Πελοπόννησον
ἀποκλείουσαν, καὶ τρίτην ἐν Δημητριάδι τὴν Αἰτω-
3 λοῖς καὶ Μάγνησιν ἐφεδρεύουσαν· ἡ δὲ βουλὴ τοὺς
Φιλίππου πρέσβεις ἤρετο τί φρονοίη περὶ τῶνδε
τῶν φρουρῶν ὁ βασιλεύς, ἀποκριναμένων δὲ ἀγνοεῖν,
Φλαμινῖνον ἔφη κρινεῖν, καὶ πράξειν ὅ τι ἂν δίκαιον
ἡγῆται. οὕτω μὲν οἱ πρέσβεις ἐκ Ῥώμης ἐπανῇσαν,
Φλαμινῖνος δὲ καὶ Φίλιππος ἐς οὐδὲν συμβαίνοντες
ἀλλήλοις αὖθις ἐς πόλεμον καθίσταντο. (Exc. de leg.
gent. 33, p. 560 de Boor)

9. Ὅτι ἡττηθεὶς πάλιν ὁ Φίλιππος περὶ συμβάσεων
ἐπεκηρυκεύετο πρὸς Φλαμινῖνον, ὁ δ' αὖθις αὐτῷ συνελθεῖν ἐς λόγους συνεχώρει, πολλὰ μὲν τῶν Αἰτωλῶν
δυσχεραινόντων, καὶ διαβαλλόντων αὐτὸν ἐς δωροδο-
κίαν καὶ καταγιγνωσκόντων τῆς ἐς ἅπαντα εὐχεροῦς
μεταβολῆς, ἡγούμενος δ' οὔτε Ῥωμαίοις συμφέρειν
οὔτε τοῖς Ἕλλησι Φιλίππου καθαιρεθέντος ἐπιπολά-
σαι τὴν Αἰτωλῶν βίαν. τάχα δ' αὐτὸν καὶ τὸ παράδοξον τῆς νίκης ἀγαπᾶν ἐποίει. συνθέμενος δὲ χωρίον

270

Malian gulf. Here, when the Rhodians, the Aetolians, and Amynander the Athamanian made complaints against Philip, Flamininus ordered him to remove his garrisons from Phocis, and instructed both parties to send ambassadors to Rome, which they did. In the Roman senate, the 2 Greeks demanded that Philip remove the three garrisons that he himself called the "fetters" of Greece; that is, the one in Chalcis that threatened Boeotia, Euboea, and Locris; the one in Corinth that closed off the Peloponnese like a gate; and the third in Demetrias, which kept watch over Aetolia and Magnesia. The senate asked Philip's envoys what the king thought about these garrisons, and when they answered that they did not know, the senate said that Flamininus would make the decision in accordance with what he thought was the right thing to do. And so the ambassadors returned from Rome, while Philip and Flamininus resumed hostilities, having failed to come to an agreement. (*Exc. de leg. gent.* 33, p. 560 de Boor)

9. After a second defeat, Philip sent heralds to Flamininus to sue for peace.[15] When he again granted him an audience, the Aetolians were very disgruntled, accused Flamininus of receiving bribes, and complained of him unscrupulously changing his mind on everything. But he was of the opinion that it would benefit neither the Romans nor the Greeks to have Philip destroyed and Aetolian power dominant. Perhaps the fact that his victory was unexpected was also influential in satisfying him. Having

[15] Appian is referring to the battle of Cynoscephalae in 197 and to the battle at the Aous river the year before.

APPIAN

οἷ τὸν Φίλιππον ἐπελθεῖν ἔδει τοὺς συμμάχους ἐκέλευσε γνώμην προαποφήνασθαι κατὰ πόλεις. τὰ μὲν
δὴ παρὰ τῶν ἄλλων φιλάνθρωπα ἦν, τό τε τῆς τύχης
ἄδηλον ἐξ ὧν ἔπαθεν ὁ Φίλιππος ὑφορωμένων, καὶ τὸ
πταῖσμα τοῦτο οὐ κατ᾽ ἀσθένειαν ἀλλὰ πλέον ἐκ συν-
τυχίας αὐτὸν παθεῖν ἡγουμένων· Ἀλέξανδρος δὲ ὁ τῶν
Αἰτωλῶν πρόεδρος ἀγνοεῖν ἔφη τὸν Φλαμινῖνον ὅτι
μηδὲν ἄλλο μήτε Ῥωμαίοις μήθ᾽ Ἕλλησι συνοίσει
2 πλὴν ἐξαιρεθῆναι τὴν ἀρχὴν τὴν Φιλίππου. ὁ δὲ Ἀλέ-
ξανδρον ἀγνοεῖν ἔφη τὴν Ῥωμαίων φύσιν, οἳ οὐδένα
πω τῶν ἐχθρῶν εὐθὺς ἀπ᾽ ἀρχῆς ἀνέτρεψαν, ἀλλὰ
πολλῶν ἐς αὐτοὺς ἁμαρτόντων, καὶ Καρχηδονίων
ἔναγχος, ἐφείσαντο, τὰ σφέτερα αὐτοῖς ἀποδόντες καὶ
φίλους ποιησάμενοι τοὺς ἠδικηκότας. "Ἀγνοεῖς δ᾽,"
ἔφη, "καὶ τοῦθ᾽, ὅτι τοῖς Ἕλλησιν ἔθνη πολλά, ὅσα
βάρβαρα τὴν Μακεδονίαν περικάθηται, εἴ τις ἐξέλοι
τοὺς Μακεδόνων βασιλέας, ἐπιδραμεῖται ῥᾳδίως. ὅθεν
ἐγὼ δοκιμάζω τὴν μὲν ἀρχὴν ἐᾶν τῶν Μακεδόνων
προπολεμεῖν ὑμῶν πρὸς τοὺς βαρβάρους, Φίλιππον
δὲ ἐκστῆναι τοῖς Ἕλλησιν ὧν πρότερον ἀντέλεγε
χωρίων, καὶ Ῥωμαίοις ἐς τὴν τοῦ πολέμου δαπάνην
ἐσενεγκεῖν τάλαντα διακόσια, ὅμηρά τε δοῦναι τὰ
ἀξιολογώτατα καὶ τὸν υἱὸν αὐτοῦ Δημήτριον, μέχρι
δὲ ταῦθ᾽ ἡ σύγκλητος ἐπικυρώσει, τετραμήνους ἀνο-
3 χὰς γενέσθαι." δεξαμένου δὲ πάντα τοῦ Φιλίππου,
τὴν μὲν εἰρήνην ἡ βουλὴ μαθοῦσα ἐπεκύρωσε, τὰς δὲ
προτάσεις τὰς Φλαμινίνου σμικρύνασα καὶ φαυλί-
σασα, ἐκέλευσε τὰς πόλεις ὅσαι ἦσαν Ἑλληνίδες ὑπὸ

272

agreed a place where Philip was required to present himself, Flamininus asked the allies to give their opinion beforehand town by town. Suspicious of the inscrutable nature of fate as evidenced by what Philip had suffered, and believing that this defeat of his had more to do with bad luck than weakness, the others were inclined to moderation; but Alexander, the Aetolian president, said that Flamininus did not understand that nothing would be of any good to either Rome or Greece, but the complete destruction of Philip's kingdom. Flamininus replied that Alexander did not understand the character of the Romans, who had never yet destroyed one of their enemies right at the beginning, but had spared many who had wronged them, most recently the Carthaginians, giving them back their possessions and making friends of those who had harmed Rome. "You also fail to understand the fact," he continued, "that the many barbarian peoples on the borders of Macedonia would easily overrun Greece, if one were to remove the Macedonian kings. That is the reason for my assessment that the Macedonian kingdom must be left to protect you against the barbarians, while Philip must retire from the places he has previously refused to give back to the Greeks, pay two hundred talents to Rome as a war indemnity, and provide hostages from the most important families, including his own son, Demetrius. There will be a four month cease-fire for the senate to validate the agreement." Philip agreed to everything, and the senate confirmed the peace when they learned of it, but they regarded Flamininus' terms as too lenient and inadequate. So, they gave orders that all Greek

2

3

Φιλίππῳ, πάσας ἐλευθέρας εἶναι, καὶ τὰς φρουρὰς
ἀπ' αὐτῶν Φίλιππον ἐξαγαγεῖν πρὸ τῶν ἐπιόντων
Ἰσθμίων, ναῦς τε ὅσας ἔχει, χωρὶς ἐξήρους μιᾶς καὶ
σκαφῶν πέντε καταφράκτων, παραδοῦναι τῷ Φλαμι-
νίνῳ, καὶ ἀργυρίου τάλαντα Ῥωμαίοις ἐσενεγκεῖν
πεντακόσια μὲν αὐτίκα πεντακόσια δὲ ἔτεσι δέκα,
ἑκάστου τὸ μέρος ἔτους ἐς Ῥώμην ἀναφέροντα, ἀποδοῦναι δὲ καὶ αἰχμάλωτα καὶ αὐτόμολα αὐτῶν ὅσα
ἔχοι. τάδε μὲν ἡ βουλὴ προσέθηκε, καὶ Φίλιππος ἐδέ-
ξατο ἅπαντα· ᾧ καὶ μάλιστα ἡ σμικρολογία Φλαμινίνου καταφανὴς ἐγένετο. συμβούλους δ' ἔπεμπον
αὐτῷ, καθάπερ εἰώθεσαν ἐπὶ τοῖς λήγουσι πολέμοις,
δέκα ἄνδρας, μεθ' ὧν αὐτὸν ἔδει τὰ εἰλημμένα καθ-
4 ίστασθαι. καὶ τάδε μὲν διετίθετο σὺν ἐκείνοις, αὐτὸς
δ' ἐς τὸν τῶν Ἰσθμίων ἀγῶνα ἐπελθών, πληθύοντος
τοῦ σταδίου, σιωπήν τε ἐσήμηνεν ὑπὸ σάλπιγγι, καὶ
τὸν κήρυκα ἀνειπεῖν ἐκέλευσεν· "Ὁ δῆμος ὁ Ῥωμαίων
καὶ ἡ σύγκλητος καὶ Φλαμινῖνος ὁ στρατηγός, Μακεδόνας καὶ βασιλέα Φίλιππον ἐκπολεμήσαντες, ἀφιᾶσι
τὴν Ἑλλάδα ἀφρούρητον ἀφορολόγητον ἰδίοις ἤθεσι
καὶ νόμοις χρῆσθαι." πολλῆς δ' ἐπὶ τούτῳ βοῆς καὶ
χαρᾶς γενομένης θόρυβος ἥδιστος ἦν, ἑτέρων μεθ'
ἑτέρους τὸν κήρυκα καὶ παρὰ σφᾶς ἀνειπεῖν μετακα-
λούντων. στεφάνους τε καὶ ταινίας ἐπέβαλλον τῷ
στρατηγῷ, καὶ ἀνδριάντας ἐψηφίζοντο κατὰ πόλεις.
πρέσβεις τε μετὰ χρυσῶν στεφάνων ἔπεμπον ἐς τὸ
Καπιτώλιον, οἳ χάριν ὡμολόγουν, καὶ ἐς τοὺς Ῥωμαίων συμμάχους ἀνεγράφοντο. καὶ δεύτερος ὅδε

towns under Philip's control were to be free; that he must withdraw the garrisons from them before the upcoming Isthmian games; that he must surrender to Flamininus all ships in his possession, except for one with six banks of oars and five decked ketches; that he must immediately pay Rome five hundred silver talents, and another five hundred talents in annual installments over the next ten years; and that he must hand back all Roman prisoners and deserters in his possession. These were the additional terms of the senate, and Philip accepted them all, which shows very clearly the deficiency of Flamininus' demands. As was their normal practice when wars came to an end, the senate sent a ten-man commission of advisors to Flamininus: together it was their job to organize the conquered territory. With their joint arrangements in place, 4 Flamininus himself went off to the Isthmian games. When the stadium was full, he signaled the trumpet to sound for silence, and ordered the herald to make the following proclamation: "The senate and people of Rome, and their general Flamininus, having defeated the Macedonians and king Philip in battle, leave Greece free from garrisons and tribute to enjoy its own customs and laws." At this, there was loud shouting, widespread joy and a most delighted clamor, as one group after another called the herald back to repeat the proclamation to them. They threw garlands and ribbons on the general, and individual towns voted to erect statues of him. They sent ambassadors to the Capitol with golden garlands, to express their gratitude, and they had themselves enrolled as allies of Rome. This was how the second war between Philip and Rome

πόλεμος Ῥωμαίοις τε καὶ Φιλίππῳ ἐς τοῦτο ἐτελεύτα.
5 οὐ πολὺ δὲ ὕστερον καὶ συνεμάχησε Ῥωμαίοις ὁ
Φίλιππος ἐν τῇ Ἑλλάδι κατ' Ἀντιόχου βασιλέως,
περῶντάς τε ἐπὶ Ἀντίοχον ἐς τὴν Ἀσίαν διὰ Θρᾴκης
καὶ Μακεδονίας ὁδὸν οὐκ εὐμαρῆ παρέπεμπεν οἰκείοις
τέλεσι καὶ τροφαῖς καὶ δαπανήμασιν, ὁδοποιῶν καὶ
ποταμοὺς δυσπόρους ζευγνὺς καὶ τοὺς ἐπικειμένους
Θρᾷκας διακόπτων, ἕως ἐπὶ τὸν Ἑλλήσποντον ἤγαγεν. ἐφ' οἷς ἡ μὲν βουλὴ τὸν υἱὸν αὐτῷ Δημήτριον
παρὰ σφίσιν ὁμηρεύοντα ἀπέλυσε, καὶ τῶν χρημάτων
ἀφῆκεν ὧν ἔτι ὤφειλεν· οἱ δὲ Θρᾷκες οἴδε Ῥωμαίους
ἀπὸ τῆς ἐπ' Ἀντιόχῳ νίκης, ἐπανιόντας, οὐκέτι Φιλίππου παρόντος, τήν τε λείαν ἀφείλοντο καὶ πολλοὺς
διέφθειραν, ᾧ καὶ μάλιστα ἐπεδείχθη ὅσον αὐτοὺς
6 ἀνιόντας ὤνησεν ὁ Φίλιππος. ἐκτελεσθέντος δὲ ‹. . .›[4]
πολλοὶ κατηγόρουν τοῦ Φιλίππου, τὰ μὲν ἀδικεῖν
αὐτόν, τὰ δὲ οὐ ποιεῖν ὧν ὥρισε Φλαμινῖνος, ὅτε διετίθετο τὴν Ἑλλάδα. καὶ Δημήτριος ἐς ἀντιλογίαν
ἐπρέσβευεν ὑπὲρ αὐτοῦ, κεχαρισμένος μὲν ἔκπαλαι
Ῥωμαίοις ἀπὸ τῆς ὁμηρείας, Φλαμινίνου δὲ αὐτὸν τῇ
βουλῇ γνωρίζοντος ἰσχυρῶς. νεώτερον δ' ὄντα καὶ
θορυβούμενον ἐκέλευσαν τὰ τοῦ πατρὸς ὑπομνήματα
ἀναγνῶναι, ἐν οἷς ἦν ἐφ' ἑκάστου, τὰ μὲν ἤδη γεγο-

[4] τοῦ κατ' Ἀντιόχου πολέμου prop. Mend.

came to an end. Not long after this, Philip fought along- 5
side the Romans in Greece against king Antiochus.[16] As
they were marching through Thrace and Macedonia on
their way to confront Antiochus in Asia, Philip accompanied them along a difficult route with his own squadrons,
supplying them with rations and expenses, making the
road passable, bridging rivers that could not be forded and
forcing a way through the hostile Thracians, until he
brought them to the Hellespont. In return for this, the
senate released back to him his son Demetrius who had
been a hostage in Rome, and wrote off the money he still
owed. When the Romans were returning after their victory over Antiochus, but no longer with Philip as escort,
these same Thracians robbed them of their booty and
killed many of them—a clear demonstration of how help-
ful Philip had been to them on their outward journey.
After the end ‹of the war against king Antiochus?›,[17] many 6
made accusations against Philip, some claiming that he
was acting illegally, others that he was failing to carry out
what Flamininus had ordained when he settled the affairs
of Greece. Demetrius went to Rome to represent Philip
in answering the charges, as he had long been popular
with the Romans from his time as a hostage, and Flamininus strongly recommended him to the senate. He was still
quite young and overawed, so the senate told him to read
his father's memorandum, which listed all the details of

[16] In 192 Antiochus III (the Great) invaded Greece, but he
was defeated in 190 at the battle of Magnesia by the consul L.
Cornelius Scipio Asiaticus.

[17] There is a lacuna in the text at this point, possibly to be filled
as suggested, but the gap could be longer.

νέναι, τὰ δὲ γενήσεσθαι, καίπερ ἀδίκως ὡρισμένα·
καὶ γὰρ τοῦτο προσέκειτο πολλοῖς. ἡ δὲ βουλὴ τὴν
ὑπόγυον αὐτοῦ ἐς Ἀντίοχον προθυμίαν αἰδουμένη,
συγγιγνώσκειν τε ἔφη, καὶ προσεπεῖπε, "Διὰ Δη-
7 μήτριον." ὁ δ' ὁμολογουμένως αὐτοῖς ἐς τὸν Ἀντιόχου
πόλεμον χρησιμώτατός τε γεγονώς, καὶ βλαβερώτα-
τος ἂν φανεὶς εἰ Ἀντιόχῳ παρακαλοῦντι συνέπραξε,
πολλὰ ἐλπίσας ἐπὶ τῷδε, καὶ ὁρῶν αὐτὸν ἀπιστούμε-
νον καὶ κατηγορούμενον καὶ συγγνώμης ἀντὶ χαρίτων
ἀξιούμενον, καὶ τῆσδε διὰ Δημήτριον, ἤχθετο καὶ
ἠγανάκτει, καὶ ἐπέκρυπτεν ἄμφω. ὡς δὲ καὶ ἐν δίκῃ
τινὶ Ῥωμαῖοι πολλὰ τῶν Φιλίππου πρὸς Εὐμένη μετ-
έφερον, ἀσθενοποιοῦντες ἀεὶ τὸν Φίλιππον, ἐς πόλεμον ἤδη λανθάνων ἡτοιμάζετο. (Exc. de leg. gent. 34,
p. 561 de Boor)

10. Ὁ δὲ Φίλιππος τοὺς ἐπιπλέοντας διέφθειρεν, ἵνα
μὴ Ῥωμαίοις λέγοιεν τὰ Μακεδόνων ἐκτετρῦσθαι.
(Suda, τ 418)

11. Ὅτι Ῥωμαῖοι ταχέως αὐξανόμενον τὸν Περσέα
ὑφεωρῶντο· καὶ μάλιστα αὐτοὺς ἠρέθιζεν ἡ τῶν Ἑλλήνων φιλία καὶ γειτνίασις, οἷς ἔχθος ἐς Ῥωμαίους
ἐπεποιήκεσαν οἱ Ῥωμαίων στρατηγοί. ὡς δὲ καὶ οἱ
πρέσβεις οἱ ἐς Βαστέρνας ἀπεσταλμένοι τὴν Μακεδονίαν ἔφασκον ἰδεῖν ἀσφαλῶς ὠχυρωμένην καὶ παρασκευὴν ἱκανὴν ⟨ἔχουσαν⟩[5] καὶ νεότητα γεγυμνασμένην, Ῥωμαίους καὶ τάδε διετάρασσεν. αἰσθόμενος

5 ἔχουσαν add. Goukowsky

what had been done and what remained to be done, even the unfair demands—a remark attached to many of the entries. The senate expressed their respect for Philip's recent enthusiastic help against Antiochus, but said that they were granting him a pardon, and added, "on account of Demetrius." Philip had pinned high hopes on the fact that, 7 as everyone admitted, he had proved extremely useful to Rome in the war against Antiochus, when he could clearly have proved extremely damaging to them if he had accepted Antiochus' invitation to join forces with him. Now seeing himself distrusted and accused, and considered deserving of forgiveness rather than gratitude, and even this only because of Demetrius, he was offended and very annoyed, but kept both feelings hidden. In their continuing attempt to weaken him, however, when the Romans used a particular dispute to transfer much of his territory to Eumenes, he finally began to make secret preparations for war. (*Exc. de leg. gent.* 34, p. 561 de Boor)

10. Philip destroyed the expedition sailing against him, making it impossible for them to tell the Romans that Macedon had been completely crushed. (*Suda τ* 418)

11. The Romans were suspicious of the rapidly expanding power of Perseus.[18] What really concerned them was the fact that he was a friend and neighbor of the Greeks, who had been driven to hatred of Rome by Rome's own generals. And when the ambassadors sent to the Bastarnae reported seeing Macedonia securely fortified, well supplied with matériel, and with their young men thoroughly trained, this too disturbed the Romans. When Perseus

---

[18] Perseus, son of Philip V, ruled Macedon from 179 to his death in 166.

APPIAN

δ' ὁ Περσεὺς ἑτέρους ἔπεμπε πρέσβεις, τὴν ὑπόνοιαν
ἐκλύων. ἐν δὲ τούτῳ καὶ Εὐμένης ὁ τῆς περὶ τὸ Πέρ-
γαμον Ἀσίας βασιλεύς, ἀπὸ τῆς πρὸς Φίλιππον
ἔχθρας δεδιὼς Περσέα ἧκεν ἐς Ῥώμην, καὶ κατηγόρει
φανερῶς αὐτοῦ, παρελθὼν ἐς τὸ βουλευτήριον, ὅτι
Ῥωμαίοις δυσμενὴς γένοιτο ἀεί, καὶ τὸν ἀδελφὸν
οἰκείως ἐς αὐτοὺς ἔχοντα ἀνέλοι, καὶ Φιλίππῳ τε
παρασκευὴν τοσήνδε κατ' αὐτῶν συναγαγόντι συμ-
πράξειε, καὶ βασιλεὺς γενόμενος οὐδὲν ἐκλύσειεν
αὐτῆς ἀλλὰ καὶ προσεξεργάσαιτο ἕτερα, καὶ τὴν Ἑλλάδα ἀμέτρως θεραπεύοι, Βυζαντίοις τε καὶ Αἰτωλοῖς
καὶ Βοιωτοῖς συμμαχήσας, καὶ Θρᾴκην κατακτῷτο,
μέγα ὁρμητήριον, καὶ Θετταλοὺς καὶ Περραιβοὺς
διαστασιάσειε βουλομένους τι πρεσβεῦσαι "Πρὸς
2 ὑμᾶς. καὶ τῶν ὑμετέρων," ἔφη, "Φίλων καὶ συμμάχων
Ἀβρούπολιν μὲν ἀφῄρηται τὴν ἀρχήν, Ἀρθέταυρον δ'
ἐν Ἰλλυριοῖς δυνάστην καὶ ἔκτεινεν ἐπιβουλεύσας,
καὶ τοὺς ἐργασαμένους ὑποδέδεκται." διέβαλλε δ'
αὐτοῦ καὶ τὰς ἐπιγαμίας βασιλικὰς ἄμφω γενομένας,
καὶ τὰς νυμφαγωγίας ὅλῳ τῷ Ῥοδίων στόλῳ παρα-
πεμφθείσας. ἔγκλημα δ' ἐποίει καὶ τὴν ἐπιμέλειαν
αὐτοῦ καὶ τὸ νηφάλιον τῆς διαίτης, ὄντος οὕτω νέου,
καὶ ὅτι πρὸς πολλῶν ὀξέως ἐν ὀλίγῳ ἀγαπῷτο καὶ

---

19 Eumenes II ruled Pergamum from 197 to 158.

20 Perseus himself married Laodice, daughter of Seleucus IV
of Syria, and gave his sister in marriage to Prusias II of Bithynia
(Polyb. 24.4.8–10; Livy 42.12.3–4). Laodice was accompanied to

learned of this, he sent another mission to allay their suspicion. Meanwhile, Eumenes, king of Pergamum in Asia,
arrived in Rome.[19] He had been an enemy of Philip and
for that reason was afraid of Perseus. He now came before
the senate and made a series of public accusations against
him: Perseus had been ill-disposed to Rome all along, and
had killed his brother for being friendly toward Rome; he
had helped Philip in collecting such an extensive armament against Rome, and on succeeding to the throne had
done nothing to reduce it, but had actually added to it; he
was currying favor with the Greeks in an unrestrained
manner, and was giving military assistance to Byzantium,
the Aetolians, and the Boeotians; he had taken possession
of Thrace, a powerful base of operations, and had caused
disagreement among the Thessalians and Perhaebians
when they wanted to make certain diplomatic representa-
tions "to you. And of your friends and allies," he contin-   2
ued, "he has deprived Abroupolis of his kingdom, and
conspired to assassinate the Illyrian prince, Arthetaurus:
those who carried out the deed he has secreted away
safely." Eumenes also attacked him for his marriages, both
of them with royal families, and for his bridal procession which had been accompanied by the whole Rhodian
fleet.[20] He even managed to complain about what was for
such a young man his careful and sober lifestyle, and about
the admiration and praise he had received from many
quarters in such a short time. Including everything that

Pergamum by the Rhodian fleet because the Seleucid fleet was
prevented by the terms of the treaty of Apamea (188) from sailing
that far north (Polyb. 21.43.14).

APPIAN

ἐπαινοῖτο. ζήλου τε καὶ φθόνου καὶ δέους μᾶλλον ἢ
ἐγκλημάτων οὐδὲν ὁ Εὐμένης ἀπολιπών, ἐκέλευε τὴν
σύγκλητον ὑφορᾶσθαι νέον ἐχθρὸν εὐδοκιμοῦντα καὶ
γειτονεύοντα.

3 Ἡ δ' ἔργῳ μὲν οὐκ ἀξιοῦσα βασιλέα σώφρονα καὶ
φιλόπονον καὶ ἐς πολλοὺς φιλάνθρωπον, ἀθρόως
οὕτως ἐπαιρόμενον καὶ πατρικὸν ὄντα σφίσιν ἐχθρόν,
ἐν πλευραῖς ἔχειν, λόγῳ δ' ἃ προύτεινεν ὁ Εὐμένης
αἰτιωμένη, πολεμεῖν ἔκρινε τῷ Περσεῖ. καὶ τοῦτ'
ἀπόρρητον ἔτι ἐν σφίσιν αὐτοῖς ποιούμενοι, Ἅρπαλόν
τε πεμφθέντα παρὰ Περσέως ἐς ἀντιλογίαν Εὐμένους,
καὶ Ῥοδίων τινὰ πρεσβευτήν, βουλομένους ἐς ὄψιν
τὸν Εὐμένη διελέγχειν, παρόντος μὲν ἔτι τοῦ Εὐμένους οὐ προσήκαντο, μεταστάντος δὲ ἐδέξαντο. καὶ οἱ
μὲν ἐπὶ τῷδε πρῶτον ἀγανακτοῦντές τε καὶ παρρησίᾳ
χρώμενοι πλέον ‹τοῦ δέοντος πολεμεῖν›⁶ βουλομένους
ἤδη Ῥωμαίους Περσεῖ καὶ Ῥοδίοις μᾶλλον ἐξηγρίω-
σαν· τῶν δὲ βουλευτῶν πολλοὶ τὸν Εὐμένη δι' αἰτίας
εἶχον ὑπὸ φθόνου καὶ δέους αἴτιον τοσοῦδε πολέμου
γενόμενον. καὶ Ῥόδιοι τὴν θεωρίαν αὐτοῦ, μόνου βασιλέων, ἐς τὴν ἑορτὴν τοῦ Ἡλίου πεμπομένην οὐκ
4 ἐδέξαντο. αὐτὸς δ' ἐς τὴν Ἀσίαν ἐπανιὼν ἐκ Κίρρας
ἐς Δελφοὺς ἀνέβαινε θύσων, καὶ αὐτῷ τέσσαρες
ἄνδρες ὑπό τι τειχίον ὑποστάντες ἐπεβούλευον. καὶ
ἄλλας δέ τινας αἰτίας οἱ Ῥωμαῖοι ἐς τὸν Περσέως
πόλεμον ὡς οὔπω κεκριμένον προσελάμβανον, καὶ

⁶ τοῦ δέοντος add. Roos; πολεμεῖν add. Schweig.

282

would provoke Roman envy, spite, and fear over and above his accusations, Eumenes told the senate to look with suspicion on a young man who was hostile, highly regarded, and their neighbor.

In fact, the senate did not want on their flanks a sensible, hardworking, and widely generous king who was a hereditary enemy and had so suddenly risen to prominence, but giving as their reason the allegations made by Eumenes, they decided to make war on Perseus. They kept this to themselves for the time being, and when Harpalus, who had been sent by Perseus to counter the accusations of Eumenes, together with a Rhodian ambassador, both wanted to refute him face to face, the senate refused to admit them as long as Eumenes was present, and only received them when he had left. Now for the first time the ambassadors showed annoyance at this and, with the intemperate language they used, irritated the Romans even more, when they already wanted to declare war against Perseus and Rhodes. Many senators, however, blamed Eumenes for causing such a great war out of personal envy and fear, and the Rhodians refused to admit to the festival of the sun his sacred envoys, alone among kings.[21] When Eumenes himself was on his way back to Asia, he went up from Cirrha to Delphi to offer sacrifice, where four men hiding behind a wall attacked him. The Romans alleged other reasons as well for the war against Perseus, as if they had not already decided on it, and they

___

[21] Rhodes was sacred to the sun god, Helios, and celebrated the games in his honor lavishly every five years.

APPIAN

πρέσβεις ἐς τοὺς φίλους βασιλέας, Εὐμένη καὶ Ἀντίοχον καὶ Ἀριαράθην καὶ Μασσανάσσην καὶ Πτολε-
μαῖον τὸν Αἰγύπτου, περιέπεμπον, ἑτέρους δ' ἐς τὴν
Ἑλλάδα καὶ Θεσσαλίαν καὶ Ἤπειρον καὶ Ἀκαρνα-
νίαν, καὶ ἐς τὰς νήσους, ὅσας δύναιντο προσαγαγέ-
σθαι· ὃ καὶ μάλιστα τοὺς Ἕλληνας ἐτάραττεν, ἡδο-
μένους μὲν τῷ Περσεῖ φιλέλληνι ὄντι, ἀναγκαζομένους
δ' ἐνίους Ῥωμαίοις ἐς συμβάσεις χωρεῖν.

5   Ὧν ὁ Περσεὺς αἰσθόμενος ἔπεμπεν ἐς Ῥώμην,
ἀπορῶν τε καὶ πυνθανόμενος τί παθόντες ἐκλήθονται
τῶν συγκειμένων καὶ πρέσβεις κατ' αὐτοῦ περιπέμ-
πουσιν ὄντος φίλου, δέον, εἰ καί τι μέμφονται, λόγῳ
διακριθῆναι. οἱ δ' ἐνεκάλουν ὅσα Εὐμένης εἴποι καὶ
πάθοι, καὶ μάλιστα ὅτι Θρᾴκην κατακτῷτο, καὶ στρατιὰν ἔχοι καὶ παρασκευὴν οὐκ ἐρεμήσοντος ἀνδρός.
ὁ δ' αὖθις ἔπεμπεν ἑτέρους, οἳ ἐς τὸ βουλευτήριον
ἐσαχθέντες ἔλεγον ὧδε· "Τοῖς μὲν προφάσεως ἐς πόλεμον, ὦ Ῥωμαῖοι, δεομένοις ἱκανὰ πάντα ἐς τὴν πρό-
φασίν ἐστιν. εἰ δ' αἰδεῖσθε συνθήκας οἱ πολὺν ἀξιοῦντες αὐτῶν λόγον ἔχειν, τί παθόντες ὑπὸ Περσέως
αἱρεῖσθε πόλεμον; οὐ γὰρ ὅτι στρατιὰν ἔχει καὶ
παρασκευήν. οὐ γὰρ ἔχει ταῦτα καθ' ὑμῶν. οὐδὲ τοὺς
ἄλλους κεκτῆσθαι βασιλέας κωλύετε· οὐδ' ἄδικον
ἀσφαλῶς ἔχειν ἐς τοὺς ἀρχομένους καὶ τὰ περίοικα,
καὶ εἴ τις ἔξωθεν ἐπιβουλεύοι. πρὸς δὲ ὑμᾶς, ὦ ἄνδρες

---

[22] Eumenes II of Pergamum, Antiochus IV Epiphanes of

sent ambassadors around to their royal friends, Eumenes, Antiochus, Ariarathes, Massinissa, and Ptolemy king of Egypt;[22] and others to Greece, Thessaly, Epirus, and Acarnania, and to all the islands they could recruit to their side. This was particularly disturbing to the Greeks, in the first place because they liked Perseus for his philhellenic policies, and then because some felt they were being forced into making an agreement with Rome.

When Perseus learned of these matters, he sent a mission to Rome to express his bewilderment and to ask what had happened to them to make them forget their agreement and send ambassadors around to speak against him, an ally of theirs, when, even if they did have a complaint, they should settle it by discussion. The senate accused him of the things Eumenes had told them and suffered at Perseus' hands, and particularly the fact that he had taken possession of Thrace, and had the army and armament of a man who was not about to keep the peace. Yet again he dispatched another mission, who were admitted to the senate house and spoke as follows: "Anything will do as an excuse, men of Rome, to those who are looking for a pretext to go to war. But if you have respect for treaties—and you claim to set great store by them—what has Perseus done to you to make you prefer war? It cannot be that he has an army and munitions, as he does not keep them for use against you, and you do not stop other kings from having them. Nor is it wrong that he makes himself safe against his subjects and neighbors, and any outsiders who might plot against him. To you on the other hand, men of

Syria, Ariarathes IV Eusebes of Cappadocia, Massinissa of Numidia, and Ptolemy VI Philometor of Egypt.

APPIAN

Ῥωμαῖοι, ὑπὲρ τῆς εἰρήνης ἐπρέσβευσε καὶ τὰς συν-
6 θήκας ἔναγχος ἀνεκαίνισεν. ἀλλ' Ἀβρούπολιν ἐξέ-
βαλε τῆς ἀρχῆς. ἐπιδραμόντα γε τοῖς ἡμετέροις ἀμυ-
νόμενος. καὶ τοῦτ' αὐτὸς ὑμῖν ἐδήλωσε Περσεύς, καὶ
τὰς συνθήκας αὐτῷ μετὰ τοῦτο ἀνενεώσασθε, οὔπω
διαβάλλοντος Εὐμένους. τὸ μὲν δὴ περὶ Ἀβρούπολιν
καὶ πρεσβύτερόν ἐστι τῶν συνθηκῶν, καὶ παρ' ὑμῖν,
ὅτε συνετίθεσθε, δίκαιον ἐφάνη. Δόλοψι γὰρ ἐπε-
στράτευσεν οὖσι τῆς ἰδίας ἀρχῆς, καὶ δεινὸν εἰ τῶν
ἑαυτοῦ λογισμὸν ὑμῖν ὀφλήσει. δίδωσι δ' ὅμως, περὶ
πολλοῦ ποιούμενος ὑμᾶς τε καὶ δόξαν ἀγαθήν. ἔκτειναν δ' οἱ Δόλοπες οἵδε τὸν ἡγούμενον αὐτῶν αἰκισάμενοι, καὶ ζητεῖ Περσεὺς τί ἂν ὑμεῖς ἐδράσατε τοὺς
ὑπηκόους τοιαῦτα πράξαντας. ἀλλὰ Ἀρθέταυρόν τινες
ἀνελόντες ἐν Μακεδονίᾳ διέτριβον. κοινῷ γε πάντων
ἀνθρώπων νόμῳ, καθὰ καὶ ὑμεῖς τοὺς ἑτέρωθεν φεύγοντας ὑποδέχεσθε. μαθὼν δὲ καὶ τοῦθ' ὅτι ἔγκλημα
7 ποιεῖσθε, ἐξεκήρυξεν αὐτοὺς τῆς ἀρχῆς ὅλης. Βυζαντίοις δὲ καὶ Αἰτωλοῖς καὶ Βοιωτοῖς οὐ καθ' ὑμῶν
ἀλλὰ καθ' ἑτέρων συνεμάχησεν. καὶ ταῦτα πρὶν ὑμῖν
ἡμέτεροι πρέσβεις ἐμήνυον, καὶ οὐκ ἐμέμφεσθε μέχρι
τῆς Εὐμένους διαβολῆς, ἣν οὐκ εἰάσατε τοὺς ἡμετέρους πρέσβεις ἐς ὄψιν αὐτὸν ἐλέγξαι. ἀλλὰ τὴν
ἐπιβουλὴν τὴν ἐν Δελφοῖς αὐτῷ γενομένην προσγρά-
φετε Περσεῖ, πόσων μὲν Ἑλλήνων, πόσων δὲ βαρβάρων κατ' Εὐμένους πρεσβευσάντων πρὸς ὑμᾶς οἷς
πᾶσιν ἐχθρός ἐστι τοιοῦτος ὤν. Ῥέννιον δὲ τὸν ἐν

286

Rome, he sent a peace mission and only recently renewed the treaty between you. But you claim that he expelled 6 Abroupolis from his kingdom. Yes, he did, but in self-defense, when Abroupolis invaded our territory. Perseus explained this to you himself, and you subsequently renewed the treaty with him, as Eumenes had not yet made his slanderous accusations. The Abroupolis affair happened before the treaty, which you found to be just when you agreed to it. You claim he campaigned against the Dolopians. Yes, he did, but they're subjects of his own kingdom, and it would surely be a strange demand if he had to account to you for his own affairs. Nevertheless, he does so, out of the high regard he has for you and his own good name. These Dolopians tortured and murdered their governor, and Perseus would like to know what you would have done to your subjects if they had behaved like this. You claim that Arthetauros' killers were able to stay on in Macedonia. Yes, they were, but in accordance with the common law of all men, which you Romans also observe when you give asylum to refugees from other countries. And when Perseus found out that you regarded this too as a ground of complaint, he banned them publicly from his whole kingdom. You claim he gave military assistance to 7 the Byzantines, Aetolians, and Boeotians. Yes, he did, but he gave it against others, not against you. Our ambassadors made all these points to you before, and you found nothing to object to until Eumenes slandered us; and then you did not even let our envoys refute his arguments face to face. You blame Perseus for the plot against Eumenes at Delphi. But how many Greeks, how many foreigners, have sent embassies to you to speak against Eumenes, whom they all hate because of the person he is? And when it

APPIAN

Βρεντεσίῳ τίς ἂν πιστεύσειεν ὅτι Περσεύς, Ῥωμαῖον
ὄντα καὶ φίλον ὑμέτερον καὶ πρόξενον, εἴληφεν ἐπὶ
τὴν τῆς βουλῆς φαρμακείαν, ὡς ἀναλῶσαι τὴν σύγκλητον δι᾽ αὐτοῦ δυνάμενος, ἢ τοὺς ὑπολοίπους εὐμε-
νεστέρους ἕξων διὰ τοὺς ἀναιρουμένους; ἀλλ᾽ Ἑρέν-
νιος μὲν ἐψεύσατο τοῖς ἐπιτρίβουσιν ἐς τὸν πόλεμον
ὑμᾶς πρόφασιν εὐσχήμονα διδούς, Εὐμένης δ᾽ ὑπ᾽
ἔχθρας τε καὶ φθόνου καὶ δέους οὐδὲ ταῦτ᾽ ὤκνησεν
ἐγκαλέσαι Περσεῖ, ὅτι πολλοῖς ἔθνεσι κεχαρισμένος
καὶ φιλέλλην, καὶ σωφρόνως ἀντὶ μέθης καὶ τρυφῆς
ἄρχει. καὶ ταῦθ᾽ ὑμεῖς αὐτοῦ λέγοντος ὑπέστητε
8 ἀκροάσασθαι. τοιγάρτοι τὴν ἐκείνου διαβολὴν αὔξετε
καθ᾽ ὑμῶν ὡς οὐ φέροντες σώφρονας καὶ δικαίους καὶ
φιλοπόνους γείτονας. Περσεὺς δ᾽ Ῥέννιον μὲν καὶ
Εὐμένη, καὶ εἴ τις ἄλλος ἐθέλοι, προκαλεῖται παρ᾽
ὑμῖν ἐς ἐξέτασιν καὶ κρίσιν, ὑμᾶς δ᾽ ἀναμιμνήσκει
μὲν τῆς ἐς Ἀντίοχον τὸν μέγαν τοῦ πατρὸς ἑαυτοῦ
προθυμίας καὶ βοηθείας, ἧς ἐπιγιγνομένης καλῶς
ᾐσθάνεσθε, αἰσχρὸν δὲ παρελθούσης ἐπιλαθέσθαι,
προφέρει δὲ συνθήκας πατρῴας τε καὶ ἰδίας πρὸς
αὐτὸν ὑμῖν γενομένας. καὶ ἐπὶ τοῖσδε οὐκ ὀκνεῖ καὶ
παρακαλεῖν ὑμᾶς, θεοὺς οὓς ὠμόσατε αἰδεῖσθαι, καὶ
μὴ πολέμου κατάρχειν ἀδίκως ἐς φίλους, μηδ᾽ ἔγκλημα ποιεῖσθαι γειτνίασιν καὶ σωφροσύνην καὶ
παρασκευήν, οὐ γὰρ ἄξιον, ὡς Εὐμένους, καὶ ὑμῶν

comes to Rhennius of Brundisium, who could believe that
Perseus suborned him, a Roman citizen, your friend and
honorary ambassador, to use poison against the senate—as
if through him, Perseus would be able to kill the whole
senate, or make the surviving senators more amenable
because he had murdered the others?[23] Rhennius lied to
those who are inciting you to war, to give them a convincing excuse. Eumenes, driven by malice, envy, and fear,
hasn't even hesitated to find fault with Perseus for being
popular with so many people, for being a friend of the
Greeks, and for ruling with sobriety, instead of being a
debauched drunk. And you agree to listen to such non-
sense from him! The truth is that giving credence to this
man's slanders works to your own disadvantage, giving the
impression that you are intolerant of sober, right-minded,
and hardworking neighbors. Perseus challenges Rhennius, Eumenes, and anyone else who is willing, to undergo
investigation and judgment by you. He reminds you of the
enthusiastic help his father gave you against Antiochus the
Great. You acknowledged it handsomely at the time; it
would be shameful to forget it now that it is in the past.
He also cites the treaties you made with his father and with
himself, and has no hesitation in calling on you to respect
the gods in whose name you swore to uphold them, and
not to begin an unjust war against friends. You should not
attach blame to someone for being your neighbor or for
their sobriety and state of military preparation. For it is
not worthy of you too to be affected by envy or fear, like

[23] The story of Rammius of Brundisium is missing from
Eumenes' list of accusations against Perseus earlier in this book,
but it is recorded in Livy (42.17).

ἅπτεσθαι φθόνον ἢ φόβον. τὸ δὲ ἐναντίον ἐστὶ σῶ-
φρον, φείδεσθαι γειτόνων ἐπιμελῶν, καὶ ὡς Εὐμένης
φησίν, εὖ παρεσκευασμένων."

9   Οἱ μὲν δὴ πρέσβεις τοιαῦτα εἶπον, οἱ δὲ οὐδὲν
αὐτοῖς ἀποκρινάμενοι τὸν πόλεμον ἐς τὸ φανερὸν
ἐκύρουν. καὶ ὁ ὕπατος ἐκέλευε τοὺς πρέσβεις ἐκ μὲν
τῆς πόλεως αὐτῆς ἡμέρας, ἐκ δὲ τῆς Ἰταλίας τριάκοντα ἄλλαις ἐξιέναι. τὰ δὲ αὐτὰ καὶ τοῖς ἐπιδημοῦσι
Μακεδόνων ἐκήρυττεν. καὶ θόρυβος αὐτίκα μετὰ τὸ
βουλευτήριον ἐπίφθονος ἦν, ἐν ὀλίγαις ὥραις ἐλαυνο-
μένων τοσῶνδε ὁμοῦ, καὶ οὐδὲ ὑποζύγια εὑρεῖν ἐν
οὕτω βραχεῖ διαστήματι, οὐδὲ πάντα φέρειν δυνα-
μένων. ὑπὸ δὲ σπουδῆς οἱ μὲν οὐκ ἔφθανον ἐπὶ τοὺς
σταθμούς, ἀλλ᾽ ἐν μέσαις ἀνεπαύοντο ταῖς ὁδοῖς, οἱ
δὲ παρὰ ταῖς πύλαις μετὰ παίδων ἑαυτοὺς ἐρρίπτουν
καὶ μετὰ γυναικῶν. πάντα τε ἐγίγνετο ὅσα εἰκὸς ἐν
αἰφνιδίῳ καὶ τοιῷδε κηρύγματι· αἰφνίδιον γὰρ αὐτοῖς
ἐφαίνετο διὰ τὰς ἔτι παρούσας πρεσβείας. (Exc. de
leg. gent. 35, p. 564 de Boor)

12. Ὅτι μετὰ τὴν νίκην ὁ Περσεύς, εἴτ᾽ ἐπιγελῶν
Κράσσῳ καὶ τωθάζων αὐτόν, εἴτ᾽ ἀποπειρώμενος
ὅπως ἔτι φρονήματος ἔχοι, εἴτε τὴν Ῥωμαίων δύναμίν
τε καὶ παρασκευὴν ὑφορώμενος, εἴθ᾽ ἑτέρῳ τῳ λογι-
σμῷ, προσέπεμπεν αὐτῷ περὶ διαλλαγῶν, καὶ πολλὰ
δώσειν ὑπισχνεῖτο ὧν ὁ πατὴρ Φίλιππος οὐ συνε-
χώρει· ᾧ καὶ μᾶλλον ὕποπτος ἦν ἐπιγελῶν καὶ πειρώ-
2   μενος. ὁ δὲ Περσεῖ μὲν ἀπεκρίνατο Ῥωμαίων ἀξίας

Eumenes. On the contrary, it is simple prudence for you to foster conscientious neighbors, who, as Eumenes says, are well prepared militarily."

This was the speech of the Macedonian mission. The 9 senate made no response, but confirmed publicly the decision to go to war. The consul[24] ordered the ambassadors to leave the city that very day, and to leave Italy within thirty days. He issued the same orders to all resident Macedonians. There was immediate and angry uproar following the meeting of the senate, with so many people displaced at the same time within a few hours, unable even to find transport animals at such short notice, or to carry everything themselves. In all the rush, some did not reach lodgings before night and rested in the middle of the road, others threw themselves down beside the city gates with their wives and children. What happened was exactly what was to be expected with such a sudden proclamation of this sort. For it seemed sudden to them because the ambassadors were still in Rome. (*Exc. de leg. gent.* 35, p. 564 de Boor)

12. After his victory, Perseus sent representatives to Crassus to discuss peace, and promised to make many concessions that his father, Philip, had refused.[25] He did this either to ridicule Crassus and mock him, or to test the current strength of his resolution, or because he was wary of Rome's power and military resources, or on some other calculation. It was particularly this promise that gave rise to the suspicion that he was making fun of Crassus and testing him. Crassus replied to Perseus that it would not 2

[24] P. Licinius Crassus (consul 171).   [25] Perseus defeated the consul P. Licinius Crassus at the battle of Callinicus in 171.

οὐκ εἶναι διαλύσεις αὐτῷ, εἰ μὴ καὶ Μακεδόνας καὶ
ἑαυτὸν ἐπιτρέψειε Ῥωμαίοις· αἰδούμενος δ' ὅτι Ῥωμαῖοι τῆς ἥττης κατῆρξαν, ἐκκλησίαν συναγαγὼν
Θεσσαλοῖς μὲν ἐμαρτύρησεν ὡς ἀνδράσιν ἀγαθοῖς
περὶ τὴν συμφορὰν γενομένοις, Αἰτωλῶν δὲ καὶ
ἑτέρων Ἑλλήνων κατεψεύσατο ὡς πρώτων τραπέντων.
καὶ τούτους ἐς Ῥώμην ἔπεμψεν. (Exc. de leg. gent. 36,
p. 567 de Boor)

13. Τὸ δὲ λοιπὸν τοῦ θέρους ἀμφότεροι περὶ σιτο-
λογίαν ἐγίγνοντο, Περσεὺς μὲν ἐν τοῖς πεδίοις ἁλω-
νευόμενος, Ῥωμαῖοι δὲ ἐν τῷ στρατοπέδῳ. (Suda, α
1383)

14. Ὃς δὲ πρῶτος ἐξῆρχε τοῦ πόνου, ἑξηκοντούτης
ὢν καὶ βαρὺς τὸ σῶμα καὶ πιμελής. (Suda, π 1605)

15. Τότε δὲ ἔθει τις δρόμῳ δηλώσων τῷ Περσεῖ
λουομένῳ καὶ τὸ σῶμα ἀναλαμβάνοντι. ὁ δὲ ἐξήλατο
τοῦ ὕδατος βοῶν ὅτι ἑαλώκοι πρὸ τῆς μάχης. (Suda,
α 1930)

16. Ὅτι Περσεὺς ἀναθαρρῶν ἤδη κατ' ὀλίγον μετὰ
τὴν φυγήν, Νικίαν καὶ Ἀνδρόνικον, οὓς ἐπὶ τὸν κατα-
ποντισμὸν τῶν χρημάτων καὶ τὸν ἐμπρησμὸν τῶν
νεῶν ἐπεπόμφει, περιποιήσαντας αὐτῷ καὶ τὰς ναῦς
καὶ τὰ χρήματα, συνίστορας ἡγούμενος αἰσχροῦ φόβου καὶ ἑτέροις ἐξαγγελεῖν, ἀπέκτεινεν ἀθεμίστως,

---

26 This refers to Q. Marcius Philippus in the year of his consulship, 169, when he was assigned the Macedonian command. See

be in keeping with Rome's dignity to grant him a treaty, unless he surrendered himself and Macedonia to the Romans. Ashamed of the fact that the Romans had been the first to flee, Crassus called a meeting at which he bore witness to the bravery of the Thessalians during the disaster, and lied in claiming that the Aetolians and other Greeks had turned tail first. These latter he sent to Rome. (*Exc. de leg. gent.* 36, p. 567 de Boor)

13. During the rest of the summer, both sides were engaged in storing up grain, Perseus doing the threshing in the fields, the Romans in their camp. (*Suda*, α 1383)

14. Although he was sixty years old, overweight, and fat, he was the first to put himself to work.[26] (*Suda*, π 1605)

15. At that moment, someone ran to tell Perseus who was refreshing himself in a bath. He jumped out of the water shouting that he had fallen into enemy hands before the battle had taken place.[27] (*Suda*, α 1930)

16. When Perseus was now gradually getting his nerve back after his flight, he had Nicias and Andronicus killed in a criminal manner.[28] He had sent them to throw his money into the sea and burn his ships, but although they had managed to save both the ships and the money for him, he believed that as witnesses of his disgraceful panic

Livy 44.4.10: *cum Romanus imperator, maior sexaginta annis et praegravis corpore, omnia militaria munera ipse inpigre obiret* (the Roman commander, although over sixty years old and very heavy in body, personally carried out all military duties with alacrity).

[27] Perseus was shocked that the Romans were so close: see Livy 44.6.1.

[28] The story is in Livy (44.10).

καὶ ἀπὸ τοῦδε εὐθὺς ἐκ μεταβολῆς ὠμὸς καὶ εὐχερὴς
ἐς ἅπαντας ἐγένετο, καὶ οὐδὲν ὑγιὲς οὐδ' εὔβουλόν οἱ
ἔτι ἦν, ἀλλ' ὁ πιθανώτατος ἐς εὐβουλίαν καὶ λογίσα-
σθαι δεξιὸς καὶ εὐτολμότατος ἐς μάχας, ὅσα γε μὴ
σφάλλοιτο δι' ἀπειρίαν, ἀθρόως τότε καὶ παραλόγως
ἐς δειλίαν καὶ ἀλογιστίαν ἐτράπετο, καὶ ταχὺς καὶ
εὐμετάθετος ἄφνω καὶ σκαιὸς ἐς πάντα ἐγένετο, ἀρχομένης αὐτὸν ἐπιλείπειν τῆς τύχης. ὅπερ ἔστι πολλοὺς
ἰδεῖν, μεταβολῆς προσιούσης ἀλογωτέρους γιγνομέ-
νους ἑαυτῶν. (Exc. de virt. 34, p. 231 Roos; Suda, π 1371
+ σ 1581)

17. Ὅτι Ῥόδιοι πρέσβεις ἐς Μάρκιον ἔπεμψαν,
συνηδόμενοι τῶν γεγονότων Περσεῖ. ὁ δὲ Μάρκιος
τοὺς πρέσβεις ἐδίδασκε Ῥοδίους πεῖσαι πέμψαντας
ἐς Ῥώμην διαλῦσαι τὸν πόλεμον Ῥωμαίοις τε καὶ
Περσεῖ. καὶ Ῥόδιοι πυθόμενοι μετέπιπτον ὡς οὐ
φαύλως ἔχοντος τοῦ Περσέως· οὐ γὰρ εἴκαζον ἄνευ
Ῥωμαίων ταῦτα Μάρκιον ἐπισκήπτειν. ὁ δ' ἀφ' ἑαυτοῦ καὶ τάδε καὶ ἕτερα πολλὰ διὰ τόλμαν[7] ἔπραττεν.
Ῥόδιοι μὲν οὖν καὶ ὡς πρέσβεις ἔπεμπον ἐς Ῥώμην,
καὶ ἑτέρους πρὸς Μάρκιον. (Exc. de leg. gent. 37, p. 568
de Boor)

18. Ὅτι Γένθιος βασιλεὺς Ἰλλυριῶν ἑνὸς ἔθνους
προσοίκου Μακεδόσι, Περσεῖ συμμαχῶν ἐπὶ τριακο-

---

[7] δι' ἀτολμίαν Exc; δι' ἀτοπίαν prop. Goukowsky; διὰ τόλμαν nos

they would tell others. From this point on he immediately changed, becoming cruel and unscrupulous toward everyone, and no longer displayed any good sense or wisdom. Apart from the occasions when inexperience let him down, he had been most persuasive in giving good advice, mentally adroit and extremely daring in battle. But now, when fortune began to abandon him, he turned into somebody totally and inexplicably cowardly and irrational, as well as unstable, fickle, and completely inept. We can see this happening in many people who, when situations change, lose their previous good sense. (*Exc. de virt.* 34, p. 231 Roos; *Suda*, π 1371 + σ 1581)

17. The Rhodians sent ambassadors to Marcius to congratulate him on what had happened to Perseus. But Marcius advised the ambassadors to persuade Rhodes to send a mission to Rome and resolve the conflict between Perseus and Rome. On hearing this, the Rhodians changed their mind: Perseus could not have been in too bad a situation, they assumed, as Marcius would not have given this advice without Rome's approval. In fact, Marcius' boldness[29] led him to act unilaterally on this and many other matters. Nevertheless the Rhodians sent a diplomatic mission to Rome and another one to Marcius. (*Exc. de leg. gent.* 37, p. 568 de Boor)

18. Genthius, king of one of the Illyrian peoples and a neighbor of the Macedonians, having allied himself to

---

[29] The manuscript reading (*di' atolmian*—"on account of his timidity") seems unlikely, as there is no other evidence for Marcius' lack of daring. Goukowsky suggests that he was acting out of "malice" (*di' atopian*); I suggest dividing the words differently (*dia tolman*—"on account of his daring").

σίοις ταλάντοις, ὧν τι καὶ προειλήφει, ἐσέβαλεν ἐς
τὴν ὑπὸ Ῥωμαίοις Ἰλλυρίδα, καὶ πρέσβεις περὶ
τούτων πρὸς αὐτὸν ἐλθόντας Περπένναν καὶ Πετίλιον
ἔδησεν. ὧν ὁ Περσεὺς αἰσθόμενος οὐκέτι τὰ λοιπὰ
τῶν χρημάτων ἔπεμπεν ὡς ἤδη καὶ δι᾽ αὐτὸν Ῥωμαίοις πεπολεμωμένον. ἐς δὲ Γέτας ἔπεμπε τοὺς ὑπὲρ
Ἴστρον, καὶ Εὐμένους ἀπεπείρασεν ἐπὶ χρήμασιν ἢ
μεταθέσθαι πρὸς αὐτόν, ἢ διαλῦσαι τὸν πόλεμον, ἢ
ἀμφοτέροις ἐκστῆναι τοῦ ἀγῶνος, εὖ μὲν εἰδὼς οὐ λη-
σόμενα ταῦτα Ῥωμαίους, ἐλπίζων δ᾽ ἢ πράξειν τι
αὐτῶν ἢ τῇ πείρᾳ διαβαλεῖν τὸν Εὐμένη. ὁ δὲ μετα-
θήσεσθαι μὲν οὐκ ἔφη, τάλαντα δ᾽ ᾔτει τῆς μὲν διαλύσεως χίλια καὶ πεντακόσια, τῆς δὲ ἡσυχίας χίλια.
καὶ ὁ Περσεὺς ἤδη Γετῶν αὐτῷ προσιέναι μισθοφόρους μυρίους ἱππέας καὶ μυρίους πεζοὺς πυθόμενος, αὐτίκα τοῦ Εὐμένους κατεφρόνει, καὶ τῆς μὲν
ἡσυχίας οὐκ ἔφη δώσειν οὐδέν (αἰσχύνην γὰρ φέρειν
ἀμφοῖν), τὰ δὲ τῆς διαλύσεως οὐ προδώσειν, ἀλλ᾽ ἐν
Σαμοθρᾴκῃ καταθήσειν μέχρι γένοιτο ἡ διάλυσις, εὐ-
μετάβολος ἤδη καὶ μικρολόγος ὑπὸ θεοβλαβείας ἐς
2 πάντα γενόμενος. ἑνὸς δὲ ὧν ἤλπισεν ὅμως οὐκ
ἀπέτυχε, Ῥωμαίοις Εὐμένους ὑπόπτου γενομένου. Γετῶν δὲ τὸν Ἴστρον περασάντων, ἐδόκει Κλοιλίῳ μὲν
τῷ ἡγεμόνι δοθῆναι χιλίους χρυσοῦς στατῆρας, ἱππεῖ
δ᾽ ἑκάστῳ δέκα, καὶ τὰ ἡμίσεα πεζῷ· καὶ τοῦτο σύμ-

Perseus in return for three hundred talents, some of which he had received in advance, launched an attack on the part of Illyria under Roman control, and arrested Perpenna and Petilius on their arrival from Rome as envoys sent to him to investigate the affair.[30] When Perseus heard this, he suspended payment of the rest of the money, in the belief that Genthius' own behavior had already made him an enemy of Rome. He also sent a mission to the Getae north of the Ister, and tried to bribe Eumenes either to come over to his side, or negotiate an end to the war, or remain neutral in the conflict. He was well aware that this would not escape Roman attention, but he hoped either to achieve one of his ends, or to cast suspicion on Eumenes in the attempt. Eumenes refused to come over to his side, and demanded one thousand five hundred talents for negotiating a peace agreement or one thousand for remaining neutral. But Perseus now learned that Getan mercenaries were on their way to him, ten thousand infantry and ten thousand cavalry, and immediately began to regard Eumenes with disdain. He said he would pay him nothing for his neutrality—that would be a disgrace to both of them—and would make no advance payment for a peace treaty, but would deposit money at Samothrace, until the treaty was actually concluded. This was how utterly unreliable and miserly he had now become in his god-sent folly. He did succeed, however, in one of his aims, in that Eumenes had become an object of suspicion to Rome. When the Getae crossed the Ister, Perseus decided that their leader, Cloelius, should be given one thousand gold staters, every cavalryman should get ten and every infan-

2

---

[30] M. Perperna and L. Petilius were later released: see Livy 44.32.1.

APPIAN

παν ἦν ὀλίγῳ πλέον πεντεκαίδεκα μυριάδων χρυσίου. ὁ δὲ χλαμύδας μέν τινας ἐπήγετο καὶ ψέλια χρυσᾶ καὶ ἵππους ἐς δωρεὰν τοῖς ἡγουμένοις, καὶ στατῆρας φερομένους μυρίους, καὶ πλησιάσας μετεπέμπετο Κλοίλιον. ὁ δὲ τοὺς ἐλθόντας, εἰ φέρουσι τὸ χρυσίον, ἤρετο, καὶ μαθὼν οὐκ ἔχοντας ἀναστρέφειν ἐπ᾿ αὐτὸν ἐκέλευσεν. ὧν ὁ Περσεὺς πυθόμενος, πάλιν αὐτὸν ἐλαύνοντος θεοῦ, κατηγόρει τῶν Γετῶν ἐν τοῖς φίλοις ἐκ μεταβολῆς ὡς φύσεως ἀπίστου, καὶ ὑπεκρίνετο μὴ θαρρεῖν δισμυρίους αὐτῶν ἐς τὸ στρατόπεδον ὑποδέξασθαι, μόλις δ᾿ ἔφη μυρίους, ὧν καὶ νεωτεριζόντων
3 κρατῆσαι δύνασθαι. ταῦτα δὲ τοῖς φίλοις εἰπὼν ἕτερα τοῖς Γέταις ἐπλάττετο, καὶ τὸ ἥμισυ τῆς στρατιᾶς ᾔτει, τὸ χρυσίον τὸ γιγνόμενον ὑπισχνούμενος δώσειν. τοσαύτης ἀνωμαλίας ἔγεμε, φροντίζων χρημάτων τῶν πρὸ βραχέος ἐς θάλασσαν μεθιεμένων. ὁ δὲ Κλοίλιος τοὺς ἀφικομένους ἰδὼν ἤρετο μετὰ βοῆς εἰ τὸ χρυσίον κεκομίκασι, καὶ βουλομένους τι λέγειν ἐκέλευε πρῶτον εἰπεῖν περὶ τοῦ χρυσίου. ὡς δ᾿ ἔμαθεν οὐκ ἔχοντας, οὐκ ἀνασχόμενος αὐτῶν οὐδ᾿ ἀκοῦσαι, τὴν στρατιὰν ἀπῆγεν ὀπίσω. καὶ Περσεὺς ἀφῄρητο καὶ τῆσδε συμμαχίας, πολλῆς τε καὶ κατὰ καιρὸν
4 ἐλθούσης. ὑπὸ δ᾿ ἀφροσύνης, ἐν Φίλᾳ χειμάζων καὶ στρατὸν ἔχων πολὺν Θεσσαλίαν μὲν οὐκ ἐπέτρεχεν, ἢ Ῥωμαίοις ἐχορήγει τροφάς, ἐς δὲ τὴν Ἰωνίαν ἔπεμπε κωλύειν τὴν ἀγορὰν τὴν ἐκεῖθεν αὐτοῖς φερομένην. (Exc. de virt. 35, p. 232 Roos)

19. Ὅτι Παύλῳ ἐπ᾿ εὐτυχίας τοσῆσδε γενομένῳ τὸ

tryman five. The total was a little over one hundred and fifty thousand gold staters. But he only brought some cloaks and gold bracelets and, as a gift for the officers, horses, which were carrying ten thousand staters. When he was near, he summoned Cloelius, who asked the approaching company if they were bringing the gold. On being told that they did not have it, Cloelius ordered them to go back to Perseus. When this was reported to him, Perseus, with some god again driving him on, changed course and began to complain about the Getae among his courtiers, saying that they were naturally unreliable. He pretended that he was uneasy about taking twenty thousand of them into his camp; indeed, he said he would scarcely have ten thousand, a number he could subdue if they mutinied. This is what he said to his courtiers, while 3 for the Getae he fabricated different lies, asking for only half their army and promising to give them the gold due. He was now a mass of contradictions, worrying about the money that shortly before he had ordered to be thrown into the sea. Cloelius shouted a question at Perseus' men when he saw them approaching, asking if they had brought the gold. They wanted to make some sort of speech, but he ordered them to talk about the gold first. When he realized they did not have it, he was not even prepared to listen to them and led his army home. So Perseus contrived to lose this military assistance too, even though it was substantial and had arrived at just the right time. In 4 his madness, while wintering at Phila with a large army, he also failed to invade Thessaly, which was supplying the Romans, but sent an expedition to Ionia intending to cut off the supplies being brought to the Romans from that direction. (*Exc. de virt.* 35, p. 232 Roos)

19. When Paullus had enjoyed such exceptional suc-

APPIAN

δαιμόνιον ἐφθόνησε τῆς εὐτυχίας. καί οἱ τεσσάρων
παίδων ὄντων τοὺς μὲν πρεσβυτέρους αὐτῶν ἐς θέσιν
ἄλλοις ἐδεδώκει, Μάξιμόν τε καὶ Σκιπίωνα, τοὺς δὲ
νεωτέρους ἄμφω συνέβη, τὸν μὲν πρὸ τριῶν ἡμερῶν
τοῦ θριάμβου τὸν δὲ μετὰ πέντε, ἀποθανεῖν. καὶ τοῦτ᾽
οὐδενὸς ἧττον ὁ Παῦλος κατελογίσατο τῷ δήμῳ.
2 ἔθους γὰρ ὄντος τοῖς στρατηγοῖς καταλέγειν τὰ πε-
πραγμένα, παρελθὼν ἐς τὴν ἀγορὰν εἶπεν ἐς μὲν Κέρ-
κυραν ἐκ Βρεντεσίου διαπλεῦσαι μιᾶς ἡμέρας, ἐκ δὲ
Κερκύρας πέντε μὲν ἐς Δελφοὺς ὁδεῦσαι καὶ θῦσαι τῷ
θεῷ, πέντε δὲ ἄλλαις ἐς Θεσσαλίαν παραγενέσθαι καὶ
παραλαβεῖν τὸν στρατόν, ἀπὸ δὲ ταύτης πεντεκαίδεκα ἄλλαις ἑλεῖν Περσέα καὶ Μακεδόνας παραλαβεῖν. οὕτω δὲ ὀξέως ἁπάντων ἐπιτυχὼν δεῖσαι "Μή τι
3 τῷ στρατῷ συμπέσοι πρὸς ὑμᾶς ἐπανιόντι. διασωθέν-
τος δὲ τοῦ στρατοῦ περὶ ὑμῶν ἐδεδοίκειν," ἔφη· "Φθο-
νερὸς γὰρ ὁ δαίμων. ἐς ἐμὲ δὲ ἀποσκήψαντος τοῦ
κακοῦ, καὶ ἀθρόως μοι τῶν δύο παίδων ἀποθανόντων,
ἐπ᾽ ἐμαυτῷ μέν εἰμι βαρυσυμφορώτατος, ἐπὶ δὲ ὑμῖν
ἀμέριμνος." ταῦτ᾽ εἰπών, καὶ καταθαυμαζόμενος ἐπὶ
πᾶσιν, οἰκτιζόμενος δὲ ἐπὶ τοῖς τέκνοις, μετ᾽ οὐ πολὺν
χρόνον ἀπέθανεν. (Exc. de virt. 36, p. 233 Roos)

20. Ἐπιθείασας δὲ καὶ τοῖσδε. Ἀππιανὸς Μακεδο-
νικοῖς. (Anecd. Bekker p. 143.11 = Περὶ Συντάξεων No.
9 Gaillard)

31 L. Aemilius Paullus, consul in 182 and 168, defeated Perseus at the battle of Pydna in 168, to bring an end to the Third
Macedonian War. His two elder sons were Q. Fabius Maximus

cess, the divinity became jealous of his good fortune. He had four sons. The two eldest, Maximus and Scipio, he had given for adoption into other families, but it so happened that the two younger ones both died, one three days before Paullus' triumph, the other five days after it.[31] He dealt with this matter fully in the report he gave the people. For it was the custom that generals give an account of 2 their actions. After entering the Forum, he said that he had sailed from Brundisium to Corcyra in one day. He had taken five days to get from Corcyra to Delphi, where he sacrificed to the god, and another five days to reach Thessaly, where he took command of the army. Fifteen days later he defeated Perseus and conquered Macedonia. With all this success coming so quickly, he was afraid "that something bad might happen to the army on its way back home. But when the army was safe," he continued, "I 3 began to be afraid on your account. For the divinity is jealous. But it is on me that the misfortune has fallen, with the death of my two sons at the same time. For myself, I am weighed down by the calamity that has befallen me, but for you I have no anxiety." With these words, he won admiration for all his achievements and pity for the death of his sons. He died not much later.[32] (*Exc. de virt.* 36, p. 233 Roos)

20. Having called on the name of the gods on these matters too. Appian in the Macedonian history. (*Anecd.* Bekker p. 143.11 = *On Syntax* No. 9 Gaillard)

Aemilianus (consul 145) and P. Cornelius Scipio Aemilianus Africanus (consul 147, 134), the destroyer of Carthage in 146 and of Numantia in 133.

[32] In fact, Aemilius Paullus was censor in 164 and did not die until 160.

IX

ΙΛΛΥΡΙΚΗ[1]

1. Ἰλλυριοὺς Ἕλληνες ἡγοῦνται τοὺς ὑπέρ τε Μακεδονίαν καὶ Θρᾴκην ἀπὸ Χαόνων καὶ Θεσπρωτῶν ἐπὶ
ποταμὸν Ἴστρον. καὶ τοῦτ' ἐστὶ τῆς χώρας τὸ μῆκος,
εὖρος δ' ἐκ Μακεδόνων τε καὶ Θρᾳκῶν τῶν ὀρείων ἐπὶ
Παίονας καὶ τὸν Ἰόνιον καὶ τὰ πρόποδα τῶν Ἄλπεων.
2 καὶ ἔστι τὸ μὲν εὖρος ἡμερῶν πέντε, τὸ δὲ μῆκος τριάκοντα, καθὰ καὶ τοῖς Ἕλλησιν εἴρηται. Ῥωμαίων δὲ
τὴν χώραν μετρησαμένων ἔστιν ὑπὲρ ἑξακισχιλίους
σταδίους τὸ μῆκος, καὶ τὸ πλάτος ἀμφὶ τοὺς χιλίους
καὶ διακοσίους.
3   2. Φασὶ δὲ τὴν μὲν χώραν ἐπώνυμον Ἰλλυριοῦ τοῦ
Πολυφήμου γενέσθαι· Πολυφήμῳ γὰρ τῷ Κύκλωπι
καὶ Γαλατείᾳ Κελτὸν καὶ Ἰλλυριὸν καὶ Γάλαν παῖδας
ὄντας ἐξορμῆσαι Σικελίας, καὶ ἄρξαι τῶν δι' αὐτοὺς
Κελτῶν καὶ Ἰλλυριῶν καὶ Γαλατῶν λεγομένων. καὶ
τόδε μοι μάλιστα, πολλὰ μυθευόντων ἕτερα πολλῶν,

[1] Ἀππιανοῦ Ἰλλυρικὴ Ῥωμαϊκῶν L

BOOK IX
PART 2

THE ILLYRIAN BOOK[1]

1. The Greeks identify as Illyrians the people who live to the north of Macedonia and Thrace, between Chaonia and Thesprotia and the river Ister. That is the length of the country, and in breadth it stretches from the mountains of Macedonia and Thrace to Paeonia and the Ionian sea, and the foothills of the Alps. It is five days' journey across, and 2
thirty lengthwise, according to the Greek accounts. The Romans surveyed the land, and it is over six thousand stades in length and about one thousand, two hundred wide.[2]

2. They say that the country is named after Illyrius, the 3
son of Polyphemus. For Polyphemus, the Cyclops, and Galatea, had three sons, Celtus, Illyrius, and Galas, who left Sicily to rule over people called, because of them, Celts, Illyrians, and Galatians. There are many other mythological versions, but this seems the most convincing

---

[1] Appian makes it clear himself (*BCiv.* 5.602) that Illyrian history joins with Macedonian into one book, even though the manuscripts call it (with minor variations) "the Illyrian book of Appian's Roman history."   [2] That is, about 670 miles from north to south, and 130 from east to west.

APPIAN

4 ἀρέσκει. Ἰλλυριῷ δὲ παῖδας Ἐγχέλεα καὶ Αὐταριέα καὶ Δάρδανον καὶ Μαῖδον καὶ Ταύλαντα καὶ Περραιβὸν γενέσθαι, καὶ θυγατέρας Παρθὼ καὶ Δαορθὼ καὶ Δασσαρὼ καὶ ἑτέρας, ὅθεν εἰσὶ Ταυλάντιοί τε καὶ Περραιβοὶ καὶ Ἐγχέλεες καὶ Αὐταριεῖς καὶ Δάρδανοι ⟨καὶ Μαῖδοι⟩[2] καὶ Παρθηνοὶ καὶ Δασσαρήτιοι καὶ Δάρσιοι. Αὐταριεῖ δὲ αὐτῷ Παννόνιον ἡγοῦνται παῖδα ἢ Παίονα γενέσθαι, καὶ Σκορδίσκον Παίονι καὶ Τριβαλλόν, ὧν ὁμοίως τὰ ἔθνη παρώνυμα εἶναι.

5   3. Καὶ τάδε μὲν τοῖς ἀρχαιολογοῦσι μεθείσθω, γένη δ' ἔστιν Ἰλλυριῶν, ὡς ἐν τοσῇδε χώρᾳ, πολλά. καὶ περιώνυμα ἔτι νῦν, χώραν νεμόμενα πολλήν, Σκορδίσκων καὶ Τριβαλλῶν, οἳ ἐς τοσοῦτον ἀλλήλους πολέμῳ διέφθειραν ὡς Τριβαλλῶν εἴ τι ὑπόλοιπον ἦν ἐς Γέτας ὑπὲρ Ἴστρον φυγεῖν, καὶ γένος ἀκμάσαν μέχρι Φιλίππου τε καὶ Ἀλεξάνδρου νῦν ἔρημον καὶ 6 ἀνώνυμον τοῖς τῇδε εἶναι, Σκορδίσκους δὲ ἀσθενεστάτους ἀπὸ τοῦδε γενομένους ὑπὸ Ῥωμαίων ὕστερον ὅμοια παθεῖν καὶ ἐς τὰς νήσους τοῦ αὐτοῦ ποταμοῦ φυγεῖν, σὺν χρόνῳ δέ τινας ἐπανελθεῖν καὶ Παιόνων ἐσχατιαῖς παροικῆσαι· ὅθεν ἔστι καὶ νῦν Σκορδίσκων 7 γένος ἐν Παίοσιν. τῷ δ' αὐτῷ τρόπῳ καὶ Ἀρδιαῖοι τὰ θαλάσσια ὄντες ἄριστοι πρὸς Αὐταριέων ἀρίστων ὄντων τὰ κατὰ γῆν, πολλὰ βλάψαντες αὐτούς, ὅμως ἐφθάρησαν. καὶ ναυτικοὶ μὲν ἐπὶ τοῖς Ἀρδιαῖοις ἐγένοντο Λιβυρνοί, γένος ἕτερον Ἰλλυριῶν, οἳ τὸν Ἰόνιον

---

[2] καὶ Μαῖδοι add. Roos

304

to me. Illyrius' sons were Encheleus, Autarieus, Darda- 4
nus, Maedus, Taulas, and Perrhaebus, and among his
daughters were Partho, Daortho, and Dassaro. From
these were descended the Taulantii and the Perrhaebi and
the Encheleis and the Autarieis and the Dardanians ‹and
the Maedi› and the Partheni and the Dassareti and the
Dorsi. It is thought that Autarieus had a son called Pan-
nonius or Paeon, and that Paeon had two sons, Scodiscus
and Triballus, from whom, in similar fashion, those bear-
ing the same names are descended.

3. But I leave this topic for the antiquarians. There are 5
many Illyrian peoples, as is to be expected in such a large
country. Still well known names are the Scordisci and
Triballi, who inhabited a large area, but did such damage
to each other in war, that the Triballian survivors fled
across the Ister to the Getae; and although they continued
to flourish as a people up to the time of Philip and Alexander, they are now extinct and the present inhabitants do
not recognize their name. The Scordisci were also re- 6
duced to extreme weakness thereafter, and later suffered
similar difficulties at the hands of the Romans, but they
took refuge on the islands of the same river, and after a
time some returned to settle at the edge of Paeonian territory. That is the reason there is still a Scordiscan people
in Paeonia. In the same sort of way, the Ardaei too, who 7
had the stronger fleet, met destruction at the hands of the
Autarieis, who had the stronger army, although they inflicted great damage on the Autarieis. Another Illyrian
people, the Liburnians, second to the Ardaei in naval capacity, used to carry out pirate raids in the Ionian sea and

καὶ τὰς νήσους ἐλῄστευον ναυσὶν ὠκείαις τε καὶ κού-
φαις, ὅθεν ἔτι νῦν Ῥωμαῖοι τὰ κοῦφα καὶ ὀξέα δίκροτα
Λιβυρνίδας προσαγορεύουσιν.

8   4. Αὐταριέας δὲ φασὶν ἐκ θεοβλαβείας Ἀπόλλωνος
ἐς ἔσχατον κακοῦ περιελθεῖν. Μολιστόμῳ γὰρ αὐτοὺς
καὶ Κελτοῖς τοῖς Κίμβροις λεγομένοις ἐπὶ Δελφοὺς
συστρατεῦσαι, καὶ φθαρῆναι μὲν αὐτίκα τοὺς πλέονας αὐτῶν πρὸ ἐπιχειρήσεως, ὑετῶν σφίσι καὶ θυέλ-
λης καὶ πρηστήρων ἐμπεσόντων, ἐπιγενέσθαι δὲ τοῖς
ὑποστρέψασιν ἄπειρον βατράχων πλῆθος, οἳ διασα-
9   πέντες τὰ νάματα διέφθειραν. καὶ ἐκ τῆς γῆς ἀτμῶν
ἀτόπων γενομένων λοιμὸς ἦν Ἰλλυριῶν καὶ φθόρος
Αὐταριέων μάλιστα, μέχρι φεύγοντες τὰ οἰκεῖα, καὶ
τὸν λοιμὸν σφίσι περιφέροντες, οὐδενὸς αὐτοὺς δεχο-
μένου διὰ τοῦτο τὸ δέος ὑπερῆλθον ὁδὸν ἡμερῶν
εἴκοσι καὶ τριῶν, καὶ τὴν Γετῶν ἑλώδη καὶ ἀοίκητον,
10   παρὰ τὸ Βαστερνῶν ἔθνος, ᾤκησαν. Κελτοῖς δὲ ὁ θεὸς
τὴν γῆν ἔσεισε καὶ τὰς πόλεις κατήνεγκε· καὶ τὸ κακὸν οὐκ ἔληγε, μέχρι καὶ οἵδε τὰ οἰκεῖα φεύγοντες
ἐνέβαλον ἐς Ἰλλυριοὺς τοὺς συναμαρτόντας σφίσιν,
ἀσθενεῖς ὑπὸ τοῦ λοιμοῦ γενομένους, καὶ ἐδῄωσάν τε
τὰ ἐκείνων, καὶ τοῦ λοιμοῦ μετασχόντες ἔφυγον καὶ
μέχρι Πυρήνης ἐληλάτουν. ἐπιστρέφουσι δ᾽ αὐτοῖς
ἐς τὴν ἕω, Ῥωμαῖοι, δεδιότες ὑπὸ μνήμης τῶν προπε-
πολεμηκότων σφίσι Κελτῶν, μὴ καὶ οἵδε ἐς τὴν
Ἰταλίαν ὑπὲρ Ἄλπεις ἐσβάλοιεν, ἀπήντων ἅμα τοῖς

---

[3] This seems a jumbled account. Molistomos led an attack on

its islands using their fast, light ships. It is after these that the Romans still call their own light, swift biremes "Liburnians."

4. They say that madness visited upon them by Apollo 8 drove the Autarieis to the very edge of destruction. For when they joined the expedition against Delphi led by Molistomus and the Celtic people known as the Cimbri, most of them were killed immediately, before the attack, when a storm hit them with heavy rain and hurricane-force winds.[3] Those who got home suffered a huge plague of frogs, whose bodies putrefied and poisoned their streams. Strange vapors rose from the ground and brought 9 disease to Illyria that killed the Autarieis in particular. Eventually they fled their homes carrying the plague with them, and after a journey of twenty-three days when no one would take them in out of fear of the disease, they came to a marshy and uninhabited part of Getan territory, where they settled beside the Bastarnae. As for the Celts, 10 the god shook their land with an earthquake and leveled their towns. And their problems did not ease until they too fled their homes and invaded the territory of the Illyrians, who had shared in their sacrilege, and had been weakened by the plague. While plundering their land, the Celts contracted the plague and fled, pillaging their way as far as the Pyrenees. When they turned back eastward, the Romans, remembering the Celts who had fought against them before, were afraid that these ones too might invade Italy across the Alps, and confronted them with the con-

the Autarieis in 310. The most famous Celtic attack on Delphi, with which the Cimbri are not otherwise associated, took place in 279/8.

11 ὑπάτοις καὶ πανστρατιᾷ διώλλυντο. καὶ τὸ πάθος
τοῦτο Ῥωμαίων μέγα δέος Κελτῶν ἐς ὅλην τὴν Ἰταλίαν ἐνέβαλε, μέχρι Γάιον Μάριον ἑλόμενοι σφῶν οἱ
Ῥωμαῖοι στρατηγεῖν, ἄρτι Λιβύων τοῖς Νομάσι καὶ
Μαυρουσίοις ἐγκρατῶς πεπολεμηκότα, τοὺς Κίμ-
βρους ἐνίκων καὶ πολὺν φόνον αὐτῶν εἰργάσαντο
πολλάκις, ὥς μοι περὶ Κελτῶν λέγοντι εἴρηται. οἱ δὲ
ἀσθενεῖς τε ἤδη γενόμενοι καὶ πάσης γῆς ἀποκλειό-
μενοι διὰ τὸ ἀσθενές, ἐς τὰ οἰκεῖα ἐπανῆλθον πολλὰ
καὶ δράσαντες καὶ παθόντες.

12   5. Τοιοῦτον μὲν δὴ τέλος τῆς ἀσεβείας ὁ θεὸς
ἐπέθηκεν Ἰλλυριοῖς τε καὶ Κελτοῖς· οὐ μὴν ἀπέσχοντο
τῆς ἱεροσυλίας, ἀλλ᾽ αὖθις, ἅμα τοῖς Κελτοῖς, Ἰλλυριῶν οἱ Σκορδίσκοι μάλιστα καὶ Μαῖδοι καὶ Δάρδανοι τὴν Μακεδονίαν ἐπέδραμον ὁμοῦ καὶ τὴν Ἑλλάδα,
καὶ πολλὰ τῶν ἱερῶν καὶ τὸ Δελφικὸν ἐσύλησαν,

13 πολλοὺς ἀποβαλόντες ὅμως καὶ τότε. Ῥωμαῖοι δ᾽
ἔχοντες ἤδη δεύτερον καὶ τριακοσιοστὸν[3] ἔτος ἀπὸ
τῆς πρώτης ἐς Κελτοὺς πείρας, καὶ ἐξ ἐκείνου πολεμοῦντες αὐτοῖς ἐκ διαστημάτων, ἐπιστρατεύουσι τοῖς
Ἰλλυριοῖς ἐπὶ τῇδε τῇ ἱεροσυλίᾳ ἡγουμένου Λευκίου
Σκιπίωνος, ἤδη τῶν τε Ἑλλήνων καὶ Μακεδόνων
προστατοῦντες. καί φασι τοὺς μὲν περιχώρους οὐ

---

3 τριακοσιοστὸν Duchesne; τριακοστὸν codd.

---

4 Cn. Mallius Maximus (consul 105) and Q. Servilius Caepio
(consul 106) were defeated by the Cimbri and Teutones at the
battle of Arausio in 105.   5 C. Marius, elected consul for the

suls, but the whole army was annihilated.[4] This Roman   11
defeat filled all Italy with great fear of the Celts, until the
Romans appointed Gaius Marius, who had recently fought
a successful war against the Numidians and Moors in Africa, to command their forces, and defeated the Cimbri,
inflicting great slaughter on them on many occasions, as I
have related in my book of Celtic history.[5] Now weakened,
and shut out from any other territory because they were
weak, the Cimbri returned home, having caused others,
and experienced themselves, a great deal of suffering.

5. Such was the payment the god exacted from the Il-   12
lyrians and Celts for their impiety. Not that they stopped
robbing temples. For along with the Celts, some Illyrians,
particularly the Scordisci, Maedi, and Dardanians, again
invaded Macedonia and Greece at the same time, plundering many temples, including Delphi, although this
time too they suffered heavy casualties. Three hundred   13
and two years after their first encounter with the Celts,
and having fought with them at intervals since then, the
Romans, now masters of Greece and Macedonia, march
against the Illyrians in response to this latest sacrilegious
raid. In command was Lucius Scipio.[6] It is said that the
surrounding population did not give military assistance

first time in 107, ended the war in Africa against Jugurtha in 105.
Consul from 104 to 100, he defeated the Teutones and Ambrones
at the battle of Aquae Sextiae in 102, and the Cimbri at the battle
of Vercellae in 101. Appian's detailed account of Marius' northern
campaigns in the Celtic book does not survive.

[6] The exact date of the raid on Delphi is difficult to identify,
but L. Cornelius Scipio Asiagenus Asiaticus had probably been
praetor in 86 and campaigned from 85 to 84 in Illyria.

συμμαχῆσαι τοῖς ἱεροσύλοις, ἀλλ᾽ ἑκόντας ἐγκαταλι-
πεῖν τῷ Σκιπίωνι ἀβοηθήτους, μνήμῃ τῶν δι᾽ Αὐτα-
14 ριέας ἐς πάντας Ἰλλυριοὺς συμπεσόντων· Σκιπίωνα
δὲ Σκορδίσκους μὲν διαφθεῖραι, καὶ εἴ τι λοιπὸν
αὐτῶν ἦν, ἐς τὸν Ἴστρον καὶ τὰς νήσους τοῦ ποταμοῦ
μετοικῆσαι φυγόντας, Μαίδοις δὲ καὶ Δαρδανεῦσι
συνθέσθαι δωροδοκήσαντα τοῦ ἱεροῦ χρυσίου. καί τις
ἔφη τῶν Ἰταλικῶν συγγραφέων ὡς διὰ τοῦτο μάλιστα Ῥωμαίοις πλεόνως μετὰ Λεύκιον τὰ ἐμφύλια
ἤκμασε μέχρι μοναρχίας.

15 6. Καὶ περὶ μὲν τῶν νομιζομένων εἶναι τοῖς Ἕλλησιν Ἰλλυριῶν τοσαῦτά μοι προλελέχθω. Ῥωμαῖοι δὲ
καὶ τούσδε καὶ Παίονας ἐπ᾽ αὐτοῖς καὶ Ῥαιτοὺς καὶ
Νωρικοὺς καὶ Μυσοὺς τοὺς ἐν Εὐρώπῃ, καὶ ὅσα ἄλλα
ὅμορα τούτοις ἐν δεξιᾷ τοῦ Ἴστρου καταπλέοντι ᾤκη-
ται, διαιροῦσι μὲν ὁμοίως τοῖς Ἕλλησιν ἀπὸ Ἑλλήνων, καὶ καλοῦσι τοῖς ἰδίοις ἑκάστους ὀνόμασι,
16 καινῇ δὲ πάντας Ἰλλυρίδα ἡγοῦνται, ὅθεν μὲν ἀρξά-
μενοι τῆσδε τῆς δόξης, οὐκ ἔσχον εὑρεῖν, χρώμενοι δ᾽
αὐτῇ καὶ νῦν, ὅπου καὶ τὸ τέλος τῶνδε τῶν ἐθνῶν, ἀπὸ
ἀνίσχοντος Ἴστρου μέχρι τῆς Ποντικῆς θαλάσσης,
ὑφ᾽ ἓν ἐκμισθοῦσι καὶ Ἰλλυρικὸν τέλος προσαγορεύουσιν. ὅπως δὲ αὐτοὺς ὑπηγάγοντο Ῥωμαῖοι, ὡμο-
λόγησα μὲν καὶ περὶ Κρήτης λέγων οὐχ εὑρεῖν τὰς
ἀκριβεῖς τῶν πολέμων ἀρχάς τε καὶ προφάσεις, καὶ
ἐς τοῦτο τοὺς δυναμένους τι πλέον εἰπεῖν παρεκάλουν·
ὅσα δ᾽ αὐτὸς ἔγνων, ἀναγράψω.

17 7. Ἄγρων ἦν βασιλεὺς Ἰλλυριῶν μέρους ἀμφὶ τὸν

to the temple raiders, but willingly abandoned them to Scipio, without helping them, mindful of what happened to the whole of Illyria because of the Autarieis. Scipio destroyed the Scordisci, and any survivors fled and took up residence on the Ister and its islands. With the Maedi and Dardanians Scipio made an agreement, having accepted a bribe, so it was said, of the temple gold. One Roman historian maintains that this was the main reason why the civil wars intensified between Lucius' time and the monarchy.

6. So much by way of introduction to those considered by the Greeks to be Illyrians. The Romans distinguish these people from each other, and in addition to them the Paeonians, Rhaeti, Norici, and European Mysians, and all their other neighbors living on the right bank of the Ister as one travels downstream—just as they distinguish the Greeks from each other—and they call each of them by their own name, but regard them all collectively as Illyria. I have not been able to find out where this notion originated, but they still use the term even now for the tax paid by the peoples between the source of the Ister and the Pontic sea: they farm it out as a single entity and call it the Illyrian tax. How the Romans subdued these peoples, and what the exact causes of and pretexts for the wars were, I admitted, when writing about Crete, that I have not been able to discover, and I invited anyone who could add something to the story to do so. What I found out by myself, I will now write down.

7. Agron was king of the part of Illyria that lies along

14

15

16

17

κόλπον τῆς θαλάσσης τὸν Ἰόνιον, ὃν δὴ καὶ Πύρρος
ὁ τῆς Ἠπείρου βασιλεὺς κατεῖχε καὶ οἱ τὰ Πύρρου
διαδεξάμενοι. Ἄγρων δ᾽ ἔμπαλιν τῆς τε Ἠπείρου τινὰ
καὶ Κόρκυραν ἐπ᾽ αὐτοῖς καὶ Ἐπίδαμνον καὶ Φάρον
καταλαβὼν ἔμφρουρα εἶχεν. ἐπιπλέοντος δ᾽ αὐτοῦ καὶ
τὸν ἄλλον Ἰόνιον, νῆσος, ᾗ ὄνομα Ἴσσα, ἐπὶ Ῥω-
18 μαίους κατέφυγεν. οἱ δὲ πρέσβεις τοῖς Ἰσσίοις συνέ-
πεμψαν, εἰσομένους τὰ Ἄγρωνος ἐς αὐτοὺς ἐγκλήματα.
τοῖς δὲ πρέσβεσιν ἔτι προσπλέουσιν ἐπαναχθέντες
Ἰλλυρικοὶ λέμβοι τῶν μὲν Ἰσσίων πρεσβευτὴν Κλε-
έμπορον, τῶν δὲ Ῥωμαίων Κορογκάνιον ἀναιροῦσιν·
19 οἱ δὲ λοιποὶ διέδρασαν αὐτούς. καὶ ἐπὶ τῷδε Ῥωμαίων
ἐπ᾽ Ἰλλυριοὺς ναυσὶν ὁμοῦ καὶ πεζῷ στρατευόντων,
Ἄγρων μὲν ἐπὶ παιδίῳ σμικρῷ, Πίννῃ ὄνομα, ἀπο-
θνήσκει, τῇ γυναικὶ τὴν ἀρχὴν ἐπιτροπεύειν τῷ παιδὶ
παραδούς, καίπερ οὐκ οὔσῃ μητρὶ τοῦ παιδίου, Δημήτριος δ᾽ ὁ Φάρου ἡγούμενος Ἄγρωνι (Φάρου τε
γὰρ αὐτῆς ἦρχε, καὶ ἐπὶ τῇδε Κορκύρας) παρέδωκεν
ἄμφω Ῥωμαίοις ἐπιπλέουσιν ἐκ προδοσίας. οἱ δ᾽ ἐπὶ
ταύταις Ἐπίδαμνον ἐς φιλίαν ὑπηγάγοντο, καὶ τοῖς
Ἰσσίοις καὶ Ἐπιδαμνίοις πολιορκουμένοις ὑπὸ Ἰλλυ-
20 ριῶν ἐς ἐπικουρίαν ἔπλεον. Ἰλλυριοὶ μὲν δὴ τὰς πολιορκίας λύσαντες ἀνεχώρουν, καί τινες αὐτῶν ἐς
Ῥωμαίους, οἱ Ἀτιντανοὶ λεγόμενοι, μετετίθεντο. μετὰ
ταῦτα δὲ ἡ Ἄγρωνος γυνὴ πρέσβεις ἐς Ῥώμην ἔπεμψε
τά τε αἰχμάλωτα ἀποδιδόντας αὐτοῖς καὶ τοὺς αὐτο-

the Ionian gulf of the Mediterranean, which Pyrrhus, king of Epirus, and his successors controlled. In contrast to them, Agron subsequently took possession of, and established garrisons in some of Epirus, and Corcyra, Epidamnus, and Pharus too. When he sailed against the rest of the Ionian, an island called Issa turned to Rome for refuge. The Romans sent their own envoys off with the Issian 18 representatives to find out what accusations Agron was making against them. While the ambassadors are still at sea, Illyrian galleys put out against them and kill Cleemporus, one of the Issian ambassadors, and Coruncanius, one of the Romans; the others outran the pursuers.[7] After 19 this incident, when the Romans attack the Illyrians with a joint naval and military expedition, Agron dies, leaving an infant son called Pinnes, and entrusting the administration of the kingdom to his wife on behalf of the boy, although she was not the mother of the child. Demetrius, Agron's governor in Pharus—he held Pharus itself and Corcyra too—treacherously handed over both places to the invading Roman fleet. In addition to Pharus and Corcyra, Rome also enrolled the people of Epidamnus as a friend, and when Issa and Epidamnus were put under siege by the Illyrians, sailed to their assistance. The Illyrians then 20 abandoned the siege and withdrew, and some of their people, called the Atintani, changed sides to Rome. After this, Agron's wife sent ambassadors to Rome to hand back the prisoners and deserters they brought with them. She

---

[7] Polybius (2.8) says that it was Teuta, Agron's wife and successor, who had Coruncanius murdered. Polybius does not mention the Issian ambassador, Cleemporus. The First Illyrian War took place in 229/8.

μόλους ἄγοντας, καὶ ἐδεῖτο συγγνώμης τυχεῖν τῶν
21 οὐκ ἐφ᾽ ἑαυτῆς ἀλλ᾽ ἐπὶ Ἄγρωνος γενομένων. οἱ δὲ
ἀπεκρίναντο Κόρκυραν μὲν καὶ Φάρον καὶ Ἴσσαν καὶ
Ἐπίδαμνον καὶ Ἰλλυριῶν τοὺς Ἀτιντανοὺς ἤδη Ῥωμαίων ὑπηκόους εἶναι, Πίννην δὲ τὴν ἄλλην Ἄγρωνος
ἀρχὴν ἔχειν καὶ φίλον εἶναι Ῥωμαίοις, ἢν ἀπέχηταί
τε τῶν προλελεγμένων, καὶ τὴν Λίσσον μὴ παρα-
πλέωσιν Ἰλλυρικοὶ λέμβοι δυοῖν πλείονες, καὶ τούτοιν
δὲ ἀνόπλοιν.

22 8. Ἡ μὲν δὴ ταῦτα πάντα ἐδέχετο, καὶ γίγνονται
Ῥωμαίοις αἵδε πρῶται πρὸς Ἰλλυριοὺς πεῖραί τε καὶ
συνθῆκαι· Ῥωμαῖοι δ᾽ ἐπ᾽ αὐταῖς Κόρκυραν μὲν καὶ
Ἀπολλωνίαν ἀφῆκαν ἐλευθέρας, Δημητρίῳ δ᾽ ἔστιν ἃ
χωρία μισθὸν ἔδοσαν τῆς προδοσίας, ἐπειπόντες ὅτι
ἐν τοσῷδε διδόασι, τὴν ἀπιστίαν ἄρα τοῦ ἀνδρὸς
23 ὑφορώμενοι. ἢ δὴ καὶ ἦρξεν αὐτοῦ μετ᾽ ὀλίγον· Ῥωμαίων γὰρ Κελτοῖς ἐπὶ τριετὲς τοῖς ἀμφὶ τὸν Ἠρι-
δανὸν οὖσι πολεμούντων, ὁ Δημήτριος ὡς ὄντων ἐν
ἀσχολίᾳ τὴν θάλασσαν ἐλῄζετο, καὶ Ἴστρους ἔθνος
ἕτερον Ἰλλυριῶν ἐς τοῦτο προσελάμβανε, καὶ τοὺς
Ἀτιντανοὺς ἀπὸ Ῥωμαίων ἀφίστη. οἱ δέ, ἐπεὶ τὰ Κελτῶν διετέθειτο, εὐθὺς μὲν ἐπιπλεύσαντες αἱροῦσι τοὺς
λῃστάς, ἐς νέωτα δὲ ἐστράτευον ἐπὶ Δημήτριον καὶ
24 Ἰλλυριῶν τοὺς συναμαρτόντας αὐτῷ. Δημήτριον μὲν
δὴ πρὸς Φίλιππον τὸν Μακεδόνων βασιλέα φυγόντα
καὶ αὖθις ἐπιόντα καὶ λῃστεύοντα τὸν Ἰόνιον κτείνουσι, καὶ τὴν πατρίδα αὐτῷ Φάρον συναμαρτοῦσαν

asked to be forgiven for what had happened, not under her rule, but under Agron's. Rome's reply was that Corcyra, 21 Pharus, Issa, Epidamnus, and the Illyrian Atintani were now subjects of Rome. Pinnes could have the rest of Agron's kingdom and be a friend of the Romans, if he kept his hands off the aforementioned places, and if no more than two Illyrian galleys, both of them unarmed, were to sail further than Lissos.[8]

8. She accepted all these terms. This is the first conflict 22 between Rome and Illyria and the first treaty. Afterward, the Romans made Corcyra and Apollonia free, and rewarded Demetrius for his treachery by giving him some strongholds, but adding that this was a temporary gift, no doubt because they suspected he was a man not to be trusted. And indeed not much later his fickle nature took complete control of him. For when the Romans were en- 23 gaged for three years in a war against the Celts living around the Po, and thus, so Demetrius believed, preoccupied, he began to launch raids by sea, taking the Istrians, another Illyrian people, into partnership, and detaching the Atintani from Rome.[9] As soon as the Romans made a settlement with the Celts, they immediately sailed against the pirates and subdue them, and the following year marched against Demetrius and his Illyrian partners in crime.[10] Demetrius took refuge with Philip, king of 24 Macedon, but when he went back to his Ionian piracy, the Romans kill him and destroyed his home town of Pharus for assisting his criminal activities. The Illyrians, however,

[8] Lissos is modern Lezha in Albania.   [9] Roman forces were fighting the Celts in northern Italy from 225 to 222.

[10] The Second Illyrian War took place in 219.

APPIAN

ἐπικατέσκαψαν, Ἰλλυριῶν δ' ἐφείσαντο διὰ Πίννην
αὖθις δεηθέντα. καὶ δεύτεραι πεῖραί τε καὶ συνθῆκαι
πρὸς Ἰλλυριοὺς αὐτοῖς ἐγίγνοντο.

25   9. Τὰ λοιπὰ δ' οὔτι μοι πάντα χρόνῳ καὶ τάξει
μᾶλλον ἢ κατὰ ἔθνος Ἰλλυριῶν ἕκαστον, ὅσα ηὗρον,
συγγέγραπται. Ῥωμαῖοι Μακεδόσιν ἐπολέμουν, καὶ
Περσεὺς ἦν ἤδη Μακεδόνων βασιλεὺς μετὰ Φίλιπ-
πον· Περσεῖ δὲ Γένθιος Ἰλλυριῶν ἑτέρων βασιλεὺς
ἐπὶ χρήμασι συνεμάχει, καὶ ἐς τοὺς Ῥωμαίων Ἰλλυριοὺς ἐνέβαλε, καὶ πρέσβεις Ῥωμαίων πρὸς αὐτὸν
ἐλθόντας ἔδησεν, αἰτιώμενος οὐ πρέσβεις ἀλλὰ κατα-
26   σκόπους ἐλθεῖν. Ἀνίκιος δὲ Ῥωμαίων στρατηγὸς λέμ-
βους τε τοῦ Γενθίου τινὰς εἷλεν ἐπιπλεύσας, καὶ κατὰ
γῆν αὐτῷ συνενεχθεὶς ἐκράτει τὴν μάχην, καὶ συν-
έκλεισεν ἔς τι χωρίον, ὅθεν αὐτῷ δεομένῳ ὁ μὲν
Ἀνίκιος ἐκέλευσε Ῥωμαίοις ἑαυτὸν ἐπιτρέψαι, ὁ δ' ἐς
βουλὴν ᾔτησε τρεῖς ἡμέρας, καὶ ἔλαβεν. ἐν δὲ ταύταις
τῶν ὑπηκόων αὐτοῦ πρὸς τὸν Ἀνίκιον μετατιθεμένων
ἠξίωσεν ἐντυχεῖν τῷ Ἀνικίῳ, καὶ γονυπετὴς ἐδεῖτο
27   αὐτοῦ πάνυ αἰσχρῶς. ὁ δὲ αὐτὸν ἐπιθαρρύνων κατ-
επτηχότα ἀνίστη, καὶ καλέσας ἐπὶ ἑστίασιν, ἀπιόντα
ἀπὸ τοῦ δείπνου προσέταξε τοῖς ὑπηρέταις ἐς φυλακὴν ἐμβαλεῖν. καὶ τόνδε μὲν ἐς θρίαμβον ἅμα τοῖς
παισὶν ὁ Ἀνίκιος ἐς Ῥώμην ἤγαγε, καὶ ὁ Γενθίου
28   πόλεμος ἅπας εἴκοσιν ἡμέραις ἐπεπολέμητο· ἑβδομήκοντα δ' αὐτοῦ πόλεις οὔσας Αἰμίλιος Παῦλος ὁ
τὸν Περσέα ἑλών, τῆς βουλῆς ἐπιστειλάσης ἐν ἀπορρήτῳ, ἐς Ῥώμην παρώδευεν ἐπίτηδες, καὶ δεδιόσιν

they spared, again at the request of Pinnes. This was the second war between Rome and Illyria, and the second treaty between them.

9. All the rest of my researches have been written up   25
not in chronological order, but taking each Illyrian people separately. Rome was at war with Macedon and Perseus, Philip's successor, was now king of Macedon. Genthius, king of other Illyrians, made an alliance with Perseus in exchange for money, and attacked the Illyrians aligned with Rome. He then arrested the Roman ambassadors who had come to him, accusing them of coming as spies rather than ambassadors. The Roman general Anicius, in   26
command of the naval expedition sent against Genthius, captured some of his galleys, engaged and defeated him in battle on land, and shut him up in a fort.[11] From here Genthius tried to negotiate, but Anicius ordered him to surrender to Rome. When he requested three days to think about it, his request was granted. In the meantime his subjects went over to Anicius, and Genthius asked for a meeting with Anicius, at which he sank to his knees and in completely ignominious fashion begged his forgiveness. Anicius encouragingly raised him from his cowering posi-   27
tion, and invited him to dinner, but ordered his attendants to throw him into prison as he was leaving after the meal. Anicius paraded him and his sons in his triumph at Rome. The whole war against Genthius was over in twenty days. On his way back to Rome, Aemilius Paullus, the conqueror   28
of Perseus, acting on secret orders from the senate, purposefully included in his itinerary the seventy towns under

[11] L. Anicius Gallus was praetor in 168 when he defeated Genthius.

APPIAN

αὐτοῖς ὑπέσχετο συγγνώσεσθαι τῶν γεγονότων, ἐὰν
ὅσον ἔχουσιν ἀργύριόν τε καὶ χρυσίον ἐσενέγκωσιν.
ὑποδεξαμένων δ' ἐκείνων συνέπεμπεν αὐτοῖς τοῦ
στρατοῦ μέρος ἐς πόλιν ἑκάστην, ὁρίσας ἡμέραν τοῖς
στρατηγοῦσι τοῦ στρατοῦ πᾶσι τὴν αὐτήν, καὶ ἐντει-
λάμενος ἅμα ἕῳ κηρύσσειν ἕκαστον ἐν ἑκάστῃ πόλει
τρισὶν ὥραις ἐς τὴν ἀγορὰν τὰ χρήματα φέρειν, συν-
ενεγκόντων δὲ τὰ λοιπὰ διαρπάσαι.

29   10. Οὕτω μὲν ὁ Παῦλος ἑβδομήκοντα πόλεις διήρ-
πασεν ὥρᾳ μιᾷ· Ἀρδεῖοι δὲ καὶ Παλάριοι, γένη ἕτερα
Ἰλλυριῶν, τὴν ὑπὸ Ῥωμαίους Ἰλλυρίδα ἐδῄουν, καὶ
οἱ Ῥωμαῖοι δι' ἀσχολίαν πρέσβεις ἔπεμψαν ἐπιπλή-
ξοντας αὐτοῖς. οὐ μεταθεμένων δὲ ἐκείνων ἐστράτευον
ἐπ' αὐτοὺς μυρίοις πεζοῖς καὶ ἱππεῦσιν ἑξακοσίοις. οἱ
δὲ πυθόμενοι, καὶ ἔτι ὄντες ἀπαράσκευοι, πρέσβεις
ἔπεμψαν μεταγιγνώσκοντες καὶ δεόμενοι. καὶ ἡ βουλὴ
τὰς βλάβας αὐτοῖς ἐκέλευσεν ἀποδοῦναι τοῖς ἠδικη-
μένοις. οὐκ ἀποδιδόντων δὲ ἐστράτευεν ἐπ' αὐτοὺς
Φούλβιος Φλάκκος. καὶ ὁ πόλεμος ἄρα μέχρι κατα-
δρομῆς ἔληξε μόνης. οὐ γὰρ ηὗρον αὐτοῦ τέλος ἀκρι-
30   βές. Ἰάποσι δὲ τοῖς ἐντὸς Ἄλπεων ἐπολέμησε μὲν
Σεμπρώνιος ὁ Τουδιτανὸς ἐπίκλην, <ἐπολέμησε δὲ>[4]
καὶ Πανδούσας Τιβέριος. καὶ ἐοίκασιν οἱ Ἰάποδες
αὐτοῖς ὑπακοῦσαι, ἐοίκασι δὲ καὶ Σεγεστανοὶ Λευκίῳ

[4] ἐπολέμησε δὲ add. Goukowsky

the control of Genthius. Although they were afraid, Aemilius promised to forgive them for what had happened, if they delivered all the gold and silver they had. This they agreed to do. Aemilius then sent a military detachment into each of their towns, ordering all the company commanders to proclaim at dawn on the same prearranged day that every person in every town had three hours in which to bring their money to the forum; when they had collected this, the rest was for plunder.

10. In this way Paullus plundered seventy towns in one   29
hour.[12] When two other Illyrian peoples, the Ardaei and Palarians, also made a raid on Roman Illyria, the Romans were too busy to do anything other than send envoys to reprimand them. When they refused to comply, the Romans sent an expedition of ten thousand infantry and one thousand six hundred cavalry against them. On hearing of this, the Illyrians, who were not yet prepared for war, changed their mind and sent a mission to ask for pardon. The senate ordered them to pay damages to the people they had wronged, but they did not do this, and Fulvius Flaccus led an expedition against them. The war, I think, petered out after a single incursion, but I could not find any details of what happened in the end.[13] Sempronius   30
Tuditanus and Tiberius Pandusa conducted operations against the Iapodes who live this side of the Alps, and the Iapodes appear to have submitted to them, just as the people of Segesta appear to have submitted to Lucius

[12] Livy (45.34) says it was the towns of Epirus that had sided with Perseus that were targeted in this way by Aemilius Paullus.

[13] The action is dated to the consulship of Ser. Fulvius Flaccus in 135.

Κόττᾳ καὶ Μετέλλῳ, ἀμφότεροι δ' οὐ πολὺ ὕστερον
ἀποστῆναι.

31   11. Δαλμάται δέ, Ἰλλυριῶν ἕτερον γένος, Ἰλλυριοὺς τοὺς ὑπὸ Ῥωμαίοις κατέθεον, καὶ πρέσβεις ἀφικομένους περὶ τοῦδε Ῥωμαίων οὐ προσίεντο. στρα-
τεύουσιν οὖν ἐπ' αὐτοὺς οἱ Ῥωμαῖοι, Μαρκίου Φίγλου
σφῶν ὑπατεύοντός τε καὶ ἐς τὸν πόλεμον ἡγουμένου.
οἱ δὲ ἄρτι τοῦ Φίγλου παραστρατοπεδεύοντος τὰς φυ-
λακὰς ἐνίκων ἐπίδραμόντες, καὶ αὐτὸν ἐκ τοῦ στρατοπέδου κατήραξαν ἐς πεδίον πρανές, μέχρι ἐπὶ Νάρωνα
32   ποταμὸν ἧκεν ὑποφεύγων. ὡς δὲ οἱ μὲν ἀνεχώρουν,
ἀρχὴ δὲ χειμῶνος ἦν, ὁ Φίγλος ἐλπίσας αὐτοῖς ἀδοκήτως ἐπιπεσεῖσθαι συνερρυηκότας ηὗρεν ἐκ τῶν
πόλεων πρὸς τὴν ἔφοδον αὐτοῦ. καὶ συνήλασεν ὅμως
ἐς πόλιν Δελμίνιον, ὅθεν ἄρα καὶ τὸ ὄνομα αὐτοῖς ἐς
Δελματέας, εἶτα Δαλμάτας ἐτράπη. οὐδὲν δὲ πρὸς
ἐχυρὰν πόλιν ἐξ ἐφόδου δυνάμενος, οὐδὲ μηχανήμα-
σιν ἔχων χρῆσθαι διὰ τὸ ὕψος, ᾔρει τὰς ἄλλας ἐπι-
θέων, ἐρημοτέρας ἀνδρῶν ὑπὸ τῆς ἐς τὸ Δελμίνιον
συνόδου γενομένας. εἶτα διπήχεας κορύνας πίσσῃ
καὶ θείῳ καὶ στυππίῳ περιβαλὼν ἐς τὸ Δελμίνιον ἐκ
καταπελτῶν ἐσφενδόνα. αἱ δ' ὑπὸ τῆς ῥύμης ἐξεκαί-
οντο, καὶ φερόμεναι καθάπερ λαμπάδες ὅπου τύχοιεν
ἐνεπίμπρασαν, ἕως πολλὰ μὲν κατεπρήσθη, καὶ τέλος
ἄρα τοῦτο ἦν τότε Φίγλῳ τοῦ Δαλματῶν πολέμου.

---

14 The expedition against the Iapodes took place in 129, when
C. Sempronius Tuditanus was consul and Ti. Latinius (?) Pandusa

Cotta and Metellus.[14] But both of them revolted not long after.

11. Another Illyrian people, the Dalmatians, also over- 31 ran Roman Illyria, and refused to admit the Roman envoys who had come in connection with the incident. So, the Romans sent an expedition against them, with Marcius Figulus, one of their consuls in command of operations.[15] He had just pitched camp near them, when the Dalmatians attacked and overpowered his guards, driving him out of the camp in headlong flight into the plain, until he escaped by reaching the river Naro. As the Dalmatians 32 were withdrawing, and it was the beginning of winter, Figulus hoped to make a surprise attack on them, but found that they had hurriedly reassembled from their towns at his approach. Nevertheless he drove them into the town of Delminium, from where, of course, they got the name Delmatians, later changed to Dalmatians. It was a strongly fortified town and Figulus could make no progress against it by assault, nor could he use siege engines because of its height. So, he attacked and captured the other towns, which were rather short of men because of the concentration of forces in Delminium. Then, taking pieces of wood two cubits long and covering them with pitch, sulfur, and tow, he used catapults to throw them into Delminium. The rush of the air got them burning and they were like torches when thrown, setting fire to wherever they landed, until much of the town was burned down. This was, in fact, the end of Figulus' war against the Dal-

was praetor. L. Aurelius Cotta and L. Caecilius Metellus were the consuls of 119.

[15] C. Marcius Figulus, consul 156.

33 χρόνῳ δ᾽ ὕστερον Καικίλιος Μέτελλος ὑπατεύων οὐδὲν ἀδικοῦσι τοῖς Δαλμάταις ἐψηφίσατο πολεμεῖν
ἐπιθυμίᾳ θριάμβου, καὶ δεχομένων αὐτὸν ἐκείνων ὡς
φίλον διεχείμασε παρ᾽ αὐτοῖς ἐν Σαλώνῃ πόλει, καὶ
ἐς Ῥώμην ἐπανῆλθε καὶ ἐθριάμβευσεν.

34   12. Τοῦ δὲ Καίσαρος ἡγουμένου Κελτῶν, οἱ Δαλμάται οἵδε, καὶ ὅσοι ἄλλοι Ἰλλυριῶν τότε μάλιστα
διηυτύχουν, Λιβυρνούς, ἕτερον ἔθνος Ἰλλυριῶν, Πρωμόναν πόλιν ἀφείλοντο· οἱ δὲ σφᾶς Ῥωμαίοις ἐπιτρέ-
ποντες ἐπὶ τὸν Καίσαρα ἐγγὺς ὄντα κατέφυγον. ὁ δὲ
ἔπεμψε μέν, καὶ προηγόρευσε τοῖς ἔχουσι τὴν Πρωμόναν ἀποδοῦναι τοῖς Λιβυρνοῖς· οὐ φροντισάντων δὲ
ἐκείνων τέλος ἔπεμψε στρατὸν πολύν, οὓς ἅπαντας
ἔκτειναν οἱ Ἰλλυριοί. καὶ ὁ Καῖσαρ οὐκ ἐπεξῆλθεν· οὐ
γὰρ ἦν οἱ σχολὴ τότε στασιάζοντι πρὸς Πομπήιον.

35 ἐκραγείσης δὲ ἐς πόλεμον τῆς στάσεως ὁ μὲν Καῖσαρ
μεθ᾽ ὅσων εἶχεν ἐκ Βρεντεσίου χειμῶνος μέσου⁵ τὸν
Ἰόνιον ἐπέρα καὶ Πομπηίῳ κατὰ Μακεδονίαν ἐπολέμει, τοῦ δ᾽ ἄλλου στρατοῦ τὸν μὲν Ἀντώνιος ἐς τὴν
Μακεδονίαν ἦγε τῷ Καίσαρι, περῶν καὶ ὅδε τὸν
Ἰόνιον χειμῶνος ἄκρου, σπείρας δὲ πεζοῦ πεντεκαίδεκα καὶ τρισχιλίους ἱππέας Γαβίνιος ἦγεν αὐτῷ διὰ
36 τῆς Ἰλλυρίδος, περιοδεύων τὸν Ἰόνιον. οἱ δὲ Ἰλλυριοὶ
φόβῳ τῶν οὐ πρὸ πολλοῦ γεγονότων ἐς Καίσαρα, τὴν
νίκην αὐτοῦ νομίζοντες ὄλεθρον γενήσεσθαι ἑαυτοῖς,
κτείνουσι πάντα τὸν ὑπὸ τῷ Γαβινίῳ στρατὸν ἐπι-

---

⁵ μέσου Mend: ἐς codd.

matians at that time. Later on, Caecilius Metellus, when   33
consul, had a vote passed for war against the Dalmatians.
They had done nothing wrong, but he wanted a triumph.
They received him like a friend and he spent the winter
with them in the town of Salona, and then returned to
Rome, where he did celebrate a triumph.

12. When Caesar was governor of Gaul, these Dalma-   34
tians and other Illyrians, who were particularly successful
at the time, took the town of Promona from the Liburnians, another Illyrian people.[16] Entrusting themselves to
Rome they fled for refuge to Caesar who was in the vicinity. He sent a message with orders that those holding Promona should give it back to the Liburnians, and when they
ignored him, he finally dispatched a strong force against
them. The Illyrians killed them all, but Caesar did not
pursue the matter, as he was involved at the time in a
struggle for power with Pompey and was too busy. When   35
this civil unrest broke out into war, Caesar crossed the
Ionian gulf from Brundisium in midwinter with all the
troops at his disposal, and began to campaign against Pompey in Macedonia. As for the rest of the army, Antony
brought one part of it to Caesar in Macedonia, he too
crossing the Ionian in the depth of winter, and Gabinius
brought him another fifteen cohorts of infantry and three
thousand cavalry by marching around the Ionian through
Illyria. The Illyrians were afraid that, because of the man-   36
ner in which they had treated Caesar not long before, it
would be disastrous for them if he won, and so they attack
and kill the entire force under Gabinius' command, apart

[16] Julius Caesar's command in Gaul began in 58, and he returned to Italy in 49.

δραμόντες, χωρὶς αὐτοῦ Γαβινίου καὶ ὀλίγων διαφυγόντων. καὶ ἐς χρήματα τότε μάλιστα καὶ τὴν ἄλλην ἰσχὺν ἐκ τοσῶνδε λαφύρων ἔστησαν.

13. Ὁ δὲ Καῖσαρ ἠσχολεῖτο μὲν ὑπ' ἀνάγκης ἐς Πομπήιον, καὶ Πομπηίου καθαιρεθέντος ἐς τὰ ὑπόλοιπα τῆς ἐκείνου στάσεως πολυμερῆ γενόμενα, καταστησάμενος δὲ πάντα ἐπανῆλθεν ἐς Ῥώμην, καὶ
37 ἐστράτευεν ἐπὶ Γέτας τε καὶ Παρθυαίους. ἔδεισαν οὖν οἱ Ἰλλυριοὶ μὴ ἐν ὁδῷ σφίσιν οὖσιν ἐπιθοῖτο, καὶ πρέσβεις πέμψαντες ἐς Ῥώμην ᾔτουν τε συγγνώμην τῶν γεγονότων καὶ ἐς φίλίαν ἑαυτοὺς καὶ συμμαχίαν ἐδίδοσαν, ὡς περὶ ἔθνους ἀλκίμου μάλιστα σεμνολογούμενοι. ὁ δὲ ἐπειγόμενος ἄρα ἐς Παρθυαίους σεμνότερον ὅμως αὐτοῖς ἀπεκρίνατο, φίλους μὲν οὐ θήσεσθαι τοὺς τοιαῦτα δεδρακότας, συγγνώσεσθαι
38 δέ, εἰ φόρους ὑποσταῖεν καὶ ὅμηρα δοῖεν. ὑπισχνουμένων δὲ ἐς ἀμφότερα αὐτῶν Οὐατίνιον ἔπεμψε σὺν στρατοῦ τέλεσι τρισὶ καὶ ἱππεῦσι πολλοῖς, φόρους τε ὀλίγους τάξοντα αὐτοῖς καὶ τὰ ὅμηρα ληψόμενον. ἀναιρεθέντος δὲ τοῦ Καίσαρος, ἡγούμενοι τὴν Ῥωμαίων ἰσχὺν ἐν τῷ Καίσαρι γεγονέναι τε καὶ διεφθάρθαι, οὐδὲν ἔτι τοῦ Οὐατινίου κατήκουον, οὔτε ἐς τοὺς φόρους οὔτε ἐς τὰ ἄλλα, βιάζεσθαι δὲ ἐγχειροῦντος αὐτοὶ πέντε τάξεις ἐπιδραμόντες ἔφθειραν, καὶ τὸν ἡγούμενον τῶν τάξεων Βαίβιον, ἄνδρα ἀπὸ βουλῆς. καὶ Οὐατίνιος μὲν σὺν τοῖς ὑπολοίποις ἐς Ἐπί-
39 λῆς. καὶ Οὐατίνιος μὲν σὺν τοῖς ὑπολοίποις ἐς Ἐπίδαμνον ἀνεχώρει· ἡ δὲ Ῥωμαίων βουλὴ τὸν στρατὸν τόνδε καὶ Μακεδονίαν ἐπ' αὐτῷ, καὶ Ἰλλυριοὺς ὅσων

from Gabinius himself and a few others who escaped. With such substantial spoils, it was at this time in particular that the Illyrians reached the zenith of their wealth and other powers.

13. Caesar was preoccupied with the necessity of dealing with Pompey, and when Pompey was killed, with his remaining partisans, who had split into many groups. Having settled all these matters, he returned to Rome and enrolled an army to fight against the Getae and Parthians. This made the Illyrians afraid that as they were on his route he might attack them, and so they sent ambassadors to Rome to ask forgiveness for what had happened and offer their friendship and military assistance, being, as they solemnly claimed, an extremely brave people. Caesar was in a hurry to set out against the Parthians, but still answered them, even more solemnly, that he would not enlist as friends anyone who had done what they had done, but that he would pardon them, if they undertook to pay tribute and handed over hostages. As they promised to do both, Caesar sent Vatinius with three legions and a large force of cavalry to exact a small tribute from them and collect hostages.[17] But then Caesar was assassinated and, believing that Roman power had resided in Caesar, and died with him, the Illyrians now refused to do what Vatinius told them either in relation to the tribute or anything else. When he tried to enforce his will, they attacked and destroyed five of his cohorts, including their commander Baebius, a man of senatorial rank. Vatinius retired to Epidamnus with the survivors. At Rome the senate transferred this army, together with Macedonia and all of Illyria

37

38

39

[17] P. Vatinius (consul in 47) was sent to Illyricum in 45.

APPIAN

ἦρχον, ἐνεχείρισε Βρούτῳ Καιπίωνι τῷ κτείναντι
Γάιον, ὅτε περ καὶ Συρίαν Κασσίῳ, καὶ τῷδε ἀνδρο-
φόνῳ Γαΐου γενομένῳ. ἀλλὰ καὶ οἵδε, πολεμούμενοι
πρὸς Ἀντωνίου καὶ τοῦ δευτέρου Καίσαρος τοῦ Σεβαστοῦ προσαγορευθέντος, ἐς οὐδὲν ἐσχόλασαν Ἰλλυριοῖς.

40   14. Οἱ δὲ Παίονές εἰσιν ἔθνος μέγα παρὰ τὸν
Ἴστρον, ἐπίμηκες ἐξ Ἰαπόδων ἐπὶ Δαρδάνους, Παίονες μὲν ὑπὸ τῶν Ἑλλήνων λεγόμενοι, καὶ ῥωμαϊστὶ
Παννόνιοι, συναριθμούμενοι δὲ ὑπὸ Ῥωμαίων τῇ Ἰλ-
λυρίδι, ὡς προεῖπον. διὸ καὶ περὶ τῶνδέ μοι δοκεῖ νῦν
41   κατὰ τὰ Ἰλλυρικὰ εἰπεῖν. ἔνδοξοι δ' εἰσὶν ἐκ Μακεδόνων δι' Ἀγριᾶνας, οἳ τὰ μέγιστα Φιλίππῳ καὶ Ἀλε-
ξάνδρῳ κατεργασάμενοι Παίονές εἰσι τῶν κάτω Παιόνων, Ἰλλυριοῖς ἔποικοι. ἐπεὶ δ' ἐπὶ τοὺς Παίονας
ἐστράτευσε Κορνήλιος, κακῶς ἀπαλλάξας μέγα δέος
Παιόνων Ἰταλοῖς ἅπασιν ἐνεποίησε, καὶ ἐς πολὺ τοῖς
ἔπειτα ὑπάτοις ὄκνον ἐπὶ Παίονας ἐλαύνειν.

42   15. Τὰ μὲν δὴ πάλαι τοσαῦτα περὶ Ἰλλυριῶν καὶ
Παιόνων ἔσχον εὑρεῖν· ἐν δὲ τοῖς ὑπομνήμασι τοῦ
δευτέρου Καίσαρος τοῦ κληθέντος Σεβαστοῦ, παλαι-
ότερον μὲν οὐδὲν οὐδ' ἐν τοῖσδε περὶ Παιόνων ηὗρον.
Ἰλλυριῶν δέ μοι φαίνεται χωρὶς τῶν εἰρημένων ἐθνῶν
43   καὶ ἕτερα Ῥωμαίων προϋπακοῦσαι. καὶ ὅπως μεν, οὐκ

18 After his father's death, M. Iunius Brutus was adopted by
his uncle, Q. Servilius Caepio, and known as Q. Servilius Caepio
Brutus.

under Roman rule, to Brutus Caepio, one of Gaius' assassins, and at the same time assigned Syria to Cassius, who was also one of the assassins of Gaius.[18] But these men too, engaged as they were in a war against Antony and the second Caesar, the one with the title Augustus, had no time at all to deal with the Illyrians.

14. The Paeonians are a big nation on the Ister, whose territory stretches from the Iapodes to the Dardanians. They are called Paeonians by the Greeks, but Pannonians in Latin, and are counted by the Romans as part of Illyria, as I noted earlier.[19] That is why I have decided to write about them here in this book of Illyrian history. They have been famous since the time of the Macedonians because of the Agrianes, who gave such vital assistance to Philip and Alexander, and who are Paeonians of lower Paeonia and neighbors of the Illyrians. When Cornelius' expedition against the Paeonians turned out badly, this caused a great fear of them throughout the whole of Italy, and for a long time later consuls were reluctant to march against them.[20]

15. This is all I have been able to find out about the Illyrians and Paeonians in ancient times. Not even in the diaries of the second Caesar, the one called Augustus, did I find any earlier information about the Paeonians. It seems to me, however, that there were other Illyrian peoples subject to Rome in the early period, besides the ones I have already mentioned. How this came about, I do not

40

41

42

43

[19] At 6.15 Appian has confused the Paeonians with the Pannonians, who were not the same people. Cassius Dio (49.36.6) makes the distinction clear.

[20] It is not known who this Cornelius was, or when he lived.

APPIAN

ἔγνων· οὐ γὰρ ἀλλοτρίας πράξεις ὁ Σεβαστός, ἀλλὰ
τὰς ἑαυτοῦ συνέγραφεν, ὡς δ' ἀποστάντας ἐς τοὺς
φόρους ἐπανήγαγε, καὶ ἑτέρους ὡς ἀρχῆθεν ἔτι ὄντας
αὐτονόμους εἷλε, καὶ πάντας ἐκρατύνατο ὅσοι τὰς κορυφὰς οἰκοῦσι τῶν Ἄλπεων ἢ τὰ πρόποδα, οἱ μὲν ἐς
τὴν Ἰταλίαν ἀνορῶντες, οἱ δ' ἐς τὸ πέραν Ἄλπεων,
βάρβαρα καὶ μάχιμα ἔθνη, καὶ κλοπεύοντα τὴν
44 Ἰταλίαν ὡς γείτονα. καί μοι θαῦμά ἐστιν ὅτι καὶ πολλοὶ καὶ μεγάλοι Ῥωμαίων στρατοὶ ἐπὶ Κελτοὺς καὶ
Ἴβηρας διὰ τῶν Ἄλπεων ὁδεύοντες ὑπερεῖδον τάδε τὰ
ἔθνη, καὶ οὐδὲ Γάιος Καῖσαρ, εὐτυχέστατος ἐς πολέμους ἀνήρ, ἐξήνυσεν αὐτά, ὅτε Κελτοῖς ἐπολέμει
καὶ δέκα ἔτεσιν ἀμφὶ τήνδε τὴν χώραν ἐχείμαζεν.
45 ἀλλά μοι δοκοῦσιν οἱ μέν, ἐφ' ἃ ἠρέθησαν ἐπειγόμε-
νοι, τῆς διόδου τῶν Ἄλπεων μόνης φροντίσαι, ὁ δὲ
Γάιος ἀμφί τε τὰ Κελτικὰ γενέσθαι, καὶ τῆς στάσεως
τοῦ Πομπηίου τὰ Κελτικὰ ἐπιλαβούσης τὸ τούτων
τέλος ὑπερθέσθαι. φαίνεται μὲν γὰρ καὶ Ἰλλυρίδος
ἅμα Κελτοῖς αἱρεθεὶς ἄρχειν, οὐ πάσης δ' ἄρα ἦρχεν
ἀλλ' ὅση τις ἦν τότε Ῥωμαίοις Ἰλλυρίς.
46   16. Ὁ δὲ Σεβαστὸς πάντα ἐχειρώσατο ἐντελῶς, καὶ
ἐν παραβολῇ τῆς ἀπραξίας Ἀντωνίου κατελογίσατο
τῇ βουλῇ τὴν Ἰταλίαν ἡμερῶσαι δυσμάχων ἐθνῶν
θαμινὰ ἐνοχλούντων. Ὀξυαίους μὲν δὴ καὶ Περθεη-
νάτας καὶ Βαθιάτας καὶ Ταυλαντίους καὶ Καμβαίους
καὶ Κινάμβρους καὶ Μερομέννους καὶ Πυρισσαίους
47 εἷλε δι' ὀλιγοστῆς⁶ πείρας· ἔργῳ δὲ μείζονι ἐλήφθησαν, καὶ φόρους ὅσους ἐξέλιπον ἠναγκάσθησαν ἀπο-

328

know. For Augustus wrote about his own achievements not those of other people, narrating how he reestablished rebels as tribute-paying subjects, how he conquered others who had been independent from the beginning, how he subdued all the inhabitants of the Alpine peaks and foothills, the former looking out over Italy, the latter looking across at the Alps, barbarous and warlike peoples, who used to raid the neighboring part of Italy. I am astonished   44
at how many large Roman armies crossed the Alps on their way to fight the Celts or Iberians, and ignored these peoples. Not even Gaius Caesar, a man of supreme military success, conquered them, when he fought the Celts and wintered for ten successive years in their very land. But   45
the others, I suppose, in a hurry to take up their appointment, thought only of getting across the Alps, while Gaius was busy with his Celtic campaigns, and when the civil conflict with Pompey interrupted them, postponed putting an end to the Illyrian situation. For he was given command, it appears, in Illyria as well as against the Celts—not, of course, in all of Illyria, only the part that was subject to Rome at the time.

16. When Augustus had taken complete control of the   46
state, he drew a comparison with Antony's indolence by recounting for the senate how he had freed Italy from the annoyance of repeated raids made by belligerent peoples. In a brief campaign he defeated the Oxyaei and the Pertheenates and the Bathiatae and the Taulantii and the Cambaei and the Cinambri and the Meromenni and the Pyrissaei. A greater effort was needed to overcome the   47

---

6 ὀλιγοστῆς Goukowsky: ὅλης codd.

δοῦναι, Δοκλεᾶταί τε καὶ Κάρνοι καὶ Ἰντερφρουρῖνοι
καὶ Ναρήσιοι καὶ Γλιντιδίωνες καὶ Ταυρίσκοι. ὧν
ἁλόντων οἱ ὅμοροι προσέθεντο αὐτῷ καταπλαγέντες,
Ἱππασῖνοί τε καὶ Βεσσοί. ἑτέρους δὲ αὐτῶν ἀποστάντας, Μελιτηνοὺς καὶ Κορκυρηνούς, οἳ νήσους ᾤκουν,
ἀνέστησεν ἄρδην, ὅτι ἐλῄστευον τὴν θάλασσαν· καὶ
τοὺς μὲν ἡβῶντας αὐτῶν ἔκτεινε, τοὺς δ' ἄλλους ἀπέδοτο. Λιβυρνῶν δὲ τὰς ναῦς ἀφείλετο, ὅτι καὶ οἵδε
48 ἐλῄστευον. Ἰαπόδων δὲ τῶν ἐντὸς Ἄλπεων Μοεντῖνοι
μὲν καὶ Αὐενδεᾶται προσέθεντο αὐτῷ προσιόντι,
Ἀρουπῖνοι δ', οἳ πλεῖστοι καὶ μαχιμώτατοι τῶνδε τῶν
Ἰαπόδων εἰσίν, ἐκ τῶν κωμῶν ἐς τὸ ἄστυ ἀνῳκίσαντο,
καὶ προσιόντος αὐτοῦ ἐς τὰς ὕλας συνέφυγον. ὁ δὲ
Καῖσαρ τὸ ἄστυ ἑλὼν οὐκ ἐνέπρησεν, ἐλπίσας ἐνδώσειν αὐτούς· καὶ ἐνδοῦσιν οἰκεῖν ἔδωκεν.

49   17. Μάλιστα δ' ἠνώχλησαν αὐτὸν Σαλασσοί τε καὶ
Ἰάποδες οἱ πέραν Ἄλπεων καὶ Σεγεστανοὶ καὶ Δαλμάται καὶ Δαίσιοί τε καὶ Παίονες, ὄντες ἑκὰς τοῖς
Σαλασσοῖς, οἳ κορυφὰς οἰκοῦσι τῶν Ἄλπεων, ὄρη
δύσβατα, καὶ στενὴ δίοδός ἐστιν ἐπ' αὐτὰ καὶ δυσ-
χερής· δι' ἃ καὶ ἦσαν αὐτόνομοι, καὶ τέλη τοὺς παρ-
50 οδεύοντας ᾔτουν. τούτοις Οὐέτερ ἐμπεσὼν ἀδοκήτως
τὰ στενὰ προύλαβε δι' ἐνέδρας, καὶ ἐπὶ διετὲς αὐτοὺς
ἐπολιόρκει. οἱ δὲ ἁλῶν ἀπορίᾳ, ὧν εἰσὶ μάλιστα ἐν
χρείᾳ, φρουρὰς ἐδέξαντο. καὶ Οὐέτερος ἀπελθόντος[7]

---

[7] ἀπελθόντος Goukowsky: παρελθόντος P

Docleatae and the Carni and the Interfrurini and the Naresii and the Glintidiones and the Taurisci, and to force them to pay the tribute they had stopped paying. Once they had been subdued, the neighboring Hippasini and Taurisci were terrified, and surrendered to Augustus. Others who had revolted from Rome, the Meliteni and Corcyreans, who were island dwellers, he utterly destroyed, because they resorted to piracy on the high seas: he killed all their young men and sold the others into slavery. Because the Liburnians also took to raiding, he confiscated their ships. Among the Iapodes who lived in the Alps, the Moentini and Avendeatae went over to his side when he approached them. The Aroupini, the most numerous and warlike of these Iapodes, moved from the villages into the town, but fled into the woods at his arrival. Octavian took the town, but did not burn it, in the hope that they would give themselves up. When they did so, he let them live there. 48

17. Those giving him particular trouble were the Salassi and transalpine Iapodes and the Segestani and the Dalmatians and the Daesii and the Paeonians, who live far from the Salassi in the high Alps, difficult mountains to climb, with a narrow and steep path up to them. Because of this they were independent, and imposed tolls on those who traveled through their territory. Vetus launched a surprise attack on them, used a trick to get control of the passes before they did, and blockaded them for two years.[21] When they ran short of salt, which they use particularly heavily, they admitted a garrison. As soon as Vetus left, 49 50

[21] The command of C. Antistius Vetus (consul 30) against the Salassi was in 35/4.

ἀποστάντες τὰς φρουρὰς ἐξέβαλον εὐθύς, καὶ τὰ
στενὰ κρατυνάμενοι τοὺς ἐπιπεμπομένους σφίσιν ὑπὸ
τοῦ Καίσαρος διέπαιζον, οὐδὲν δρᾶν μέγα ἔχοντας.
51 ὅθεν αὐτοῖς ὁ Καῖσαρ, προσδοκωμένου τοῦ πρὸς
Ἀντώνιον πολέμου, συνέθετο αὐτονόμους ἐάσειν, καὶ
ἀκολάστους τῶν ἐπὶ Οὐέτερι πραχθέντων. οἱ δ᾽ ἅτε ἐν
ὑποψίᾳ ταῦτ᾽ ἔχοντες ἄλας πολλοὺς ἐσώρευον, καὶ
τὴν Ῥωμαίων κατέθεον, μέχρι Μεσσάλας Κορουῖνος
αὐτοῖς ἐπιπεμφθεὶς λιμῷ παρεστήσατο.

52   18. Καὶ Σαλασσοὶ μὲν οὕτως ἐλήφθησαν, Ἰάποδες
δὲ οἱ πέραν Ἄλπεων, ἔθνος ἰσχυρόν τε καὶ ἄγριον, δὶς
μὲν ἀπεώσαντο Ῥωμαίους, ἔτεσί που ἀγχοῦ εἴκοσιν,
Ἀκυληίαν δ᾽ ἐπέδραμον καὶ Τεργηστὸν Ῥωμαίων
ἄποικον ἐσκύλευσαν. ἐπιόντος δ᾽ αὐτοῖς τοῦ Καίσαρος ὁδὸν ἀνάντη καὶ τραχεῖαν· οἱ δ᾽ ἔτι μᾶλλον αὐτὴν
53 ἐδυσχέραινον αὐτῷ, τὰ δένδρα κόπτοντες. ὡς δ᾽ ἀνῆλ-
θεν, ἐς τὴν ἄλλην ὕλην αὐτοὶ συνέφυγον καὶ προσι-
όντα ἐλόχων. ὁ δέ (ὑπώπτευε γὰρ ἀεί τι τοιοῦτον) ἐς
τὰς ἀκρωρείας τινὰς ἔπεμπεν, οἳ ἑκατέρωθεν αὐτῷ
συνέθεον προβαίνοντι διὰ τοῦ χθαμαλοῦ καὶ κόπτοντι
τὴν ὕλην· οἱ δὲ Ἰάποδες ἐπεξέθεον μὲν ἐκ τῶν ἐνέδρων
καὶ πολλοὺς ἐτίτρωσκον, ὑπὸ δὲ τῶν ἐν τοῖς ἄκροις
ἐπιτρεχόντων κατεκόπτοντο οἱ πλείους. οἱ δὲ λοιποὶ
πάλιν ἐς τὰ λάσια συνέφευγον, τὴν πόλιν ἐκλιπόντες,
ᾗ ὄνομα Τέρπωνος. καὶ αὐτὴν ὁ Καῖσαρ ἑλὼν οὐκ

however, they revolted and immediately expelled the garrison, and having taken control of the passes, made fun of the troops Octavian sent against them, unable, as they were, to make any substantial progress. In view of this, with war against Antony expected, Octavian agreed to leave them independent and unpunished for their treatment of Vetus. But they found this suspicious, and stockpiling large supplies of salt, continued to raid Roman territory. Eventually, Messalla Corvinus was sent against them and starved them into submission.[22]

18. This was how the Selassi were subjected. The transalpine Iapodes, on the other hand, a powerful and fierce people, repelled the Romans twice in the space of about twenty years, made an attack on Aquileia and plundered the Roman colony of Tergestus. Octavian moved against them up a steep and rough road, which they made even more difficult for him by cutting down trees. When he reached the top, they fled to another part of the forest, where they set an ambush for him as he advanced. He was always suspicious of this sort of thing, and sent some men to occupy the ridges, who kept pace with him on either side as he moved forward over the lower ground cutting his way through the trees. The Iapodes dashed out from their place of ambush and wounded many Romans, but most of them were cut down by the Romans attacking from the high ground. The survivors escaped back into the undergrowth and abandoned their town, which was called Terponus. Octavian took possession of it, but did not burn

[22] A command of M. Valerius Messalla Corvinus (consul 31) against the Selassi is not otherwise recorded. The Selassi were finally subdued in 25.

ἐνέπρησεν, ἐλπίσας καὶ τούσδε ἐνδώσειν· καὶ ἐνέδω-
καν.

54   19. Ἐπὶ δ' ἑτέραν πόλιν ἐχώρει, Μέτουλον, ἣ τῶν
Ἰαπόδων ἐστὶ κεφαλή, κεῖται δ' ἐν ὄρει σφόδρα ὑλώ-
δει ἐπὶ δύο λόφων, οὓς διαιρεῖ χαράδρα στενή. καὶ ἡ
νεότης ἦν ἀμφὶ τοὺς τρισχιλίους μαχίμους τε καὶ
σφόδρα εὐόπλους· οἳ Ῥωμαίους τὰ τείχη σφῶν περι-
στάντας εὐκόλως ἀπεκρούοντο. οἱ δὲ χῶμα ἤγειρον·
καὶ οἱ Μέτουλοι τό τε χῶμα νυκτὸς καὶ ἡμέρας ἐκτρέ-
χοντες ἠνώχλουν, καὶ τοὺς ἄνδρας ἀπὸ τοῦ τείχους
μηχαναῖς κατεπόνουν, ἃς ἐσχήκεσαν ἐκ τοῦ πολέμου
ὃν Δέκμος Βροῦτος ἐνταῦθα ἐπολέμησεν Ἀντωνίῳ τε
55   καὶ τῷ Σεβαστῷ. πονοῦντος δὲ κἀκείνοις ἤδη τοῦ τείχους, οἴδ' ὑπετείχισαν ἔνδοθεν, καὶ τὸ κεκμηκὸς ἐκλιπόντες μετεπήδησαν ἐς τὸ νεότευκτον· οἱ δὲ Ῥωμαῖοι
τὸ μὲν ἐκλειφθὲν λαβόντες ἐνέπρησαν, κατὰ δὲ τοῦ
ἄλλου δύο χώματα ἔχουν, καὶ ἀπ' αὐτῶν γεφύρας
τέσσαρας ἐξέτεινον ἐς τὸ τεῖχος. γενομένων δὲ τούτων
ὁ Καῖσαρ περιέπεμψέ τινας ἐς τὰ ὀπίσθια τῆς πόλεως,
περισπᾶν τοὺς Μετούλους, τοῖς δ' ἄλλοις προσέταξε
περᾶν ἐς τὰ τείχη διὰ τῶν γεφυρῶν. καὶ αὐτὸς ἐς
ὑψηλὸν πύργον ἀναβὰς ἑώρα.

56   20. Οἱ βάρβαροι δὲ τοῖς περῶσιν ὑπήντων τε ἐκ
μετώπου κατὰ τάχος,[8] καὶ ὑφεδρεύοντες ἕτεροι τὰς γεφύρας μακροῖς δόρασιν ὑπεκίνουν, μᾶλλόν τε ἐθάρ-
ρησαν μιᾶς γεφύρας καὶ δευτέρας ἐπ' ἐκείνῃ πεσού-

------

[8] τάχος P: τὸ τεῖχος BJ

it, in the hope that these too would give themselves up. And they did.

19. He then advanced to another town, called Metulum, which is the capital of the Iapodes. It is situated on a heavily wooded hill on two heights divided by a narrow ravine. The town had about three thousand young men, ready for battle and extremely well armed, and they easily beat off the Roman force surrounding the walls. So the Romans began to build a mound, and the people of Metulum sent out sorties day and night to damage it, while from their position on the walls they fired at the enemy using artillery acquired in the war that Decimus Brutus fought there against Antony and Augustus.[23] When their wall too began to give way, they built another wall inside it, abandoned the damaged one and jumped over to the new one. The Romans occupied the abandoned wall, burned it and set about raising two mounds to deal with the new wall, to which they extended four bridges from the mounds. While this was going on, Octavian sent some men round to the back of the town to distract the Metulians, and ordered the others to attack the wall across the bridges. He himself climbed a high tower to view the situation.

20. The barbarians quickly confronted the Romans crossing the bridges face to face, while others hid under the bridges and stabbed upward with their long spears. They were greatly encouraged when one bridge, then a

54

55

56

[23] Appian is confused. Decimus Iunius Brutus did fight Marc Antony, but at Mutina in Gaul, not in Illyria. Gaius Antonius was besieged, and captured, by Marcus Iunius Brutus at Apollonia in Illyria in 43.

σης. ὡς δὲ καὶ ἡ τρίτη συνέπεσε, φόβος ἤδη παντελὴς
τοὺς Ῥωμαίους ἐπεῖχε, καὶ οὐδεὶς τῆς τετάρτης ἐπέβαινεν, ἕως ὁ Καῖσαρ ἐκ τοῦ πύργου καταθορὼν ὠνεί-
διζεν αὐτούς. ἀλλὰ καὶ ὡς οὐκ ἐρεθιζομένων, αὐτὸς
57 ἀσπίδα λαβὼν ἐπὶ τὴν γέφυραν ἵετο δρόμῳ. συνέθεον
δ᾽ αὐτῷ τῶν ἡγεμόνων Ἀγρίππας τε καὶ Ἱέρων[9] καὶ ὁ
σωματοφύλαξ Λοῦπος[10] καὶ Ἀονιόλας,[11] τέσσαρες
οἵδε μόνοι, καὶ τῶν ὑπασπιστῶν ὀλίγοι. ἤδη δ᾽ αὐτοῦ
τὴν γέφυραν περῶντος, ἐν αἰδοῖ γενόμενος ὁ στρατὸς
ἀνεπήδησεν ἄθρους. καὶ πάλιν ἡ γέφυρα βαρηθεῖσα
καταπίπτει, καὶ οἱ ἄνδρες ὑπ᾽ αὐτῆς ἀθρόοι κατεχών-
νυντο, καὶ οἱ μὲν ἀπέθανον αὐτῶν, οἱ δὲ συντριβέντες
58 ἐφέροντο. ὁ δὲ Καῖσαρ ἐπλήγη μὲν τὸ σκέλος τὸ δεξιὸν καὶ τοὺς βραχίονας ἄμφω, ἀνέδραμε δ᾽ ὅμως
εὐθὺς ἐπὶ τὸν πύργον μετὰ τῶν συμβόλων, καὶ ἑαυτὸν
ἔδειξεν ἐρρωμένον, μή τις ὡς ἀποθανόντος γένοιτο
θόρυβος. ἵνα δὲ μηδ᾽ οἱ πολέμιοι νομίσειαν αὐτὸν ἐνδώσειν ἀναχωρήσαντα, εὐθὺς ἑτέρας ἐπήγνυτο γεφύρας. ὃ καὶ μάλιστα κατέπληξε τοὺς Μετούλους ὡς
ὑπὸ γνώμης ἀμάχου πολεμουμένους.

59   21. Καὶ τῆς ἐπιούσης πρεσβευσάμενοι πρὸς αὐτὸν
ὁμήρους τε πεντήκοντα ἔδοσαν, οὓς ὁ Καῖσαρ ἐπελέ-
ξατο, καὶ φρουρὰν ὑποσχόμενοι δέξεσθαι τὸν ὑψη-
λότερον λόφον τοῖς φρουροῖς ἀπέλιπον, αὐτοὶ δὲ μετ-

---

9 Ἱέρων codd: Νέρων prop. Schweig: Κικέρων prop. Goukowsky   10 Λοῦπος Goukowsky: Λοῦτος PB
11 Ἀονιόλας Goukowsky: Οὐόλας P

second, collapsed. And when the third one went, a general panic affected the Romans, and no one would venture onto the fourth bridge, until Octavian jumped down from his tower and reprimanded the men. As they were still not roused to action, he grabbed a spear himself and ran onto the bridge. Of his officers, Agrippa and Hiero ran beside 57 him, along with his bodyguard, Lupus, and Aviola, just the four of them, and a few shield bearers.[24] He had almost reached the other end of the bridge, when the troops were shamed into charging after him in large numbers. Again the bridge could not take the weight of the men and it collapsed, and those on it fell on top of each other, some dying, others carried away with broken bones. Octavian 58 was wounded in his right leg and both arms, but immediately scrambled onto the tower with his insignia of rank, to show that he was alive and well, and avoid any confusion arising from a report of his death. And to prevent the enemy from thinking that he would give up and withdraw, he immediately started to build new bridges. This particularly shocked the inhabitants of the town, as they seemed to be fighting against irresistible willpower.

21. Next day the Metuli sent ambassadors to Octavian 59 and gave him fifty hostages whom he chose himself. They also undertook to accept a garrison to be stationed on the higher hill which they evacuated and went across to the

[24] Of Octavian's four companions, only Agrippa is identifiable (as the famous M. Vipsanius Agrippa). The other names have been corrupted. Various suggestions have been made, perhaps most interestingly Cicero (for Hiero), the son of the great Cicero.

APPIAN

εχώρουν ἐς τὸν ἕτερον. ἐπεὶ δὲ ἐσελθοῦσα ἡ φρουρὰ
τὰ ὅπλα αὐτοὺς ἐκέλευεν ἀποθέσθαι, οἱ δὲ ἠγανάκτη-
σάν τε, καὶ τὰ γύναια σφῶν καὶ τοὺς παῖδας ἐς τὸ
βουλευτήριον συγκλείσαντες, καὶ φυλακὴν ἐπιστή-
σαντες, οἷς εἴρητο, εἴ τι ἀηδὲς γίγνοιτο περὶ αὐτούς,
ἐμπρῆσαι τὸ βουλευτήριον, ἐπεχείρουν τοῖς Ῥωμαίοις
60 αὐτοὶ μετ' ἀπονοίας. οἷα δ' ὑψηλοτέροις ἐπιχειροῦντες
ἐκ ταπεινοῦ, συνεχώσθησαν ἀθρόοι, καὶ οἱ φύλακες
τὸ βουλευτήριον κατέπρησαν, πολλαί τε τῶν γυναικῶν ἑαυτάς τε καὶ τὰ τέκνα διεχρῶντο, αἱ δὲ καὶ ζῶν-
τα ἔτι φέρουσαι ἐς τὸ πῦρ ἐνήλαντο, ὡς ἀπολέσθαι
τῶν Μετούλων τήν τε νεότητα πᾶσαν ἐν τῇ μάχῃ καὶ
61 τῶν ἀχρείων τὸ πλέον τῷ πυρί. συγκατεφλέγη δὲ
αὐτοῖς καὶ ἡ πόλις, καὶ οὐδὲν ἦν ἴχνος μεγίστης
ἐκεῖθι γενομένης. Μετούλου δ' ἁλούσης οἱ λοιποὶ τῶν
Ἰαπόδων καταπλαγέντες ἑαυτοὺς ἐπέτρεψαν τῷ Καίσαρι. Ἰάποδες μὲν οὖν οἱ πέραν Ἄλπεων τότε πρῶτον
Ῥωμαίων ὑπήκουσαν· καὶ αὐτῶν Ποσηνοὺς ἀποχωρή-
σαντος τοῦ Καίσαρος ἀποστάντας ἐπιπεμφθεὶς αὐτοῖς
Μᾶρκος Ἕλουιος εἷλε, καὶ τοὺς μὲν αἰτίους ἔκτεινε,
τοὺς δὲ λοιποὺς ἀπέδοτο.

62   22. Ἐς δὲ τὴν Σεγεστικὴν γῆν οἱ Ῥωμαῖοι δὶς
πρότερον ἐμβαλόντες οὔτε ὅμηρον οὔτε ἄλλο τι εἰλή-
φεσαν· ὅθεν ἦσαν ἐπὶ φρονήματος οἱ Σεγεστανοί. ὁ
δὲ Καῖσαρ αὐτοῖς ἐπήει διὰ τῆς Παιόνων γῆς, οὔπω
63 Ῥωμαίοις οὐδὲ τῆσδε ὑπηκόου γενομένης. ὑλώδης δ'
ἐστὶν ἡ Παιόνων, καὶ ἐπιμήκης ἐξ Ἰαπόδων ἐπὶ Δαρδάνους. καὶ οὐ πόλεις ᾤκουν οἱ Παίονες οἵδε, ἀλλ'

338

other hill. But when the garrison troops entering the town ordered them to lay down their weapons, they were extremely angry. They shut their wives and children in the senate house, set guards over it, and told them to burn the building if anything bad happened to them. They then launched a desperate attack on the Romans, but advancing from below against men on an elevated position, they were completely wiped out. The guards set fire to the senate house, and many women killed themselves and their children, while others leaped into the fire with their children alive in their arms. And so all the young men of Metulum died in the battle, and most of the civilians in the fire. The town was also consumed with them in the flames, and no trace of it was left, even though it had been the biggest town in the area. The remaining Iapodes were horrified by the sack of Metulum, and surrendered themselves to Octavian. So it was at this time that the transalpine Iapodes first became subjects of Rome. When Octavian withdrew, the Poseni revolted and Marcus Helvius was sent against them. He defeated them, executed those responsible, and sold the rest into slavery.[25]

22. On two previous occasions, Rome invaded the land of Segesta, but had failed to take hostages or anything else. As a result, the Segestani had become overconfident. Octavian advanced on them through Paeonian territory, which was also not yet subject to Rome. Paeonia is a heavily wooded country, stretching from the Iapodes to the Dardanians. These Paeonians did not live in towns, but

60

61

62

63

[25] Metulum was destroyed in 35. M. Helvius' expedition was in 34.

ἀγροὺς ἢ κώμας κατὰ συγγένειαν· οὐδ᾽ ἐς βουλευ-
τήρια κοινὰ συνῄεσαν, οὐδ᾽ ἄρχοντες αὐτοῖς ἦσαν ἐπὶ
πᾶσιν. οἱ δ᾽ ἐν ἡλικίᾳ μάχης ἐς δέκα μυριάδας συν-
ετέλουν. ἀλλ᾽ οὐδ᾽ οὗτοι συνῄεσαν ἀθρόοι δι᾽ ἀναρ-
64 χίαν. προσιόντος δ᾽ αὐτοῖς τοῦ Καίσαρος, ἐς τὰς ὕλας
ὑποφυγόντες τοὺς ἀποσκιδναμένους τῶν στρατιωτῶν
ἀνῄρουν. ὁ δὲ Καῖσαρ ἕως μὲν ἤλπιζεν αὐτοὺς ἀφίξε-
σθαι πρὸς αὐτόν, οὔτε τὰς κώμας οὔτε τοὺς ἀγροὺς
65 ἐλυμαίνετο, οὐκ ἀπαντώντων δὲ πάντα ἐνεπίμπρη καὶ
ἔκειρεν ἐπὶ ἡμέρας ὀκτώ, ἐς ὃ διῆλθεν ἐς τὴν Σεγεστανῶν, καὶ τήνδε Παιόνων οὖσαν, ἐπὶ τοῦ Σάου ποταμοῦ, ἐν ᾧ καὶ πόλις ἔστιν ἐχυρά, τῷ τε ποταμῷ καὶ
τάφρῳ μεγίστῃ διειλημμένη, διὸ καὶ μάλιστα αὐτῆς
ἔχρῃζεν ὁ Καῖσαρ, ὡς ταμιείῳ χρησόμενος ἐς τὸν
Δακῶν καὶ Βαστερνῶν πόλεμον, οἳ πέραν εἰσὶ τοῦ
Ἴστρου, λεγομένου μὲν ἐνταῦθα Δανουβίου, γιγνομέ-
66 νου δὲ μετ᾽ ὀλίγον Ἴστρου. ἐμβάλλει δ᾽ ὁ Σάος ἐς τὸν
Ἴστρον· καὶ αἱ νῆες ἐν τῷ Σάῳ Καίσαρι ἐγίγνοντο,
αἳ ἐς τὸν Δανούβιον αὐτῷ τὴν ἀγορὰν διοίσειν ἔμελλον.

67   23. Διὰ μὲν δὴ ταῦτα τῆς Σεγέστης ἔχρῃζεν ὁ
Καῖσαρ· προσιόντι δὲ αὐτῷ οἱ Σεγεστανοὶ προσέπεμ-
ψαν, πυνθανόμενοι τίνος χρῄζει. ὁ δὲ φρουρὰν ἐσα-
γαγεῖν ἔφη, καὶ ὁμήρους ἑκατὸν λαβεῖν, ἵν᾽ ἀσφαλῶς
ταμιείῳ τῇ πόλει χρῷτο ἐπὶ Δάκας. ᾔτει δὲ καὶ σῖτον,
ὅσον δύναιντο φέρειν. ταῦθ᾽ οἱ μὲν πρωτεύοντες ἠξίουν δοῦναι· ὁ δὲ δῆμος ἐξαγριαίνων τὰ μὲν ὅμηρα
διδόμενα περιεῖδεν, ὅτι ἴσως οὐ παρὰ σφῶν ἀλλὰ τῶν

they formed kinship groups on the land and in villages. They did not meet in representative councils, and they had no overall political leadership. Although they could muster nearly one hundred thousand men of fighting age, even so they never came together in a single force because of the lack of leadership. When Octavian advanced against 64 them, they took refuge in the woods, and killed any Roman stragglers, but he refrained from ravaging their fields or villages as long as he thought they might come over to him of their own accord. But when they failed to present them- 65 selves, he cut and burned everything for eight days, until he came to the territory of Segesta. This is also in Paeonia, situated on the river Sava, where there is a secure town, protected by the river and a very big ditch. For this reason Octavian was particularly keen to have it, to use as a base for the war against the Dacians and Bastarnae. These lived on the other side of the Ister, called the Danube at this point: it becomes the Ister a little further downstream. The Sava flows into the Ister. Octavian constructed ships 66 on the Sava, intending to use them to bring supplies to him on the Danube.

23. These, then, were the reasons Octavian needed 67 Segesta. As he approached, the Segestans sent representatives to ask what he wanted. He said he wanted to station a garrison there and to take one hundred hostages, so that he could use the town as a safe base against the Dacians. He also demanded as much grain as they could give him. The leading men of the town were minded to agree to these terms, but the ordinary people were angry. They put up with the handing over of hostages, perhaps because the children came from the leading families, not their own,

APPIAN

68 πρωτευόντων παῖδες ἦσαν, προσιούσης δὲ τῆς φρου-
ρᾶς τὴν ὄψιν οὐκ ἐνεγκόντες ὁρμῇ μανιώδει τὰς πύλας
αὖθις ἀπέκλειον καὶ αὑτοὺς τοῖς τείχεσιν ἐπέστησαν.
ὁ οὖν Καῖσαρ τόν τε ποταμὸν ἐγεφύρου, καὶ χάρακας
καὶ τάφρους πάντοθεν ἐποιεῖτο, ἀποτειχίσας δ' αὐτοὺς
δύο χώματα ἔχου. οἷς ἐπέδραμον μὲν οἱ Σεγεστανοὶ
πολλάκις, οὐ δυνηθέντες δ' ἑλεῖν λαμπάδας καὶ πῦρ
πολὺ ἄνωθεν ἐπέβαλλον. προσιούσης δ' αὐτοῖς Παιόνων ἑτέρων βοηθείας, ὁ Καῖσαρ ὑπαντήσας ἐνήδρευσεν αὐτήν· καὶ οἱ μὲν ἀνηρέθησαν, οἱ δ' ἔφυγον, καὶ
οὐδεὶς ἔτι Παιόνων ἐβοήθει.

69   24. Οἱ Σεγεστανοὶ δὲ πᾶσαν πολιορκίαν ὑποστάντες ἡμέρᾳ τριακοστῇ κατὰ κράτος ἐλήφθησαν, καὶ
τότε πρῶτον ἤρξαντο ἱκετεύειν. καὶ αὐτοὺς ὁ Καῖσαρ
ἐπαίνῳ τε τῆς ἀρετῆς καὶ ἐλέῳ τῆς ἱκεσίας οὔτε ἔκτεινεν οὔτε ἀνέστησεν, ἀλλὰ χρήμασιν ἐζημίωσε, καὶ
τῆς πόλεως μέρος διατειχίσας ἐσήγαγεν ἐς αὐτὸ
70 φρουρὰν πέντε καὶ εἴκοσι σπειρῶν. καὶ ὁ μὲν τάδ'
ἐργασάμενος ἐς Ῥώμην ἀνέζευξεν, ὡς ἦρος ἐπανήξων
ἐς τὴν Ἰλλυρίδα. φήμης δ' ἐπιδραμούσης ὅτι τὴν
φρουρὰν οἱ Σεγεστανοὶ διέφθειραν, ἐξέθορε χειμῶνος.
καὶ τὸ μὲν τέλος τῆς φήμης ψευδὲς ηὗρε, τὴν δὲ
αἰτίαν ἀληθῆ· ἐγεγόνεσαν γὰρ ἐν κινδύνῳ, τῶν Σεγεστανῶν αὐτοὺς ἄφνω περιστάντων, καὶ πολλοὺς τὸ
αἰφνίδιον ἀπωλωλέκει, τῆς δ' ἐπιούσης προελθόντες
ἐκράτουν τῶν Σεγεστανῶν. ὁ οὖν Καῖσαρ ἐπὶ Δαλμάτας μετῄει, γένος ἕτερον Ἰλλυριῶν, Ταυλαντίοις
ὅμορον.

342

but they could not bear to see the garrison troops ap-   68
proaching, and on a mad impulse closed the gates again,
and stationed themselves on the walls. At this, Octavian
bridged the river, dug ditches and built palisades everywhere, and having cut the town off, began to raise
two siege mounds. The Segestans made frequent sorties
against them, and although they were unable to destroy
them, they threw a large number of torches and firebrands
down on them. When a relief force from other Paeonians
was approaching the town, Octavian went to confront
them and set an ambush for them: some were killed, the
rest fled, and no Paeonians came to their assistance any-
more.

24. Having endured the whole siege, Segesta was cap-   69
tured in an assault on the thirtieth day, and only then for
the first time did its people begin to present themselves as
suppliants. Out of admiration for their courage and pity
for their entreaties, Octavian neither executed nor banished them, but punished them with a fine. He walled off
a section of the town, installed a garrison of twenty-five
cohorts in it, and, with his work complete, returned to   70
Rome. He intended to return to Illyria in the spring, but
when a rumor spread that the Segestans had massacred
the garrison, he rushed over during the winter. He discov-
ered, however, that the substance of the rumor was false,
but that there was a real reason for it. The garrison had
been in danger when the inhabitants of Segesta suddenly
surrounded it, and the element of surprise had caused the
death of many, but next day the troops made a sortie and
brought the population under control. So, Octavian then
attacked the Dalmatians, another Illyrian people, neighbors of the Taulantii.

APPIAN

71 25. Οἱ Δαλμάται δ᾽ ἐξ οὗ τὰς ὑπὸ Γαβινίῳ πέντε[12]
τάξεις ἀνῃρήκεσαν καὶ τὰ σημεῖα εἰλήφεσαν, ἐπαρ-
θέντες ἐπὶ τῷδε τὰ ὅπλα οὐκ ἀπετέθειντο ἔτεσιν ἤδη
δέκα, ἀλλὰ καὶ τοῦ Καίσαρος ἐπιόντος αὐτοῖς συμμα-
72 χήσειν ἀλλήλοις συνετίθεντο. καὶ ἦσαν οἱ μαχιμώτατοι μυρίων καὶ δισχιλίων πλείους, ὧν στρατηγὸν
Οὐέρσον αἱροῦνται. ὁ δὲ Προμόναν αὖθις, τὴν τῶν
Λιβυρνῶν πόλιν, καταλαβὼν ὠχύρου, καὶ τἆλλα οὖσαν ἐκφυῶς ὀχυρωτάτην· ὄρειον γάρ ἐστι τὸ χωρίον,
καὶ αὐτῷ περίκεινται λόφοι πάντοθεν ὀξεῖς οἷα πρίο-
νες. ἐν μὲν δὴ τῇ πόλει τὸ πλέον ἦν, ἐν δὲ τοῖς λόφοις
διέθηκεν Οὐέρσος φρούρια· καὶ πάντες ἐφεώρων τὰ
73 Ῥωμαίων ἀφ᾽ ὑψηλοῦ. ὁ δὲ Καῖσαρ ἐς μὲν τὸ φανερὸν
πάντας ἀπετείχιζε, λάθρᾳ δὲ τοὺς εὐτολμοτάτους
ἔπεμπε ζητεῖν ἄνοδον ἐς τὸν ἀκρότατον τῶν λόφων.
καὶ οἱ μέν, τῆς ὕλης αὐτοὺς ἐπικαλυπτούσης, νυκτὸς
ἐμπίπτουσι τοῖς φύλαξιν εὐναζομένοις, καὶ κτείνουσιν
αὐτούς, καὶ τῷ Καίσαρι κατέσεισαν ὑπὸ λύγῃ· ὁ δὲ
τῆς τε πόλεως ἐς πεῖραν ᾔει τῷ πλέονι στρατῷ, καὶ
ἐς τὸ εἰλημμένον ἄκρον ἑτέρους ἐφ᾽ ἑτέροις ἔπεμπεν,
74 οἳ τοῖς ἄλλοις λόφοις ἐπικατῄεσαν. φόβος τε καὶ
θόρυβος ἦν τοῖς βαρβάροις ὁμοῦ πᾶσιν ἐπιχειρουμέ-
νοις πάντοθεν· μάλιστα δὲ οἱ ἐν τοῖς λόφοις ἔδεισαν
διὰ τὸ ἄνυδρον, μὴ τῶν διόδων ἀφαιρεθῶσιν. καὶ
συμφεύγουσιν ἐς τὴν Προμόναν.

---

[12] πέντε codd: πεντεκαίδεκα Goukowsky

25. After they had destroyed the five companies under 71 the command of Gabinius and taken the standards, the Dalmatians, encouraged by this success, did not lay down their arms for the next ten years.[26] When Octavian attacked, the Dalmatians all made a mutual defensive alliance. They had more than twelve thousand fighting men, 72 and choose Versus as commander in chief. He again occupied Promona,[27] the town belonging to the Liburnians, and fortified it, even though it was naturally extremely well protected. For it is in a mountainous location, surrounded by sharp ridges on all sides that look like the teeth of a saw. Most of the Dalmatian forces remained in the town, but Versus did station some guard posts on the ridges, and they all looked down on the Romans from their high position. In full view, Octavian began to build a wall to cut 73 them all off, but secretly sent his bravest men to look for a route up to the highest ridges. With the woods hiding them, these men fell on the sleeping guards at night, killing them, and signaling to Octavian in the dawn light. He advanced to make an attempt on the town with the main part of his force, and sent one unit after another onto the ridge that had been captured, from where they moved down onto the other heights. The barbarians were alarmed 74 and confused by being attacked from all directions at the same time. Those on the hills had no water supply and were, therefore, particularly afraid that they would be cut off. So they all retreated together into Promona.

[26] Appian (*Ill.* 12.35–36) earlier talked of fifteen cohorts (*speirai*) under Gabinius. It is not clear whether the five companies (*taxeis*) mentioned here are different units, or the number five is a mistake. [27] For the earlier occupation of Promona, see above, *Ill.* 12.34.

APPIAN

75   26. Ὁ δὲ Καῖσαρ αὐτήν τε καὶ δύο λόφους, οἳ ἔτι
ἐκρατοῦντο ὑπὸ τῶν πολεμίων, ὁμοῦ περιετείχιζε, τεσσαράκοντα σταδίων περίμετρον. κἀν τούτῳ Τέστιμον
Δαλμάτην, στρατὸν ἕτερον ἄγοντα τοῖς ἐν Πρωμόνῃ
συμμάχον, ὑπαντήσας ἐδίωκεν ἐς τὰ ὄρη, καὶ ἐφορῶν-
τος ἔτι τοῦ Τεστίμου τὴν Πρωμόναν εἷλεν, οὔπω τῆς
περιτειχίσεως τετελεσμένης. ἐκδραμόντων γὰρ τῶν
ἔνδον καὶ συνελαυνομένων ὀξέως, οἱ Ῥωμαῖοι φεύγουσιν αὐτοῖς ἐς τὴν πόλιν συνεσέπεσον, καὶ τὸ τρίτον
τούτων ἔνδον ἔκτειναν· οἱ λοιποὶ δ᾽ ἐς τὴν ἄκραν ἀνέ-
76 δραμον. καὶ σπεῖρα Ῥωμαίων ἐφύλασσεν αὐτοὺς ἐπὶ
τῶν πυλῶν. ᾗ προσπίπτουσιν οἱ βάρβαροι νυκτὸς
τετάρτης, καὶ ἐξέλιπεν ἡ σπεῖρα τὰς πύλας ὑπὸ δέους.
ὁ δὲ Καῖσαρ τοὺς μὲν πολεμίους ἀνέκοψε τῆς ὁρμῆς,
καὶ τῆς ἐπιούσης εἷλε παραδόντας ἑαυτούς· τὴν δὲ
σπεῖραν ᾗ τὸ φυλάκιον ἐξέλιπε διακληρώσας, ἐζημίωσε θανάτῳ τὸ δέκατον, καὶ λοχαγοὺς ἐπὶ τῷ δεκάτῳ
δύο. καὶ τοῖς λοιποῖς ἐκέλευεν ἐκείνου τοῦ θέρους κρι-
θὴν ἀντὶ σίτου τραφῆναι δίδοσθαι.

77   27. Οὕτω μὲν ἑάλω Πρωμόνα, Τέστιμος δ᾽ ὁρῶν
διεσκέδασε τὸν στρατὸν ἑαυτοῦ, φεύγειν ἄλλους ἀλ-
λαχοῦ· ὅθεν αὐτοὺς οὐκ ἐδύναντο οἱ Ῥωμαῖοι διώκειν
ἐς πολύ, τήν τε διαίρεσιν σφῶν τὴν ἐς πολλὰ δείσαν-
τες, καὶ τὴν ἀπειρίαν τῶν ὁδῶν καὶ τὰ ἴχνη τῆς φυγῆς
78 συγκεχυμένα. Συνόδιον δ᾽ αἱροῦσι πόλιν ἐν ἀρχῇ τῆς
ὕλης, ἐν ᾗ τὸν Γαβινίου στρατὸν ἐνήδρευσαν οἱ Δαλμάται περὶ φάραγγι βαθείᾳ καὶ ἐπιμήκει καὶ μέσῃ
δύο ὀρῶν, ἔνθα καὶ τὸν Καίσαρα ἐνήδρευον. ὁ δὲ τό

346

26. Octavian now surrounded the town and the two   75
ridges still held by the enemy with a wall forty stades long.
Meanwhile, Testimus, a Dalmatian, brought up another
army to give assistance to those in Promona, but Octavian
confronted him, chased him into the mountains, and with
Testimus still looking on, captured Promona before the
encircling wall had been completed. For when the defenders made a sortie and met with a sharp reverse, the
Romans rushed with them into the town as they fled, and
killed a third of their force inside the walls. The rest ran   76
for protection up to the citadel, where a Roman cohort
took up guard at the gates. Four nights later the barbarians
attacked and the cohort abandoned the gates in fear, but
Octavian halted the enemy's charge and next day took
them prisoner when they gave themselves up. He made
the cohort who had abandoned their guard post draw lots,
and had every tenth man punished by death, along with
two centurions as well. He also gave orders that all the
others were to be given rations of barley that summer
rather than wheat.

27. This was how Promona was captured. When Testi-   77
mus saw it, he disbanded his army, telling them all to flee
in different directions. Because of this the Romans were
not able to pursue them very far, as they were afraid to
divide their force into many units, they did not know the
roads, and the tracks of the fugitives were all confused.
They do capture the town of Synodium at the edge of the   78
forest where the Dalmatians had ambushed Gabinius'
force in a deep and long ravine between two mountains.
Here too they waited in ambush for Octavian. But, after

τε Συνόδιον ἐνέπρησε, καὶ ἐς τὰ ὅρη περιπέμψας ἄνω
στρατὸν ἑκατέρωθεν αὐτῷ συμπαρομαρτεῖν, αὐτὸς ἤει
διὰ τῆς φάραγγος, κόπτων τὴν ὕλην καὶ τὰς πόλεις
αἱρῶν, καὶ πάντα ἐμπιπρὰς ὅσα κατὰ τὸν Ἀδρίαν[13]
79 ᾕρει. πολιορκουμένης δὲ πόλεως Σετουΐας, ἐπῄει τις
αὐτοῖς συμμαχία βαρβάρων, ἣν ὁ Καῖσαρ ὑπαντήσας ἐκώλυσεν ἐσδραμεῖν ἐς τὴν Σετουΐαν. κἀν τῷ
πόνῳ τῷδε ἐπλήγη λίθῳ τὸ γόνυ, καὶ ἐς πολλὰς
ἡμέρας ἐθεραπεύετο. ῥαΐσας δὲ ἐς Ῥώμην ἐπανῆλθεν,
ὑπατεύσων σὺν Οὐολκατίῳ Τύλλῳ, Στατίλιον Ταῦρον
ἐς τὰ λοιπὰ τοῦ πολέμου καταλιπών.

80   28. Νουμηνίᾳ δ᾽ ἔτους ἀρξάμενος ὑπατεύειν, καὶ
τὴν ἀρχὴν αὐτῆς ἡμέρας παραδοὺς Αὐτρωνίῳ Παίτῳ,
εὐθὺς ἐξέθορεν αὖθις ἐπὶ τοὺς Δαλμάτας, ἄρχων ἔτι
τὴν τῶν τριῶν ἀρχήν· δύο γὰρ ἔλειπεν ἔτη τῇ δευτέρᾳ
πενταετίᾳ τῆσδε τῆς ἀρχῆς, ἣν ἐπὶ τῇ προτέρᾳ σφί-
81 σιν αὐτοῖς ἐψηφίσαντο καὶ ὁ δῆμος ἐπεκεκυρώκει. οἱ
Δαλμάται δ᾽ ἤδη κάμνοντες ὑπὸ λιμοῦ, τῶν ἔξωθεν
ἀγορῶν ἀποκεκλεισμένοι, ἐρχομένῳ τῷ Καίσαρι ὑπήντων καὶ σφᾶς παρέδοσαν σὺν ἱκετηρίᾳ, ὅμηρά τε
δόντες ἑπτακοσίους παῖδας, οὓς καὶ ὁ Καῖσαρ ᾔτει,
καὶ τὰ Ῥωμαϊκὰ σημεῖα τὰ Γαβινίου· τὸν δὲ φόρον
τὸν ἀπὸ Γαΐου Καίσαρος ἐκλειφθέντα ἀποδώσειν

13 τὸν Ἀδρίαν P: τὴν ὁδὸν BJ

setting fire to Synodium, Octavian sent troops up onto the high ground on both flanks to keep pace with him, while he made his way through the ravine. He cut down trees, captured towns and burned everything he seized along the Adriatic coast. While he was besieging Setovia, he confronted a barbarian relief force and prevented it from rushing into the town. In this engagement he was wounded on the knee by a stone, and needed several days of treatment. When he recovered, he returned to Rome to assume the consulship with his colleague, Volcatius Tullus, leaving Statilius Taurus to finish the campaign.[28]

79

28. Taking up his consulship on the first day of the year, Octavian handed over his office to Autronius Paetus the same day, and immediately hurried back against the Dalmatians, as he still held triumviral power.[29] For there were two years of this office left in the second five-year term which the triumvirs had voted for themselves and which the people had confirmed. As the Dalmatians were now suffering from hunger and their external supply routes were cut off, they went to meet Octavian at his approach and voluntarily surrendered as suppliants. They handed over seven hundred of their children as hostages in compliance with Octavian's demand, and gave back the Roman standards of Gabinius. They also undertook to bring up-to-date their tribute payments which they had stopped

80

81

[28] Octavian and L. Volcatius Tullus were elected consuls for 33. T. Statilius Taurus had been consul in 37.
[29] Replacing Octavian as suffect consul on January 1, 33, was L. Antonius (not Autronius) Paetus. Antony, Lepidus, and Octavian were first given triumviral powers in 43, and the triumvirate was renewed in the summer of 37.

82 ὑποστάντες, εὐπειθεῖς ἐς τὸ ἔπειτα ἐγένοντο. τὰ σημεῖα δὲ ὁ Καῖσαρ ἀπέθηκεν ἐν τῇ στοᾷ τῇ Ὀκταουία
λεγομένῃ. Δαλματῶν δ᾽ ἁλόντων καὶ Δερβανοὶ προσ-
ιόντα τὸν Καίσαρα συγγνώμην ᾔτουν σὺν ἱκετηρίᾳ,
καὶ ὁμήρους ἔδοσαν, καὶ τοὺς ἐκλειφθέντας φόρους
ὑπέστησαν ἀποδώσειν. τῶν δὲ <. . .> οἷς μὲν ὁ Καῖσαρ ἐπλησίασε, <καὶ συνέθεντο>[14] καὶ ὁμήρους ἐπὶ
ταῖς συνθήκαις ἔδοσαν· ὅσοις δ᾽ οὐκ ἐπλησίασε διὰ
νόσον, οὔτ᾽ ἔδοσαν οὔτε συνέθεντο. φαίνονται δὲ καὶ
83 οἵδε ὕστερον ὑπαχθέντες. οὕτω πᾶσαν ὁ Καῖσαρ τὴν
Ἰλλυρίδα γῆν, ὅση τε ἀφειστήκει Ῥωμαίων, καὶ τὴν
οὐ πρότερον ὑπακούσασαν αὐτοῖς, ἐκρατύνατο. καὶ
αὐτῷ ἡ βουλὴ θρίαμβον Ἰλλυρικὸν ἔδωκε θριαμβεῦ-
σαι, ὃν ἐθριάμβευσεν ὕστερον ἅμα τοῖς κατ᾽ Ἀντωνίου.
84 29. Λοιποὶ δ᾽ εἰσὶ τῆς ὑπὸ Ῥωμαίων νομιζομένης
Ἰλλυρίδος εἶναι πρὸ μὲν Παιόνων Ῥαιτοὶ καὶ Νωρι-
κοί, μετὰ Παίονας δὲ Μυσοὶ ἕως ἐπὶ τὸν Εὔξεινον
Πόντον. Ῥαιτοὺς μὲν οὖν καὶ Νωρικοὺς ἡγοῦμαι
Γάιον Καίσαρα πολεμοῦντα Κελτοῖς ἐπιλαβεῖν, ἢ τὸν
Σεβαστὸν χειρούμενον Παίονας· ἐν μέσῳ γάρ εἰσιν
ἀμφοτέρων, καὶ οὐδὲν ηὗρον ἴδιον ἐς Ῥαιτοὺς ἢ Νωρικοὺς γενόμενον· ὅθεν μοι δοκοῦσι τοῖς ἑτέροις τῶν
γειτόνων συναλῶναι.

[14] καὶ συνέθεντο add. Roos

[30] Something has fallen out of the text at this point, but perhaps not very much.

since the time of Gaius Caesar, and they remained compliant thereafter. Octavian dedicated the standards in what is known as the Portico of Octavia. After the conquest of the Dalmatians, the Derbani too presented themselves as suppliants when Octavian advanced against them: they asked for a pardon, gave hostages, and promised to pay their arrears of tribute. ‹The remaining peoples?›[30] approached by Octavian also negotiated a treaty with him and gave hostages in compliance with the terms of their agreement. There were some peoples he did not go near because they were affected by disease. These did not give hostages or sign a treaty at the time, but they too appear to have been subdued later. This was how Octavian became master of all Illyrian territory, both the parts that had revolted against Rome, and those that had not been subject to Roman rule before. The senate granted him permission to hold a triumph over Illyria, which he celebrated later along with that for his victories over Antony.[31]

82

83

29. The rest of those forming part of what the Romans consider as Illyria are, on this side of Paeonia, the Rhaeti and the Norici, and on the other side of Paeonia as far as the Euxine Sea, the Mysians. I believe, then, that Gaius Caesar annexed Rhaetia and Noricum when he was campaigning against the Celts, or else it was Augustus when he was subduing Paeonia, for they are situated between the Celts and Paeonians. I could find nothing specific relating to the Rhaeti or the Norici, which leads me to conclude that they were subdued at the same time as their other neighbors.

84

[31] Octavian in fact celebrated a triple triumph on August 13, 29, for his victories over Dalmatia and Illyria, over Antony at the battle of Actium, and over Egypt.

APPIAN

85   30. Μυσοὺς δὲ Μᾶρκος μὲν Λεύκολλος, ὁ ἀδελφὸς
Λικινίου Λευκόλλου τοῦ Μιθριδάτῃ πολεμήσαντος,
κατέδραμε, καὶ ἐς τὸν ποταμὸν ἐμβαλών, ἔνθα εἰσὶν
Ἑλληνίδες ἓξ πόλεις Μυσοῖς πάροικοι, Ἴστρος τε
‹καὶ Καλλατὶς›[15] καὶ Διονυσόπολις καὶ Ὀδησσὸς καὶ
Μεσημβρία, ‹καὶ Ἀπολλωνία›.[16] ἐξ ἧς ἐς Ῥώμην μετ-
ήνεγκε τὸν μέγαν Ἀπόλλωνα τὸν ἀνακείμενον ἐν τῷ
86   Παλατίῳ. καὶ πλεῖον οὐδὲν ηὗρον ἐπὶ τῆς Ῥωμαίων
δημοκρατίας ἐς Μυσοὺς γενόμενον, οὐδ᾽ ἐς φόρου
ὑπαχθέντας οὐδ᾽ ἐπὶ τοῦ Σεβαστοῦ· ὑπήχθησαν δὲ
ὑπὸ Τιβερίου τοῦ μετὰ τὸν Σεβαστὸν τοῖς Ῥωμαίοις
87   αὐτοκράτορος γενομένου. ἀλλά μοι τὰ μὲν πρὸ ἁλώσεως Αἰγύπτου πάντα ὑπὸ νεύματι τοῦ δήμου γενόμενα ἐφ᾽ ἑαυτῶν συγγέγραπται, ἃ δὲ μετ᾽ Αἴγυπτον
οἱ αὐτοκράτορες οἴδε ἐκρατύναντο ἢ προσέλαβον, ὡς
ἴδια αὐτῶν ἔργα, μετὰ τὰ κοινὰ εἴρηται· ἔνθα καὶ περὶ
88   Μυσῶν ἐρῶ πλέονα. νῦν δ᾽, ἐπεὶ τοὺς Μυσούς τε οἱ
Ῥωμαῖοι τῆς Ἰλλυρίδος ἡγοῦνται, καὶ τὸ σύγγραμμά
μοι τοῦτο Ἰλλυρικόν ἐστιν, ὡς ἂν εἴη τὸ σύγγραμμα
ἐντελές, ἐδόκει προειπεῖν ὅτι καὶ Μυσοὺς Λεύκολλός
τε τῷ δήμῳ στρατηγῶν ἐπέδραμε καὶ Τιβέριος εἷλε
κατὰ τὴν μόναρχον ἐξουσίαν.

15 καὶ Καλλατὶς add. Roos
16 καὶ Ἀπολλωνία add. Roos

32 M. Terentius Varro Lucullus (consul 73) was governor of
Macedonia in 72 and 71, when he brought the towns at the mouth
of the Danube within the Roman orbit. His brother, L. Licinius

30. As for the Mysians, Marcus Lucullus, brother of the   85
Licinius Lucullus who fought against Mithridates, overran
their territory and advanced to the river where there
are six Greek towns bordering on Mysia, namely, Istrus
and Callatis and Dionysopolis and Odessus and Mesem-
bria and Apollonia.[32] It was from Apollonia that Lucullus
brought to Rome the large statue of Apollo which now
stands on the Palatine. I have found no other Roman un-   86
dertaking with regard to Mysia in the Republican period.[33]
And it was not even in Augustus' time that the Mysians
were made tribute-paying subjects: they were reduced by
the Tiberius who became emperor of Rome after Augustus. All the regions that came under the will of Rome   87
before the annexation of Egypt, I have written about in
separate books for each country. The conquests and acqui-
sitions these emperors made after Egypt, I have treated
after the period of the Republic, as being their personal
achievements. I will have more to say about Mysia at that
point. But for now, since the Romans regard the Mysians   88
as part of Illyria, and this is my Illyrian history, in order
to make it complete, I decided to say in advance that
Lucullus invaded Mysia too when he held command for
the Republic, and that Tiberius annexed it in the time of
the monarchy.

Lucullus (consul 74), commanded Roman forces in the Third
Mithridatic War, from 73 to 69.

[33] Appian frequently, as here, uses the word "democracy" of
what we call the Republic, but by Appian's time it had lost any
close connection with its original meaning, and he applies it to
almost any form of government, however oligarchic, that was not
sole rule.